D0850339

Hierarchical Concepts
in Psychoanalysis

Hierarchical Concepts in Psychoanalysis

Theory, Research, and Clinical Practice

Edited by

ARNOLD WILSON
JOHN E. GEDO

THE GUILFORD PRESS
New York   London

Chapter 4 © 1991 Analytic Press. From *The Biology of Clinical Encounters* (pp. 25–44) by John E. Gedo. Reprinted by permission.

Chapter 6 © 1992 The American Psychoanalytic Association. From Hierarchies, Boundaries, and Representation in a Freudian Model of Mental Organization by W. I. Grossman, 1992, *Journal of the American Psychoanalytic Association, 40*(1), 27–62, 1992. Adapted by permission.

Chapter 7 © 1992 Analytic Press. From *Self and Motivational Systems: Toward a Theory of Psychoanalytic Technique* (pp. 35–59) by Joseph D. Lichtenberg, Frank M. Lachmann, and James L. Fossage. Reprinted by permission.

Printed in the United States of America

This book is printed on acid-free paper.

Last digit is print number: 9 8 7 6 5 4 3 2 1

Library of Congress Cataloging-in-Publication Data

Hierarchical concepts in psychoanalysis : theory, research, and
  clinical practice / edited by Arnold Wilson, John E. Gedo.
      p. cm.
  Includes bibliographical references and index.
  ISBN 0-89862-987-X
  1. Psychoanalysis. 2. Hierarchies. I. Wilson, Arnold, 1952–
II. Gedo, John E.
  [DNLM: 1. Psychoanalytic Therapy. 2. Psychoanalytic Theory.
3. Mental Processes. WM 460 H633 1993]
RC504.H54 1993
616.89′17 – dc20
DNLM/DLC
for Library of Congress   92-12380
                                                                    CIP

To Linda and Mary

Contents

Part III. Clinical Contributions

Part IV. Overview

Contributors

WILMA BUCCI, Ph.D., Professor of Psychiatry, Derner Institute, Adelphi University, Garden City, New York.

KENNETH FEINER, Psy.D., Department of Psychiatry, Health Science Center at Brooklyn, Brooklyn, New York; and Department of Psychology, New York University Postdoctoral Program in Psychotherapy and Psychoanalysis, New York, New York.

JOHN E. GEDO, M.D., Retired Training and Supervising Analyst, Chicago Institute for Psychoanalysis, Chicago, Illinois.

STANLEY GRAND, Ph.D., Department of Psychiatry, Health Science Center at Brooklyn, S.U.N.Y., Brooklyn, New York; and Department of Psychology, New York University Postdoctoral Program in Psychotherapy and Psychoanalysis, New York, New York.

WILLIAM I. GROSSMAN, M.D., Training and Supervising Analyst, The New York Psychoanalytic Institute, New York, New York.

EDWARD J. KHANTZIAN, M.D. Associate Clinical Professor of Psychiatry, Harvard Medical School, Cambridge, Massachusetts; Principle Psychiatrist for Substance Abuse Disorders, The Cambridge Hospital, Cambridge, Massachusetts; and Associate Chief of Psychiatry, Tewksbury Hospital, Tewksbury, Massachusetts.

FRED LEVIN, M.D., Department of Psychiatry, Northwestern University Medical School, Chicago, Illinois; and Training and Supervising Analyst, The Institute for Psychoanalysis, Chicago, Illinois.

JOSEPH D. LICHTENBERG, M.D., Clinical Professor, Georgetown University Department of Psychiatry, and Faculty, Washington Psychoanalysis Institute.

STEVEN PASSIK, Ph.D., Attending Psychologist Sloan Kettering Memorial Hospital, New York Hospital, Cornell Medical Center, New York, New York.

STEVEN REISNER, Ph.D., Department of Psychiatry, Regent Hospital, New York, New York; and Department of Psychology, Teachers College, Columbia University, New York, New York.

MICHAEL ROBBINS, M.D., Department of Psychiatry, Harvard Medical School, Boston, Massachusetts; and McLean Hospital, Belmont, Massachusetts.

ARNOLD WILSON, Ph.D., Associate Professor, Graduate Faculty, Department of Psychology, New School for Social Research, New York, New York.

Preface

Hierarchical conceptions of the regulation of the functions that sustain living organisms have an ancient pedigree; they entered the study of behavioral regulation in the second half of the 19th century through the neurological theories of Hughlings Jackson. As William Grossman argues in this volume (Chapter 6), Sigmund Freud's concepts of mental function were always organized similar to the hierarchical model suggested by Jackson, although this matter was not explicitly articulated in psychoanalytic discourse for many years. Stimulated in large measure by the example of Piaget, it was David Rapaport—probably the foremost methodologist within psychoanalysis—who called upon future theoreticians to reintroduce hierarchical concepts into contemporary psychoanalysis.

In the past generation Rapaport's challenge has provoked a number of more or less ambitious responses, including those talked about by the editors of this volume (see Chapters 3 and 4). These developments have taken place parallel to the rise of a number of competing clinical theories within the field, theories whose advocates neglected to ascertain whether the hypotheses they espoused dealt adequately with the clinical observations reported by others, or for that matter, with contemporary findings in cognate scientific disciplines such as neurophysiology (see Chapter 5) or cognitive psychology (see Chapter 1). We have solicited contributions for this volume with the conviction that a hierarchical approach to the data contributed by the various observers of human behavior can provide an integration that should transcend the current fragmentation of psychoanalysis into irreconcilable camps (in the most common version of the status quo, those of "ego psychology" versus "object relations theories").

If it were feasible to piece together what we have learned about intrapsychic conflicts (under the aegis of ego psychology) with the prestructural phenomena and the undifferentiated transactional field of early childhood (illuminated through the lens of object relations theories), it should be possible to establish conceptual links with contemporary scientific findings in cognate disciplines. While the complex model or models we may hope to develop on such foundations are still only distant goals, a hierarchical approach makes it possible to aim for a definitive synthesis of hitherto uncoordinated bits of knowledge, without sacrificing any of the hard-won clinical insights accumulated over the past century. To prepare the reader for the varied contributions to this book, which represent several viewpoints rather than a consensus, it may be helpful to spell out the one idea that unites all of our authors — their commitment to a shared definition of what a hierarchical viewpoint in psychoanalysis entails.

The definition we discern in their work is as follows: In a hierarchical conception, multiple levels of phenomena (usually, but *not necessarily* ranked according to developmental considerations) are invariably viewed in relation to one another. Moreover, the transformational principles that define the interrelationship of the various levels must be specified, and the ways in which transformations from level to level alter the nature of available data are made explicit. As the differences among the authors included in this volume will show, the foregoing definition allows for a variety of plausible hierarchical conceptions in psychoanalysis. Nonetheless, every contribution in this book illuminates the fact that hierarchically ordered psychological experiences originating in early life are rarely lost; rather, they are preserved in a multitude of ways and ever remain potentially accessible, mainly as a consequence of regressive developments but also through a number of alternative avenues.

In principle, two kinds of hierarchical approaches are possible: those based on the concept of "stages," and those involving "epigenesis." Epigenetic theories, currently favored in psychoanalysis, are set apart from stage theories by the assumption that the various levels they encompass interrelate both continuously (i.e., they are quantitatively related in terms of "more/less" gradients measuring the phenomena considered) and categorically (i.e., they are qualitatively different in other ways). In other words, stage theories focus on the content of their various levels (cf. the emphasis on dynamic considerations in most clinical theories within psychoanalysis), while epigenetic theories emphasize the principles of transformation from level to level.

Thus an *epigenetic* hierarchical approach is likely to postulate the following: (1) That there is a sequence of interactions between a person and his/her environment that possesses causal significance in terms of later developments; (2) that earlier (and more undiffer-entiated) structures in the person interact with the environment so as to cause more differentiated structures to unfold in that person; (3) that these structures unfold in a series of levels, stages, or modes; (4) that these structures come to possess increased levels of complexity, dif-ferentiation, and organization; (5) that each new level is characterized by particular new qualities that may be viewed as "emergent." Hence, each particular level or mode is characterized by a specifiable degree of complexity and structural differentiation; it possesses specific emer-gent qualities and denotes a particular interplay between the person and the environment. In addition, each level is causally related to all past and future modes by means of the nature of the object relations that characterize it. These, in turn, create a structural reorganization and new possibilities for human transactions.

One of our goals in collecting the papers for this book is to initiate the expansion of the set of working assumptions embodied in an epigenetic hierarchical model so that they will fit the observational data collected in the psychoanalytic situation. In other words, we wish to elevate the optimal conceptualization of intrapsychic hierar-chies to a position of the greatest urgency for psychoanalytic theory, leaving behind the status quo wherein other considerations (such as the issues best illuminated by the tripartite model Freud proposed in 1923 [ego psychology] or those dealt with in terms of object relations) have occupied the forefront of attention.

The need for multiple models, implicit in an overall hierarchical conceptualization, has finally become evident as a consequence of the demonstrated limitations of each of the models of the mind previ-ously used in psychoanalysis. As long ago as 1968 ego psychology was judged to be insufficient by George Klein, who noted that the "ego" has had so many functions assigned to it that the term has lost specific meaning: It has been put in the position of having to explain virtually all phenomena considered by academic psychology. Hence, as Klein also pointed out, it has become virtually impossible to differentiate data about the acquisition of ego functions from those of studies not specifically informed by psychoanalytic theory.

In addition, Klein demonstrated that ego psychology has used the term "ego" in an illogically conflicting sense. On the one hand, it refers to the central organizing agency of the mind; on the other hand, it also pertains to various functions supposedly regulated by this organizing agency. Clearly, the same structure cannot regulate and be regulated simultaneously (see also Gedo & Goldberg, 1973). Further, as Schafer (1976) and others have observed, the propositions of Freud's structural theory may not provide explanations at all, even if detailed criticisms about their internal coherence could be overcome.

Theories of object relations have been subjected to equally severe criticism. Although the development of these theories (like Freud's proposals of 1923) proved to be heuristically useful in pointing to the possibility of widening the range of applicability of psychoanalysis as treatment, the propositions themselves have not attained internal consistency. American versions of object relations theory (e.g., those of Jacobson [1964], Mahler et al. [1975], or Kernberg [1976]) have relied on drive concepts, while the crux of the observations they are intended to explain—early communicational and affective phenomena, the differentiation of self from others, etc.—are best considered from points of view divorced from terminology pertaining to the drives (Eagle, 1984; Gedo, 1986).

It has been pointed out that object relations theories tend adultomorphically and pathomorphically to impute to infants activities that characterize adults, especially adult psychotics (Peterfreund, 1978). In other words, these theories have overlooked data on infant–mother transactions: They have failed satisfactorily to reconcile "the reconstructed child" (inferred on the basis of psychoanalytic data) with "the observed child" in vivo. Analysts who have reviewed the data of infancy research (Lichtenberg, 1983; Stern, 1985) have concluded that these invalidate the accounts of development contained in existing object relations theories. From a different vantage point, object relations theories have also been found wanting in failing to maintain a consistently intrapsychic frame of reference, often lapsing instead into the study of interpersonal transactions without the prioritizing of the mind.

One of the defining characteristics of the current era in psychoanalysis, an era that has been called "post-metapsychological," is that present developments in psychology seem increasingly to be available to synthesize with the observations gathered within the psychoanalytic situation. For example, modern cognitive science studies "tacit" knowledge and "modular" and "representational" models of the mind, not unlike unconscious mentation and psychic structure. Thus cognitive science has spawned methods and models that are readily translated into psychoanalytic terms; its sophisticated experiments produce data that psychoanalysis may usefully incorporate (Holtzman and Aronson, 1992). Another example of relevant bodies of data is that of linguistics, especially from studies of how words are used to accomplish a task, i.e., the role of "speech acts."

Ever since Freud (1905) described the stages of libido development, the axis of developmental lines, eventually formalized by Anna Freud (1965), has served as one of the most important tools for attributing meaning to clinical data. This task was optimally accomplished when viewed in an epigenetic, hierarchical manner. In parallel with these psychoanalytic conceptualizations, Jean Piaget demonstrated the complicated relationship of operations to sequences of stages in cognitive development; he conceptualized the relations of various operations to each other within a developmental hierarchy, creating a model of qualitative and quantitative change in cognitive functioning. Another parallel advance was the contemporaneous work of Lev Vygotsky. Lev Vygotsky emphasized word meanings, the transformations of language that undergo hierarchical reordering over time. Wertch (1991) has aptly termed Vygotsky's theory one of "heterogeneity as genetic hierarchy." Clearly, there is much more to be done in bridging such work with psychoanalysis.

This volume represents one effort to address some of these questions. We have organized the book into four sections: (1) Research Contributions; (2) Theoretical/Historical Contributions; (3) Clinical Contributions; and (4) Overview. The section on Clinical Contributions were contributed by seasoned analytic clinicians who have extended the boundaries of the field into areas such as borderline and psychotic states or drug addiction. The theoretical section makes use of scholars who have attempted to integrate the realms of psychoanalysis, neurophysiology, infant research, and linguistics in the context of the intellectual history of the discipline. The section on Research Contributions includes Wilma Bucci's novel attempt to integrate psychoanalysis and cognitive science and reports by two teams of investigators (Grand, Feiner, and Reisner from Kings County Hospital; Wilson and Passik from the New School for Social Research) who have conducted extensive empirical studies based on epigenetic hierarchical assumptions.

We hope that these contributions will form the basis for discussion among the partisans of various viewpoints about the role of hierarchies in psychoanalytic conceptualization—a discussion that ought to continue after this book is published. The editors have tried to initiate such dialogues by preparing the overview chapter that concludes this volume. There, we attempt to highlight the issues, debates, and conundrums raised and left unsettled by our various contributors.

REFERENCES

Eagle, M. (1984). *Recent developments in psychoanalysis: A critical evaluation.* New York: McGraw-Hill.

Freud, A. (1965). *Normality and pathology in childhood.* New York: International Universities Press.

Freud, S. (1888). *On aphasia.* New York: International Universities Press, 1953.

Freud, S. (1905). Three essays on the theory of sexuality. *Standard Edition* (Vol. 7, pp. 130–243). London: Hogarth Press.

Freud, S. (1923). The ego and the id. *Standard Edition* (Vol. 19, pp. 3–68). London: Hogarth Press.

Gedo, J. (1986). *Conflict in psychoanalysis: Essays in history and method.* New York: Analytic Press.

Gedo, J., & Goldberg, A. (1973). *Models of the mind.* Chicago: University of Chicago Press.

Holtzman, P., & Aronson, G. (1992). Psychoanalysis and its neighboring sciences: Paradigms and opportunities. *Journal of the American Psychoanalytic Association, 40,* 57–89.

Jacobson, E. (1964). *The self and the object world.* New York: International Universities Press.

Kernberg, O. F. (1976). *Object relations and clinical psychoanalysis.* New York: Aronson.

Klein, G. S. (1968). Psychoanalysis: Ego psychology. In *International encyclopedia of the social sciences* (pp. 11–31). New York: Macmillan & Free Press.

Lichtenberg, J. (1983). *Psychoanalysis and infant research.* Hillsdale, NJ: Analytic Press.

Mahler, M., Pine, F., & Bergman, A. (1975). *The psychological birth of the human infant.* New York: Basic Books.

Peterfreund, E. (1978). Some critical comments on psychoanalytic conceptions of fantasy. *International Journal of Psychoanalysis, 59,* 427–442.

Schafer, R. (1976). *A new language for psychoanalysis.* New Haven: Yale University Press.

Stern, D. (1985). *The interpersonal world of the infant.* New York: Basic Books.

Wertsch, J. (1991). *Voices of the mind.* Cambridge, MA: Harvard University Press.

New York and Chicago
September 1992

Arnold Wilson
John E. Gedo

I

Research Contributions

1

The Development of Emotional Meaning in Free Association: A Multiple Code Theory

WILMA BUCCI

> Only connect. That was the whole of her sermon. Only connect the prose and the passion, and both will be exalted and human love will be seen at its height. Live in fragments no longer. Only connect, and the beast and the monk, robbed of the isolation that is life to either, will die.
>   Nor was the message difficult to give. It need not take the form of a good "talking." By quiet indications the bridge would be built and span their lives with beauty.
>   But she failed.
>
> —*Forster (1921, p. 187)*

THE REFERENTIAL CYCLE

Psychoanalysis focuses on the emotional meanings of events, rather than their features as objectively defined. The goal of treatment is change in such emotional meanings; changes in behavior or physiological states may follow from this. By emotional meanings, we refer to perceptions of other people, and wishes, expectations, and beliefs about them—how we see them, what we want or need from them, how we expect they will make us feel. Such meanings may be nonverbal only, but in adults they are usually represented in referential schemata that connect verbal and nonverbal elements. New emotional meanings develop in the shared analytic discourse through activation of both intrapsychic and interpsychic connections, linking the several components of each individual's representational system and linking their separate, subjective worlds. These connecting processes take place, sequentially and repeatedly, in the course of a "referential cycle," which is played out in the free association and in the therapeutic relationship.

The referential cycle has three main phases; each phase is characterized by dominance of a particular type of connecting process: nonverbal, referential, or verbal. The patient first attempts to retrieve private emotional experience—the passion, the terror, the rage—in a halting, indirect and lonely quest, then connects the private nonverbal representations that have surfaced to the communicative verbal code, and finally reflects upon this in the shared therapeutic discourse. Optimally, the collaborative contemplation of this material, within the intensity of the therapeutic relationship, will lead to the opening of new emotional structures, thus continuing the cyclic progression on a deeper level.

The concepts of emotional meaning and the referential cycle are defined in the theoretical context of a multiple code model of mental representation, derived from current work in cognitive experimental psychology and neurophysiology. In this chapter I will first briefly describe the multiple code theory and the concept of the referential cycle. I will then describe the evolution of emotional meaning through the three stages of this cycle and place this characterization of the therapeutic discourse in the context of current empirical research. The development of emotional meaning in the referential cycle may also be characterized as a process with some epigenetic characteristics, as will be discussed below, following the presentation of the theory and its applications.

Outline of the Multiple Code Theory and Its Applications to Psychoanalysis

The multiple code theory is the general case of a dual code model described elsewhere (Bucci, 1985, 1989). The earlier dual code formulation (Bucci, 1985), based on work by Paivio (1971, 1986) and others, focused on the distinction between the nonverbal and verbal systems, and the implication of this duality for psychoanalytic theory and research. The current development of the multiple code aspect of the model retains the basic structure of separate verbal and nonverbal representational systems, but also explicitly recognizes the massively parallel nature of processing within the nonverbal system. Thus the new model reflects major advances in cognitive science and neurophysiology over the past several years (Gazzaniga, 1985; Kosslyn, 1987; Rumelhart, McClelland, & the PDP Research Group, 1986).

The multiple code model, as applied to psychoanalysis, may be characterized briefly as follows: All information is registered in the mind in verbal or nonverbal form. The *verbal* system is the code of language and logic, the external, shared code of communication with others; and the internal code that humans use to regulate themselves, to direct attention, and to direct and modify behavior. The elements of the verbal system are words, connected sequentially in sentences or "strings." The store of verbal knowledge is largely organized in category systems, in which concrete and specific elements are classified on the basis of common features in categories of increasing generality and abstractness. The semantic networks of the verbal system may be defined as hierarchical, and are the only components of the representational system that can be so characterized. Through the verbal schemata, the meaning of words *in terms of other words* is derived.

The elements of the *nonverbal* system incorporate representations of imagery in all sensory modalities, including taste, touch, smell, and sound as well as visual imagery. The nonverbal system also includes representations of motoric activity and autonomic, visceral, and somatic experience. All of these experiential representations are organized in highly complex and differentiated networks, built on nonverbal organizing principles, such as similarity of perceptual features, or function, or contiguity in time and place. Thus, things, people and events are associated because they look or feel alike, or share common functions, or because they occurred together in the same events of one's life. Condensation and displacement are systematic laws of operation of the nonverbal system, based on these organizing principles (Bucci, Severino, & Creelman, 1991). Episodic memory, based on specific events (Tulving, 1984) and repetitions of these, constitutes a major, but not the only, type of organization in the nonverbal system. The nonverbal schemata are massively parallel, taking in and processing information in many channels simultaneously; they have their own intrinsic organization, independent of language, but may also be redirected or regulated by connection to language.

Emotion in the Multiple Code Model

Emotions are major organizing structures of the nonverbal system, composed of all the elements of that system—including sensory and motoric representations as well as visceral experience. The emotional schemata include images of the object of the emotion, the person we hate or fear or desire, and representations of actions associated with the emotion—attacking, fleeing, caressing. These emotional schemata constitute expectations or beliefs about how people will act toward us, and how we will act towards them.[1] The special nature of the emotional schemata, differentiating these from other nonverbal representational structures, is that these expectations or beliefs are associated with activation of visceral or autonomic states—what we *feel*, bodily, when we are angry or afraid or in love.

The aspect of visceral or autonomic activation that figures in the emotional structures is the *central representational* component of the arousal; we are concerned with activation of the central neural pathways that subserve the experience of arousal, not with peripheral activation or "drives." The autonomic or visceral experience may be activated, via the associative networks of the nonverbal system, by internal as well as by external events. Just as visual images occupy some of the same neural pathways as are occupied by a perceptual visual experience, so an expectation of danger or a memory of a beautiful evening will activate neural pathways associated with the bodily component of an emotional state. Images and memories of significant people may activate such emotional structures, as may a familiar song, an old photograph, or a special food. It follows that motivation is not conceptualized in terms of need reduction or drive discharge but, more precisely, in terms of the representational and directive properties of the emotional structures themselves.

The emotional schemata—the particular expectations and beliefs we have about other people, with their associated visceral states—are developed through interactions with caretakers and others from the beginning of life. Emotional schemata represent the experience of one's life in complex and intricate networks in memories and expectations of painful longing, terror, murderous rage, or conflictual desire. They are in place before language is acquired; in an open system, emotional meanings continue to develop in changing and evolving interpersonal contexts throughout life. However, the ongoing development of these structures may be aborted if they are closed or warded off, as will be discussed further below. Like all representational structures, the emotional schemata have the status of hypothetical constructs, inferred from external events, rather than from phenomenological experience—although we are each aware of their phenomenological face within ourselves.[2]

This outline of the interaction of perceptual, motoric, autonomic, and visceral components of the nonverbal system is consistent with current views of the neurophysiological basis of emotion (McLean, 1949; Panksepp, 1982; Winson, 1985). Thus, the emotion mediating circuits of the central nervous system collect sensory and perceptual information from the temporal and frontal lobes, connect these to the limbic system (including the hippocampus and amygdala), the hypothalamus, which is the head ganglion of the autonomic nervous system, and the basal ganglia, which are involved in final motor action. These circuits may be activated by sensory information concerning environmental events as well as stimuli arising from internal states. Once activated, the emotion-mediating circuits arouse and organize related arrays of somatic, hormonal, and visceral sensory-motor processes; these are organized structures composed of elements of the nonverbal system, as postulated above.

The Referential Process

The two systems, with different contents and different organizing principles, including contents that are accessible to awareness and contents that have been warded off, are joined and affect each other through the referential links. The referential connections are bidirectional, permitting us to name what we see and to point to what has been named—or in more general terms, to translate our own experience into words, and to translate the words of others back into nonverbal representations in our own minds. The making of a referential connection requires joining the multichanneled, parallel and analogic contents of the nonverbal schemata, which are often private and unique to an individual's life, to the discrete, sequential and logically organized verbal modality, which is the shared communicative code. This is a difficult task that can be accomplished only partially, even where dynamic factors of resistance and defense do not interfere. The fundamental phylogenetic advance, with the advent of language, was the acquisition of the system of referential connections linking the separate representational domains, not the acquisition of speech forms per se.

The referential connections, like the connections within the nonverbal system itself, develop in the infant–caretaker interaction. The caretaker's emotional response provides the first external "reference" for the child's inner experience. The development of the referential function is intimately connected to the development of object representations; if the mother can accept her child's fear and delight, and respond appropriately, the ground is laid for the child's own acknowledgment of these emotions. Failures and distortions of the connections to others will also affect an individual's capacity to connect personal emotional experience to words; the effect spirals downward, feeding back to diminish connection to other people still further. The development of the referential process, in transactions with others, is centrally involved in the development of the self schema, beginning in the preverbal transactions of infancy, continuing through adult life, and played out again in the therapeutic discourse.

Activity of the referential connections may vary between individuals as a matter of competence or capacity and may also vary within an individual over time as a function of interpersonal situation or inner (emotional or physiological) state. Where referential linkage is active, the schemata of the two systems will interact and may help to reorganize one another. Where referential linkage is sparse or inactive, the systems retain their intrinsic organizational modes.

The referential connections are most direct for specific concrete entities or properties and the words that refer to them (e.g., "orange," "apple," "juicy," "sweet"). They are less direct for category terms such as "fruit" and still less direct for higher order category terms such as "food" and abstract terms such as "human needs," "truth," or "justice." Such abstract, category terms are usually connected to nonverbal imagery only indirectly, through working down the categorical hierarchies to the level of concrete exemplars. The so-called "concreteness" effect—the effect of concrete and specific language in evoking imagery—has been demonstrated in many experimental studies during the past two decades (Marschark, Richman, Yuille, & Hunt, 1987; Paivio, 1971, 1986).

Similarly, representations on the nonverbal side differ in how readily they may be put into words; the difficulties of verbalizing emotions may be understood in this light. For most of us, it is extremely difficult to express strong emotion verbally. Instead, we may express the intensity of an emotion *by the very fact that it goes beyond speech*: "My heart is too full for speech"; "I was struck dumb with awe"; "My mouth hung open, I was absolutely speechless"; "My heart was in my mouth." Lovers stammer and cannot say how they feel. Love songs are full of this verbal paralysis: "I can't begin to tell you how much you mean to me"; "It's just too wonderful, too wonderful for words." The capturing of emotional experience in words is the gift of the poet; the poet communicates emotion, not by naming it directly, but by creating concrete images through which the emotion is evoked:

> How beautiful you are, how charming,
>   my love, my delight!
> In stature like the palm tree,
>   its fruit clusters your breasts.
> "I will climb the palm tree," I resolved,
> "I will seize its clusters of dates".
> —*Song of Songs*, ascribed to Solomon

The process of connecting verbal and nonverbal systems, through the activity of the referential connections, is a distinct aspect of cognitive functioning, which we have termed Referential Activity (RA). Differences in RA are reflected systematically in measurable differences in language style. The RA measures provide operational definitions for some key psychoanalytic concepts and give this approach some of its power in empirical psychoanalytic research, as will be illustrated below.

Evidence for Multiple Coding and the Referential Process: New Neurophysiological Support

Evidence for dual or multiple coding and the referential process has been developed in experimental cognitive psychology, in neuropsychology, and in our own experimental, clinical, and psychotherapy research, as summarized elsewhere (Bucci, 1985, 1988, 1989; Bucci & Miller, in press; Paivio, 1986). Recent research on cerebral lateralization and modularity of function, by Gazzaniga (1985), Kosslyn (1987), Farah (1984), and others, supports the new multistage formulation of the referential cycle; the new work takes us well beyond the simple bicameral left-brain–right-brain dichotomy that was initially postulated in the early cerebral lateralization research.

Gazzaniga (1985) has argued that the human brain is organized into relatively independent functioning units, or modules, that work in parallel; many processes may go on in parallel to conscious thought. In Gazzaniga's terms these are classified as "coconscious but nonverbal mental modules" (p. 117). These modules can discharge and produce ideas, images, and even behaviors that may not have corresponding verbal representations and thus may not be accessible to, or known by, the verbal system. The notion of modularity of function makes possible new and more precise analyses of the component processes of the referential function linking the verbal and nonverbal domains. Thus, there is general agreement that modules associated with linguistic functions are primarily localized in the left hemisphere, while many imagistic and other nonverbal representational processes, including coordinate spatial representation, are largely right-brain functions. However, there is also evidence that some important imagistic functions, in particular, the processes underlying the generating of discrete images, are located in the left rather than right hemisphere (Farah, 1984; Kosslyn, 1987). These are the types of imagery that are more amenable to being named.

These neurophysiological findings have important implications for the model of the referential cycle. Thus the underlying neurophysiological substrate for the referential process would include activation of analogic and global nonverbal representations, which are dominant in the right hemisphere; connections across the corpus collosum to the more discrete, "nameable" images that we now find to be associated with the left; processing by the image-generating component of the left hemisphere; and connections within the left hemisphere, which is primarily a symbol-processing mechanism between discrete images and words.

The dimension of consciousness cuts across the verbal/nonverbal distinction; both language and imagery function outside of as well as within awareness. The notion of consciousness, in the cognitive sense, may be understood in terms of focus of attention. The dynamic unconscious, or the concept of representations that are "warded off," involves additional explanatory factors, particularly in terms of the origin and nature of neural inhibition and disconnections between systems.

The distinction between nonverbal and verbal processing does not correspond directly to the quality of the primary and secondary processes as it is generally understood, but involves a reformulation of this basic psychoanalytic dichotomy. Freud (1900) distinguished the primary and secondary processes on the basis of mobility of cathexis, such that primary process thought is characterized by a high degree of mobility of energy and a tendency for full and rapid discharge, while secondary process thought is characterized by bound energy and delayed discharge. The concept of the primary process is then associated, within the topographic model, with systemic and genetic regression, and regulation by the pleasure principle. In contrast, processing in the nonverbal, as in the verbal system, is a standard mode of mentation, occurring in rational, mature, adult waking life; processing in either system may become regressive or pathological when the systems are dissociated and infantile expectations and beliefs persist.

Several writers, such as McLaughlin (1978) and Noy (1969) have characterized primary process thought in terms that are largely compatible with the notion of the nonverbal system as formulated here. Arlow and Brenner (1964) have also pointed to changes in the concepts of the primary and secondary process, within the structural theory, which correspond to the formulation proposed here. Nevertheless, the traditional linkage of these concepts to Freud's energy model remains widely accepted today. Thus, according to Arlow and Brenner, "The concepts of primary and secondary processes should be defined in terms of varying degrees of mobility of cathexes" (p. 102), within the structural, as within the topographic theory. The reformulation of these concepts as this emerges from the new multiple code theory, without reliance on energic notions, is discussed in Bucci and Miller (in press), and in more detail in Bucci (1992).

Operation of the Defenses in a Multiple Code Theory

Some of the expectations and beliefs about others, as represented in the emotional structures of the nonverbal system, may be painful, even overwhelming or catastrophic, or intensely conflictual. Closeness may evoke dread and expectation of annihilation; lack of closeness, the panic of abandonment. The same objects may evoke approach and avoidance, love, fear, humiliation, rage, or desires to be close, to attack, to escape. Occurrence of any element of a dreaded emotional structure—a word, a memory, an image—may activate expectations of the actual events, with their autonomic and visceral concomitants. Such an event may even activate traces of the somatic experiences themselves. We try to avoid such conflictual or painful mental representations as we would the painful event itself. Since images are internal rather than external to us, we may avoid them by turning away attention, rather than by turning physically away. If an emotion, such as rage or desire, is activated toward a forbidden object, the visceral and motoric elements of the schema may be split off; thus the objects are represented without emotional valence, and the somatic and motoric aspects without objects. The visceral or motoric elements may also be turned toward more neutral objects that share certain perceptual and functional characteristics with the forbidden one. Thus anger may be directed not at one's mother, or later, one's lover, but at another person less necessary for survival; anger might also be turned against the self, directed at one's own body or mind.

The construct of repression takes on an extended range of meaning within this formulation. It may refer to inhibition of referential connections or to dysfunction of connections within either system. Within the nonverbal system, dissociation may occur among the autonomic experience, the object of the emotion, and the potential consummatory act, or between the discrete image and words. In these terms, a componential model of repression can be generated, based on specific types of dissociations within the emotional schemata.

While defenses are defined primarily as dysfunctions of connections between different types of representational components, nonverbal processing is not in itself viewed as defensive or regressive. This is a fundamental implication of the multiple code theory and a major way in which it differs from the standard psychoanalytic model. A systematic multiple code formulation thus permits us to account directly for normal and adaptive preverbal internalization and other preverbal processes of organized thought, as well as for regressive forms.

The effectiveness of psychoanalytic treatment depends on activity of all the connections that have been outlined above: connections within the nonverbal and verbal systems, referential connections between nonverbal representations and words, and connections between patient and therapist. The patient needs to retrieve and organize emotional experience, and translate this into words that will evoke similar experience in the therapist's mind; the therapist needs to translate the words that the patient has spoken into nonverbal experience in his own mind. The reverse operations (therapist to patient) have to take place as well, for the words of the therapist to reach the patient's emotional structures, not to be processed in the verbal system only. We will first describe the verbal, nonverbal, and referential processes and their interaction as these operate in general in mental life before discussing their application in the analytic discourse.

Three Types of Processing

The model stresses the importance of indigenous, independent organization in the nonverbal system, as well as the emergence of new organization by integration with language. In terms of this theory, there are three distinct ways of representing and processing information associated with the nonverbal, verbal and referential processes. These operate in all persons to varying degrees, and at different times, but they may also be relatively dominant in some individuals as special capacities or talents.

1. *Processing where the nonverbal system is dominant.* Some people — artists, athletes, musicians, dancers, chefs, wilderness guides, wine tasters, safecrackers — have exceptionally complex and elaborated nonverbal structures within specific sensory or motoric modalities, or clusters of modalities. Such individuals are able to delve deeply into their nonverbal systems, to organize and direct them intentionally, and to carry out extensive processing in them. The nonverbal representations may be highly differentiated on visual-spatial or other sensory dimensions. Many of these dimensions may not be translatable to verbal form. In such domains, the meaning of an action or an object is expressed essentially and intrinsically in the format of the

modality itself, and does not have to be expressed in verbal form. The painter does not set his goals for a project verbally, and often does not wish to, indeed cannot translate his vision into words. It is almost impossible for most dancers to break down the sequence of steps and actions so as to verbalize them; their mode of communication is to demonstrate and to guide motorically. The same applies, in different ways, for the other nonverbal processes and skills. Apprenticeships rather than textbooks are often required for learning in such fields.

In a very different domain, some natural scientists and mathematicians also see themselves as primarily engaged in nonverbal processing. In his response to an inquiry by Hadamard concerning his mode of scientific thought, Einstein deals directly with several distinctions of interest to us here:

> (A) The words of the language, as they are written or spoken, do not seem to play any role in my mechanism of thought. The psychical entities which seem to serve as elements in thought are certain signs and more or less clear images which can be voluntarily reproduced and combined.
>
> There is, of course, a certain connection between those elements and relevant logical concepts. It is also clear that the desire to arrive finally at logically connected concepts is the emotional basis of this rather vague play with the above mentioned elements. . . .
>
> (B) The above mentioned elements are, in my case, of visual and some of muscular type. . . .
>
> (C) . . . the play with the mentioned elements is aimed to be analogous to certain logical connections one is searching for.
>
> (D) . . . In a stage when words intervene at all, they are, in my case, purely auditive. (Hadamard, 1945, pp. 142–143)

Among developmental psychologists, only Werner & Kaplan (1963) have systematically examined the continued development of nonverbal processing and nonverbal representational modes throughout life. In their developmental theory, they introduced the concept of two distinct lines of cognitive processing, which they termed "geometric-technical" and "physiognomic-dynamic." Both of these continue and are elaborated throughout life; the emphasis on one or the other of these cognitive paths vary among individuals. No one would question the differentiated nature of the thought of Einstein, or of Balanchine, Picasso, or Bach, each working in a different nonverbal modality, with linguistic mediation either absent or playing a limited role.

Perhaps the earliest systematic investigation of nonverbal representation was the work of Galton (1883), who developed a questionnaire about vividness of mental imagery in various sense modalities. Later, Betts (1909) developed the widely used Questionnaire upon Mental Imagery (QMI) based on Galton's approach, and a shorter version was produced by Sheehan (1967). Some of the performance subtests of the Wechsler Adult Intelligence Scale–Revised (Wechsler, 1981), such as Picture Completion, also tap dominantly nonverbal functions, particularly in the visual imagery domain (Bucci, 1985, 1989).

2. *Dominantly verbal processing.* The second category of functions are those in which the logical organization of the verbal networks is most heavily engaged. Lawyers, historians, literary critics, philosophers, and others who are concerned with the study of texts rather than things, may have particular facility within this system and depend most heavily on this. Logicians trace the implications of relationships among propositions within the hierarchical organization of the verbal networks. Similarly, precise wording is crucial in the interpretation of the law and in the search for legal precedent.

Formal, symbolic processing is seen as the optimal mature form by most developmental psychologists, as in the stage of formal operations as characterized by Piaget. Abstract verbal intelligence is also prized most highly in the scoring of such intelligence tests as the Similarities or Vocabulary subtests of the WAIS or WISC. When a child is asked in what way an orange and an apple are alike, the highest score is given for the name of the category to which the two entities belong, that is, fruit. This is the link between them in the hierarchical verbal system. An answer based on a sensory property that they both share, which would reflect a connection in the organizing networks of the nonverbal system (e.g., sweet, juicy, have peels) receives a lower score.

According to the multiple code theory, processing dominated by the logical organization of the verbal mode is far less central than has been customarily assumed. Even in those fields where verbal processing appears to dominate, many people describe the use of nonverbal structures, usually visual-spatial in nature, as guiding their thought (Huttenlocher, 1968), as reflected in the comments by Einstein, above.

3. *The referential process.* The third type of capacity, or function, implied by the multiple code model, is the referential process linking the nonverbal with the verbal system. This has been studied by Paivio (Paivio, Clark, Digdon, & Bons, 1989), but has not generally been recognized as a function in its own right by developmental psychologists, psychometricians, cognitive psychologists, or psycholinguists. The new neurophysiological research discussed above shows promise

of bringing the mechanisms underlying the referential function to light for the first time. The referential process leads to the emergence of "referential structures," which incorporate both verbal and non-verbal elements, and also permits each modality to have far-reaching impact upon the other.

The work of creative writers, and many mathematicians and scientists, rests most heavily on this type of function in elaborated and highly developed form. Talented psychoanalysts, who are able to listen well with the "third ear" to find the underlying thread, must also depend on activation of the referential process, moving back and forth flexibly between the patient's emotional experience and words and their own emotional and verbal experience.

The theory implies that physical scientists and mathematicians are necessarily engaged in referential processing, although the nonverbal component may be phenomenologically salient for them, as it was for Einstein. Thus, the play with visual and motoric elements, which constitutes the central substance of Einstein's work, is "aimed to be analogous to certain logical connections one is searching for," presumably existing in formal, and in some cases verbal, form. An interactive process of guidance by the verbal system, and play with nonverbal elements, seems to have been taking place for Einstein, although he did not focus on this.

The referential function has been studied in depth in our own research. This function is reflected at different levels in a wide range of tasks, including speed of naming simple objects, use of metaphoric terms in describing and differentiating visual stimuli (Bucci, 1984), use of hand movements integrated with rhythm and intonation patterns of speech, and performance on certain verbal intelligence tasks, such as the Comprehension subtest of the WAIS, which requires "common sense" knowledge and integration of systems (Bucci & Freedman, 1978). Some performance tasks, for instance, tests of spatial relations such as the Block Design subtest of the WAIS, are actually referential tasks, in depending on the logical verbal system to guide manipulation of visual designs (Bowen, 1987; Rapaport, Gill, & Schafer, 1968). All of these functions tap the integration of systems, connecting nonverbal to verbal representations, moving flexibly between and within systems. In several studies, intercorrelations have been found among the types of referential processes and tasks mentioned here, supporting the construct validity of the referential function (Bucci, 1989). The referential function is, of course, particularly necessary for the patient and the analyst, as they connect to their own inner experience and to the other.

The Referential Cycle and the Creative Process

The kind of processing that underlies creative scientific or literary work differs from the processing that occurs in psychotherapy, in the contents of the nonverbal schemata, but is quite similar in the basic nature of the referential process itself. The three kinds of processing that have been identified here—nonverbal, verbal, and referential—constitute phases in a "referential cycle"—an ordered sequential pattern, which characterizes thought in the referential domain. The description by Hadamard (1945, p. 56) of the process of inventive or creative thought is strikingly parallel to this formulation. Hadamard identifies four stages in this process: preparation, incubation, illumination, and verification.

1. *Preparation*. This is the preliminary period of systematic labor, in which conscious attacks on the problem are made. The scientist asks himself some questions, makes some progress, then is blocked. The story of Poincaré's great discovery of the uniformization theorem, establishing the fundamental relationship between topology and algebra, is famous in this regard.[3] Poincaré works vainly for a fortnight, attempting to prove that there could not be any functions with the particular defining features that he had specified, a conjecture that was to prove false. During a sleepless night, he first builds up one class of those functions; then he wishes to find a mathematical expression for them, and has a conscious idea of the properties and form that this expression must have.

2. *Incubation*. Without having found this expression, he turns his attention to other matters:

> Just at this time, I left Caen, where I was living, to go on a geologic excursion under the auspices of the School of Mines. The incidents of the travel made me forget my mathematical work.

3. *Illumination*. The new idea that has been sought arrives as a surprise:

> Having reached Coutances, we entered an omnibus to go some place or other. At the moment when I put my foot on the step, the idea came to me, without anything in my former thoughts seeming to have paved the way for it, that the transformations I had used to define the Fuchsian functions were identical with those of non-Euclidean geometry.

4. *Verification and making precise.* Following upon the flash of inspiration, he carries out a systematic formal proof, although he himself did not need to be convinced of the truth of his idea:

> On my return to Caen, for conscience's sake, I verified the result at my leisure.

There are many similar examples of successful cognitive work carried out outside of the formal, intentionally directed information processing system in reports by other scientists and mathematicians:

> Thus Gauss, referring to an arithmetical theorem which he had unsuccessfully tried to prove for years, writes: "Finally, two days ago, I succeeded, not on account of my painful efforts, but by the grace of God. Like a sudden flash of lightning, the riddle happened to be solved. I myself cannot say what was the conducting thread which connected what I previously knew with what made my success possible." (Hadamard, 1945, p. 15)

The phenomenon of sudden illumination coming from an unidentified, experientially external source is not restricted to mathematics or the sciences. As the poet Paul Valéry has described it, the state or process known as poetic inspiration is essentially similar to this:

> The man whose business is writing experiences a kind of flash—for this intellectual life, anything but passive, is really made of fragments; . . . elements very brief, yet felt to be very rich in possibilities, which do not illuminate the whole mind, which indicate to the mind, rather, that there are forms completely new which it is sure to be able to possess after a certain amount of work. Sometimes I have observed this moment when a sensation arrives in the mind; it is as a gleam of light, not so much illuminating as dazzling. This arrival calls attention, points, rather than illuminates, and in fine, is itself an enigma which carries with it the assurance that it can be postponed. You say, "I see, and then tomorrow I shall see more." (Valéry, quoted in Hadamard, 1945, p. 17)

Valéry, Hadamard, Poincaré, and others who have written about the phenomenon of apparent sudden illumination have recognized to some degree, its actual basis in the years of preparatory work. In these apparently fruitless struggles, the poet or the scientist gradually builds up the structures from which the answer will finally, seemingly without effort, emerge. Some observations of Poincaré provide an unusual insight into his experience of the preparation and incubation phases. Thus he describes the following experience, which occurred during the night of sleeplessness referred to above:

> One evening, contrary to my custom, I drank black coffee and could not sleep. Ideas arose in crowds; I felt them collide until pairs interlocked, so to speak, making a stable combination. . . .
>
> It seems, in such cases, that one is present at his own unconscious work, made partially perceptible to the over-excited consciousness, yet without having changed its nature. Then we vaguely comprehend what distinguishes the two mechanisms or, if you wish, the working methods of the two egos. (Poincaré, quoted in Hadamard, 1945, pp. 14–15).

Hadamard terms this process "looking at one's unconsciousness" and characterizes it as strange and exceptional (pp. 14–15). I suggest that the process might appear less strange if it were understood as looking at one's *nonverbal* rather than *unconscious* system, that is, work performed in a domain not as yet fully accessible to the verbal system—the coconscious, in Gazzaniga's terms. It also seems likely that people differ greatly in their capacity to direct attention in this way. Poincaré, like Einstein, for example, may have had special gifts in this regard.

In the context of the componential view of nonverbal and referential processing, formulated above, it is possible to distinguish different levels of intentional access to the representations of the nonverbal or coconscious systems, corresponding to the degree to which the imagery has been organized in discrete and specific form. Thus the special experience described by Poincaré may involve access to a preformative level of visual processing, involving organization of prototypic visual representations in terms of spatial coordinates without specific, discrete imagery being formed. This is largely a right-hemisphere function, and for most people cannot be intentionally retrieved or directed. The work that goes on in the preparation and incubation periods, prior to the illumination, which seems to be out of awareness or external to oneself, may to a large extent consist of this type of preformative processing, occurring in different ways in the various sensory domains. The imagery to which most people commonly have access is that which has already been organized in discrete form, with specific contents that are amenable to being named.

Similar processes are also reflected in dreams. The day residue and conscious concerns of the day are the preparation. The person goes to sleep with something "on his mind"—the problems of the day, an interpersonal difficulty, a worry, a feeling that is troublesome but not acknowledged or understood. The latent contents constitute the preformative or incubation phase of processing of the dream thoughts, as the dreamer begins to make connections within the emotional structures and to retrieve elements of these. These may be global imagery or visceral trace elements that are not readily named. The manifest contents are the first stage in the referential process, laying the groundwork for the illumination, as the analogic, somatically dominated patterns of the latent content are connected to specific, concrete—and nameable—images. The dream report and associations continue the expansion and elaboration of the associative network, now in the verbal as well as nonverbal system. The verification and making precise then occur in the interpretation of the dream and the working through, as new connections in the verbal and referential systems are made.

APPLICATION TO THE TREATMENT PROCESS:
A CLINICAL ILLUSTRATION

The sequence of these three types of processes—verbal, nonverbal, and referential—form a referential cycle, which occurs repeatedly within a session and more globally over a series of sessions. Each of these phases of the referential cycle may be reflected in systematic, operational measures, as will be discussed below. Thus they are, in principle, and even to some extent now in practice, amenable to empirical research. I will first illustrate the cycle as it plays out clinically in a session and then introduce the project of finding empirical evidence for this.

In all cases described above, in scientific or literary invention, and in dreaming as well, the preformative nonverbal and referential processing must initially have been primed by intentional and directed preparatory search. The same applies in treatment. The work of setting the problems, including thoughts about the general issues that bring the patient to treatment and the specific experiences of the day, constitute a counterpart of a preparation phase, carried out outside of the session itself. The referential cycle as this occurs in free association in the therapeutic discourse consists of the emotional counterparts of the other three phases.

1. *Turning inward; incubation and accretion; letting the nonverbal system lead.* The patient turns inward to delve and forage around

within his own subjective, private representations, his memories and images, to capture the nonverbal material that has been incubating. Just as the mathematician is attempting to capture a mathematical structure that has not yet been identified, the patient is attempting to capture an emotional structure that exists in the format of the nonverbal system, including diffuse motoric and visceral representations, which may not ever have been connected to words and may not yet be connected to specific images or events. He may begin with an intense and global feeling of pain or excitement, related to some expectation or past event, but not clearly articulated. He "feels anxious" or "feels upset" or "feels excited," but may not "know" *why*, he may not "know" quite *what* he feels, or somatic experience may be salient but split off from the emotional meaning of events.

In *East of Eden*, Steinbeck describes vividly this state of generalized, somatically experienced emotional distress:

> An ache was on the top of his stomach, an apprehension that was like a sick thought. It was a *Weltschmerz*—which we used to call "Welshrats"—the world sadness that rises into the soul like a gas and spreads despair so that you probe for the offending event and can find none. (1952, p. 232)

In terms of our model, we can say that the patient's emotional representation, at this stage, lies in a component of the nonverbal representational continuum that is far removed from language and whose contents are inaccessible because they are not organized in discrete images as well as because they are defended and warded off. The referential connections are not yet in place; the verbal and nonverbal lines of representation are distant and divergent at this phase; the nonverbal line dominates and directs the associative process. This is similar to the incubation phase of creative scientific or literary work. The difference is that here the patient must carry out the nonverbal search in an interpersonal context and must report it verbally, as fully as possible, *while it is going on*. This is, of course, a major distinction, which is crucial for a creative search where interpersonal issues are intrinsically involved.

The following example is from the middle phase of the analysis of a young male patient. He is successful in his work in an engineering field, but has difficulties in establishing a relationship with a woman and is increasingly bereft as his circle of male friends is depleted by marriage.

He opens the session with an immediate reference to bodily experience, dissociated from emotional state:

PATIENT: I see it's cold in here today. I guess it's the ah, yeah, I can feel the ah cold coming through the mattress. Ah, it's not my imagination. It's the temperature.

[He then goes on to tell how he was stood up by a date last night; he did not feel angry at this:]

PATIENT: So, ah, what, what was I feeling then? Well, I tried to, at this point I tried to understand it right then and there. I didn't feel anything. I said, boy, am I taking this calm and cool, huh? Didn't (*stutters*) didn't, didn't get upset, didn't do anything. Took it real calm and cool.

[He goes on to talk about how he "got very lonely, all of a sudden," later that same evening and called some friends; his attention then turns to aspects of somatic experience:]

PATIENT: . . . and I called this one, and called that one, okay, just to touch base, to uh—I have a terrible itch here—just, just to call base, ah, call base, touch base.

THERAPIST: Call base.

PATIENT: Yeah.

THERAPIST: An itch, what's underneath trying to get to the surface?

PATIENT: Well, (*stammers; inaudible*) . . . was itching, uhm.

THERAPIST: Where?

PATIENT: Ah, ah right here, it's on the penis, an itch, you know, it itches, you got to scratch it.

THERAPIST: And what flashes to mind?

PATIENT: What flashes to mind? That my penis just fell off. I don't know.

THERAPIST: Yes.

PATIENT: I don't know what flashes to mind. Ah—

THERAPIST: (*Inaudible*)

PATIENT: I thought I'd be somewhat original.

THERAPIST: See where your images and feelings take you.

PATIENT: Well, fell off, went into a, into a, into a river and down a sewer or down a drain and disappeared forever. Ah, images don't take me (*inaudible*) anywhere, anywhere, anywhere. When I say (*inaudible*) I don't know, images, any bare, anywhere, (*stutters*) bare, bare, naked, naked. Ah when I think of bare and naked, I think of a kid, a child. Anyway, I'm still itching. And I'll keep on scratching. Ah I'm, don't—the thing that bothered me is, was, or is, ah my total lack of feeling. I was calm as, cool as ice. Ah.

Somatic and motoric experience (feeling cold, itching, scratching) are salient for the patient at this stage. His language is at times disorganized and diffuse, perhaps deliberately so, and for a complex set of reasons. The analyst's interventions encourage him to elaborate his experiential associations. He seems to be manifestly resistant, but does nevertheless expand his exploration of the nonverbal domain:

PATIENT: Anyway, so I scratch. What does that mean? (*inaudible*) so when you say what, what does it, what do you think of? I think I'm losing my penis. I'm scratching it ah, oh, to show you how lonely I felt last night—(*mutters*) ah, ah, (*inaudible*) I'm losing my voice—to show you how lonely I felt last night. I intended to masturbate too. Just to, I don't know what the hell what for. I fell asleep, before I even got around to it. And ah there was loneliness. So let's see now. I fell asleep and I did dream, and I'll get to those dreams in a minute.

2. *The referential phase; illumination; the surprise.* In the referential phase, the speaker connects the generalized emotional or somatic experience to discrete and specific images, for which the referential connections are most active; he then connects these to words. Dreams are particularly suited for the concrete and specific instantiation of previously nonverbalized and dissociated emotional representations. After the phase above, dominated by dissociated somatic and emotional experience and vague imagery, the patient reports a long and detailed dream from the previous night. He is riding a bicycle or unicycle with one or more male friends. He is in a village square with three movie theaters; he feels the scene has appeared in his dreams before; he describes the scene and his actions in elaborate detail. He is supposed to tell his friend which movie to go to, but he misses the theaters. He experiences his parents as criticizing him for this:

PATIENT: I think in terms of my mother right now, saying you never did, or my father, you never did (*inaudible*) you never do anything properly, you ah, you don't go into any detail. You touch the surface sort of thing.

Then the scene shifts and he is in an upstairs apartment with his single friends. He describes an image of a room seen through a door, in which there is a couch and a chair. All of his friends are in the room; he is having a great time talking to them. Then he sees five good-looking girls in the doorway, who intrude on this. He first says that the dream ended there; then, as an afterthought, he remembers another part:

PATIENT: There's one point that I missed that's quite important. I guess going from downstairs to upstairs, I got quite upset. I had to go to the bathroom. Now—so I took a crap—now for some reason there was no toilet, and I ended up holding the feces in my, not in my hand, but in paper, toilet paper in my hand. (*Stutters*) I had, I had no place to put it. And I went upstairs, that's what it was, and I couldn't find anything. Under a table there was a wastepaper basket, so I dumped the whole thing in there and then covered it up. I was hoping that it wouldn't smell, you know. And I was sort of embarrassed, and I got to itch again. And ah here we go, dumped the feces into the ah, into the basket, and I'm itching. Now that's got to be totally sexual, going back to my childhood.

He then spends much of the remainder of the session associating to this dream. The associative links of the emotional schema enable him to access and verbalize previously dissociated elements. Through the building of these referential connections, emotional experience may be named.

PATIENT: I'm afraid of women, I tell you, I am. They scare me. They're not compassionate and not reasonable like men, ah, (*pause*) ah, well, so I understand it and intellectualize. Still, the feelings, I don't know what the feelings were. Embarrassing with the feces, and annoyance with the women, frustration that I couldn't find the ah right movie. And I wasn't doing a good job. Ah, those were the feelings.

THERAPIST: Suppose the bowel movement and the shit represented some kind of very violent feeling that is hidden behind that image, what would it be? If you suddenly blurted it out.

PATIENT: Rage.

THERAPIST: Yes?

PATIENT: Rage, what right does that girl got to do to stand me up. That's it. I'm pretty important. I'm a pretty good guy. Rage, that would be the feeling.

As the process of associating to the dream continues, the emotional meaning of rage is connected to the feelings in the session, the early memories, and the events of the previous night. This is an interactive process, opening referential connections to new emotional schemata:

PATIENT: I got the feeling . . . my mother must have been sitting there with her hand out waiting for the goddamn thing, you know, and maybe I, ah, that would be a funny one, it's as though that it was a battle between me and my mother who'd get hold of my shit. She wanted it, and I wanted it. She wanted it, by getting it she had possession of me, or something. I don't know.

Where referential connections have been activated, the surprise, the new piece of the pattern is likely to emerge, as in the illumination phase of the creative scientist or writer:

PATIENT: (*Pause*) another interesting thing, the feces were very small and I sort of questioned whether (*chuckle*) whether they were mine or not. Because in my present sized body, my adult sized body, this was definitely baby's feces. They were little, little ones. And that's something else too.

Uhm, here's another one. When my father was dying at the house, on PQV Street, one day I guess I went to his john and he had, hadn't flushed the toilet and there was his feces there. It was long and it was thin and it was small like a baby's and ah, it was sort of frightening. I guess he didn't eat much, his rectum was closing up or this or that. And I'm not sure if this reminds me of that. But if it did man, I could see why I want to get rid of that stuff. This might be, this might be ah, a curve I'm throwing but that comes to mind.

3. *Insight; making the verbal links; verification; making precise.* In the next phase, the patient begins to reflect upon the connections that have been made and evaluates these. The analyst helps him to acknowledge the new meanings, and to contain and explore them. The two together continue the collaborative work begun in the referential phase; the analyst may be the leader at this point.

THERAPIST: Looks as though you retreated from sort of the excitement of the world (*inaudible*) and the anxiety to this upstairs room, with the couch and with the man, holding all this dirty filthy stuff in your hand.

PATIENT: Ah, a better way of, maybe (*stutters*) maybe if that's so, maybe this (*stutters*) is, I have the dirty stuff in my hand, got to get rid of it. But (*clears throat*) I retreated from the ah challenge of mixing, okay?

THERAPIST: Uhum. Because if you mix what—

PATIENT: You make, you mix, you mix, you might get involved.

THERAPIST: Yes, and what's going to happen?

PATIENT: I lose my penis in a girl.

THERAPIST: Yes.

PATIENT: I don't know, maybe it's (*inaudible*).

THERAPIST: Yes.

PATIENT: I lose my, I lose my identity. I lose my oneness. It's a threat. I'm no longer a selfish individual who has only me to care for. Ah, as I'm going upstairs, what, what's safer than a room like this, a couch, nothing but males and in the dark room there's some women, and I, (*makes noise*) the enemy. Well, that's it.

THERAPIST: One meaning of it is the analysis. You multiply everything. Everything is multiplied, but it's, you're with the man. (*Inaudible*) This image, the female keeps trying to intrude and you want her to stay the hell out. Because it's too frightening. There seem to be two kinds of dangers you've been through. One is she takes something from you. She takes the shit, she takes the penis, and the second is you do something very violent and filthy and dirty and destructive.

PATIENT: I really punish her when I do that, (*clears throat*) you know. I got to punish myself if I do something dirty, filthy, and violent and destructive. So what do I do, punish myself with a celibate life or whatever you want to call it?

THERAPIST: Stay with the feelings.

The events of this session have illustrated the construct of the tripartite referential cycle in which emotional meanings are developed. The patient first speaks about the event of being stood up, bodily experience—including feeling cold and his penis itching—actions of scratching, planning to masturbate, and feelings of loneliness. But he does not connect these in an integrated schema. The dream and associations to it introduce many specific objects, people, actions, and events: infantile feces in his hand, his dying father's feces, the room upstairs with his male friends and "with the man," and the women at the door. Through these images, which he can name, referential structures are formed, which connect some of the previously dissociated representations. Eventually the patient is able to assign emotional meaning to the schemata of motoric and perceptual imagery with their autonomic and visceral components: first being afraid of women, then rage. The therapist adds to the structure with his interpretations. The word "anger" did not have emotional meaning for the patient at the beginning of the session; he looked for the feeling, expected it to be there, but felt calm and cool, cold as ice. The words "rage" and "fear" have emotional meaning now, because specific imagery has been retrieved and connected to previously dissociated feelings, and referential connections have been made.

We would expect to see this repeating cycle played out in a session or in a series of sessions over time. The danger of this phase, as the analyst appears to recognize here, is that it will be foreclosed; in our terms, that the patient will impose the connections of the verbal schemata prematurely, reducing the scope of exploration of the nonverbal terrain.

While we can see a number of alternative interpretations of the material of this hour, as well as alternative views of the analyst's technique, the process emerges clearly in the terms of the proposed model. The analyst first supported the patient's exploration of his somatic and emotional experience, before interpreting the emotional meaning of the previous night's events. New and surprising nonverbal imagery emerged in the associations to the dream, leading finally to the image of his infantile feces, "little, little ones," which looked like those of his dying father. While the analyst may have led the patient in some ways, the emergence of the new imagery indicates that the patient's referential connections had been activated and his own nonverbal representations had been retrieved.

The model as proposed here lays the basis for a program of research; it provides a framework for constructing questions that are amenable to empirical study, rather than a set of answers or solutions. Thus, we can begin to develop a systematic approach to the question of suggestibility; the model implies that there can be indications in language style and content of the degree to which the patient's utterances reflect referential connections to his own private emotional experience rather than suggested or shared verbal associations only. We can also begin to set some interesting questions: How does the somatic experience expressed by the patient in the beginning of the session relate to the concrete and specific imagery of the dream? How can we show that it does? To what degree does the analyst's leading of the patient to name the violent feeling connected to his images account for his acknowledgment of rage, which had been inaccessible to him emotionally until then? How can we demonstrate the validity of this verbalization to his actual inner state?

CONVERGING EVIDENCE FOR THE REFERENTIAL PROCESS: THE NOMOLOGICAL NET

The multiple code theory provides a theoretical framework or "nomological network" (Feigl, 1956; Cronbach & Meehl, 1955) that permits empirical validation of the construct of the referential cycle. A nomological net connects hypothetical constructs and intervening variables to one another and to observable indicators, in language and behavior, through which the underlying constructs may be operationally defined (Bucci, 1989). The availability of a nomological net then permits convergent and divergent validation of independent measures, and validation of theoretical constructs, in an interactive, theory driven empirical approach. We will illustrate this approach as applied to the fifth session of a fully recorded analysis of a young woman, which was to go on for seven or eight years, and which served as a specimen hour for study by several independent researchers, as reported in Dahl, Kaechele, and Thomä (1988).

MEASURES OF REFERENTIAL ACTIVITY

The referential cycles are identified using measures of Referential Activity (RA), defined as activity of the referential connections between verbal and nonverbal representations. The RA measures are based on the premise outlined above, that referential connections are most direct between specific and concrete entities and words referring to them, less direct for abstract concepts and words. The conceptual basis for the RA measures and empirical evidence for them, in both experimental and clinical work, has been presented briefly above and in detail elsewhere (Bucci, 1989; Bucci & Miller, in press). The methods for scoring RA include qualitative rating scales and objective measures based on quantifiable linguistic features. The RA rating scales measure the *Concreteness*, *Imagery* level, *Specificity*, and *Clarity* of speech.

Concreteness is based on degree of perceptual or sensory quality, including references to all sense modalities, action, and bodily experience (not cognitive concreteness in a regressive or deficit sense). *Imagery* refers to the degree to which the language evokes corresponding experience in the reader or hearer. These two scales are usually highly correlated, and their scores are combined to produce the composite scale "CONIM," interpreted as measuring the level of sensory imagery in a text.

Specificity refers to amount of detail; a highly specific text involves explicit descriptions of persons, objects, places, or events. *Clarity* refers to clarity of an image as seen through the language, how well focused is the linguistic image. These two scales are combined to yield the composite scale "CLASP," defined as tapping the organizational quality of discourse.

In addition to the scales, a number of specific linguistic features have been identified as related to the RA dimension. These include metaphors, which represent abstract thought or emotional experience in concrete and specific form, and linguistic features that impart a quality of immediacy to spoken language, such as direct quotes and stylistic use of the present tense in describing past events ("So he comes into the room and he sits down, and he says to me . . . "). Computer assisted procedures for scoring RA are also being developed (Bucci & Miller, in press) using procedures developed by Mergenthaler (1985). The RA measures have been applied to many types of texts, including brief monologues, early memories, and TAT protocols, as well as transcripts of therapy sessions (Bucci, 1988, 1989).

RA Fluctuation and Other Measures of the Referential Cycle

In scoring a session for RA, it is first divided into segments, then scored for the scales and other features, using procedures outlined in the RA scoring manual (Bucci, Kabasakalian-McKay, & the RA Research Group, in press). Interrater reliability of .80 or better has consistently been obtained for judges scoring these scales.

The RA scores for the specimen hour—hour 5 of the fully recorded analysis of a young woman, referred to above[4]—are shown in Figures 1.1 and 1.2. The figures show RA scores for patient speech segments, as identified in the published version of this session (Dahl et al., 1988, pp. 15–28). Only RA scores for patient speech segments two lines or longer are shown here. The first 22 speech segments of this session consisted of th patient's continuous speech without interruption. Segments 23 to 45 consisted primarily of dialogue, with only a few scoreable patient segments, as shown. The patient then spoke without interruption in segments 46 to 48, and segments 52 to 62, which closed this session. (Nonscoreable phases including dialogue and therapist interventions are indicated by vertical breaks on the horizontal axis.)

Figure 1.1 shows scores for overall RA, an average of the four component scales. Two referential cycles were identified in this session, indicated by vertical lines on the graphs. The cycles are identified by local peaks above the midpoint of the RA scales, preceded and followed by relatively low RA. The first cycle begins at segment 10, peaks at segment 19, and ends at segment 22, when the

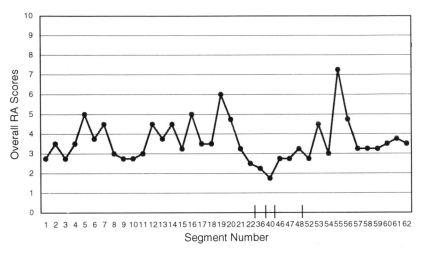

FIGURE 1.1. Overall RA scores applied to patient speech.

analyst intervenes for the first time. The second cycle begins at segment 40, peaks at segment 55, and continues to the end of the session. (A potential cycle may be seen at the beginning of the session, but this does not meet the criterion of overall RA rising above the midpoint of the scale.)

Figure 1.2 shows average standardized scores for the RA subscale

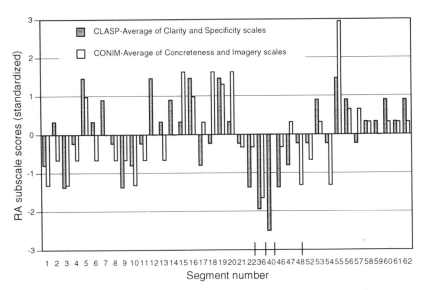

FIGURE 1.2. Comparison of RA subscales applied to patient speech.

of CLASP, which is an average of the Clarity and Specificity of language scales, and reflects the organizational quality of the discourse, compared to the subscale of CONIM, which is an average of the Concreteness and Imagery scales, and reflects the level of sensory imagery in a text. Here, the cycles are delineated not only in terms of overall RA level, but also in terms of relationships between these subscales.

Table 1.1 shows RA and other measures for three segments representing each of the three phases of these referential cycles. I will illustrate this patterning with material from the second cycle, near the close of the session and then discuss convergence of research methods in identification of both cycles.

Phase One: Nonverbal Dominance, Incubation

According to the model, the nonverbal and verbal modes of representation are proceeding separately; the patient seeks to retrieve and communicate nonverbal and emotional experience in language, but can do this only partially and in a dissociated way. The following is an

TABLE 1.1. Converging Measures of the Referential Cycle in the Specimen Hour (Hour 5)

(1) Phase	(2) Segment	(3) Overall RA	(4) CONIM[a]	(5) CLASP[a]	(6) Experiencing scale	(7) CCRT	(8) jxr	(9) Frames[b]
Nonverbal dominance	10	3.0	−1.32	−0.81	4	—	—	—
	40	1.75	−0.01	−2.51	4,4	—	—	DC,DC
	46	2.75	−0.34	−1.37	5	—	—	—
Referential	15	5.0	1.63	0.33	2,3	Father	x2	DST
	18	6.0	1.63	−0.24	2	Boys and their parents	—	TD$\overline{\text{S}}$ TS$\overline{\text{C}}$
	55	7.25	2.94	1.46	4,2,4	Teacher	x1	$\overline{\text{CDT}}$
Verbal dominance	9	2.75	−0.66	−1.37	2	—	—	—
	20	3.25	1.63	0.33	—	—	—	D$\overline{\text{C}}$C
	56	4.75	0.65	0.90	3	Teacher	r, x	$\overline{\text{D}}$CC

[a]Standard scores.
[b]Each of the emotional frame structures and their negations are represented by a sequence of letters denoting the component themes: S = a wish for reassurance or support; T = a wish for togetherness; D = a defense of delay; C = a defense of control. A negation of a theme is represented by a bar over the theme letter.

example from the nonverbal dominant phase, which begins the second cycle of this session. The patient is responding to the analyst's questions concerning her delay in telling him about a significant event that had occurred prior to the previous day's session:

PATIENT: (Segment 40) (*Interrupting*) I can't remember whether it even, you know, did come into my mind yesterday. It may have, but uhm, you know, sometimes I, especially when I first come in, I find I am here and I just have a flood of things, but nothing's really, but yet there's nothing. I'd –, it's hard to explain. You know, there are – perhaps I'm selecting now, I don't want to talk about that, no I can't about that, and you know, then I'm selecting what I can (*chuckle*) talk about or feel I can, but uhm, I don't, I don't even remember that – I'm, I'm not sure how, how long after I spoke to the mother I even began to think I shouldn't have done it too. You know, how long it took me to react to what I'd said. Oh, I must have reacted right away, but perhaps that was one of the things that I pushed away from my mind and wouldn't face that I'd made a mistake on, because I will do that too.

This segment was low on all measures, receiving an overall RA score of 1.75 as shown in Table 1.1, column 3. In terms of standardized scores for the component subscales, this segment was essentially at zero (the mean of her distribution of scores) CONIM and 2.5 standard deviations below her mean for the CLASP subscales, as shown in columns 4 and 5.

In addition to the low RA level that defines this phase of the cycle, we would expect to find convergent validation in paralinguistic indicators, including vocal quality and speech rate. Speech in this phase is likely to be characterized by pauses, repetitions, and other aspects of disfluent speech. The patient's struggles at this stage might also be reflected through paralinguistic indicators, such as body movements, which may be either self-soothing or agitated, facial expressions, crying, and other nonverbal indicators of affect.

Convergent Validation: The Experiencing Scale

We would also expect to seek additional convergent validation in measures of emotional expression by other psychotherapy researchers. For example, the nonverbal dominant phase may be captured empirically on a verbal level in the Gendlin Experiencing Scale (Klein, Mathieu, Gendlin, & Kiesler, 1970). This well-known and widely used scale, developed in the theoretical context of the client-centered approach (Rogers, 1951, 1961), directly assesses the patient's subjective, phenomenological sense of emerging feelings, rather than the specific, external details valued as objective correlatives in the Referential Activity approach. The seven-point scale ranges from the lowest level of focus on external events, with impersonal, detached treatment, to the highest levels of easy and expansive presentation of emerging feelings and their impact.

The specimen session was scored for the Experiencing Scale by Marjorie Klein, in a study reported elsewhere (Price & Bucci, 1986). Most of this session, early in the treatment of this relatively obsessional and high functioning neurotic patient, was rated as low on the Experiencing Scale as shown in Table 1.1, column 6. Scores generally ranged between 2 and 4, primarily indicating focus on external events, behavioral descriptions, and limited self-descriptions. The highest Experiencing scores in the session were several ratings of 4 and one borderline 5, reflecting some emergent focus on feelings. These were found almost exclusively in the nonverbal dominance phases, as shown in Table 1.1. For instance, the nonverbal dominance excerpt above received a score of 4 on the Experiencing Scale.

Phase Two: The Referential Phase, Illumination

This is the phase of activity of the referential links, in which the verbal and nonverbal systems are brought together. The patient is able to connect to some emotional experience through the specific objective details of a memory, a dream, or an event replayed in her mind and reported in the session, or through an event in the relationship. She may connect to this experience, even though she is not aware of its meaning at the time. It is in this sense that the ground may be laid for the illumination, the surprise, by which the emotional schemata are opened further.

In the discourse following the excerpt above, the analyst addressed the patient's need for reassurance and approval from others and her expectation that she will not get it from him. The patient then goes on to talk about her need to criticize others before she can feel friendly toward them. The analyst then questions whether she may have criticisms of him. The patient goes on to wonder if "all this really does get anywhere," if it (the analysis) "isn't some sort of a hoax." She then talks about her general fear of making personal remarks. This leads to the peak RA passage of the session.

PATIENT: (Segment 55) In fact, I was kind of horrified last night at myself. I had a course a__ after I left here and uhm, (*sniff*) it uhm, it's an art course for teachers (*sniff*) and we were working on rubbing things for texture. And at one point I noticed the professor's tie, which was a very nubby coarse woven one, and although it would have been too soft to rub, I just (*chuckle*) reached out and held it out and said, "Well, this has a wonderful texture," which it did. But I was horrified at myself, because I've just never done anything like that before. And then I was sure his reaction was horror too, that I had been so forward. I don't know what it was actually, but at the time I was sure it was just horror (*pause*).

The RA measures reached a peak in this utterance, with an overall RA score of 7.25. The CONIM score was also the highest of the session. As the standardized scores show, it was almost 3 standard deviations above the mean CONIM scores for this hour. In this excerpt, the patient finds a specific and concrete story that embodies her inner experience and provides a communicable metaphor for it. She may not have recognized its emotional meaning, but following the basic rule, she reports the incident that comes to mind, trivial or irrelevant as it may seem. She may never have permitted herself to *do* "anything like that" before; she may also rarely have permitted herself to tell a story in such a vivid and expressive way.

The connection to emotional experience, as indicated by high RA, is not reflected in the Experiencing Scale. The passages scored as relatively high in RA generally receive low Experiencing scores of 2 and 3, reflecting focus on external events. The peak RA segment above received a score of 4 for the first and last parts of the passage, in which the speaker refers to being horrified at herself, but only 2 for the description of the actual event, the action and the objects with their sensory qualities. The deviation of the RA and Experiencing Scores on this passage illustrates the distinction between the two approaches. The passage would actually have received a higher score on Experiencing had it not included the explicit description of the action and the feel of the object. We suggest that it would not have been as effective in making a link to the sensory and emotional schema that underlies the manifest content of the event without these descriptions. According to the multiple code formulation, as has been presented here, an emotion needs to be embodied in concrete and specific exemplars, incorporating specific objects, which may be accessed via the referential connections and connected to words, before the overall emotional structure of desire, or rage, or shame is named.

It follows that a major claim of the multiple code theory is that the stories in the RA peaks embody the dominant emotional schemata, played out in relation to specific objects in dreams, in memories, and in the transference. Thus we would expect measures of recurrent structure, and transference-related phenomena, as identified independently by other researchers, to converge in this phase. These would include Luborsky's measure of the "Core Conflictual Relationship Theme" (CCRT) (Luborsky & Crits-Cristoph, 1988), Hoffman and Gill's judgment of the patient's allusions to the relationship (jxr) (1988), and Teller and Dahl's frames (Dahl, 1988). In the collaborative project reported in Dahl et al. (1988), these measures were applied to the specimen hour, with converging results.

CCRT Assessment of Hour 5

In searching for the Core Conflictual Relationship Theme, scorers first locate Relationship Episodes (REs), which are narratives about significant events. Then they identify the central wish, the response expected from the other and the response expected from the self, as expressed in these episodes. The REs in this session were located primarily in the high RA peaks of the patient's discourse, as shown in Table 1.1. The exceptions were those REs identified directly in the ongoing patient–therapist interaction itself, not shown in the table. The dominant CCRT for the session included the patient's wish to be assertive and to exert control, an expectation that the other will control, disapprove, not reassure; and an expectation that she will have no control over herself, will blame herself, be annoyed, angry, upset. This CCRT emerges directly and fully in the high RA excerpt of Segment 30, as played out with the teacher. It emerges in other stories, about her father, her husband, and the boys in her class and their parents, in other high RA segments of the text (some of which are referred to in Table 1.1). No CCRTs were found in passages in the nonverbal dominance phases.

Jxr Scoring

Hoffman and Gill's assessment of the central transference themes in a session is based primarily on judgments (j) of allusions to the relationship (r) in narrative material (x) that is not manifestly about the relationship. In their procedure for coding the jxr, they identify disguised allusions to the transference relationship in stories about other people; and then demonstrate a connection of these to specific statements about the analyst. The story about the teacher's tie was scored as such a disguised allusion to the transference and was the pivotal point in their discussion of the session, receiving both a retrospective and prospective jxr coding.

Hoffman and Gill interpret the latent meaning of the passage as follows:

> Being here alone with you, a man, I feel the impulse to be forward with you, but I am horrified at that impulse and feel you too would be horrified if I pursued any kind of intimacy with you.

They support their judgment concerning the core significance of this passage by its connection to statements that are manifestly about the relationship, both preceding and following this passage. The retrospective coding is based on two prior paragraphs concerning her feelings about lying down on the couch "with just you, being a man, in the room" and her difficulty in making personal remarks. The prospective coding is based on a direct allusion to the relationship occurring somewhat later:

PATIENT: (Segment 61) Because that (*chuckle*) is, well even this I find hard to say, and it's, it's silly, but just in thinking about clothes and wearing what you want, uhm, just in, in noticing what you've worn since I've started coming and the, the variety and the freedom that you have and, and I think I've been sort of envious of that. (*Sniff*) I feel very embarrassed (*chuckle*) saying that.

The second segment to receive an x coding using the Hoffman and Gill method was a story concerning her father that occurred in segment 15 in the earlier referential phase. As in the previous example, no jxr elements were identified in the nonverbal dominant phases.

Frame Structures

As defined by Teller and Dahl (1986), frame structures are repetitive patterns, reflecting underlying emotional structures, manifested with different objects and in different contexts. They may be detected through observation of behavior and may also be identified through a pattern matching procedure in the free association of an analytic patient. Four frame structures were identified in this hour.[5] These included two major types of wishes: desires for support and reassurance (S) and a wish for closeness and togetherness (T) and two major expectations: that the wishes will not be fulfilled and that her action in seeking gratification is likely to be uncontrolled. From these expectations the defensive structures that emerge are to delay the action of seeking gratification of the wishes (D) and to control the action as well as the experience of the wish itself (C). As shown in Table 1.1, the wish structures (S and T) emerged only in the referential phase of the cycle; the defense structures (D and C) also emerged in this phase, but in some cases were overridden or negated. In contrast, the only structures that were identified in the nonverbal dominance and verbal dominance phases were defenses; these were sometimes negated in the latter case.

The independent evaluation of this session using the CCRT, jxr, and frame structure methods support the formulation proposed here. The dominant emotional and transference-related themes of the session, concerning conflictual desires and fears focused on particular persons, are contained in narrative material in the referential phase. The meaning of the narrative material, as of the story about the teacher's tie in this session, was found both in stories of events long past and in the current relationship. The narratives may emerge without the patient's recognizing the meaning that they carry; this will then need to be explicated in the succeeding discourse, often in a collaborative way.

Phase Three: Verbal Dominance, Insight, Making Precise

The expression of the emotional experience then sets the stage for the phase of testing and filtering, in which the shared verbal system may lead. In effective analytic work, the patient, or the two together, now begin to explicate the new material that has been brought forth. The danger in this phase is that the nonverbal exploration will be prematurely foreclosed, as discussed above. The next patient speech segment, which occurred immediately after the RA peak above, indicated some reflection upon the material that was retrieved there, but also considerable pulling back from the more direct emotional connections of the referential phase:

PATIENT: (Segment 56) Because several things have occurred to me while I've just been talking, shall I get off the other subject (*chuckle*)? (*Sniff*) I can't decide whether to—well, maybe I'll come back to it. Uhm, well, one thing is just a variation on my talking too much. When, at this same course last night, uhm—I'm, I'm usually very quiet when I'm, am new in a course and, and I don't like to say anything. But once I stop feeling that, once I've said something, whatever it is, then I just go the opposite way completely, and I get extremely aggressive. And at the time I don't realize I'm taking over, but then afterwards, if I think about it, I can see that I really did kind of take over or ins−, keep pushing myself into the conversation to the point where others might just say, oh well, I'm not going to bother trying to talk. And I do this, I've noticed, sometimes in conversations too, that I'll either try to anticipate what somebody's going to say and then continue on with what I'm thinking, or keep talking when I should stop because they're about to say something and then they won't, then they'll never say it. And that way I control the conversation. But the conversation might not get anywhere, or certainly nowhere near where it could have if I had stopped talking when it was time to.

In this segment, the patient is speaking in a more abstract, and general way, seemingly tracking the implications of what she has said to some extent. The emotional structures are expressed in prototypic form, rather than in the specific instantiation of the referential phase. The connection between emotional experience and words is far less direct than in the preceding segment. The overall RA score drops to 4.75; CONIM drops more than 2 standard deviations to a standardized score of less than 1 standard deviation above the session mean, while CLASP declines only slightly. Some indicators of emotional structures are also found in this phase, including one CCRT referring back to the teacher. Hoffman and Gill identify a reference to the relationship in the patient's hesitancy about changing the subject and assign an x coding for her reference to taking over conversations. Both Control and Defense frames are also identified, and in some cases negated, in this phase, in contrast to the nonverbal dominance phase.

Convergent validation for this phase might also be found in measures of insight (e.g., Broitman, 1985) which assess the patient's recognition of habitual patterns of behavior and emotion, and her understanding of the implications of what she has experienced and said. A project including this Insight measure in the identification and validation of referential cycles in a large sample of therapy sessions is now in progress. Vocal quality and paralinguistic indicators may also show characteristic patterns of this processing mode.

Using the various measures described above, we can now establish convergent validity for the phases of the referential cycle, and we can begin to see the structure of this session in terms of these sequential patterns. In the first cycle, the patient ruminates and speaks in a disconnected way; she goes on to tell stories about her father and about her husband, and then reflects upon these stories. The analyst points out that she is enacting a similar event with him. The second cycle centers around a story about her teacher. The Hoffman and Gill analysis suggests that she is experiencing the same pattern of expectations, as expressed in this story, with the analyst, although he does not explicitly make that interpretation here. The patient talks most concretely and specifically about events reflecting prototypic emotional schemata, activated in the here and now. The pattern of covariation among the RA, experiencing, and transference-related measures provides validation for all three constructs.

In contrast to the previous illustration, the patient in this early session does not enter very deeply into any of the three phases that we have identified here. She does not access new somatic or other experiential material in the nonverbal phase, and wards off the implications of the emotional meanings that she has unearthed, rather than exploring further in the reflection or verbal dominance phase. The analyst does not intervene at all following the emergence of the narrative in segment 55, and its transferential implications are not addressed, presumably being left to a time that appeared more technically appropriate to him.

CONCLUSION: A MULTIPLE CODE MODEL OF THE THERAPY PROCESS

The referential cycle has been illustrated here in two quite different sessions. In the second example, we have introduced the project of validating this theoretical formulation through converging operational measures of language, emotional expression, and underlying themes. Similar cycles have also been identified in other sessions in work now under way (Bucci & MIller, in press).

The implication of this model is that we do not expect RA to remain uniformly high in a successful session or a treatment, but rather that the referential cycles will repeat systematically. While we do not claim that such cycles will be clearly identifiable in every session or in every treatment, we would hypothesize that the occurrence of this type of fluctuation reflects the basic rhythm of therapeutic discourse: a recurrent pattern of retrieving private emotional experience, connecting it to words, and passing it through the logic and reality filters of the shared verbal code.

Free association may now be understood as following the tracks of the nonverbal schemata without the connections necessarily being apparent in the hierarchical organization of the verbal system. The fundamental rule may be seen as a technique that loosens the hold of the verbal system on the associative process and gives the nonverbal mode the chance to drive the representational and expressive systems. The patient needs to permit his private, "coconscious" nonverbal system of associations to lead the discourse, to find what is "known" only to himself, and only to part of him.

When Lieutenant Joe Leaphorn of the Navajo Tribal Police is asked by Kennedy, the local FBI officer, to look for a killer's tracks on a sagebrush flat, he walks in widening circles and crisscrosses the terrain:

"What were you looking for?" Kennedy asked. "Besides tracks."
"Nothing in particular," Leaphorn said. "You're not really looking for anything in particular. If you do that, you don't see things you're not looking for." (Hillerman, 1989, p. 23)

On a cognitive level, the lifting of logical constraints facilitates the activation of associative connections within the nonverbal system and the emergence of discrete images that can be named. On a dynamic level, the warded-off emotional schemata can perhaps best be entered by retrieving material that is peripherally connected to the schema but has not been verbally identified as connected, that is, close enough to activate some traces of the emotion, but sufficiently distant not to arouse the core distress. Ultimately this nonverbal processing is necessary to permit the "surprise," the "things you're not looking for," to emerge. The moment of enlightenment may appear in many forms—a narrative of a remembered event, a report of a dream, an incident in the treatment itself—and is the psychoanalytic counterpart of creative inspiration or a visit from the muse.

The nonverbal phase in psychoanalytic treatment is similar to the incubation phase of creative thought in that the logical aspect of verbal thought is not dominant; however the communicative aspect of verbalization remains. The flow of free association is determined, not by internal experience alone, but by the interpersonal context, and the requirement to share the subjective material as it emerges. The process of developing new emotional meanings in therapy is dependent on the patient's trust in the analyst's attending, whether he speaks or not. This is not inner speech or talking to oneself; this is inner speech for another—a new species of verbalization, perhaps existing to some extent in literature and poetry, but with great and substantial differences.

We have illustrated the cycles locally, that is, within sessions. We would also expect to see global patterns extending over days or weeks. The patient may struggle for a series of sessions, attempting to bring new emotional schemata into focus sufficiently to verbalize them, and may then have a period of apparently effortless and expansive access to this new domain, leading to reorganization of the underlying schemata in the insight phase. The global phases would direct the general level of processing, within which local fluctuation would be played out.

We would also predict systematic and general changes in the structure of these cycles in the course of treatment. Most basically, all phases, including the collaborative aspects of the referential phase, will deepen in a successful treatment. This is suggested by the comparison of the two sessions above. We would expect that the dissociation between the nonverbal and verbal representations—shown in the second session discussed above—will diminish as more material can be shared, more useable imagery becomes accessible, and insight is carried in emotion-laden terms. This might then be reflected in greater correspondence of the Experiencing, RA, and insight measures, rather than their occurrence in the different phases of the cycle. Nevertheless, any patient, at any phase of the treatment, may still find himself at times frustrated, alone, and without apparent direction in his incursions into the nonverbal domain.

A "Quasi-epigenetic" Formulation

The connections that are made in the construction of emotional meanings have certain characteristics of epigenetic development, in the sense described by Wilson and Passik (Chapter 3, this volume). Nonverbal experience is transformed when it is represented in the verbal code; one individual's experience is transformed when it is represented in the mind of another. Both types of transformations involve connection of distinct and different representational structures; both appear to have, in different ways, the qualities of discontinuity, "gappiness," and emergence that characterize epigenetic development. Both shifts occur through successive interactions between an individual and an aspect of the environment: in one case, the interaction, within an individual, between private, nonverbal representation and the verbal code, which is the internalization of shared cultural forms; in the other, the interaction between two separate, subjective worlds. In both types of transformation, each new connection brings emergent properties, but the separate structures, formed through indigenous processes prior to the transformation, continue to function and develop in their own ways.

However, the nature of connection and transformation, as defined within the multiple code theory, also differs from that generally understood by other authors in this volume and elsewhere, in several major respects:

1. *Focus on the psychological domain.* The connections and transformations that lead to emergence of new emotional meanings are not characterized in terms of movement from psychobiological to more explicitly psychological functioning but as occurring entirely within the psychological domain, that is, as mental representations and processes that occur in and between the nonverbal and verbal systems. This epistemological reformulation does not in any sense eviscerate the notion of emotional meaning. Nonverbal representations and processes, as defined here, include somatic, visceral, and emotional functions, as well as motoric and sensory imagery; thus they incorporate the body as represented in the mind.

It is important to stress that by psychological here we do not mean phenomenological. The epistemology of cognitive science has permitted us to characterize mental representations and processes, in any modality, as hypothetical constructs inferred from a wide range of converging evidence, rather than as experiential processes known through introspection. Representations in the minds of others can, in fact, only have the epistemological status of such constructs, inferred from a wide range of observable indicators, although we do not generally think in such terms. Phenomenology has a very limited domain; we each have direct access only to the representations in one mind and only in part to those, as psychoanalysts know best of all. Inferences to the representations of others are made continually, unsystematically, and without conscious examination in all the interpersonal interactions of our lives. The knowledge that we have finally caught a waiter's attention, that a crying baby is unhappy, or a snarling dog is angry is based on inference, as is the more complex recognition that a friend is upset or hurt before she has acknowledged this. Analysts constantly make inferences about the emotional structures of their patients from observation of behavior and speech, as well as from their own experiential states; in research, systematic validation for such inferences is required.

While the model has been formulated on the psychological level of the hypothetical construct, we also assume that all psychological functions, processes of "mind," have a biological substrate in the processes of the brain. Thus there are three distinct levels at which the same events can potentially be defined: at the phenomenological level, at the biological level, and at the level of the psychological construct. We can potentially look at the same event on any of these ontological levels. Insofar as they are each ontological "whole cloth," it is meaningless to postulate shifts between different levels. We suggest that many of the processes referred to by some authors as psychobiological are in fact what we have characterized here as nonverbal. It is the assumed dominance of verbal thought in the psychoanalytic model of the mental apparatus that causes nonverbal representation to be somehow relegated to a nonpsychological, or psychobiological domain.

2. *Parallel rather than hierarchical organization.* A second major factor differentiating the multiple code theory from a standard epigenetic formulation is that the system as a whole is not hierarchical. The notion of hierarchical organization is applicable only *within* the logical and semantic networks of the verbal system. The nonverbal system is organized as a network rather than as a hierarchy, with many parallel modular processors with their own rules and own organizing principles. Furthermore, the nonverbal system is distinct from the verbal, but not less complex or advanced. It follows that the retrieval of nonverbal imagery and emotional experience, and the processing of such material, is not characterized as regressive. This is a crucial implication of the multiple code model, distinguishing it from epigenetic theories as usually understood. In the multiple code theory, *regression* is the loss or abandonment of the links within the nonverbal and verbal systems, and between these representational domains. Analytic patients regress when the new referential structures that have been built are inhibited or abandoned, so that they can no longer acknowledge or identify their emotions as such, and revert, instead, to intellectualization and acting out.

ONLY CONNECT

We may now return to Forster's heroine, Margaret, to whom Forster refers in the excerpt that opens this chapter. In her hope that the connecting of the monk and the beast would lead to their disappearance as individuals, Margaret was doomed to disappointment; not only because Henry was "obtuse," but, more basically, because the human representational system is essentially a multiple code device. The representational systems (beast and monk, passion and prose) continue to develop and to function separately, in some respects, throughout life.

The more realistic expectation, for Margaret, would have been that through connecting the two systems, they might each affect and bring about change in the other, leading to new emergent structures, while continuing to operate appropriately in their own domains. This is the particular aspect of epigenetic development that has been considered here. The nonverbal and verbal systems, the passion and prose, continue to develop throughout life; they are connected and affect each other through the referential links. Through these connections, a new kind of representational entity—the referential structure—is constructed, incorporating both verbal and nonverbal elements.

In the terms of this model, *insight* is defined as articulation of emotional meanings that have not previously been acknowledged through opening new referential connections, linking verbal and nonverbal representational structures. Emotions are the organizing structures; the feeling of anger or fear toward a particular type of object, in effect, determines the category linking manifestly disparate events. *Intellectualization* is articulation of meanings based on connections within the verbal system only. Conversely, in *acting out*, connections to motoric activation occur within maladaptive emotional structures, without mediation by the logic and reality filters of the verbal code.

The goal of treatment is building of the new referential structures (i.e., insight), leading ultimately to change in the emotional structures themselves, that is, *structural change*, so that the world actually "looks different," "feels different," impulses operate differently, rather than simply being understood. The patient would not only acknowledge his fear, rage, and perhaps his desire, but, later, feel less fear and rage and more unconflictual desire. While actual recoding within the nonverbal emotional structures may be achieved at best partially, and, to varying degrees, it represents a theoretical goal of deep psychoanalytic treatment and the only definition of successful outcome in psychoanalytic terms. To bring about structural change, the activation and acknowledgment of many specific instances of a pattern, repeated over and over in different contexts and forms, in memories, dreams, and the transference—that is, *working through*—is required.

Thus the goal of treatment may be stated here, not as making the unconscious conscious, nor as locating ego where id has been, nor as imposing the secondary process on primary process thought, but as connecting the verbal to the nonverbal system, to acknowledge and recognize emotional meanings and bring about change in them. The construction of new emotional meanings in the therapeutic discourse parallels, in some respects, the development of emotional meanings in the early life of the child. However, in the construction of new emotional meanings in psychoanalysis, language plays a more central role. Ultimately, the development of new referential structures permits the individual to claim his emotional structures as his own. In contrast to emotions per se, and in contrast to past events, *meanings*, including emotional meanings, are what humans are able to regulate and reconstruct.

NOTES

1. This formulation of emotional structures is based in part on Dahl's (1978) model of the emotions, derived in turn from Freud's (1900) formulation of wishes as attempts to achieve perceptual congruence with a previous experience of satisfaction.
2. The ontological basis of this approach to theory construction, including the characterization of the representational system as a set of hypothetical constructs, and its relationship to both physiological and phenomenological levels, is discussed briefly below and in more detail in Bucci (1989).
3. From Poincaré's lecture (Hadamard, 1945, p. 13).
4. Graphs prepared at Ulm Textbank, University of Ulm, Germany.
5. Analysis carried out by G. Moroz, reported in Dahl (1988) and Bucci (1988).

REFERENCES

Arlow, J., & Brenner, C. (1964). *Psychoanalytic concepts and the structural theory.* New York: International Universities Press.

Betts, G. H. (1909). *The distribution and functions of mental imagery.* Contributions to Education Series, No. 26. New York: Columbia University, Teachers College.

Bowen, J. (1987). *The relationship between imagery and referential activity.* Unpublished doctoral dissertation, Derner Institute, Adelphi University, Garden City, NY.

Broitman, J. (1985). Insight, the mind's eye: An exploration of three patients' processes of becoming insightful. *Dissertation Abstracts International, 46*(8), 2797-B.

Bucci, W. (1984). Linking words and things: Basic processes and individual variation. *Cognition, 17,* 137–153.

Bucci, W. (1985). Dual coding: A cognitive model for psychoanalytic research. *Journal of the American Psychoanalytic Association, 33,* 571–607.

Bucci, W. (1988). Converging evidence for emotional structures: Theory and method. In H. Dahl, H. Kaechele, & H. Thomae (Eds.), *Psychoanalytic process research strategies* (pp. 29–50). New York: Springer-Verlag.

Bucci, W. (1989). A reconstruction of Freud's tally argument: A program for psychoanalytic research. *Psychoanalytic Inquiry, 9,* 249–281.

Bucci, W. (1992). *Cognitive science and psychoanalysis: A multiple code theory.* Manuscript in preparation.

Bucci, W., & Freedman, N. (1978). Language and hand: The dimension of referential competence. *Journal of Personality, 46,* 594–622.

Bucci, W., & Kabasakalian-McKay, & the RA Research Group. (in press). *Instructions for scoring Referential Activity (RA) in transcripts of spoken narrative texts.* Ulm, Germany: Ulmer Textbank.

Bucci, W., & Miller, N. (in press). Primary process: A new formulation and an analogue measure. In N. Miller, L. Luborsky, J. Barber, & J. Docherty (Eds.), *Handbook of dynamic psychotherapy research and practice.* New York: Basic Books.

Bucci, W., Severino, S. K., & Creelman, M. L. (1991). The effects of menstrual cycle hormones on dreams. *Dreaming, 1,* 263–275.

Cronbach, L., & Meehl, P. E. (1955). Construct validity in psychological tests. *Psychological Bulletin, 52,* 281–302.

Dahl, H. (1978). A new psychoanalytic model of motivation: Emotions as appetites and messages. *Psychoanalysis and Contemporary Thought, 1,* 373–408.

Dahl, H. (1988). Frames of Mind. In H. Dahl, H. Kaechele, & H. Thomae (Eds.), *Psychoanalytic process research strategies* (pp. 51–66). New York: Springer-Verlag.

Dahl, H., Kaechele, H., Thomae, H. (Eds.). (1988). *Psychoanalytic process research strategies,* New York: Springer-Verlag.

Farah, M. J. (1984). The neurological basis of mental imagery: A componential analysis. *Cognition, 18,* 245–272.

Feigl, H. (1956). Some major issues and developments in the philosophy of science of logical empiricism. In H. Feigl & M. Scriven (Eds.), *The foundations of science and the concepts of psychology and psychoanalysis* (pp. 3–37). Minneapolis: University of Minnesota Press.

Forster, E. M. (1921). *Howards end* New York: Vintage Books.

Freud, S. (1900). The interpretation of dreams. *Standard Edition* (Vols. 4 & 5). London: Hogarth Press, 1953.

Galton, F. (1883). *Inquiries into human faculty and its development.* London: Macmillan.

Gazzaniga, M. (1985). *The social brain.* New York: Basic Books.

Hadamard, J. (1945). *The psychology of invention in the mathematical field.* New York: Dover.

Hillerman, T. (1989). *The talking god.* New York: Harper Paperbacks.

Hoffman, I. Z., & Gill, M. M. (1988). A scheme for coding the patient's experience of the relationship with the therapist (PERT): Some appplications, extensions, and comparisons. In H. Dahl, H. Kaechele, & H. Thomae (Eds.), *Psychoanalytic process research strategies* (pp. 67–98). New York: Springer-Verlag.

Huttenlocher, J. (1968). Constructing spatial images: A strategy in reasoning. *Psychological Review, 4,* 550–560.

Klein, M. H., Mathieu, P. L., Gendlin, E. T., & Kiesler, D. J. (1970). *The experiencing scale: A research and training manual.* Madison: Wisconsin Psychiatric Institute, Bureau of Audio Visual Instruction.

Kosslyn, S. M. (1987). Seeing and imagining in the cerebral hemispheres: A computational approach. *Psychological Review, 94*, 148–175.

Luborsky, L., & Crits-Cristoph, P. (1988). The assessment of transference by the CCRT method. In H. Dahl, H. Kaechele, & H. Thomae (Eds.), *Psychoanalytic process research strategies* (pp. 99–108). New York: Springer-Verlag.

Marschark, M., Richman, C. L., Yuille, J. C., & Hunt, R. R. (1987). The role of imagery in memory: On shared and distinctive information. *Psychological Bulletin, 102*, 28–41.

McLaughlin, J. T. (1978). Primary and secondary process in the context of cerebral hemispheric specialization. *Psychoanalytic Quarterly, 47*, 237–266.

McLean, P. D. (1949). Psychosomatic disease and the "visceral brain": Recent developments bearing on the Papez theory of emotion. *Psychosomatic Medicine, 11*, 338–353.

Mergenthaler, E. (1985). *Textbank systems: Computer science applied in the field of psychoanalysis*. Heidelberg: Springer-Verlag.

Noy, P. (1969). A revision of the psychoanalytic theory of the primary process. *International Journal of Psycho-Analysis, 50*, 155–178.

Paivio, A. (1971). *Imagery and verbal processes*. New York: Holt, Rinehart & Winston.

Paivio, A. (1986). *Mental representations: A dual coding approach*. New York: Oxford University Press.

Paivio, A., Clark, J. M., Digdon, N., & Bons, T. (1989). Referential processing: Correlates of naming pictures and imaging to words. *Memory and Cognition, 17*, 163–174.

Panksepp, J. (1982). Towards a general psychobiological theory of emotions. *Behavioral and Brain Sciences, 5*, 407–467.

Price, A., & Bucci, W. (1986, May). *The use of language in psychoanalysis and experiential psychotherapy*. Paper presented at the Annual Conference of the Society for the Exploration of Psychotherapy Integration (SEPI), Toronto, Ontario.

Rapaport, D., Gill, M. M., & Schafer, R. (1968). *Diagnostic psychological testing*. New York: International Universities Press.

Rogers, C. (1950). A current formulation of client-centered therapy. *Social Science Review, 24*.

Rogers, C. R. (1951). *Client-centered therapy*. Boston: Houghton Mifflin.

Rogers, C. R. (1961). *On becoming a person*. Boston: Houghton Mifflin

Sheehan, P. W. (1967). A shortened form of Betts' questionnaire upon mental imagery. *Journal of Perceptual and Motor Skills, 24*, 386–389.

Steinbeck, J. (1952). *East of eden*. New York: Penguin Books.

Rumelhart, D. E., McClelland, J. L., & the PDP Research Group (1986). *Parallel distributed processing: Explorations in the microstructure of cognition*. Cambridge, MA: MIT Press.

Teller, V., & Dahl, H. (1986). The microstructure of free association. *Journal of the American Psychoanalytic Association, 34*, 763–798.

Tulving, E. (1984). Precis of elements in episodic memory. *Behavioral and Brain Sciences, 7*, 223–268.

Wechsler, D. (1981). *Wechsler Adult Intelligence Scale-Revised*. San Antonio, TX: Psychological Corporation.

Werner, H., & Kaplan, B. (1963). *Symbol formation*. Hillsdale, NJ: Erlbaum, 1984.

Winson, J. (1985). *Brain and psyche: The biology of the unconscious*. New York: Anchor Press/Doubleday.

2

The Level of Integrative Failure in Borderline and Schizophrenic Pathology

STANLEY GRAND, KENNETH FEINER, AND STEVEN REISNER

It is a well accepted fact that psychological development entails the progressive integration and differentiation of hierarchically organized structures and functions. This progression, in which earlier undifferentiated forms serve as precursors to later, more complex organizations, has been termed the epigenetic principle in psychic life. Traditionally, psychoanalytic models for the classification of psychopathology have relied heavily upon this principle and are organized around conceptual frameworks that emphasize the unfolding of maturational sequences in development. Freud's (1905, 1911) developmental line from autoerotism through narcissism to object relatedness is one such model, tracing the epigenetic unfolding of a maturational sequence in which earlier levels of development are subsumed under and incorporated within mature object relatedness. A somewhat different epigenetic unfolding is given in Freud's (1913, 1923b) model of libidinal development in which oral, anal, and phallic organizers of experience are ultimately included within and subsumed by the genital organization of libidinal wishes. Both models have been useful for the psychoanalytic understanding and treatment of psychopathology.

A number of other approaches to the organization and unfolding of maturational sequences (e.g., Erikson's [1950] psychosocial stages; Spitz's [1959] conception of psychic organizers; A. Freud's [1965] developmental lines; Mahler's [Mahler, Pine, & Bergman, 1975] stages of separation–individuation; Horner's [1975] stages and processes of object relating; and Gedo & Goldberg's [1973] and Gedo's [1979] hierarchy of mental organizations ranging from the consolidation of body boundaries to the formation of a repressive barrier) have served to fill out our conception of both early and later phases of human development in interaction with the maternal and social requirements for human adaptation. Nowhere, however, is the epigenetic principle as applied to the development of psychopathology spelled out more clearly than in Gedo's (1988) most recent work. There, Gedo has extended his earlier views on mental organization to include psychological issues that remain outside of the sphere of conflict. Thus, Gedo extends his focus upon the maladaptive ways in which the mind processes the content of thought to dysfunction in those mental operations at the beginning of psychological organization.

The work that we will present in this chapter likewise follows closely upon the application of the epigenetic principle to the full range of psychopathology.[1] It is based upon previous work (Grand, Freedman, Feiner, & Kiersky, 1988) on a system for assessing psychopathology that organizes symptoms along a developmental continuum and that takes account of the major crises of adaptation confronting human growth and development. The system views symptoms conceptually as the manifestations of failure to integrate developmentally relevant capacities and functions necessary to meet life's major tasks. Thus, symptoms are viewed as the expression of a failure to integrate major adaptive requirements for the adequate development and structuralization of mental experience at each level of human growth.[2]

Specifically, we propose that symptoms reflect a failure in the integration of three main foci of human experience: that is, bodily cohesion; psychic cohesion; and the internal organization of the representational world. In terms of our system, these foci are called the body ego, the self, and object relations.

The clinical implications of our model for understanding symptoms is clear and straightforward. The epigenetic unfolding of development in which early issues of body integrity are subsumed by issues pertaining to the establishment of a psychologically based sense of self-cohesion that, in turn, is ultimately subsumed by the establishment of a fully articulated internal world of object related experiences, reflects a progression in which structures develop, differentiate, and thereby rapidly become implicated in dynamic conflict. According to this view, structuralized conflict is contingent upon the emergence of the conceptual differentiation of self and object. Prior to such differentiation, or when such differentiation is impaired, symptoms may only reflect the disintegration of these early structural organizations per se. Thus, while adult psychopathology invariably entails a mixture of both structural and conflictual issues, dysfunction early in development, prior to the differentiation of self and object, may simply entail a global response to the waxing and waning of undifferentiated drive tensions (Hartmann, 1958; Jacobson, 1964). Structuralized conflict appears to be conditional upon and specific to the encoding of drive pressures, the differentiation of self and object, and the establishment of aims with respect to objects.[3] Viewing symptoms in regard to both structural and functional considerations allows us to assess the relative weight attributable to both preconflictual and conflictual experience in the total makeup of the individual's psychopathology. Thus, patients can be seen as having a range of structural and dynamic issues deriving from both earlier preconflictual and later conflictual stages of development. It is the dominance of one or the other form of symptom that establishes the predominant level at which a particular patient functions at any moment of his or her life.[4]

Our model for understanding symptoms considers development within the perspective of six levels of integrative functioning. At the earliest level, psychoanalytic and cognitive theorizing generally assumes that the first task of neonatal development entails the regulation and integration of bodily processes that are precursors to mental operations. These are the bio-organic, sensory, and attentional processes, involving in turn the regulation and cyclical viscissitudes of the primary bodily functions, the organization of primary sensations attendant on these bodily functions and on bodily experiences generally, and the awareness and mediation of these bio-organic and sensory processes in the promotion of bodily viability and optimal functioning. These processes constitute the biological substrate or precursors (Resch & Grand, 1984) to the earliest phase in the development of bodily integrity, or the unit characteristic of the evolving organism (cf. Freud's [1923a] Body Ego; Piaget's [1954] sensorimotor stage; Lichtenberg's [1978] first stage of body self).

Theoretically, we assume that the next level of integrative functioning entails the establishment of the integrity of bodily experience. This is a stage at which awareness of openings, gaps, or disruption in body surfaces or boundaries results in confusion of inside and outside. At this stage, experience is primarily directional in that it consists of vectors moving into or out of the interior of the organism. Referential and perceptual systems are primitively organized around loci of experience on the body surface, such as the mouth, anus, nostrils, and ear canals (Glover's [1943] "ego nuclei";

Spitz's [1959] "psychic organizers"; Lichtenberg's [1978] "Id–ego nuclei"). Primitive ideation is organized around projective and intro-jective processes, so that painful stimulation is projected and experi-enced as external to the body or taken in and experienced as threats from within. This level of integrative development is a precursor to the beginning differentiation of a self-representation (Lichtenberg's [1978] second stage of bodily cohesion) and forms the nuclei of the self-representational system that will begin to be established at the next phase of development.

Subsequent developments in the third stage assume the integra-tion of a primitive mental self characterized by an awareness of differentiated thoughts and feelings, which are experienced as dis-tinct from bodily sensation (Fast, 1985; Giovacchini, 1986; Nagera, 1981). This primitive mental self, not yet functionally independent of the external object, nor fully cohesive, requires the active presence of the external object for its completion (cf. Greenacre's [1958] "impos-ter"; Deutch's [1942] "as if" personality). The task for the infant at this stage of development is, therefore, one of integrating, through introjective mechanisms, the functions of the external object (cf. Kernberg, 1966). The eventual accomplishment of this goal estab-lishes the mental self as cohesive and provides the growing infant with the experience of adaptive sufficiency.

The fourth level of development entails the further elaboration of a cohesive self-representation. The integration of the functions of the external object is relatively complete at this stage, and the child now begins to experience a sense of illusory narcissistic self-sufficiency (Kohut, 1971; Modell, 1976; Volkan, 1976). As the external object is no longer felt to be a necessary aspect of self-experience, the child lives in an illusory world of grandiose omnipotent isolation from the object (Ferenczi, 1913). This is the stage of the child's "love affair with the world" (Kaplan, 1978). The adaptive task at this stage is the integra-tion of the polar experiences of illusory self-sufficiency and depen-dency on the object.

At the next level of development, adaptive sufficiency requires the integration of internal and external reality. The development of a unified cohesive self, the presence of a constant, albeit ambivalently experienced object, and the differentiation of an internal world of wishes, affects, and prohibitions result in the capacity to experience reality more fully, as well as the ubiquitous conflicts engendered by the attempts to satisfy needs in relation to this reality. The effort to satisfy inner needs within the context of external requirements for adaptation co-occurs with a growing capacity for reflective awareness of the self in relation to the world, and this reflective capacity serves as an adaptive mechanism for steering the child toward effective satisfaction of needs in reality (Jacobson's [1964] stage of depersonification and abstraction of the ego ideal).

The highest level of adaptation entails the integration of aims and goals with reality. At this level, the person has acquired the capacity to organize his or her life in ways that have long-term adaptive significance. The essential problems at this stage of development center around frustrations over the difficulties in attaining such long-range goals. Problem solving through thinking and logic form the adaptive mechanisms for meeting frustrations. At this level, thought is truly experimental action (Freud, 1911). Indeed, the major characteristic of this stage of development is flexible problem solving that does not result in chronic inhibition in functioning or constriction in affective relations with the object world (Jacobson's [1964] stage of the mature, autonomous superego; also, Erikson, 1956; Klein, 1960; Saul, 1960).

In our previous report (Grand et al., 1988), we summarized the manual for codifying symptoms within this model, we provided reliability data on the instrument used for obtaining relevant clinical material for assessment, and we presented two clinical case reports of patients treated at the Health Science Center at Brooklyn to illustrate the usefulness of our classification system for assessing changes in developmental level resulting from psychotherapeutic treatment. In the present chapter, we report on the progress of our work in establishing the validity of our developmental model of psychopathology by (1) applying our assessment system to the symptomatic expressions of two groups of severely disturbed patients treated at our hospital—borderline and schizophrenic groups; (2) factor analyzing the symptom scores of our entire sample in order to establish the underlying psychological dimensions that are tapped by our scale for measuring the levels of integrative failure.

In brief, our manual for assessing symptomatic behavior and the semistructured interview for tapping such behavior target five areas of experience relevant to adaptive functioning. We attempt, through an open-ended semistructured interview format, to elicit symptom expression in the areas of thought, perception, affect, self, and behavior/volition. The assessment manual codifies symptomatic experience in each of these areas along a developmental continuum ranging from Disintegration at the Level of Body Ego precursors; Disintegration at the Level of Body Ego; Disintegration at the Level of Self and Object Experiences; Disintegration at the Level of the Grandiose, Omnipotent Self; Disintegration at the Level of Internal and External Reality; to Disintegration of Aims and Goals with Respect to Reality.

THE LEVELS OF INTEGRATIVE FAILURE

We turn now to a summary of the predominant symptomatic expressions of crises in integration that are parallel to and coordinated with the six levels of normal development.[5] A manual for assessing these levels of integrative failure and a semistructured interview for eliciting expressions of integrative failure have both been developed. These are currently the subject of validation studies at our research center. Here we wish to present only the conceptual framework for assessing symptoms at each level of integrative failure and the reliability of scoring such failures.

Level I: Disintegration at the Level of Body Ego Precursors

We assume that this level of mental disorganization parallels the stage of primary autism of earliest infancy, when the organism is struggling to regulate and coordinate bodily processes in the interest of physiological viability. When dysfunction of these processes occurs, it is reflected in symptomatic behavior involving irregularities in somatic and sensory processes, such as temperature sensations, tactile and muscular sensations, vestibular sensations, and all other sensory modalities. The issues for adult psychopathology are those of organization versus chaos, of holding together versus falling apart, of existence versus nonexistence as a physical entity. In all respects, experiences at this level of integrative failure are global, diffuse, amorphous, and chaotic, reflecting the minimal and tenuous nature of the individual's sense of body integrity and the overwhelming quality of the threats to it.

Thus, at Level I, integrative failures are scored when

- *thought* lacks organization, direction, or focus and is characterized by blocking, looseness, and perseveration; or
- *perception* is primarily hallucinatory, involving amorphous sensations that are raw, unformed sensory products; or
- *affect* is extremely labile and subject to immediate discharge; or
- *self* does not appear as the center of experience, and
- *behavior* is randomly discharged and not directed.

Level II: Disintegration at the Level of the Body Ego

Pathology at Level II is assumed to entail the disruption of or threats to the individual's sense of body boundaries and body integrity. We propose that failure in the integration of the unit character of the body ego leads to symptomatic states in which fluidity or rigidity of the boundary function predominates, and there is a loss of continuity and of the vectorial quality in behavior. The threats to body integrity are experienced physically, manifested in concrete behavior, or they are symbolized in hallucinations and delusions. The threats may be experienced as coming either from without or from within; they may also have to do with the movement of materials into or out of the body. The individual may be unable to defend himself or herself from the invasive forces, or he or she may develop more or less elaborate and bizarre defenses against them. At Level II, integrative failures are scored when

- *thought* is organized around primitive introjective and projective mechanisms and is characterized by neologisms, delusions, and stereotypy; or
- *perception* is primarily hallucinatory but now involves more formed experiences centering on bodily surfaces and openings; or
- *affect* is undifferentiated and inappropriate to the content of speech or action; or
- *self* is symbiotic and undifferentiated from objects; or
- *behavior* is inappropriate, disorganized, peculiar, or bizarre.

Level III: Disintegration at the Level of Self and Object Experiences

Level III pathology assumes a failure to integrate the functions of the external object and a consequent extreme dependence of the self-concept upon the support of others, with resultant annihilation anxiety at threats of abandonment. As the existence and viability of the body and its physiological systems were the crucial issue at Level I, so at Level III the crucial issue is the survival of the self. This survival is dependent on the proximity and facilitating functions of an important object, whom the individual does not experience as being completely independent or different from himself or herself. Illusional thinking serves to ward off such fears at this level.

Level III is scored when

- *thought* is overinclusive and dominated by need gratification and colored by magical illusions and suspiciousness; or
- *perception* is essentially realistic with occasional misperceptions or derealization; or

- *affect* is intense and characterized by reactions of rage at threats of abandonment; or
- *self-centeredness* is extreme with little understanding of the needs, thoughts, or feelings of others; or
- *behavior* is oriented toward maintaining the integrity of a fragile self-structure and is manipulative, impulsive, and unstable.

Level IV: Disintegration at the Level of the Grandiose, Omnipotent Self

Until the sense of self becomes more resilient and less dependent on the maintenance of the illusion of omnipotence, the individual has difficulties with the regulation of self-esteem. This is assumed to be one of the hallmarks of Level IV pathology. A relatively fragile sense of self seeks to buttress itself through illusions of self-sufficiency and omnipotence. When the reality inevitably falls short of the illusion, then the individual's self-esteem plummets, reminding the individual of the vulnerability of his or her previously dependent state. To avoid this happening, the individual must maintain the omnipotent illusion, arranging his or her mental life so that he or she is in the center of it and awareness of his need for others is minimized. Level IV is scored when

- *thought* is characterized by fantasies of unlimited success, power, brilliance, beauty, or ideal love; or
- *perception* is in the service of screening out aspects of the external world that contradict fantasy constructions; or
- *affect* is reactive to threats to the maintenance of self-esteem; or
- *self-centeredness* is characterized by illusions of omnipotent self-sufficiency and grandiosity; or
- *behavior* is organized around avoiding the disillusionment of the omnipotent fantasy and is characterized by exhibitionism, exploitativeness, and self-aggrandizement.

Level V: Disintegration at the Level of Internal and External Reality

Pathology at Level V reflects the difficulty of reconciling one's goals and responsibilities in life with the adaptive possibilities that exist in reality. Conflict over contradictory wishes and fears, and ambivalence about the actualization of wishes, result in the inhibition of thought and action and, through various defensive maneuvers, lead to maladaptive compromise solutions to ubiquitous ambivalent tendencies. Inhibition and constriction of one's interests, warding off unpleasant affect, limitations in one's capacity to relate to others in an affectively rich and subtle manner, frustration in the capacity to satisfy one's needs and wishes, and limitations in one's ambitions form the central features of pathology at this level. Level V is scored when

- *thought* is characterized by difficulties integrating one's goals and responsibilities with the adaptive possibilities in reality; or
- *perception* involves distortions in testing and relating to external reality due to conflict in one's own needs; or
- *affect* is characterized by contradictory and antagonistic wishes that lead to either compromises that inhibit full affective experience or result in strongly ambivalent feelings; or
- *self* is caught up in conflict over incongruous aspects of one's needs and wishes, and self-experience is colored by anxiety and insecurities; or
- *behavior* is characterized by inhibitions that prevent the full actualization of one's potential to be socially and personally productive.

Level VI: Disintegration of Aims and Goals with Respect to Reality

The essential characteristic of pathology at Level VI centers around frustrations over the difficulties in attaining long-range aims and goals with respect to reality. Whereas thought, perception, affect, and behavior are still subject to inevitable conflicts and ambivalence around impulses and wishes, problem solving is characterized by consideration of alternative strategies for adaptation, perception remains relatively attuned to external reality, a wide range of affective experiences can be tolerated, and one's enjoyment in work is enriched by the capacity to sublimate impulses and wishes in realistic ways. At this level, solutions to integrative struggles are most effectively absorbed in ego-syntonic characterological structures that are more or less effective in resolving adaptive crises. Level VI is scored when

- *thought* is characterized by knowledge of one's goals and responsibilities, but frustrations occur with respect to the need to integrate these goals with the adaptive possibilities in reality; or
- *perception* entails only minor interference with the capacity to test and relate to reality, which are the result of conflicting needs and wishes; or

- *affect* is characterized by relatively brief interferences with the capacity to master emotional experience, so that one's ability to love, hate, and derive satisfaction from one's relationships and work are only mildly affected; or
- *self* is characterized by a sense of integrity that has been achieved despite conflict, and one has learned to live with oneself in relative comfort; or
- *behavior* is characterized by the capacity to work and be socially and personally productive.

Some General Qualifications in Our Understanding of the System

There are two important considerations to keep in mind in any attempt to link symptomatic expression to developmental level. First, there is the consideration that a symptom per se does not define the developmental level of the person exhibiting that symptom. People may exhibit a wide range of symptomatic behaviors, from those revealing integrative difficulties around body ego precursors to those reflecting difficulties with the integration of aims and goals with respect to reality. Our focus in scoring is upon the symptom not the person. While this may complicate our diagnostic impressions of people insofar as their having a range of developmental failures, we do consider the modal level of integrative failure as being close to the dominant level at which the person functions. The spread between highest and lowest levels of integrative failure may provide a view of the potential range of progressive and regressive movement.[6]

Second, in targeting the level at which any particular symptom may fall, it is important to tap the person's own understanding of the symptom and the context within which it is elicited. Thus, "anxiety" per se cannot be targeted at a specific developmental level. But such a level can be determined if we know both the *context* within which the anxiety emerges (e.g., conflict around triadic relationships or separation from a dyadic relationship) and the *meaning* that this anxiety has for the patient (e.g., fear of competitiveness or fear of being alone). In this sense, our study of symptoms is close to the way clinicians themselves classify symptomatic states in their clinical work. Our semistructured interview questionnaire was constructed with these considerations in mind, and it was designed to tap both the context and meaning that surround any symptomatic expression.

One final consideration should be kept in mind in regard to the way we view our data. Our effort to tap symptomatic behaviors in the areas of thought, perception, affect, self, and behavior/volition reflect our interest in being comprehensive with respect to *modalities* in which symptoms may appear. These modalities represent surface qualities, or the medium through which "deeper" psychological dimensions are expressed. The underlying dimensions are thought to manifest themselves along the same developmental continuum we have already suggested for each of the surface qualities we observe. It is clear, for example, that perception may be primitive and unstructured, as in an amorphous hallucinatory experience, or highly differentiated and structured, as in complex pattern recognition. Or, thought may be primitive, loose, and perseverative, as in autism, or more clearly structured, as in delusions, or highly articulated, as in a statement of complex logical relations. Each of those distinctions can be viewed as manifestations of different levels of a developmental continuum. One goal of the present study is to begin the process of identifying the psychological dimensions underlying these manifest symptoms and to articulate their characteristics along the developmental continua to which they give rise.[7]

The findings that we will present in this study are tentative since clinical considerations made it difficult to obtain a large sample. As such our data are only suggestive and will require further validation in subsequent studies. We feel, however, that the commonsensical nature of our findings is, in itself, an indicator of their validity, and we therefore present these data for the purpose of communicating what we feel is an important method for assessing psychopathology. In line with others in this field (Adams, Doster, & Calhoun, 1977; Frances & Cooper, 1981; Karasu & Skodol, 1980; Michels, 1984; Persons, 1986; Rosenzweig, 1982; Vaillant, 1984), we feel that "we need structures in order to discuss, study and learn about those features which we believe to be relevant to our patients and their lives" (Michels, 1984, p. 548).

METHOD

Our semistructured clinical interview was administered to 30 inpatients at the State University of New York, Health Science Center at Brooklyn. Of the 30 patients, 15 were diagnosed at discharge as having a schizophrenic illness and 15 were diagnosed as having a borderline personality disorder. The interviews that were conducted during the week of admission to the hospital were tape-recorded and subsequently transcribed for scoring. The patients' responses to items designed to tap their symptoms and concerns were assigned a level of integrative failure according to the manual developed for that purpose. Levels were determined by assessing the context or conditions under which symptoms appeared and the specific purpose the symptom served at the time of its occurrence. Criteria and examples for scoring these symptom reports are provided in our scoring manual. Our scoring procedure yields several scores that establish both the predominant *level* on which the symptom falls (determined by its focus on the body, self, or object world) and *mode* of symptomatic expression (thought, perception, affect, self, and behavior/volition), as well as a range of pathology across both level and mode of functioning.

For reasons similar to those articulated by Wilson and Passik (Chapter 3, this volume), we consider interrater reliability the most appropriate form of reliability for the Level of Integrative Failure (L.I.F.) scale. Gamma, a chance corrected statistic, appropriate for continuous or ordinal level data, is well suited to this scale because the levels are ordered on a continuum with the lowest levels tapping the most severe forms of psychopathology and the higher levels tapping highly adaptive characteristics. This statistic also allows evaluation of reliability using different degrees of stringency in defining agreement between raters. The strictest criterion requires exact agreement about the level on which a symptom falls. However, agreement can also be defined by ratings within a half step of one another, which also represents a fairly strict criterion, or a full step apart, which we would consider a relatively loose standard for agreement. The results of our reliability trials are based on agreement within a halfstep.

Although we are currently collecting data from a large sample of subjects, the data we have collected thus far only constitute a limited sample. Thus, while results of our previous reliability study (Grand et al., 1988) were quite promising, those results must be replicated with a larger sample and with a wider range of diagnostic groups to ensure that interrater agreement will still be attainable.

In the reliability trials for the present study, in order to ascertain the interrater agreement on scoring of the interview data, three raters independently scored 15 protocols after consensually scoring 5 others. Of the three raters, two were considered advanced (postdoctoral level) and the third was considered intermediate (internship level). The results of the less experienced judge were not included because she did not meet our criteria for qualification as an expert rater, which required a significant level of agreement within a half step of either of the other raters. Using gamma, the level of agreement between the two advanced raters was assessed separately for each subject. The overall average (.846) was derived from scores ranging between .650 and .998. For this type of data, this represents an extremely high degree of interrater agreement. We believe comparable levels of agreement are attainable given adequate preparation and training.

Extensive preparation is needed before undertaking a reliability trial. The necessary training of raters includes a thorough familiarity with the scoring manual. The manual provides operational descriptions of each of the levels and gives examples of subjective reports that clarify the meaning of typical symptoms at each of the levels of the scale. Additionally, raters should consensually score several protocols with a qualified expert rater to increase familiarity with the inference process that informs the L.I.F. system. As with the Epigenetic Assessment Rating Scale (EARS) (Wilson & Passik, Chapter 3, this volume), clinical experience and understanding of how clinical inferences are made enhances raters' ability to make the kinds of inferences necessary in scoring of L.I.F. protocols. The scoring of L.I.F. data is based as much as possible on manifest reports given by subjects about the meanings of their symptoms and the purposes they serve. Additionally, practice is necessary to familiarize raters with subtle distinctions between levels and with the theoretical basis for these distinctions. Understanding the theoretical principles that underlie L.I.F. gives the rater a basis for scoring the diverse responses that subjects give to the interview questions.

The data obtained from patients' responses to our original 72-item semistructured interview were subjected to an item analysis for the purpose of assessing the internal consistency of the interview questionnaire. At this stage in the development of our questionnaire our goal was to determine whether each of the 72 items contributed significant information to the overall assessment of symptom levels and modes or whether there were specific problems with items that precluded their usefulness for this purpose.[8] In this analysis we focused on the elimination of items that patients consistently could not answer, or those items that raters were consistently unable to score because of lack of sufficient responses. Beyond these criteria, we eliminated those questions that were found to be statistically unreliable, using Cronbach's alpha. By this method we determined that 25 questions did not produce scorable responses in at least one third of the sample. These items were eliminated from our interview schedule. Eleven items were discarded because they correlated poorly with all other items. Furthermore, in two cases, items appeared to yield the same or similar material, and these redundant items were eliminated. Finally, on the basis of several preliminary factor analyses, 10 of the remaining 34 items were eliminated on the basis of their failure to load above .60 on any of the emergent factors. Thus, the factor analytic data reported in this study are based on 24 items of the original pool of 72 items using Varimax rotation and mean substitution for missing values.[9]

Our procedure for assessing the validity of the L.I.F. scale was to first factor analyze the scores for the pool of our remaining 24 items in order to determine the underlying factor structure. Since our items were selected to tap a variety of psychological functions deemed to be important in the assessment of psychopathology (i.e., thought, perception, affect, self, and behavior/volition), we were especially interested to see whether the items clustered according to these functional categories or whether deeper-level structures were being tapped by our questionnaire.

Once the factor analysis was complete, subjects were assigned scores on each factor. We were interested in which factor scores, if any, would be helpful in predicting a given subject's diagnosis. A discriminant function analysis was undertaken to help determine this. In addition, we wanted to know which factor scores in particular differentiated diagnostic groups from one another. To this end, we performed t tests on the scores of our two sample populations on each factor. Thus, the discriminate function analysis was undertaken to help us predict a subject's likely diagnosis, given a particular set of factor scores. The t test was employed as a validity measure to ascertain whether subjects whose diagnoses were known were accurately differentiated by factor scores.

We were interested, as well, in determining whether valid distinctions could be made *within* diagnostic categories using the individual factors that emerged. To assess the validity of differentiating personality styles within a diagnostic category, we compared the L.I.F. factor scores with a known measure of character style. Our measure of comparison was Blatt and Schichman's (1983) distinction between anaclitic and introjective character styles. A discharge summary of each patient in the study was scored by two independent raters and labeled according to Blatt's criteria.

The raters determined that of our sample of 15 Borderline patients, 11 were of the anaclitic type, while 4 were rated as introjective. Among our sample of 15 schizophrenics, 2 were classified as anaclitic and 13 as introjective. Interrater reliability was found to be adequately high ($\chi^2 = 10.8$; 1 df, $p < .01$).

RESULTS

The factor analysis yielded six factors with eigenvalues greater than unity, accounting for 76% of the total variance. An item was assigned to a factor if it was found to have a loading above .60 on only one factor. We chose this stringent criterion because of the preliminary nature of our study and the small subject pool. By this criterion, 19 of the 24 items were included in the six factors. Presented in Table 2.1

TABLE 2.1. Factor Loadings of Items on Each of Six Factors

Factor 1: Impulse regulation (accounting for 46.8% of the variance)

Item	Loading	
49	.766	Do you ever wish you would die or have thoughts about killing yourself?
		Have you ever felt so desperate that you formed a plan about how you might kill yourself?
		Have you ever behaved self-destructively — tried to kill yourself?
53	.684	Can you describe your daily activities?
		Do you have any habits that you perform every day?
		Are you able to work?
		What work do you do?
46	.607	How is your appetite?
		Have you lost or gained a great deal of weight recently?
		Do you tend to binge when you eat?
14	.604	Are you aware of any particular sexual fantasies?
		What fantasies do you have while engaged in masturbation or intercourse?
32	.601	What are your sexual practices?
		Do you masturbate?
		How often?

Factor 2: Self-definition (accounting for 7.4% of the variance)

Item	Loading	
70	.891	Do you tend to try to be with people you admire?
		For what reason?
		Do you try to be like these people?
		How come?
60	.764	Do you see yourself as being the same person in all situations or different?
16	.729	What is one of the most creative things you have ever done?

Factor 3: Emotional relatedness (accounting for 6.8% of the variance)

Item	Loading	
35	.862	How often do you get feelings of unworthiness or of being no good, and/or do you often feel elated or invulnerable?
39	.711	Have you ever loved someone?
		Do you love someone now?
		Is your love returned?
		What is it like for you to be "in love"?
28	.707	Have you ever lost a person you feel close to?
		How did you react?
		Do you feel that someone rejected or abandoned you?
		What was this like?
40	.612	Do you find any experiences pleasurable?
		How about unpleasurable?
		Can you give an example?

(cont.)

TABLE 2.1. *(cont.)*

Factor 4: Psychic cohesiveness (accounting for 5.9% of the variance)

Item	Loading	
12	.707	Do you sometimes have so many thoughts it is difficult to focus on only one thing? What is this like for you?
69	.698	Is it difficult for you to remember what someone is like when they are not in your presence? Can you say more about this? Do you feel calmer and more stable when you are with someone?
58	.695	Do you feel like you are part of another person, like you are merged or fused with someone? What is that like for you?

Factor 5: Interpersonal relatedness (accounting for 4.9% of the variance)

Item	Loading	
68	.724	Do you watch carefully to avoid being hurt in relationships? What is this like for you? How do you react? Do you generally expect people to let you down?
73	.651	Have you found that no matter how hard you try to avoid them, the same difficulties crop up in most important relationships? Do you keep getting involved with the same type of person? What kind of person is he or she?

Factor 6: Representational differentiation (accounting for 4.4% of the variance)

Item	Loading	
11	.893	Do you get suspicious about other people's intentions toward you such as they might be following you or want to hurt you? Do you feel concerned about what other people are saying about you?
62	.664	Do you think you are special in any way? Positively or negatively? Do you think you have special powers or that you are in any way superhuman, invulnerable? Is it important for you to think you are in a special relationship with someone (or God)?

are the six factors that emerged in the analysis, along with the specific items that make up each factor. Factor 1, which accounted for a substantial percentage of the total variance (46.8%), was formed of a cluster of questions concerning daily activities, impulses, and their regulation. Since the predominant concerns tapped by these items seem to coalesce around issues of managing impulses, we named this factor Impulse Regulation.

Factor 2, consisted of items addressing issues of self-reflection, self-continuity, self-aspiration, and creativity, and this factor accounted for 7.4% of the variance. We named this factor Self-Definition.

Factor 3, which accounted for 6.8% of the variance, consisted of items tapping emotional responses to object related experience. We named this factor Emotional Relatedness.

Factor 4, accounting for 5.9% of the total variance, consisted of items tapping cohesion of thought, memory, and self-experience. We named this factor Psychic Cohesiveness.

Factor 5, accounting for 4.9% of the variance, consisted of two items, both addressing issues of relationship with others. Therefore, we named this factor Interpersonal Relatedness.

Factor 6, which accounted for 4.4% of the variance, consisted of two items, both of which addressed experiences reflecting boundary disturbances: in one, the projection of malevolent impulses, and in the other, the expansion of the boundary in grandiose and special relations with others. We tentatively named this factor Representational Differentiation to reflect variations in the level of the capacity to maintain boundaries between self and object representations.

Although we speculated that items might cluster around the surface organizational categories of thought, perception, affect, self, and behavior/volition, this hypothesis was not validated by the factor analysis. While Factor 1 (Impulse Regulation) is similar to the category we described as "behavior," and Factor 2 (Self-definition) and Factor 3 (Emotional Relatedness) include many of the items we had subsumed under the categories of "self" and "affect," the results of this factor analysis suggest that deeper-level structures are being tapped by the L.I.F. questionnaire.

The discriminant function analysis, undertaken to ascertain which, if any, of the factors could be used to predict a given subject's diagnosis, revealed that four of the six factors contributed significantly to making such a determination ($p < .01$). Thus, we found statistical support for our belief that our scale could be used to determine diagnosis according to scores on a hierarchical measure of psychological functioning.

Two of these four factors, Factors 1 and 2 (Impulse Regulation and self-definition, respectively), were found to significantly differentiate subjects according to their known diagnosis, ($p < .05$). The other two, Factors 3 and 4 (Emotional Relatedness and Psychic Cohesiveness, respectively) showed a trend in that direction ($p < .08$). The remaining two factors did not differentiate the two groups to any significant degree.

We attempted to ascertain the usefulness of factors in differentiating personality subtypes within our two diagnostic samples. Using a 2 × 6 analysis of variance, we compared subjects within diagnostic categories according to Blatt's subtypes across factors. The results of this analysis were not significant. We suspected that this lack of significance might be the result of the small number of subjects within each diagnostic category (n = 15). However, using 2-way analyses of variance for each factor separately, we found a significant interaction effect for diagnosis and personality subtype on two of the six factors. For Factor 4 (Psychic Cohesiveness), we found that among schizophrenics, anaclitic (i.e., undifferentiated) patients scored significantly lower than introjective (i.e., paranoid) patients. This difference was not noticeable among our borderline patients.

On Factor 6 (Representational Differentiation), anaclitic (i.e., undifferentiated) schizophrenics scored lower than introjective (i.e., paranoid) schizophrenics. On this factor, the reverse was true for borderline patients; that is, introjective (narcissistic–schizoid) borderline patients scored lower than anaclitic (hysterical–dependent) borderline patients.

DISCUSSION

When we undertook this study, it was our assumption that the borderline experience could be differentiated from the schizophrenic experience on the basis of *epigenetically* determined organizations of psychological functions that underlie the two forms of mental impairment. That is, the distinctions between these two diagnostic groupings would be more apparent in terms of their *levels* of organization and focus rather than in terms of distinct and different aspects of psychic dysfunction. Different organizational *issues* would be involved in each of these pathological groupings, but these issues would reflect concerns that are relevant to the adaptive requirements of different levels of the developmental progression of psychic functions and structure, and not to different organizations per se.

The results of this study confirmed our expectations and also validated to some extent the utility of the L.I.F. scale as an instrument for differentiating borderline patients from schizophrenic patients. The logic of our study required that our data analysis proceed from an identification of psychological factors underlying the responses of all of our patients to the L.I.F. scale to a discriminant function analysis that could articulate the distinctive organization of factors that discriminated the borderline and schizophrenic patients. Finally, analysis of individual differences in the factor scores made possible a more precise pinpointing of two of the factors that contributed most importantly to the distinctions between the two groups.

Of the six factors that emerged in the factor analysis, four were found by the discriminant function analysis to be conceptually related to the definitions of the borderline and schizophrenic experience. The profile of factors that contributed significantly to the discrimination of these two groups included, in the following order, Factor 1: Impulse Regulation; Factor 2: Self-definition; Factor 3: Emotional Relatedness; and Factor 4: Psychic Cohesiveness. It was the level of organization and focus of meaning of the psychological issues defined by this powerful quartet of factors that were relevant to the distinction between borderline and schizophrenic experience. These two groups exhibited developmentally relevant differences in the meaning, significance, and concerns that they attached to their experiences and symptomatic expressions in these four areas. It is equally interesting to note that Factors 5 (Interpersonal Relatedness) and 6 (Representational Differentiation) did not distinguish the two groups. Apparently, in these two areas of experience, borderline and schizophrenic patients were likely to exhibit similarities in regard to the levels at which the meanings, significance, and nature of their underlying concerns were expressed.

The clinical picture that emerges, then, in this study shares certain common features with the clinical pictures that have emerged in the work of others in this field (e.g., Gunderson, 1977; Gunderson & Kolb, 1978; Kernberg, 1966). Gunderson (1977) for example, described the clinical picture of borderline patients as including intense negative affect, poor impulse control, and a proneness to intense clinging and to shallow relationships. Gunderson and Kolb (1978) identified five areas of functioning that they felt could be useful in distinguishing borderline from schizophrenic and neurotic patients. These five realms of functioning included social adaptation, impulse-action patterns, affects, psychotic symptoms, and interpersonal relations. Similarly, Kernberg (1966) advanced a configuration of impaired ego integration in borderline patients that subsumes lower anxiety tolerance, impulse control, and sublimatory capacity in the context of intact reality testing and identity diffusion. In all of this work, the regulation and control of impulses, self-definition, affect discharge, and psychological cohesion seem to be central aspects of the pathological picture. What we have been able to add to this picture here is that it is the *developmental level* of organization and focus of meaning of these qualitative dimensions that are crucially involved in the distinction between these two diagnostic groupings. In this sense, our findings are consistent with Gedo's (1979, 1988) emphasis on the hierarchical organization of psychopathology centering around different developmentally relevant issues of content and structure that define experience from the very beginning of psychological organization.

A case in point is made by our schizophrenic patients who displayed more primitive mechanisms and meanings than the borderline patients in their discharge of impulses. Typically, action, even in the performance of the most mundane of daily activities, was either grossly disorganized or served the function of preserving body integrity in the schizophrenic patients. In contrast, the borderline patients' behavior and action was clearly more goal-directed and oriented toward a higher level of developmental concerns centering upon the maintenance of a cohesive sense of self.

Further, the factor of Emotional Relatedness, which is distinct from Interpersonal Relatedness, centered, in our borderline patients, upon threats of loss, separation, and abandonment. Typically, and in sharp contrast, our schizophrenic patients were quite isolated and fearful of deeper emotional relationships. Their subjective responses to the L.I.F. questionnaire were characteristically impoverished in their concerns about others or their emotional relatedness to others. The qualities of emotional relatedness found here for borderline patients were quite similar to those found by Gunderson, whose own sample of borderline patients consistently exhibited marked distress and difficulties in the face of possible loss, as well as related tendencies to avoid relationships where the possibility of separation exists.

The remaining two factors (Self-definition and Psychic Cohesiveness) that contributed to the discrimination of borderline and schizophrenic groups in our study are related to failures in the integration of a stable, cohesive, and continuous sense of self. Here, again, our data are in agreement with Kernberg (1966), who viewed identity diffusion as one of the defining characteristics of borderline patients and with Pao (1979), who emphasized the disruption of self-continuity as a major aspect of the schizophrenic process. In respect, then, to both cohesiveness and continuity of self-experience, borderline patients appear to achieve a higher level of integration than do the schizophrenic patients.

For the schizophrenic patient, self-experience is organized around body integrity. For these patients, the body experience may consist of feelings of bodily disintegration, fragmentation, or breaking apart. Self-continuity in this group is expressed in terms of beliefs that their bodies have been altered in some way. Their subjective concerns center around issues of physical existence and physical survival. By contrast, within the group of borderline patients, the sense of self is always organized around mental contents, that is, psychically. While threats to survival and existence are present in regard to expressions of fragmentation of the self, these threats are always articulated in terms of emotions, or mental content rather than in relation to the body and physical sensations arising from it. As distinct from the bodily sense of self in the schizophrenic patient, the borderline fears the dissolution of the psychological self. Notably, the factors obtained in our study that differentiated borderline patients and schizophrenic patients are consistent with the characteristics posited by Robbins (Chapter 10, this volume) in distinguishing schizophrenic patients and patients with primitive personality organization. In differentiating these groups, Robbins emphasizes schizophrenic patients' "inability to actively recruit an object; inability to actively, externally, and adaptively mobilize aggression in the service of identity maintenance . . . ; [and] inability to integrate mental processes . . . to make adaptive projective use of an object for sensorimotor–affective enactments (p. 296). These characteristics are consistent with those that distinguished our schizophrenic group from the borderline subjects. We observed in our schizophrenic patients marked isolation, fear of object relatedness, fragility of their sense of identity, and disintegration of physical sensations, all of which are comparable to those that Robbins posited.

We compared only borderline and schizophrenic patients, but we are currently collecting data in a variety of settings that will enable us to compare schizophrenic, borderline, narcissistic, and affective disordered (including depressed and bipolar) patients as well as subjects from nonclinical settings.

In summary, then, our findings indicate that borderline patients achieve higher level of integrative failure than do schizophrenic patients and that different levels of the factors we have identified contribute to the discrimination of these two groups. This conclusion was supported by the significant ($p < .05$) differences that emerged between borderline and schizophrenic patients on Factor 1 (Impulse Regulation) and Factor 2 (Self-definition) and the trends ($p < .08$) in that direction for Factor 3 (Emotional Relatedness) and Factor 4 (Psychic Cohesiveness). While the findings regarding the interactive effects of anaclitic versus introjective borderline and schizophrenic patients are suggestive, the sample size is too small for us to speculate about their meanings.

ON THE QUALITY OF THE BORDERLINE
AND SCHIZOPHRENIC EXPERIENCES

A close examination of patients responses to the L.I.F. questionnaire sheds light on the differences we found in the meaning, significance, and nature of the concerns that borderline and schizophrenic patients attach to their symptoms. We believe that these differences support aspects of our developmental model that posits an epigenetic sequence from the lowest levels (Levels I and II), where experience centers on the body through Levels III and IV, where mental or psychic content becomes dominant. As the existence and integrity of the body are established, the crucial issues at Level III are the survival of a psychologically based sense of self and the establishment of self-cohesion. At this level, the achievement of these tasks is dependent on the proximity and facilitating functions of an important object whom the individual does not experience as being completely independent or different from himself or herself and without whom there is regression to primitive levels of anxiety.

Schizophrenic patients who are at the lower end of our scale (Levels I and II) describe subjective experiences of bodily fragmentation and threats to body integrity, or they may exhibit integrative failures manifest in thought processes that lack organization and direction, qualities that are characterized by looseness or incoherence of speech. Typical of the lower level, one patient stated:

"I am falling apart. I feel like my body is all over the room."

Another patient exhibited the absence of psychic cohesion in her confused and loose associations:

"I feel confused all the time—everything is breaking in on me at one time. From the end of November, I met a guy and my mother tells me not to pray for her and let go or I'll be the one to fall."

The faulty cohesion characteristic of the borderline, or Level III, patients in our sample, was exemplified by two patients who had clearly established a psychologically based sense of self that was subject to threats to its cohesion and stability. One responded:

"I have so many thoughts—it's like a whirlwind—if I'm sitting and talking to someone, so many of my thoughts come out jumbled. I sound like a babbling idiot. . . . It's like my brain won't shut off."

In a similar vein, another patient indicated:

"I get scared at times because I get confused when I have too much on my mind. I'm thinking about my relationships—all these things on my head. I get confused and frightened. I panic and have to say, calm down."

These responses illustrate a shift from a lower level, where the ability to maintain the organization and coherence of their thought processes is lost and communication reveals the disintegration of goal-directedness and coherence, to Level III, where the logical organization and cohesion of thought processes is retained and psychic, as opposed to bodily, concerns prevail.

At the lower levels (Levels I and II) affect is extremely labile and subject to immediate discharge, and behavior tends to be random, undirected, or delusionally based, as is evidenced by a patient whose scores fell at the lower end of our epigenetic scale. He states:

"I was supposed to take a test to become a doctor and someone stole my books. I started hearing voices and seeing little green yellowish bulbs. I got home and the same thing happened, and I went into the bathroom and tried to drink some shoe dye . . . to kill myself."

In contrast, at Level III, affect is intense and characterized by reactions of rage or helplessness to threats of abandonment. Behavior is oriented toward maintaining a cohesive sense of self and may be manipulative and impulsive. Typifying this level, one patient began to articulate his suicidal feelings by stating:

"I feel I have nothing going. I'm never going to have a good relationship. . . . If I'm not gonna be loved, what am I living for? I lost out—it's a waste of time being there without love and affection."

The factor we refer to as self-definition includes the issue of self-continuity. On this factor, at Level I, patients experience a disruption in the sense of the body's continuity. At Level II, bodily continuity is established, but experience is still organized around the body. It is not until Level III that mental or psychic contents become important. Yet, self-continuity is still tenuous. Finally, by Level IV, self-continuity is established psychically.

The following responses given by a schizophrenic and borderline patient exhibit disruptions in the sense of the body's continuity and continuity of the self, respectively.

Schizophrenic Patient

"I used to have a beauty mark, a little black mole, that was part of my creation at birth. . . . My head used to go around like that, and I feel like my head is getting square now. . . . I've changed as far as features is concerned."

Borderline Patient

"I'm not the same person all the time—this is me. At different times I have characters that'll pop up. . . . Sometimes I feel like different characters I've picked up, when I admire someone I add it to myself."

Finally, Factor II, Emotional Relatedness, is characterized by the experience of love, pleasure, and states of unworthiness. In our schizophrenic patients, these emotional experiences were delusionally based and or organized around sensory or bodily experiences. For example, one schizophrenic patient responded to a question about his feelings of unworthiness by revealing a self that is merged with and represented by a nonhuman life form (Searles, 1960).

"I feel like animals from inside and we got to eat flesh. It makes us wrinkled and old."

A response to the same question given by a borderline patient shows one of the more significant distinguishing features of this type of pathology, that is, the degree to which the critical functions of external objects are internalized. He states:

"I don't feel I've done anything to make anyone proud of me. I've done a lot of bad things—made a lot of people unhappy. I don't deserve anything."

Unlike the schizophrenic patients who either showed an autistic mode of relatedness to objects, or who viewed object relatedness as entailing grave dangers to the self, the borderline patients' sense of well-being was typically dependent upon the continuing support and presence of others.

Using these factors, composite pictures of borderline and schizophrenic patients can be drawn that portray the salient differences in the nature and meaning of symptoms and subjective experiences that characterize patients in these two groups.

The "typical" schizophrenic patient is dominated by a continual struggle to establish or preserve a stable sense of body integrity in the face of threats of annihilation, overwhelming helplessness, and loss of physical cohesion or vital bodily contents. Chaotic and confused states are common and are frequently the result of failures in the differentiation of inner and outer experience—particularly confusion about the source of sensory experiences. Behavior is often random and undirected, organized by delusional ideas, and/or often, through self stimulation, used to restore a sense of body integrity, physical continuity and coherence. For these patients, interpersonal and object related experiences tend to be frightening, overwhelming, or over-stimulating. These experiences tend to jeopardize the tenuous self–object boundaries or bodily integrity that the patient has been able to achieve and result in the adoption of autistic modes of relatedness to others or more complete isolation.

Our findings reveal a picture of borderline patients dominated by fears of object loss and abandonment. For these patients, their sense of well-being, the establishment of a sense of psychic- or self-cohesion, and a psychologically based sense of self-continuity are dependent upon the continuing and supportive presence of others. Reactions of rage, helplessness, and depression, states of self-dissolution and/or fragmentation, merciless self-criticism, as well as impulsive suicide gestures and other forms of acting out occur in connection with threats of abandonment or object loss. Behavioral reactions are often oriented toward discharging tension and/or the restoration of a stable, constant object tie and a cohesive and continuous sense of self.

NOTES

1. We share Gedo's (Chapter 4, this volume) view, that shifts from one level of development to another are not limited to isolated achievements. Rather they represent transformations in the modes of organization that are manifest in the availabilities of sets of more advanced adaptive possibilities.
2. See Wilson and Passik (Chapter 3, this volume) for a similar perspective on the conceptualization of epigenesis.
3. We agree with Loewald (1971) that encodings of undifferentiated drive tensions by the mother transform these tensions into more highly organized motivations or aims.
4. These distinctions have clinical significance. Like Gedo (1979; Chapter 4, this volume), we believe there are different therapeutic requirements at each level of integrative failure. Aibel (1990) identified six categories of therapist intervention that vary along a continuum from regulation to interpretive intervention. The categories include; (1) regulation of somatic state and perception; (2) regulation of adaptive behavior; (3) regulation of communicative behavior; (4) focus on inner states; (5) focus on the organization of inner states; and (6) focus on the interpretation of inner states. Although it is not the central concern of this paper, Aibel's findings are worth noting as they document the clinical usefulness of Level of Integrative Failure (L.I.F.) system (to be presented in this chapter) and are suggestive of the value of this instrument for training beginning clinicians. Aibel found that category 1 and 2 interventions tend to predominate in

work with low L.I.F. (Levels I and II) patients, while category 5 predominates in patients with higher L.I.F. levels. This research was carried out by Dr. Iona Aibel under the supervision of Dr. Norbert Freedman as part of Dr. Aibel's dissertation requirements at New York University.

5. While early development informs our understanding of adult functioning, it is neither identical to nor necessarily causal of later integrative failures. The relation between early and later processes and functions is a complex one, the understanding of which goes far beyond the scope of the present chapter.

6. Wilson and Passik (Chapter 3, this volume) indicate in relation to the Epigenetic Assessment Rating Scale (EARS) that the concept of a static level of organization fails to account for the momentary shifts in intrapsychic functioning. We have also observed that the modal level of integrative failure is indicative of a frequent or dominant level of functioning, rather than a uniform level. Our conception of "potential range" provides a novel way to view fluctuations and their relation to regression and progression.

7. Consistent with this idea, in an investigatory study of phobic patients, we found that L.I.F. level distinguished simple phobic patients from agoraphobics, with the latter group obtaining significantly lower scores. Additionally, patients with higher L.I.F. scores had better results in psychotherapy, and L.I.F. level predicted these results better than a self-report questionnaire and a brief symptom-focused interview.

8. It should be noted that most items consisted of a cluster of questions tapping similar issues. The answers to all of the questions were treated as one response. A single level was assigned to the group of questions. After completing the item analysis, we decided to reduce each item to a single question. On the basis of a clinical analysis of those items that were still included in the interview after the item analysis, we selected the question in each group that elicited the most easily scored material.

9. This reduction in the number of items in the semistructured interview has substantially simplified the task of scoring patients responses and hopefully will enhance further interrater reliability.

REFERENCES

Adams, H. E., Doster, J. A., & Calhoun, K. S. (1977). A psychological based system of response classification. In A. R. Aminero, K. S. Calhoun, & H. E. Adams (Eds.), *Handbook of behavioral assessment* (pp. 47–78). New York: Wiley.

Aibel, I. (1990). *On the concept of level-appropriate intervention: An investigation of therapist verbal activity in psychoanalytically informed treatment with psychiatric inpatients.* Unpublished doctoral dissertation, New York University.

Blatt, S. J., & Schichman, S. (1983). Two primary configurations of psychopathology. *Psychoanalysis and Contemporary Thought, 6*, 187–254.

Deutch, H. (1942). Some forms of emotional disturbance and their relationship to schizophrenia. *Psychoanalytic Quarterly, 11,* 301–321.

Erikson, E. H. (1950). *Childhood and society.* New York: Norton.

Erikson, E. (1956). The problem of ego identity. *Journal of the American Psychoanalytic Association, 4,* 56–121.

Fast, I. (1985). Infantile narcissism and the active infant. *Psychoanalytic Psychology, 2,* 153–170.

Ferenczi, S. (1913). Stages in the development of the sense of reality. In *Contributions to psychoanalysis: Vol. 1. Sex in psychoanalysis* (pp. 213–239). New York: Basic Books, 1950.

Frances, A., & Cooper, A. M. (1981). Description and dynamic psychiatry: A perspective on DSM-III. *American Journal of Psychiatry, 138,* 1198–1202.

Freud, A. (1965). *Writings of Anna Freud: Vol. 6. Normality and pathology in childhood.* New York: International Universities Press.

Freud, S. (1900). The interpretation of dreams. *Standard Edition* (Vols. 4 & 5, pp. 1–627). London: Hogarth Press, 1953.

Freud, S. (1905). Three essays on the theory of sexuality. *Standard Edition* (Vol. 7, pp. 135–243). London: Hogarth Press, 1953.

Freud, S. (1911). Formulations on the two principles of mental functioning. *Standard Edition* (Vol. 12, pp. 215–225). London: Hogarth Press, 1958.

Freud, S. (1913). The disposition to obsessional neurosis. *Standard Edition* (Vol. 12, pp. 313–326). London: Hogarth Press, 1958.

Freud, S. (1923a). The ego and the id. *Standard Edition* (Vol. 19, pp. 13–66). London: Hogarth Press, 1961.

Freud, S. (1923b). The infantile genital organization. *Standard Edition* (Vol. 19, pp. 141–145). London: Hogarth Press, 1961.

Gedo, J. E. (1979). *Beyond interpretation: Toward a revised theory for psychoanalysis.* New York: International Universities Press.

Gedo, J. E. (1988). *The mind in disorder.* Hillsdale, NJ: Analytic Press.

Gedo, J. E. & Goldberg, A. (1973). *Models of the mind.* Chicago: University of Chicago Press.

Giovacchini, P. L. (1986). *Developmental disorders.* Northvale, NJ: Jason Aronson.

Glover, E. (1943). The concept of dissociation. In *On the early development of mind* (pp. 307–323). New York: International Universities Press, 1956.

Grand, S., Freedman, N., Feiner, K., & Kiersky, S. (1988). Notes on the progressive and regressive shifts in levels of integrative failure: A preliminary report on the classification of severe psychopathology. *Psychoanalysis and Contemporary Thought, 11,* 705–740.

Greenacre, P. (1958). The impostor. *Psychoanalytic Quarterly, 27,* 359–382.

Gunderson, J. G. (1977). Characteristics of borderlines. In P. Hartocollis (Ed.), *Borderline personality disorders: The concept, the syndrome, the patient* (pp. 173–192). New York: International Universities Press.

Gunderson, J. G. & Kolb, J. E. (1978). Discrimination feartures of borderline patients. *American Journal of Psychiatry, 135*(7), 792–796.

Hartmann, H. (1958). Comments on the scientific aspects of psychoanalysis. *Psychoanalytic Study of the Child, 13,* 127–146.

Horner, A. J. (1975). Stages and processes in the development of object relations and their associated pathologies. *International Review of Psycho-Analysis, 2,* 95–105.

Jacobson, E. (1964). *The self and the object world.* New York: International Universities Press.

Kaplan, L. J. (1978). *Oneness and separation: From infant to individual.* New York: Simon & Schuster.

Karasu, T. B., & Skodol, A. E. (1980). VI Axis for DSM-III: Psychodynamic evaluation. *American Journal of Psychiatry, 137,* 607–610.

Kernberg, O. (1966). Structural derivatives of object relationships. *International Journal of Psycho-Analysis, 47,* 236–253.

Klein, M. (1960). On mental health. *British Journal of Psychology, 32,* 237–241.

Kohut, H. (1971). *The analysis of the self: A systematic approach to the psychoanalytic treatment of narcissistic personality disorders.* New York: International Universities Press.

Lichtenberg, J. (1978). The testing of reality from the standpoint of the body self. *Journal of the American Psychoanalytic Association, 26,* 357–384.

Loewald, H. (1971). On motivation and instinct theory. In *Papers on psychoanalysis* (pp. 102–137). New Haven, CT: Yale University Press, 1980.

Mahler, M., Pine, F., & Bergman, A. (1975). *The psychological birth of the human infant.* New York: Basic Books.

Michels, R. (1984). A debate on DSM-III. First rebuttal. *American Journal of Psychiatry, 141,* 548–551.

Modell, A. (1976). The holding environment and the therapeutic action of psychoanalysis. *Journal of the American Psychoanalytic Association, 24,* 285–304.

Nagera, H. (1981). *The development approach to childhood psychopathology.* New York: Jason Aronson.

Pao, P. N. (1979). *Schizophrenic disorders.* New York: International Universities Press.

Persons, J. B. (1986). The advantages of studying psychological phenomena rather than psychiatric diagnoses. *American Psychologist, 41,* 1252–1260.

Piaget, J. (1954). *The construction of reality in the child.* New York: Basic Books.

Resch, R., & Grand, S. (1984). On the precursors to psychic structure: Notes on the treatment of a two-year-old autistic toddler. In E. Galenson & R. L. Tyson (Eds.), *Frontiers of infant psychiatry* (pp. 415–427). New York: Basic Books.

Rosenzweig, N. (1982). Diagnosis and the concept of mental illness. *American Journal of Social Psychiatry, 2,* 47–80.

Saul, L. J. (1960). *Emotional maturity.* Philadelphia: Lippincott.

Searles, H. (1960). *The nonhuman environment in normal development and in schizophrenia.* New York: International Universities Press.

Spitz, R. A. (1959). *A genetic field theory of ego formation: Its implications for pathology.* New York: International Universities Press.

Vaillant, G. E. (1984). The disadvantages of DSM-III outweigh its advantages. *American Journal of Psychiatry, 141,* 542–545.

Volkan, V. D. (1976). *Primitive internalized object relations.* New York: International Universities Press.

3

Explorations in Presubjectivity

ARNOLD WILSON AND STEVEN PASSIK

One way to bridge the domains of psychoanalytic practice and research is in the development of an empirical method that can be employed by researchers in a manner similar to how psychoanalysts listen and then respond to their patients. That is to say, the clinical inference processes—of the rater asking a research question of his or her data and the analyst listening and then reacting to a patient—can be approximated and treated as analogic processes. Usually, the *in vivo* ambiguities and richness of the clinical situation are viewed as incompatible with the scientific value of parsimony when studying analytic processes. Then too, the requirements of many research programs limit or minimize the role of the rater of various scales, making the measure, rather than the person and his or her clinical skill, the object of reliability and validity claims. Such an elimination of the clinical factor inevitably distances empirical findings from the daily urgencies of the clinical analyst. We have sought to reach for what we believe are these necessary, if not sufficient, approximations, by including in our method the clinical inferences of the rater rather than focusing exclusively upon the measure. This emphasis undergirds the Epigenetic Assessment Rating System (EARS), an empirical approach to the identification of levels of dimensions of psychic structure. The EARS is meant to explicate a usually implicit clinical inference-making procedure. It systematizes the analyst's task of inference-making in the clinical situation. The construction of the EARS follows from our view that research that speaks to the concerns of psychodynamic clinicians must attempt to measure complex and fluid variables without undue simplification.

The EARS is a theoretical system. It has to date been applied to three specific data bases, which are types of narrative speech samples: Thematic Apperception Test (TAT) narratives, 5-minute speech monologues, and relationship anecdote paradigm stories (RAPS). These applications of the EARS are called, respectively, the EPI-TAT, the EPI-LOG, and the EPI-RAP. The EARS can be applied to many forms of verbal samples spontaneously generated by a speaker. We began our work by first adapting it to TAT narratives, the EPI-TAT. Then the EPI-LOG and EPI-RAP were developed. Applications to other narrativized speech samples are currently under investigation, including transcripts of psychoanalytic hours.

The EARS has as its theoretical basis a hierarchical, epigenetic approach to conceptualizing the personality organization. An assumption of the authors is that sound clinical inference-making is usually both sequential and hierarchical in nature. Clinical inference-making is sequential in that over time inferences are made on the basis of how one thing follows another in an orderly manner. Understanding the how and why of this sequence yields important clinical information. Clinical inference-making is hierarchical in that the level of organization of clinical data is key to making sense of what is inferred about patients. Hence, clinical material is seen as a complex condensation and fusion of multiple levels of meaning occurring at any time. Thus, the same clinical data can be given alternative interpretations when viewed from the vantage point of different levels. Wilson (1989) has demonstrated how this is the case for the narcissistic personality disorder. Most hierarchically based psychoanalytic approaches tend to be identifiable by their use of explanatory concepts based on similar assumptions. Some examples of hierarchical approaches include multimodal models of personality dynamics and analytic intervention (Gedo, 1979, 1984), levels of integrative failure in diagnosis (Grand, Feiner, & Reisner, Chapter 2, this volume), multiple levels of discourse properties (see Chapter 1), and the development of multiple domains of self-experience (Stern, 1985; Lichtenberg, Chapter 7, this volume). The EARS is a system that is designed to provide empirical referents for psychoanalytic concepts defined according to epigenetic principles, which tend to emphasize the progressive and regressive movement of clinical phenomena within a particular theoretical hierarchy of personality organization.

A hierarchical approach is a more general case of the epigenetic approach. All epigenetic approaches are hierarchical, whereas not all hierarchical approaches are epigenetic. A hierarchical approach simply asserts that there are multiple levels of a structure available or at play simultaneously, whereas an epigenetic approach defines the relationship between the levels, focusing on the transformational regularities. In contrast to the other hierarchies described in this volume (e.g., Bucci, Chapter 1; Lichtenberg, Chapter 7), ours is explicitly epigenetic.

The EARS is constituted of 10 hierarchically, epigenetically ordered dimensions, selected in accordance with our view of their clinical and research importance. These dimensions are Affect Tolerance, Affect Expression, Uses of an Object, Empathy, Temporality, Defensive Operation, Adaptive Needs, Centration–Decentration, Threats to the Self, and Personal Agency. Before beginning a discussion of the ways in which the EARS system has been empirically employed, we will first further elaborate its theoretical basis.

THE EARS: THEORETICAL FRAMEWORK

Each of the 10 EARS dimensions was assigned five epigenetically defined levels.[1] Each dimension scaled at each modal level was then carefully defined. Each dimension was characterized in such a way that at least one modal level of each must be present and discernible in any narrative speech sample. We made reference to a normative developmental psychology and psychoanalytic theory to define equivalent scale points for the dimensions. We sought to avoid a perennial problem in related research approaches, wherein scale points of different dimensions are not equivalent to one another with reference to some superordinate theoretical system. In the EARS, the scale points of the different dimensions are yoked to one another according to the principles of developmental psychoanalysis. The problem of a lack of coordination between scale points places serious limitations on the making of any comparisons between dimensions. The developmental chronology of the EARS is largely derived from empirical evidence from prospective and retrospective approaches, which we joined in both our choice and construction of the dimensions.

As is the case with much of what is now often termed developmental psychoanalysis, the EARS is derived from both a normative developmental psychology that is psychoanalytically informed as well as classical psychoanalytic theory. These and related contributions tend to begin with the observation of behaviors and then infer inner states that help explain the behaviors. A recent and well-known example of this infusion of new evidence from the direct observation of caregivers and their children is offered by Stern (1985). Stern inferred a series of infantile "senses of self," that are hypothesized to exert a profound experiential tone on later mental life, although the origins are beyond memorial recollection. These senses of self pivot around such developmental acquisitions as language acquisition, separation responses, and related object relational phenomena. Three senses of self (emergent, core, and self-with-other) precede the lexical self and determine some aspects of experience that may or may not later be appropriated by the linguistic self. Here we see a theoretical commentary on how early preverbal mental life exerts a profound impact upon the content and structures of human development. Sander (1964, 1980) provides another illustrative observational model emphasizing preverbal factors in his discussion of what he terms an "epigenetic sequence of adaptive issues" that every caregiver–infant dyad must navigate in order for the infant to develop a capacity for successful self-regulation. These joint tasks include what Sander calls basic regulation, focalization, self-assertion, recognition, and self-constancy. The tasks are epigenetic because the successful negotiation of each task depends upon and is partially determined by the successful traversing of the previous one. However, since Sander's papers were published, the particular tasks described as central to an epigenetic sequence have been further elaborated through microanalyses of caregiver–infant interaction by infant observers. Sander's, though, was an early psychoanalytically informed model grounded in direct observation that explicitly shifted from a linear cause–effect to a diachronic systems model and emphasized a sophisticated epigenetic perspective on development.

The observation-based theories of Stern, Sander, and others are constructed from the bottom up—viewing early development prospectively, with an eye toward what is to come. Traditionally, many clinical psychoanalysts utilize a more top-down approach—reconstructing infancy from the (transference) data of adult analysands, with an eye toward what has occurred before. In constructing the EARS, we strove as best we could to integrate both versions of childhood, the "observed" and "reconstructed" child, in arriving at the empirical definition of each dimension and each modal level within the dimensions.

It has been repeatedly noted that the reconstructed child tends to be adultomorphized and pathomorphized (see Peterfreund, 1978). The more recent emphasis on observation adds a necessary corrective by focusing on normal development, allowing for clarification of the divergent paths along which the mind develops in normal and abnormal ways. Our integrative stance certainly has epistemological implications, and it is a product of our conviction that psychoanalytic concepts can be derived from, and be responsive to, not only the inferences obtained within the clinical situation but also from extra-clinical domains of psychological knowledge, including the observations of infants and their caregivers. The inclusion of extraclinical evidence into psychoanalytic theory construction, however, is not without problems. A number of analysts, notably Klein (1976), have cautioned about the lack of compatibility of these two streams of data. He observed that, from the perspective of ego psychology, it is at times difficult to distinguish observations concerning the acquisition of ego functioning from other developmental research not specifically informed by any psychoanalytic understanding. Moreover, the explanatory use of these data in the clinical situation constitutes a theoretical conundrum. How data on children are to be used to make inferences about adults, and vice versa, remains an open question that invites dialogue. Pine's (1981) suggestion that such inferences should possess a certain "psycho-logic" and that they be based on observations that, from the outside, look as though they bear on the phenomena later to be known from the inside is a good start for specifying cogent translation rules between these two domains of evidence. Pine's argument is important; there are correct and incorrect methods for making inferences in any scientific endeavor—and the rules should be publically negotiated so that there is clarity about the inferential leaps built into the inductive reasoning necessary for psychoanalytic theorizing.

One effort in this integrative direction can be found in the psychoanalytic model initially proposed by Gedo and Goldberg (1973) and then further elaborated by Gedo (1979, 1981, 1984, 1986, 1988; Chapter 4, this volume). Gedo has outlined a hierarchically organized model for conceptualizing activities of the mind composed of five epigenetically defined modes of functioning. His multimodal approach emphasizes the strategy of the clinician's formulation of specific forms of clinical intervention that match the modal functioning of the patient and address mode-specific dangers and dilemmas. Gedo's hierarchical model served as a touchstone for the EARS. Like the EARS, his view places a premium on the earliest content and processes of experience, which constitute the fundamental common denominators to be integrated and transformed in all future development. As we in this chapter and many others describe, a central task of the earliest periods of epigenesis is the regulation of stimulation and sensation in various ways; this, then, is part of the foundation upon which the later edifice of human personality and psychic conflict rests.

The remainder of this chapter is intended to clearly explicate the approach we have taken with the EARS and to place this instrument within its theoretical context for the reader. To set the stage for the reporting of our results, we will present reliability and validity data that have arisen from some of the research done to date. We will then proceed to: first, demonstrate the interrater reliability and internal clusters of the EARS; second, highlight the sensitivity of the EARS to shifts in the predominant mode of responding in normals from low- to high-arousal conditions; third, demonstrate differences between predominant mode of responding between normals and psychiatric inpatients under both high- and low-arousal conditions; fourth, examine differences between normals, heroin addicts, and cocaine addicts on the EPI-TAT; and fifth, examine which and how well certain dimensions of the EPI-LOG can predict certain aspects of the object relations of schizophrenic adults and their parents. The data we are reporting here are summarized from several studies, each of which is a step toward the validation of the EARS.

However, before we move into a discussion of these empirical findings, it is important to further elaborate the theoretical context for the current work. The EARS is predicated upon an intersection of two streams of thought within psychoanalysis—epigenetic views of development and the psychology of narrative speech productions. The germane aspects of these will now be discussed.

Epigenesis

Epigenesis has been used by theorists interested in models of development in the psychological sciences as a way of conceptualizing a superordinate principle that explains the movement from psychobiological to more explicitly psychological functioning. Its origins lie in and have been borrowed from general biology, specifically the ontogenesis of organisms. To briefly summarize the biological view of epigenesis, it has five distinctive features: (1) it postulates a causal sequence of interactions between organism and environment; (2) earlier and more undifferentiated structures in the organism interact with the environment and cause more differentiated structures to unfold in the organism; (3) these structures unfold in a series of levels, stages, or modes; (4) these structures come to possess increased levels of complexity, differentiation, and organization; and (5) particular "emergent" qualities characterize each new level. (See Kitchener [1978] for a critical discussion of whether these are sufficient and necessary for a psychological developmental perspective.)

When remade into psychological theory, corollaries that follow from this definition of epigenesis are that a particular level or mode:

(1) is characterized by a specifiable degree of complexity and differentiation of structure; (2) possesses certain emergent qualities; (3) denotes a particular interplay between organism and environment; and (4) is causally related to all past and future modes through the nature of successive transactions that reorganize structure and experience. This leads to a primary focus on the transformational properties and principles of structure and a secondary focus on content, or the phenomenon that is undergoing transformation. One advantage of this approach is that we can understand changes in mental life that are in part qualitatively discontinuous. In the EARS, an example of discontinuity within overall continuity is the notion of phase-specific dangers. Although there are continual threats to the self that the person must master in order to avoid pathology, the specific form and content of what constitutes a "danger" is markedly different for each developmental phase. The excitation resulting from overstimulation can be contrasted with the excitation that results from the guilt from having acted in discord with one's conscience. The epigenetic view that focuses primarily on transformational principles and secondarily on content (what is transformed) can thus be usefully applied to human development. Werner (1948), and Werner and Kaplan (1963) first articulated the most clearly epigenetic theory to human development. As Werner noted, "the normal adult['s] . . . mental structure is marked by not one but many functional patterns, one lying above the other." (1948, p. 38). In the Russian Vygotsky's treatment of "heterogeneity," we see a similar claim, that

> one cannot think of . . . the various processes of shifting among various forms of thinking . . . as a purely mechanistic process in which each new phase emerges when the previous one is completely finished and completed. The picture of development turns out to be much more complex. Different genetic forms coexist, just as in the earth's core the deposits of quite different geological epochs exist. (1956, p. 204)

After Werner, many Western theorists interested in human development began using the concept of epigenesis in order to understand changes in mental life that are in part qualitatively discontinuous. According to Werner (1948), such changes involve qualities of "gappiness" (a lack of forms characterizing intermediate change states) and "emergence" (nonreducible changes between later and earlier states).

Most sophisticated contemporary developmental psychoanalytic perspectives are epigenetic in nature. The principle of epigenesis has been applied to psychoanalytic theory, initially, of course, by Erikson (1959). Erikson employed the concept to elaborate the psychosocial as a parallel to the psychosexual. In our application, we adduce several primary postulates that characterize the importation of epigenesis to psychoanalytic theory: (1) that the formation of psychic structure is the result of successive reorganizing transactions between the child and the caregiving environment; (2) that the form or structuralization of each mode of organization depends upon the outcome of each previous mode and the subsequent effects of experience; (3) that each mode integrates previous modes and results in new and more differentiated and articulated levels of organization and regulation; and (4) that each mode is defined by its own emergent properties.

Furthermore, there are two important corollaries we append that follow from these postulates: (1) that once a given mode has been integrated by a higher mode, the more archaic form nonetheless continues to exist as a potential end point of regression, at which time it can become the overriding organizer of experience, and (2) that although having yielded to developmental transformation, lower modes are contained within and can continue to exert influence over higher-order advanced psychological processes.

Conceptualizing a layering of the organization of the psyche, dimensions of psychic structure can be seen as subject to more-or-less constant regressive and progressive influences in response to factors that are both intrapsychic as well as biosocial. These qualities that define the developmental–epigenetic transformations are captured in the conceptualization of each modal level for each dimension of the EARS. Through the use of the EARS, the clinician/rater is enabled to detect the progressive and regressive flux of the dimensions, if provided with an adequate speech sample. This claim is reminiscent of Archimedes's boast that he could use his lever to move the world if provided the right location. What constitutes an adequate speech sample has been a vexing and crucial problem in virtually all psychotherapy research, known as the "unit problem." Speech units necessarily are encoded in a way that renders them "slower" than intrapsychic processes. Speech units must be articulated in such a way that they can be apprehended by a listener, whereas thought has no such limitation. On the EARS, we have not solved the unit problem, but we have adopted a particular approach that frames our work. The subject responds to the demand of the task with a narrative, and thus makes the unit himself or herself. Thus, in the different EARS applications, a subject may tell a TAT story (EPI-TAT), speak open-endedly for 5 minutes (EPI-LOG), or describe an interaction with an important other (EPI-RAP).

The notion of "level of organization" viewed from our perspective tilts too much toward a rigid, insufficiently fluid view of structure; a level of organization is better thought of as imputing the modes in which a person may function most, but not all, of the time. Thus, psychotics can be expected to be assessed most often in the least advanced modes, neurotics in the most advanced, and borderlines at various points in-between. Most clinical realities are more fluid than is suggested by the notion of level of organization. Much psychoanalytic research runs the risk of erroneously labeling transient states as consistent and stable traits, thereby creating an illusory appearance of continuity. Instead, the application of sampling strategies such as that in the EARS, or what is called "time intensive sampling," provides a different picture. The closer scrutiny of naturally occurring phenomena provided by repeated sampling leads to an appreciation of the volatility of change and its patterns, a pattern that has been called "second-order consistency." This is a remarkably difficult research task. We will return to this question of temporal instability of psychic structure later. Clearly, an appreciation of the instability of psychic structure runs contrary to traditional definitions of this concept, which emphasize stability. For example, in Rapaport and Gill's (1959) definition, structures are hypothetical entities that are enduring, characterized by a slow rate of change—within which, between which, and by means of which mental processes take place— are hierarchically ordered, and inferred from actions.

Narration

A second important theoretical influence upon this research is the theory of narration. There has been a good deal of attention paid to narrative theory in psychoanalytic circles in recent years (e.g., Schafer, 1983; Spence, 1982, 1987). Impetus for this line of thinking has emerged from psychologists interested in postmodern epistemological questions, *how* we know rather than *what* we know. When how we know achieves parity with what we know, structure achieves parity with content, preverbal with verbal, pragmatics with syntax and semantics. Bruner (1986), arguing for narrative as a mode of thought, persuasively argues that humans actively "construct" their realities through the implementation of their psychological tools, particularly language. He describes how people are not passive possessors of knowledge that is a "copy" of what they are provided from outside, but rather are active creators of worlds that then pass as "objective." It is the appreciation of newer perspectives on linguistics that characterizes this general epistemological movement. The importance of these perspectives for clinical psychoanalysis is examined by Wilson and Weinstein (1992a, 1992b).

An aspect of our use of narrativity, thus, is that the narratives people create reflect crucial aspects of their life history and personality organization. Note that this is a psychological and not an epistemological proposition. Chafe (1980) has argued in support of the essential interface between narration, perception, and autobiography. He notes that

> [S]imilar principles are involved in the way information is acquired from the environment, in the way it is scanned by consciousness during recall, and in the way it is verbalized. All three processes may be guided by a single executive mechanism. (Chafe, 1980, p. 16)

Chafe's views suggest to us that in order to understand the psychodynamics of the person, the analysis of how people narrate should be amenable to the same sorts of study as are perceptual responses. A similar theoretical approach has informed the "story grammars" of Mandler and Johnson (1977). Our hypothesis has considerable evidential support and is allied with some recent developments in cognitive science. A person's narrative productions can be studied for their thematic and structural elements and content. Theorists who have tried to characterize psychoanalysis as primarily a hermeneutic science have argued to the contrary. They have used the concept of narration in a controversial way, to bridge psychoanalysis with the "human" sciences. In this way, psychoanalysis becomes subject to other epistemological truth claims than are traditionally thought to characterize psychology. However, narration can be studied empirically. This view of narrativity thus stands in contrast to the hermeneutically inspired [four truth] claims of narration in the psychoanalytic situation put forth by Ricoeur (1977), which eschew any empirical referents and put forward a separate truth claim for stories than for other naturally occurring phenomena.

One major shortcoming of the narrative perspective, from a clinical point of view, has been its primary focus upon the narrative that is told. The reliance on semantics as a data base is limiting. As has been described elsewhere, the branch of linguistics of native concern to psychoanalysis should include pragmatics, or what is done with "speech acts," as well as semantics and syntax (Wilson & Weinstein, 1992b).

Clinically, the interpretation of the solely semantic content of a narrative leads to the exclusion of important preverbal representations, namely those represented in earlier symbolic and presymbolic forms, such as images, archaic fantasies, enactments, and pre-linguistic word meanings (Bruner, 1964; Freedman, 1985; Wilson & Weinstein, 1992a). A major theoretical disjunction occurs when these subjectively accessible contents are not tied to their preverbally coded underpinnings found in repetitions, behavioral enactments, un-spoken feeling states, and other clinical phenomena that are not subjectively accessible. Influences from different hierarchical levels become accessible as various modes become the predominant orga-nizers of experience at any one time. Thus, the early modal elements can also figure prominently in narrativity. The overlooking of pre-verbal elements in the clinical understanding of narration is especially problematic for clinicians who study and treat severely disturbed patients. Such patients are more profoundly affected by developmen-tally early factors than are neurotics. This specific way of analyzing narratives was foreshadowed many years ago by Schafer (1967) in a seminal paper on the TAT called "How Was This Story Told?" Crucial diagnostic information was available, Schafer argued, not only in the actual content of the narrative but in an analysis of its formal dimensions. Our instrument, which was constructed to be sensitive to both streams of narrativized data, in many ways formalizes Schafer's analysis and extends it.

The EARS approach thus ascribes to the notion that the mean-ings patients convey through discourse that are of concern to psy-choanalysts are best understood through a complementarity of para-verbal as well as verbal emphases. For example, what type of narratives might the thought disordered verbal productions of a schizophrenic patient constitute? These archaic echoes may be part of a hidden, unspoken, or even a prelinguistic narrative, represented in sensorimotor or imagistic forms. Preverbal influences are subject to limited and indirect illumination through semantic analysis of spoken content. The schizophrenic with the delusion of thought withdrawal is telling an important preverbal narrative about feelings of perme-ability, loss of autonomy and reversal of agency, inability to create lexical meaning, and poor stimulation regulation. Such a "story" is likely closer to his or her experience than is the simple content-laden story of persecutors who may operate bizarre machines that steal his or her thoughts. Additionally, this example shows how some pre-verbal narratives are not only poorly illuminated but deformed by communication through the avenue of lexicality. In the research to be discussed, we will be conceptualizing modes of content and theme that are beyond or prior to subjectivity and reflective self-awareness (which we will discuss later as Modes I and II in the EARS hierarchy).

To do this in a manner that is synchronous with the epigenetic perspective, we will adopt a broad concept of the "narrative creation" that encompasses all of the behaviors, verbalizations, movements, and tropes that occur during the period allocated for the subject to respond. Our research to date demonstrates that these and other nonverbal elements can be reliably inferred and deduced from a person's construction of a narrative.

THE DEVELOPMENT OF THE EARS

Modal Organization of the EARS

As discussed, the EARS has been specifically designed to be sensitive to the manifestations of the lower modes of organization. This is one of the unique aspects of the EARS that separates it from more traditional (e.g., self report) assessment techniques, a point similar to one made by Holt (1978) in his discussion of "guided clinical systems." There are many problems with self report instruments that make assessment of preverbal phenomena problematic. For example, patients often do not recognize and therefore cannot endorse certain self report items because they are unable to apply the proper words to describe their feeling states. In its most extreme form, this is called alexithymia (Taylor, 1987). Further, on self report instruments, subjects are required to report on a trait or state about which they are often not conscious.[2]

We constructed the EARS to account for five broadly defined epigenetic modes of personality organization. Briefly, the modes have the following general features, common to all of the 10 psychological dimensions to be described later:

1. Mode I is understood as a presubjective period of human development. There is a limited distinction between self and other. Information is encoded in sensorimotor or action-oriented forms. The primary feeling states are pleasure and unpleasure. Avoidance of global unpleasure is the predominant defensive activity. Overstimulation is the primary danger.

2. Mode II is understood as a transitional period between sensorimotor representations and representations encoded in imagistic forms. Others, especially significant others, are represented as "separate but attached" because they provide for basic needs, such as soothing. This leads to the other being represented in a polarized fashion — good–bad. Intense attachment to and/or extreme avoidance of others is prominent. The independent volition of others tends not

to be understood, and projection is the predominant defensive activity. Separation and issues of autonomy and intrusiveness are the primary danger situations.

3. Mode III is a period in which the proper positioning of the self in relationship to the object world is the superordinate developmental task. Self-enhancement and the maintenance of self-esteem are key concerns. A powerful need is the protection of those wishful illusions about one's and important others' capabilities and capacities, particularly those that support and bolster one's self-esteem. Denial and disavowal are the predominant defensive activities, and the primary danger situation is prohibition from external authority figures. Lexical representational capacities develop along with a mature communicational ability.

4. Mode IV is a period of oedipal level conflicts. Moral anxieties and derivatives of castration fears are the main sources of threat. Subjectively accessible intrapsychic ideational conflict, especially around competition and self-assertion, is the principal danger. There is guilt over sexuality, but genital sexuality is also desired. The predominant defensive activity is repression (proper).

5. Mode V is a period characterized by the benevolent resolution of conflict. Creativity and generativity are the basic needs. Aggression is well contained; competition is not a major threat. There is a sense of containment deriving from one's realistic appraisal of a place and role in the object world. The primary dangers come from undistorted reality factors (real threats), and the predominant defensive activity is renunciation.

Reliability and Validity of the EARS

In order to examine the reliability and validity of the EARS, we first examined narratives produced in response to TAT cards. The TAT is a projective task. A projective instrument can be particularly useful in studying the psychology of narration. The so-called projective hypothesis (Rapaport, Gill, & Schafer, 1968) stipulates that in responding to an open-ended or unstructured ambiguous stimulus, an individual through projection onto the stimulus reveals much about his or her characteristic and conflictual styles of thinking, feeling, and perceiving. The description provided by Rapaport and his coauthors is similar to what we previously identified as the psychological processes explicitly involved in narrativizing. The analysis of TAT narratives provides an excellent medium to study how an individual constructs his or her psychological world, one that can vary relative to changing environmental demands and his or her intrapsychic organization.

From a practical standpoint, the TAT narrative, outside of a patient's communications in treatment, is one of the most common forms of narrative a clinician encounters and interprets. We have focused on TAT narratives initially for the purpose of attaining validity and reliability for the EARS. As noted, we call this application the EPI-TAT.

Each TAT card elicits narratives with a range of themes. Some are more arousing than others. With this in mind, we implemented a controlled situation that regulated the stimuli with which the individual was faced while constructing his or her narrative. A basic assumption of projective assessment is that increased arousal is produced by heightened degrees of perceptual ambiguity (both thematic and perceptual) and by sexual or aggressive stimuli. A secondary assumption is that heightened arousal results in a regressive mode of responding (Schachtel, 1945; Schafer, 1954).

Under conditions of low arousal or low stress, an individual is presumed to be operating in his or her most frequently preferred modal organization. Under more difficult situations, ones that present integrative challenges, an individual momentarily may regress to a lower-modal organization. Low and high arousal conditions represent endpoints between which a subject will regress and progress. In the past, researchers have operationalized arousal level by either a video presentation of scenes of graphic violence, or by presenting electric shocks. We, in contrast, rely upon the perceptual activation of intrapsychic processes, elicited by TAT stimuli. The EPI-TAT is designed to tap a person at a high and low level of arousal, which we have specified is parallel to degree of regression. Subjects responded to specific TAT cards judged to possess high-arousal or low-arousal stimulus properties. These cards were chosen in two ways. First, three senior clinicians provided us with their opinion of high- and low-arousal rankings on the full set of TAT cards. Card 13MF—depicting a man standing with downcast head buried in his arm, while behind him is the figure of a woman, naked to the waist, lying in bed—was chosen unanimously to be the most arousing card. The least arousing card was Card 1, depicting a young boy contemplating a violin that rests on the table in front of him. Second, there is empirical evidence at hand that lends some support to the hypotheses that Cards 13MF and 1 are the most and least arousing cards, respectively, and that arousal is linked with regression. This classification was empirically tested for variables theoretically linked to arousal states associated with levels of regression. In a doctoral dissertation at the New School for Social Research, Ehrenreich (1989) examined five TAT cards (1, 2, 3BM, 12M, 13MF) and rated them according to directness/intensity of drive experiences and level of defenses exhibited, both of which are theoretically associated with degree of regression. Card 13MF consistently elicited the most drive expressions (2.62 per narrative), which were also the most consistently "direct-unsocialized" (38.2% of all scoreable responses). Cards 1 and 2 were virtually identical in having the least drive expressions (fewer than 0.75 per card) and also pulled for responses that were primarily "direct-socialized" and secondarily "weak-disguised" (only 10% of the scoreable responses were "direct-unsocialized" on Card 1). A similar pattern held for defenses exhibited, with responses to Card 13MF yielding "lower-level" defenses and those to Card 1 "higher-level" defenses. Although certainly not decisive, these results lend some empirical support to our linkage of level of arousal with degree of regression. In sum, the clinical opinion of the clinicians and the empirical evidence of Ehrenreich provided us with an *a priori* determination of low- and high-arousal situations. This circumvents the potential circularity of defining arousal on the basis of the regression manifest in the subject's narratives. Our initial hypothesis was that the low-arousal condition presented a situation in which the subject will function at higher modal levels of organization. Conversely, we hypothesized that the high-arousal condition, replete with difficult integrative challenges, would cause the subject to regress to a lower modal level of organization. As will be seen in the studies that follow, we did observe both regressive and progressive shifts along the epigenetic continuum for each dimension included on the EARS hierarchy according to arousal level.

We recognize one potential criticism of this approach; regardless of the clinicians' agreement about the objective difficulty posed by one card or another, the perception of arousal will be subject to varying individual differences. This caveat is perhaps more germane to an ipsative focus upon a single subject. In this type of research, the emphasis is upon the derivation of a more extensive profile of an individual. To that end, several TAT cards would be employed to elicit a wide range of adaptive and maladaptive regressions and progressions. Specifically arousing situations that serve as triggers to regression for that individual could then be identified. For our present purposes, we have sacrificed this kind of information in order to study more general between-group trends, based on the definition of high and low arousal described above. A between-group analysis of this sort is the preferred design to attain the validity information necessary in the early stages of exploring the validity of an instrument.

Reliability

Interrater reliability is the most appropriate form of reliability for our scale. Although all forms of reliability are usually thought of as placing a ceiling on validity, such a relationship will not hold up with a scale such as the EPI-TAT, in which underestimation of reliability in other than interrater form is built in. Split-half or alternate-form reliabilities are not appropriate because, except in overgeneralized terms, one could not predict equivalent halves or forms of TAT stimuli that would hold up across subjects. Internal consistency is not applicable because TAT stimuli present such highly heterogeneous content. Test–retest reliability is likewise not applicable (Atkinson, 1980) because the constellation of themes competing for expression on the TAT changes from Time 1 to Time 2, while nevertheless condensing the same underlying motives. We rely exclusively on interrater reliability in our evaluation of the EPI-TAT because it is the only one that does not lead to automatic underestimation of reliability. Since all forms of reliability statistically place a ceiling on validity, we chose the sole form of measuring reliability in which underestimation is not built in.[3]

The EARS possesses characteristics of both a continuous and a categorical scale. For example, it suggests qualities of "more" and "less" along a dimension, yet each modal level is also qualitatively different.[4] Whereas a Pearson r, or conceptually related statistic, is often used with a continuous scale, reliability on a categorical scale is usually evaluated with a kappa coefficient. Briefly, any Pearson correlation assesses the strength of association between scales and raters, but it does not require exact agreement, and it assumes that scores can be meaningfully averaged. A kappa coefficient is a chance-corrected agreement measure that assumes categorical data and, therefore, does not lend itself to averaging across categories. To illustrate the difference between a continuous and a categorical variable: Whereas one can average amounts of anxiety two or more people have, it is not possible to average a schizophrenic patient and a narcissistic patient and come up with a borderline patient. The reliability approach used will also depend on how any particular researcher wants to use a scale. Both the Pearson and the kappa approaches to reliability have many forms and variations (see Kraemer, 1981), which will not be addressed in this chapter. Accordingly, since the EARS possesses characteristics of both a continuous and categorical scale, we recommend that both be used when calculating interrater reliability (Bartko & Carpenter, 1976) and that a researcher be clear how and why any reliability approach is used in any particular instance.

In our first interrater reliability trials, even raters with relatively limited clinical exposure have demonstrated that they can reach a reliability criterion that qualifies them as an expert rater. Our first reliability trials involving several graduate students in clinical psychology were begun following a series of readings, discussions, and practice protocols supervised by the first author. Of the five students, two were considered "advanced" (internship level), one was considered "intermediate" (predoctoral level), and two were "beginners" (preclinical masters level). In addition to the training mentioned above, all had been involved in the preparation of a training manual for the scoring of EARS dimensions. Blind to the diagnoses, each student was given several TAT protocols to score and provided 10 judgments per card per subject. Protocols of normal (undiagnosed) subjects, subjects with character disorders, and subjects with psychotic symptoms were assessed. We set the criteria for qualification as an expert rater at the following level: 90% of the judgments had to be between $+1$ and -1 scale point of those of an already qualified expert rater, with a minimum of 50% exact matches. The results of this first trial fell slightly short of our criteria for satisfactory interrater reliability. Overall, 82% of the judgments fell between $+1$ and -1 scale point of an expert rater, with 45% exact matches. However, only the two beginning level students had failed to qualify as expert raters. Following discussion of the protocols, and further training and rewriting of unclear EPI-TAT items, all the raters were given the same TAT protocols of other patients and were again blind to their diagnoses. The results of this second trial met our criteria for expert rater status for each of the five raters. Pearson product–moment correlations of the scores provided by each rater ranged from .85 (the beginning students) to .92 (the advanced students). Final Spearman–Brown coefficient of reliability scores were calculated for the entire set of raters, which provide an average of pairwise correlations. This coefficient was .88, supporting the high interrater reliability possible on the EPI-TAT after intensive training and immersion in the theory underlying the scale. Kappa coefficients were used in later reliability work and in both of the advanced experiments reported later in this chapter. Here, too, we found that adequate coefficients were obtainable with proper training that includes knowledge of the theoretical underpinnings of the approach.

Since these initial reliability trials, we have trained, using similar procedures, over 15 graduate students who have attained expert rater status. Although time-consuming and requiring lengthy preparation, we have found that able clinical psychology graduate students who have begun supervised clinical work with patients are usually capable of being trained to criterion. Students earlier in their training tend not to be quite so ready for this type of training. Clinical experience and proper supervision provides a basis for grasping how the inferences of the EARS are made.

We want to reemphasize that interrater reliability was achieved with raters who, although novices in a clinical career, had an extensive background working with the concepts underlying the construction of the EPI-TAT. New raters may have difficulty attaining a satisfactory reliability criterion unless they receive extensive education in the theoretical principles informing the inference process captured by the EPI-TAT. In much the same way as one cannot expect an untrained psychometrician to adequately interpret a Rorschach without training in a guiding theoretical framework to channel inferences (Schafer, 1954), so too will the interpreter of the EPI-TAT require familiarity with the theoretical/clinical network of constructs informing the derivation of this instrument.

In later research, we tried a different and far more stringent tack for scoring any EARS protocol, including the EPI-LOG and the EPI-RAP. First, dummy protocols were inserted every 10th narrative to ensure that no rating drift was occurring. Second, ratings for each item were done independently by two trained raters who had already reached expert rater status. The scores that were not identical matches were then rated by a newly constituted group of three new raters, each of whom had also reached expert rating status. These new raters discussed the response and the reasoning behind each rater's score until a consensus decision was reached. These discussions were not attempts at compromise; rather, the three raters explored the reasoning behind each decision until there was agreement on the one deemed most suitable.

On the basis of our different reliability investigations, we recommend three additional possibilities for obtaining and ensuring reliability. First, using different raters for different dimensions might maximize the ability to capture intraindividual differences on the dimensions. One focus of our training has been to minimize the tendency to score modes perseveratively within subjects. This was done with the experiment to be described on heroin and cocaine abusers. Raters must be very sensitive to subtle distinctions between dimensions and be careful to score them independently rather then allow one score to bias another for a particular subject. Second, establishing additional checks of reliability after every 10 or 15 subjects rated is important. When we did this, we found some drift in our raters, which we were able to preempt by conducting ongoing "refresher" training sessions during the period that the ratings were being done. This way of checking reliability helps insure that each rater is consistently using the same internal scale throughout the entire rating procedure. Third, as described by Parducci (1974), judges often tend to slide toward the middle rather than use either extreme end of a rating scale. This is a tendency that can be examined as part of rater training.

Based on these reliability studies, interrater reliability on the EPI-LOG and EPI-RAP was obtained in two independent investigations. On the EPI-LOG (Passik, 1990), 20% of the protocols dispersed throughout a large sample were scored by each of two expert raters who has already qualified on the EPI-TAT. Reliability was tested, treating the dimensions as both categorical and continuous variables. When treated as categorical variables, a statistically significant Scott's Pi was found for each of the dimensions, indicating a high level of consistency in the judgments made by the two expert raters. When treated as continuous variables, statistically significant Spearman-Brown and intraclass correlations were found for all the dimensions. Since the EPI-LOG protocols that served in reliability trials had been dispersed throughout the sample, these results also indicate no evidence of drift in ratings.

On the EPI-RAP (Faude, 1991), two raters already qualified as experts on the EPI-TAT scored narratives from 10 subjects in a pilot study of reliability. The degree of exact agreements was 64%, and 96% fell within one modal level of each other. In the study proper, 30% of the sample protocols were scored by the two raters. Exact agreement was obtained on 65% of the protocols, and 93% of the ratings fell within one modal level of one another.

Validity

The first step in assessing the validity of the EPI-TAT was to demonstrate that each of the psychological dimensions we have defined are relatively statistically independent, thus actually measuring different components. To this end, we combined the data from several studies, to form one aggregated data set consisting of 80 subjects. A total of 20 variables, representing the 10 psychological dimensions crossed with the 2 levels of arousal, were used in a principal components analysis and rotated to Varimax criterion. This analysis showed that each dimension factored relatively independently on a rotated component. That is to say, each dimension appeared with a high loading on one component (between .533 and

.886), while all of the other dimensions on a given component appeared with a loading of .366 or less. We are not presenting these statistical data in a table since it is so unwieldy to report a 20 × 20 matrix. It is, of course, true that any one dimension in and of itself cannot completely define a factor. It is also true that we are speaking of relative rather than absolute orthogonality. Nonetheless, the principal components analysis we employed did yield evidence that the 20 dimensions were relatively orthogonal to one another. This supported our hypothesis that there were 20 separable constructs being measured (10 psychological dimensions by 2 levels of arousal).

Prior to further validity testing of the EPI-TAT per se, we examined whether arousal as we defined it was a meaningful parameter. Using the same data set, we set out to determine if partitioning psychological dimensions by level of arousal would lead to meaningful differences in how the data are distributed. An inspection of the correlations within each of the studies supported the hypothesis that arousal exists as a separate and meaningful entity. If the correlations are broken down by arousal condition, a consistent pattern of results holds up across the data. Correlations of low-arousal dimensions with themselves and correlations of high-arousal dimensions with themselves are higher than the correlations obtained when low-arousal dimensions are correlated with high-arousal dimensions. This proved to be true within the same dimension. This pattern can be seen by comparing the medians of the correlations of homogenous arousal dimensions with those for heterogenous arousal dimensions within each study. In the first two validity studies reported, there were 35 correlations involving the low-arousal condition, 35 correlations involving the high-arousal condition, and 70 correlations when high and low arousal were compared. In our first study the medians of the correlations were .447, .654, and .348, for the low–low, high–high, and low–high sets of correlations, respectively. Similarly, in our second study, the median correlations were .730, .718, and .586 for the low–low, high–high, and low–high sets of correlation. Although the medians of the correlations vary between the studies, the pattern within the studies remains the same. The correlations involving variables of different arousal levels are considerably lower than those involving the same arousal level.

In sum, a principal components analysis and inspection of the correlations within and across arousal supports the hypothesis that the EARS measures 10 relatively independent dimensions of personality organization that change relative to level of arousal. Further work is thus necessary to establish discriminant and concurrent validity with other and related measures and criteria. Let us now turn to some of this work.

EXPERIMENTAL INVESTIGATION AND FINDINGS:
INITIAL VALIDITY STUDIES

The results of the reliability investigations, including the principal components analysis, set the stage for establishing the validity of the EARS. According to epigenetic theory, one would expect to observe regressive or progressive movement within EARS dimensions as a function of changes in the stress or arousal that a person experiences. We attempted to demonstrate this phenomenon in our first empirical investigation utilizing the EARS with normal subjects. Next, epigenetic theory also predicts that it should be possible to observe differences in the predominant mode of organization between normal subjects and psychiatric inpatients. Furthermore, one would predict observable changes in the modal level in response to varying degrees of stress or arousal in these two populations. Thus, we assessed whether degree of psychopathology (i.e., normal versus psychiatric inpatient) predicts the predominant mode of organization in these groups and whether there are differences in their responses to varying levels of arousal.

Following these initial studies, we and other members of our research group applied the EARS to a number of samples with different psychiatric diagnoses to determine whether the EARS could bring epigenetic theory to bear on a number of clinical problems. In the next stage of more advanced construct validity studies, we present a summary of EARS findings by Keller and Wilson (1992) comparing the affective and object relational aspects of cocaine abusers and heroin addicts. Finally, we present the findings of Passik (1990) in which the EARS was utilized to investigate affective and object relational variables as key aspects of the relationship between schizophrenic patients and their parents.

Fluctuations in the Predominant Mode
of Responding in Normal Subjects from Low-
to High-Arousal Conditions

At the heart of epigenetic psychoanalytic theory as we see it lies the notion that dimensions of the personality organization are flexible and responsive to changing internal and external conditions. Thus, in our earliest exploration with the EARS, we hypothesized that normal subjects would be found to score at different modal levels of personality organization on the 10 psychological dimensions on the EARS under conditions of high and low arousal. We expected that subjects in the low-arousal condition would produce higher scores on the EARS (reflecting more differentiated and sophisticated psychological functioning) than in the high-arousal condition.

We examined 40 volunteers, 20 male and 20 female, who were students in an urban university clinical psychology graduate program. We refer to them as normals, although they were not formally screened for psychopathology. The subjects ranged in age from 23 to 44, with a mean age of 28 years.

A full set of TAT cards was presented to each subject with a consistent order of presentation (1, 5, 15, 14, 10, 13MF, 12M, 3BM, and 16). The TAT was administered in the standard manner, as recommended by Allison, Blatt, and Zimet (1968). Trained research assistants administered the TAT cards and recorded the responses verbatim. In addition, the assistants were trained to record significant nonverbal behaviors, including changes of affectivity, tone of voice, movements, posture, and so on, that occurred during the administration. The scores for all the EARS dimensions for Cards 1 (low arousal) and 13MF (high arousal) were then selected out for analysis. The trained raters were blind to the hypotheses of the study and to the experimental design.

A series of *t* tests for related samples, with alpha set a priori at .05, were used to compare the mean response levels of the normal subjects. Level of arousal was the independent variable. The dependent variable was the mean modal level of responses given by the subjects for each of the EARS dimensions within the high- and low-arousal conditions. The mean level of response was computed by summing the scores each subject obtained on the 10 EARS dimensions and dividing by the total number of dimensions (10) in each arousal condition.

For all of the dependent variables, the low-arousal mean was statistically greater than the high-arousal mean. The one exception was the temporality dimension. The mean scores of subjects on a particular dimension under both arousal conditions are presented in Table 3.1. The results of the *t* tests are shown in Table 3.2.

As can be seen in Tables 3.1 and 3.2, the results from this experiment indicate that EARS scores for undiagnosed normal graduate students are responsive to changes in arousal conditions. Specifically, there is a significant drop in modal level of organization when comparing a low-arousal to a high-arousal condition. In the low-arousal condition the normal subjects across dimensions tended to score at a mean level near but below Mode IV; under high arousal this mean level dropped to near but below Mode III. These findings support an epigenetic psychoanalytic hypothesis that predicts that

TABLE 3.1. Results of Normal Subjects on EPI-TAT Dimensions under High and Low Arousal

Dimension—level of arousal	Min.	Max.	$\bar{x}$	SD
Affect Expression—high	1.00	4.00	2.85	.813
Affect Expression—low	2.00	5.00	3.72	.697
Affect Tolerance—high	1.00	4.00	2.67	.863
Affect Tolerance—low	2.00	5.00	3.67	.816
Use of an Object—high	1.00	4.00	2.57	.816
Use of an Object—low	2.00	5.00	3.57	.674
Centration-Decentration—high	2.00	4.00	3.05	.667
Centration-Decentration—low	2.00	5.00	3.77	.716
Personal Agency—high	1.00	4.00	2.87	.666
Personal Agency—low	2.00	5.00	3.67	.730
Defense—high	1.00	4.00	2.75	.881
Defense—low	2.00	5.00	3.67	.674
Threats to the Self—high	1.00	4.00	3.05	.857
Threats to the Self—low	3.00	5.00	3.97	.678
Adaptive Needs—high	2.00	4.50	3.05	.686
Adaptive Needs—low	2.00	5.00	3.77	.803
Empathy—high	2.00	4.00	3.00	.743
Empathy—low	2.00	5.00	3.45	.724
Temporality—high	2.00	5.00	3.27	.786
Temporality—low	2.00	5.00	3.57	.748

even in a normal population, the various levels of personality dimensions as defined by the EARS are responsive to changing levels of stress.

The results summarized above have important implications for the epigenetic model. Under low arousal, the mean scores of our normal population was at just below Mode IV. This modal level is characterized by conflict over subjectively accessible ideational and oedipal concerns, such as neurotic conflicts over sexuality, rivalry, moral anxiety, competence, and guilt. Mode IV, thus, represents an epigenetic level of personality generally consistent with normal or neurotic concerns. However, under high-arousal conditions, on the

TABLE 3.2. Paired *t*-Tests Comparing Psychological Dimensions on the EPI-TAT and Level of Arousal

Dimension—level of arousal	x̄ difference	Standard error	*t*	*p*
Affect Expression—high vs. Affect Expressions—low	−0.875	0.841	4.65	.001
Affect Tolerance—high vs. Affect Tolerance—low	−1.000	0.778	5.74	.001
Use of an Object—high vs. Use of an Object—low	−1.000	0.811	5.51	.001
Centration-Decentration—high vs. Centration-Decentration—low	−0.725	0.769	4.22	.001
Personal Agency—high vs. Personal Agency—low	−0.800	0.715	5.00	.001
Defenses—high vs. Defenses—low	−0.925	0.893	4.63	.001
Threats to the Self—high vs. Threats to the Self—low	−0.925	1.055	3.92	.001
Adaptive Needs—high vs. Adaptive Needs—low	−0.725	1.032	3.14	.005
Empathy—high vs. Empathy—low	−0.450	0.667	3.01	.007
Temporality—high vs. Temporality—low	−0.003	0.992	1.35	.197

average, the normals' mean dropped to Mode III. Mode III is generally concerned with self-esteem maintenance, the protection of illusions concerning the self in relationship to others, dispelling illusions about one's proper place in the social world, and the preservation of autonomy over thought and action. Further, we have suggested that moving from a higher to a lower mode in the EARS paradigm is an empirical instantiation of the phenomenon of regression. We believe that people who respond this way in the testing situation may experience a similar regressive pull in a real-life context, in particular the psychoanalytic setting. On occasion, shifts to even lower levels, which we construe as yet deeper regressions, were also observed and seem to constitute a commonly occurring aspect of some normals' experience.

These findings suggested that, quite in line with epigenetic thinking, predictable patterns of cognition and emotion characterizing lower modal levels are employed by individuals usually organized at a higher level. As such, normal subjects—when stressed—possess personality characteristics similar to those seen in more disturbed subjects. This is virtually an empirical analogue of the concept of regression.

The logical next step was to compare the changes that normal subjects undergo in response to arousal to those that might be observed in an inpatient psychiatric sample. This was explored in our next experiment.

Differences between Predominant Mode of Responding of Normal Subjects and Psychiatric Inpatients under High- and Low-Arousal Conditions

We went on to compare the modal level of responses of a normal sample versus an inpatient sample relative to degree of arousal. We were specifically concerned with comparing the means of each group under high- and low-arousal conditions. We hypothesized that the inpatient sample would exhibit a lower mean modal level in their responses under both conditions than the mean modal level observed in the normal sample. We hypothesized further that the inpatients would "regress further" (i.e., the difference between their high- and low-arousal scores would be greater) than would the normal subjects.

This experiment involved two groups: a normal group and a psychiatric inpatient group. Each group consisted of 8 males and 7 females, thereby forming two groups of 15 subjects each, distributed virtually evenly by gender. Subjects ranged in age from 16 to 54, with a mean age of 28. The normal group was composed of 15 students at an urban university, screened for Axis 1 and Axis 2 diagnoses. The inpatient group was composed of an aggregate of 15 hospitalized psychiatric patients, in three subgroups by DSM-III-R (1987) Axis 1 (primary) diagnoses: 5 with a diagnosis of schizophrenia, 5 with a diagnosis of bipolar disorder, and 5 with a diagnosis of schizoaffective disorder. The hospitalized patients were screened for signs of organic pathology and subnormal intelligence, and they were not included in the study if such signs were found in their records. For normals, the procedure for administering the TAT and preparing the data for analysis was identical to that followed in the first study. For inpatients, the diagnoses were made on the basis of admissions interviews, independent of the administration of the TAT. Since retrospective chart review was used to select the inpatient sample, there was no control over when the TAT was administered during the admission. Thus, there was no way to determine the degree of psychotic disturbance at the time of testing.

The statistical results were examined via a 2 × 2 factorial analysis of variance: two levels of arousal crossed with the two sample groups. Arousal is a within-subject factor and group membership is a between-subject factor. Means for arousal levels are reported in Table 3.3. Post

TABLE 3.3. Results of Normal Subjects and Inpatients on EPI-TAT Dimensions under High and Low Arousal

Dimension—level of arousal	Min.	Max.	$\bar{x}$	SD
Affect Expression — low				
Normals	3.00	5.00	4.17	0.645
Inpatients	2.00	5.00	3.10	0.930
Affect Expression — high				
Normals	2.00	5.00	3.67	0.699
Inpatients	1.00	3.00	1.73	0.623
Affect Tolerance — low				
Normals	3.00	5.00	4.10	0.632
Inpatients	1.00	4.00	2.80	0.751
Affect Tolerance — high				
Normals	2.00	5.00	3.47	0.855
Inpatients	1.00	3.00	1.93	0.729
Use of an Object — low				
Normals	3.00	5.00	4.03	0.581
Inpatients	2.00	4.00	3.03	0.611
Use of an Object — high				
Normals	2.00	4.50	3.30	0.649
Inpatients	1.00	3.00	1.83	0.699
Centration-Decentration — low				
Normals	3.00	5.00	4.07	0.651
Inpatients	2.00	5.00	3.13	1.125
Centration-Decentration — high				
Normals	2.00	5.00	3.83	0.699
Inpatients	1.00	4.00	1.93	0.766
Personal Agency — low				
Normals	3.00	5.00	4.07	0.776
Inpatients	2.00	5.00	2.83	0.880
Personal Agency — high				
Normals	2.00	5.00	3.33	0.957
Inpatients	1.00	3.00	2.00	0.802
Defence — low				
Normals	3.00	5.00	4.23	0.530
Inpatients	2.00	5.00	2.83	0.880
Defense — high				
Normals	2.00	5.00	3.33	0.645
Inpatients	1.00	3.00	1.87	0.812
Threat — low				
Normals	3.00	5.00	4.27	0.495
Inpatients	1.00	5.00	2.97	1.109
Threat — high				
Normals	2.00	4.50	3.33	0.699
Inpatients	1.00	3.00	2.07	0.776

(cont.)

TABLE 3.3. *(cont.)*

Dimension—level of arousal	Min.	Max.	$\bar{x}$	SD
Need—low				
Normals	3.00	5.00	4.23	0.594
Inpatients	1.00	5.00	3.03	0.972
Need—high				
Normals	2.00	5.00	3.57	0.776
Inpatients	1.00	3.50	1.87	0.640
Empathy—low				
Normals	3.00	5.00	3.90	0.573
Inpatients	2.00	5.00	3.03	0.849
Empathy—high				
Normals	1.00	5.00	3.60	0.767
Inpatients	1.00	3.00	2.00	0.627
Temporality—low				
Normals	1.00	5.00	3.53	0.972
Inpatients	2.00	5.00	3.07	1.100
Temporality—high				
Normals	2.00	5.00	3.60	0.737
Inpatients	1.00	3.50	2.37	0.767

hoc tests were done using Fisher's LSD method. Univariate results of these analyses are reported in Table 3.4. Table 3.5 shows the significance tests for the decrement between arousal levels in each dimension, with the data pooled from both groups.

The results show that the responses of normals and inpatients are significantly different from one another on all 10 dimensions, such that normals score significantly higher than inpatients on each dimension (Tables 3.3 and 3.4). The results also indicate that for both normal and inpatient subjects, responses differed significantly under the two arousal conditions (Table 3.5). The mean level of response across dimensions for normals is Mode IV under the low-arousal condition and Mode III under high arousal. This result replicated our earlier finding. Further, we see that inpatients generally score at or around Mode III under the low-arousal condition and drop to Mode II and below under the high-arousal condition. Thus the degree of regression is similar in the two groups. Both normals and severely disturbed inpatients score one mode lower under the high-arousal condition. Thus, the hypotheses that the inpatient group would have a greater difference between their high- and low-arousal scores was not supported. However, this result led to the suspicion that it is the qualities of the beginning and end points of their fluctuation that may

TABLE 3.4. Univariate *F* Tests Comparing Normal Subjects' and Inpatients' Mean Scores on EPI-TAT Dimensions

	SS	df	MS	F	p
Affect Expression	33.750	1	33.750	42.792	0.001
Error	22.083	28	0.789		
Affect Tolerance	30.104	1	30.104	51.293	0.001
Error	16.433	28	0.587		
Uses of an Object	22.817	1	22.817	44.728	0.001
Error	8.417	28	0.301		
Centration–Decentration	30.104	1	30.104	34.034	0.001
Error	24.767	28	0.885		
Personal Agency	24.704	1	24.704	21.471	0.001
Error	32.217	28	1.151		
Defense	28.107	1	28.107	39.956	0.001
Error	19.633	28	0.701		
Threat	24.704	1	24.704	30.184	0.001
Error	22.917	28	0.818		
Needs	31.538	1	31.538	46.467	0.001
Error	19.000	28	0.679		
Empathy	22.817	1	22.817	37.324	0.001
Error	17.117	28	0.611		
Temporality	10.838	1	10.838	9.842	0.004
Error	30.833	28	1.101		

have greater significance, not the absolute length of their decrement on the scales from one condition to another.

Our results showed that psychiatric inpatients and normals significantly differed in their overall modal levels of organization. Normals scored at a higher modal level than did the inpatient sample, under both high- and low-arousal conditions. The inpatients, under high arousal, displayed a drop to Mode II or below. The reader is reminded that the typical concerns of Mode II pertain to issues of self-regulation, to a psychobiologically dominated representational period that bridges sensorimotor and imagistic representational capacities, polarized experiences of self and other, and acute anxieties over separation phenomena. When in Mode II, an other is *necessary* in order to maintain a continuity of self, much as Winnicott (1956) stated that the presence of the facilitating caregiver is necessary in order for the child to be enabled to keep "going on being." This regression has as its end point dimensions of personality defined as not subjectively accessible to the adult's memorial retrieval. Based on this conceptualization, the inpatients' change in responding from Mode III to II is

TABLE 3.5. Effect of Arousal Condition on EPI-TAT Dimension Scores for Normal and Inpatient Sample

	SS	df	MS	F	p
Affect Expression	13.067	1	13.067	45.076	0.001
Error	8.117	28	0.290		
Affet Tolerance	8.438	1	8.438	16.035	0.001
Error	14.733	28	0.526		
Use of an Object	14.017	1	14.017	46.630	0.001
Error	8.417	28	0.301		
Centration–Decentration	7.704	1	7.704	15.227	0.001
Error	14.167	28	0.506		
Personal Agency	9.204	1	9.204	29.011	0.001
Error	8.883	28	0.317		
Defense	15.000	1	15.000	36.207	0.001
Error	11.600	28	0.414		
Threat	12.604	1	12.604	26.469	0.001
Error	13.333	28	0.476		
Empathy	6.667	1	6.667	16.495	0.001
Error	11.317	28	0.404		
Temporality	1.504	1	1.504	2.777	0.107
Error	15.167	28	0.542		

clinically more problematic than the normals' regressive change from Mode IV to III. In regressing from Mode III to II, an individual is likely to draw objects into primitive enactments around pressing self-regulatory demands that are difficult to understand through introspection. The boundary between Modes II and III, thus, is a critical Rubicon of sorts, and a regressive crossing brings about serious challenges to a patient's capacity for therapeutic alliance and treatability using the expressive assumptions of psychoanalytic therapy.

We suggest that this frontier between Modes II and III signals the need for a change in the clinician's stance toward the patient because they become entwined in an interindividual, mutually regulating style that is necessary for the success of the treatment. In other words, one can regress from an intramental to an intermental organization (Wertsch, 1991). Inpatients, at their highest organization as reflected by their low-arousal narratives, retain the ability to self-regulate (see Wilson, Passik, & Faude, 1990). They maintain a fragile system for maintaining inner tensions and self-esteem while not requiring the containing presence of another. Under high arousal, though, the inpatients temporarily regress from Mode III to Mode II, and in some individual cases to Mode I. In these states they seek inner regulation of tension and other rudimentary affect states through symbiotic-like strivings, which explains why hospitalization is often necessary and helpful for such individuals. The regression to Mode II appears to signal a return to a reliance upon objects who can "metabolize" (Kernberg, 1975) projected mental content to preverbal patterns that characterize the fragile and volatile instability of the self at this level (Wilson, 1986). Depending upon character style, some people at times dimensionally organized at Mode II may recruit others to serve this containing function, whereas others may express rage that sequesters them from a regulating other (Malatesta & Wilson, 1988). Therefore, the difference between normals and inpatients is not merely one of more or less stability of a personality organization. More clinically important is "where" the regressions begin and end, particularly whether they end at a level in which self-regulation fails or cannot be autonomously maintained and thus there is a requirement for a regulating other.

There were also significant interaction effects between group membership and degree of arousal on three of the dimensions: Affect Expression, Centration–Decentration, and Empathy. The effects were as follows: Affect Expression: $F(2,28) = 9.717$, $p < .005$; Centration–Decentration: $F(2,28) = 6.926$, $p < .014$; Empathy: $F(2,28) = 4.990$, $p < .034$. In all cases the interaction effects are attributable to the change in the inpatient sample mean under high arousal when contrasted with the lack of a change in the normal sample on these dimensions. As can be seen in Table 3.3, on the dimension Affect Expression, the normal sample scored at a mean level of 4.17 for low arousal and 3.67 for high arousal, whereas the inpatient sample scored at a mean level of 3.10 for low arousal and 1.73 for high arousal. For the dimension Centration–Decentration, the normal sample scored at a mean level of 4.07 for low arousal and 3.83 for high arousal, whereas the inpatient sample scored at a mean level of 3.13 for low arousal and 1.93 for high arousal. For the dimension Empathy, the normal sample scored at a mean level of 3.90 for low arousal and 3.60 for high arousal, whereas the inpatient sample scored at a mean level of 3.03 for low arousal and 2.00 for high arousal. For the inpatient sample the degree of the change on the dimensions that have a significant interaction with arousal level are similar to the fluctuations on those dimensions that do not exhibit such interaction effects. However, for the normal sample, there was no pronounced downward change in those dimensions involved in the significant interaction effect. Thus, severe psychopathology might be particularly identifiable on the basis of EARS scores on these dimensions. The interaction effects for Affect Expression, Centration–Decentration, and Empathy suggest that these dimensions are the most stable and least susceptible to regression in normals. Our interpretation of this finding is that because inpatients remain vulnerable to regression along these dimensions, it is possible that these dimensions are linked to those psychological dilemmas that precipitate hospitalization. Future research is necessary to help us understand the ways in which these dimensions are related to symptoms of major psychiatric diagnoses. On the basis of this result, one might for now view the severely disturbed inpatient as possessing three particular areas of vulnerability as compared to normals, who have particular strengths in these areas: (1) under high arousal, inpatients tend to be unable to modulate, control, and express a wide and appropriate affect array (Wilson & Malatesta, 1989), whereas normals retain these capacities; (2) under high arousal, inpatients lack differentiation of self and other and struggle over enmeshment and issues of internal and external control, whereas normals maintain a sense of differentiation and capacities associated with intact self–other and inner–outer boundaries; (3) under high arousal, inpatients' knowledge and understanding of others is markedly impaired, whereas normals retain a well understood sense of the other.

In sum, these investigations have shown that the EARS is capable of distinguishing between normals and inpatients in terms of level of personality dimensions across arousal conditions. The EARS scores highlighted specific dimensions of personality in which normals remain stable while inpatients continue to change. In the next section we will describe in some detail two studies that represent examples of the "second generation" of EARS investigations. In the studies described above, some of the basic assumptions of epigenetic thinking were empirically explored. Having demonstrated that indeed there are measurable changes within dimensions of the EARS, that these changes are detectable in subjects at all levels of organization, and that such changes seem to occur in response to levels of arousal, the way was cleared to begin a second generation approach to the validation of the EARS. This group of studies involves turning to specific diagnostic groups (e.g., drug abusers, schizophrenics, depressives) and testing specific hypotheses that arise from a number of sources. As our research group has previously demonstrated, the epigenetic model and concepts arising from it (such as self-regulatory failures [Wilson et al., 1990]) can be used to organize sometimes divergent psychoanalytic and general clinical observations of these populations. Observations and research data arising from both within psychoanalysis and disciplines such as developmental psychology can be framed in hypotheses that can be empirically tested utilizing the EARS. This process allows both epigenetic psychoanalytic theory, and more specifically, the EARS to garner empirical support and construct validity, respectively.

ADVANCED EMPIRICAL INVESTIGATIONS

Opiate Abusers, Cocaine Abusers, and Normals: A Study of Their Affective Differences[5]

Psychoanalytic theorists interested in the phenomenon of substance abuse have suggested that the affectivity in such people is profoundly impaired, resulting in a need for self-medication (Greenspan, 1977; Khantzian, 1978; Krystal & Raskin, 1970; Treece, 1984; Wurmser, 1974). Based on this point of view, several interrelated subhypotheses were set forth. For example, it was proposed that substance abusers use drugs to offset difficulties in tolerating and giving verbal expression to painful affects (Krystal, 1975). Wurmser (1978) has referred to problems in the verbal expression of affects as "hyposymbolization," whereas Krystal (1987) describes them as primarily a form of alexithymia.

An idea related to the self-medication hypothesis is that the particular drug selected to modulate affects is not random (Milkman & Frosch, 1973). Rather, a "drug of choice" helps the abuser substitute a preferable for an unpreferable affect state, based upon an interaction between the pharmacologic effect of the drug and the psychodynamics of the individual. Wieder and Kaplan (1969) have called this the "pharmacogenic effect." They and others (e.g., Greenspan, 1979; Krystal, 1975) have postulated that such pharmacologically induced affect states serve as correctives for disturbances in affectivity deriving from preverbal periods of human development.

Based on a thorough review of psychoanalytic investigations of drug abuse, Keller and Wilson (1992) hypothesized that both preferential opiate and cocaine abusers would appear significantly more impaired than normals in Affect Tolerance and Affect Expression. It was also hypothesized that opiate abusers would appear significantly more impaired than cocaine abusers on these dimensions. Furthermore, cocaine abusers were predicted to score in the Mode III range, while the opiate abusers were predicted to score in the Mode II range on these variables. In addition, Keller and Wilson attempted to construct a multitrait–multimethod matrix for the affective variables by including several other measures of affect. They hypothesized that there would be pronounced differences in affective functioning between the normals and two drug abuse groups, as manifested on these other affect measures, with the same order of impairment.

Thus, as was described above, an attempt was made to both test the application of the epigenetic model to psychoanalytic observations of these groups and to further the construct validation of the EARS.

The subjects were 25 cocaine abusers, 25 opiate abusers, and 25 non-drug/alcohol-abusing volunteers who served as normal controls. Subjects were matched across age, sex, and social class (Hollingshead & Redlich, 1958). Substance abusers were patients admitted for either cocaine or opiate abuse or dependence at the Yale University Substance Abuse Treatment Unit. All met DSM-III-R (1987) criteria for cocaine or opiate abuse or dependence, respectively. All scored in the pathological range of the Millon Clinical Multiaxial Inventory (MCMI) Drug Abuse Scale. All stated they preferred either cocaine or opiates to all other drugs. Normals were volunteers recruited at several northeastern urban universities, though not all were college students. These subjects were screened for drug and alcohol abuse as well as psychiatric disorder by means of the MCMI. Volunteers were included in the normal sample only if they did not score in the pathological range of any MCMI scale. Table 3.6 presents a summary of subjects' characteristics.

The instruments used in the study included the Thematic Apperception Test (TAT), scored using the EPI-TAT application of the EARS system for the dimensions Affect Tolerance and Affect Expression, the Minnesota Multiphasic Personality Inventory (MMPI)

TABLE 3.6. Subject Characteristics

	Cocaine	Opiate	Normal
Age			
$\bar{x}$	29.3	28.9	28.3
Range	19–44	23–45	19–41
Sex			
M	16	16	9
F	9	9	9
Drug use (yrs)			
$\bar{x}$	3.68	3.44	—
Range	1–10	1–8	—
Route of administration			
Intranasal	10	1	—
Intravenous	6	19	—
Freebase	9	0	—
Oral	0	5	—

Under- vs. Over-control of Impulses Scale (EC-5) (Block, 1965), and the Toronto Alexithymia Scale (TAS) (Taylor, Ryan, & Bagby, 1985).

To prevent confounding effects of order of presentation, half the subjects in each group received the TAT cards first followed by the self report inventories (EC-5 and TAS), while the other half of the subjects received the self report inventories first followed by the TAT cards. Self report inventories were presented in a randomized fashion. TAT cards were presented to subjects in the manner described by Allison et al. (1968). The presentation of the TAT cards (1 and 13MF) was counterbalanced. Self report inventories and TAT responses were scored by research assistants blind to the hypotheses of the study and group membership. In scoring the EPI-TAT, two raters who had achieved expert status scored the responses. To minimize potential perseverative tendencies to score modes consistently within subjects, one rater scored half the subjects' responses on dimensions for Affect Tolerance, Uses of an Object, Temporality, Adaptive Needs, Threats to the Self, and another scored the other half, dimensions for Affect Expression, Empathy, Defensive Operation, Centration–Decentration, and Personal Agency. The second rater scored the first half of subjects on dimensions for Affect Expression, Empathy, Defensive Operation, Centration–Decentration, and Personal Agency, and the second half of subjects on dimensions for Affect Tolerance, Uses of an Object, Temporality, Adaptive Needs, and Threats to Self.

The hypotheses of the study were tested using two instruments employed to measure group performance on each of the affective dimensions: The EPI-TAT Affect Tolerance scale and the EC-5 for Affect Tolerance and the EPI-TAT Affect Expression scale and the TAS for Affect Expression.

The EPI-TAT data were analyzed in a 3×2 factorial design (groups $\times$ level of arousal). Both Affect Tolerance and Affect Expression variables were analyzed for statistical significance using analysis of variance with repeated measures. Arousal was the repeated measure. Means and standard deviations for each of these EPI-TAT variables at each arousal level are presented in Table 3.7. As predicted, the group means were significantly different on the EPI-TAT Affect Tolerance dimension, $F(2,72) = 10.30$, $p < .0001$. The effect of arousal was also significant, $F(1,72) = 60.54$, $p < .0001$. The groups $\times$ arousal interaction was nonsignificant. Post hoc Fisher's LSD tests were performed to estimate where group differences derived. The cocaine and opiate abusers scored significantly lower on Affect Tolerance than normals (cocaine: $p < .05$; opiate: $p < .002$). How-

TABLE 3.7. Means and Standard Deviations for Normals, Cocaine Abusers, and Opiate Abusers on the EPI-TAT Affect Tolerance and Affect Expression Scales under Low and High Arousal

	Low arousal		High arousal	
	$\bar{x}$	SD	$\bar{x}$	SD
Affect Tolerance				
Normals	4.04	0.61	3.40	0.91
Cocaine	3.64	0.75	2.64	1.07
Opiate	3.12	0.83	2.48	0.77
Affect Expression				
Normals	3.96	0.73	3.32	0.85
Cocaine	3.52	0.91	2.72	0.74
Opiate	2.96	0.68	2.20	0.76

ever, opiate abusers did not score significantly lower than cocaine abusers as predicted, though group means were in the predicted direction, as can be seen in Table 3.7. It should be pointed out that under high arousal both substance abusing groups scored well within the Mode II range, where the more primitive, psychobiological forms of affect tolerance predominate.

Affect Tolerance was also assessed by the EC-5. Means and standard deviations for the EC-5 are presented in Table 3.8. These data were analyzed by 1-way analysis of variance. The findings parallel those obtained on the EPI-TAT. The groups were significantly different, $F(2,72) = 5.62$, $p < .005$. Post hoc Fishers LSD tests revealed that both substance abusing groups scored significantly lower than normals on the EC-5 but were not significantly different with respect to one another.

The results of this study provide strong support for the hypothesis that the three groups would significantly differ on Affect Expression. On the EPI-TAT Affect Expression dimension, the groups were significantly different, $F(2,72) = 17.00$ $p < .0001$; the effect of arousal was also significant, $F(1,72) = 49.79$, $p < .0001$; and the groups ×

TABLE 3.8. Means and Standard Deviations for Normals, Cocaine Abusers, and Opiate Abusers on the EC-5

	Min.	Max.	$\bar{x}$	SD
Normal	6.00	19.00	14.72	3.31
Cocaine	5.00	21.00	12.32	4.41
Opiate	2.00	24.00	10.76	4.73

arousal interaction was nonsignificant. Post hoc Fisher's LSD tests revealed that both cocaine and opiate abusers scored significantly lower than normals (cocaine: $p < .05$; opiate: $p < .0001$). This time, however, opiate abusers scored significantly lower than cocaine abusers as had been predicted ($p < .05$). Inspection of Table 3.7 indicates that the three groups are quite evenly spaced apart under both arousal conditions on the EPI-TAT Affect Expression scale. It is worth noting that whereas opiate abusers' Affect Expression scores are at the upper end of Mode II, that is, the more primitive and psychobiologically dominated mode, cocaine abusers are well within Mode III under low arousal and regress to Mode II only under the high-arousal condition.

The results of the TAS parallel the results obtained on the EPI-TAT Affect Expression scale. Means and standard deviations for the TAS are presented in Table 3.9. A 1-way analysis of variance for the total TAS scores revealed that the groups were significantly different, $F (2,72) = 16.72$, $p < .0001$. Post hoc Fisher's LSD tests revealed that both cocaine and opiate abusers were significantly more alexithymic than normals ($p < .05$) but were not significantly different from one another. Nevertheless, the TAS is comprised of four factors, the second of which specifically measures ability to verbalize affects. The TAS factors were analyzed for statistical significance utilizing Multivariate analysis of variance. On Factor 2, the groups were significantly different, $F (2,72) = 4.38$, $p < .016$. However, the post hoc test revealed that only opiate abusers were significantly more impaired than normals on the TAS Factor 2 ($p < .05$). Cocaine abusers were not significantly different from either normals or opiate abusers, paralleling the EPI-TAT Affect Expression findings.

Another goal of this study was to provide construct validity for the EPI-TAT Affect Tolerance and Affect Expression dimensions by

TABLE 3.9. Means and Standard Deviations for Normals, Cocaine Abusers, and Opiate Abusers on the TAS

	Min.	Max.	$\bar{x}$	SD
TAS — Total				
Normal	29.00	76.00	50.84	10.72
Cocaine	47.00	94.00	64.20	11.64
Opiate	51.00	98.00	69.08	12.22
TAS — Factor 2				
Normal	7.00	25.00	15.16	5.13
Cocaine	11.00	34.00	17.36	5.38
Opiate	13.00	31.00	19.84	4.49

utilizing the EC-5 and TAS, both well-established, reliable, and valid instruments. By analyzing two traits (Affect Tolerance and Affect Expression) with two different methods (projective and self report), it was possible to test for construct validity according to the multitrait–multimethod procedure described by Campbell and Fiske (1959). For construct validity, correlations between the same trait measured by different methods should be statistically different from zero and should exceed the correlations between different traits measured by the same method as well as the correlations between different traits measured by different methods.

Table 3.10 presents the multitrait–multimethod correlation matrices for the present study. Although we failed to meet the stringent criteria set forth by Campbell and Fiske for both arousal conditions, it should be noted that the results of the analysis of the TAS approximate their criteria under high arousal. As can be seen in Table 3.10, the TAS–EPI-TAT Affect Expression correlation is significantly different from zero (0.373), is greater than the TAS–EPI-TAT Affect

TABLE 3.10. Multitrait–Multimethod Matrices for EPI-TAT Affect Tolerance, Affect Expression, EC-5, and TAS at Low and High Arousal

| | | Method 1 (EPI-TAT) | | Method 2 | |
	Traits	Affect Tolerance	Affect Expression	EC-5	TAS
		Low arousal			
Method 1 (EPI-TAT)	AT	1.000			
	AE	0.458****	1.000		
Method 2	EC-5	0.048	0.060	1.000	
	TAS	0.313*	0.296*	0.209	1.000
		High arousal			
Method 1 (EPI-TAT)	AT	1.000			
	AE	0.388***	1.000		
Method 2	EC-5	0.014	0.004	1.000	
	TAS	0.338**	0.373***	0.209	1.000

*$p < .012$. **$p < .005$. ***$p < .001$. ****$p < .0001$.

Tolerance correlation (0.338), and equals the EPI-TAT Affect Tolerance–Affect Expression correlation (0.338). These results are very encouraging for the eventual demonstration of this form of construct validity, given the relatively small size of the sample in this study.

Use of the EPI-LOG to Examine Parental Object Relations in Schizophrenic Adults[6]

Introduction and Hypotheses

Based on a thorough review of psychoanalytic investigations of schizophrenia, Passik (1990) hypothesized that schizophrenics' symptoms would be correlated with different aspects of parental object relations as measured by the EARS. The psychoanalytic theory of schizophrenia has evolved profoundly since Freud's well-known original writings on the subject. Recent psychoanalytic observations of schizophrenia (e.g., Grotstein, 1977, 1989) have attempted to integrate empirical findings of researchers and clinicians working from a biological and genetic point of view. Meanwhile the hypothesized role of early object relations in schizophrenia has changed. The idea that parents engender schizophrenia in their developing children has been replaced by an acknowledgment of the complex interaction of biological, psychological, and interpersonal factors in schizophrenia and upon parent–child interactions. Grotstein (1977, 1989) describes how schizophrenic patients have complicated relationships with their parents that vary over time from highly enmeshed and dependent, to avoidant, to more mutual and adult forms of interrelating. The "withdrawal from objects," as Freud termed it, is still considered an important aspect of schizophrenic object relations. These recent reworkings of psychoanalytic positions on schizophrenia have helped to understand this withdrawal as an overdetermined and complex phenomenon. Thus, at times schizophrenics may be defensively motivated to avoid the traumatic overstimulation to which they are prone because of an underlying inherited vulnerability. At other times, the withdrawal seen in schizophrenia may also be a biological aspect of the type of schizophrenia dominated by negative syndrome (Andreasen, 1985). (The negative syndrome is described below.)

Parents may become involved in archaic interactions with their schizophrenic offspring for a variety of reasons, ranging from aspects of their own needs stemming from personal functioning or psychopathology to a genuine attempt to mediate the multitude of cognitive and psychological deficits in their children.

The epigenetic hierarchical model of the self-organization can be helpful in bringing an ordered conceptual framework to such complex theoretical and clinical phenomena. Earlier in this chapter, we described how we have investigated inpatient psychotic adults, using the EARS. Under conditions of low and high arousal these patients' predominant epigenetic modes of functioning were in the middle and lower ranges of the hierarchical model, respectively. Interpersonal relationships stemming from these modes are focused upon regulatory and dependency needs. They are characterized by poor differentiation between self and other. Thus, Passik (1990) used the EARS system to study the other participant in the most crucial of all interpersonal relationships—a parent with whom the patient has frequent contact. We set about to understand how the parents themselves might display signs of functioning in these lower modes, as a correlate of the developmental course of the illness and the type of symptomatology displayed by the patient.

In particular, Passik drew upon the recent distinction between the deficit and nondeficit syndromes in schizophrenia to formulate his hypotheses. Negative symptoms refer to affective abnormalities, such as restricted or "blunted" affect and diminished affective range; social abnormalities, including decreased interpersonal interest and some forms of isolativeness; and "alogia," or a marked constriction of ideation and volition. Andreasen and Olsen (1982) attempted to validate subtypes of schizophrenia involving positive and negative symptom clusters. The negative subtype is marked by a relative absence of positive symptoms (hallucinations and delusions), and the presence of anhedonia, psychomotor retardation, poverty of content of speech, restricted affect, and alogia. In further validation work on the existence of distinct positive and negative subgroups, Andreasen and Olsen (1982) investigated the functional characteristics and adaptation of the two groups and found that the negative symptom group had lower levels of education, employment, and premorbid adaptation than the positive group and greater levels of impairment at admission and discharge, as well as greater neuropsychological impairments on the Mini Mental State examination. Computed tomography (CT) studies found the negative symptom group to have greater evidence of ventricular enlargement (loss of brain mass).

Passik hypothesized that those patients with the deficit or negative syndrome, with its associated long-standing and chronic affective, interpersonal, cognitive, and volitional deficits, are likely candidates for the development of an overly enmeshed form of object relationship between parent and child. The various qualities of the deficit syndrome render the schizophrenic patient liable to overstimulation, as is characteristic of functioning in the lowest epigenetic mode (Mode 1). Further, the particular social/interpersonal manifestations of this syndrome, that is, the use of isolation and withdrawal to avoid intense interpersonal interactions (Carpenter, Heinrichs, & Wagner, 1988) are examples of the use of defensive maneuvers and attachment manifestations of Mode II in the epigenetic hierarchy. These tendencies would "draw in" the parent in an attempt to mitigate the patient's social and cognitive impairments.

The EARS scoring system when applied to 5-minute monologues, is called the EPI-LOG. Passik used the EPI-LOG to assess whether a parent involved in a relationship with such an offspring manifests qualities also lower in epigenetic mode. Additionally, Passik examined a variable studied by many schizophrenia researchers – the Expressed Emotion (EE) paradigm. A detailed description of this research program is beyond the scope of the present chapter. However, in brief, high degrees of Expressed Emotion in the households of schizophrenic patients has been shown to predict relapse and rehospitalization. EE status is determined on the basis of two attitudes expressed by the parents in a structured family interview, namely Emotional Overinvolvement (EOI) and Critical Comments (CC). Passik included EOI to examine the relationship between this consciously held attitude and patients' symptoms, and then he compared this relationship to the one between EARS scores and patients' symptoms.

Passik used five dimensions of the EARS (Empathy, Uses of an Object, Affect Tolerance, Affect Expression, and Personal Agency). He hypothesized that parents whose children had a poor premorbid course and a high level of negative symptoms would be those who displayed lower modal scores on these EARS dimensions.

The subjects in the study were 50 pairs, each pair consisting of a recently hospitalized schizophrenic patient and one parent with whom the patient had frequent contact. The patients were between the ages of 18 and 40; had a DSM-III-R (American Psychiatric Association, 1987) diagnosis of schizophrenia ($n = 42$), schizoaffective disorder ($n = 5$), or schizophreniform disorder ($n = 3$); and maintained frequent contact with one member of their family origin. Frequent contact was defined as living with or spending 5 or more hours together per week, for at least 1 month prior to admission.

The patient group was comprised of 36 males and 14 females with a mean age of 27.5 years. The parent group was comprised mainly of mothers ($n = 45$). The Structured Clinical Interview for the DSM-III-R, Psychotic Disorders (SCID-PD) was used to establish the patients' diagnoses during the first week of their hospitalization.

The patients were assessed with the following instruments:

1. The Premorbid Adjustment Scale (PAS) (Cannon-Spoor, Potkin, and Wyatt, 1982): The PAS is a rating scale that evaluates level of psychosocial adjustment in four major areas: social accessibility–isolation, peer relationships, ability to function outside of the nuclear family, and sociosexual ties. Adjustment is evaluated for age-appropriate functioning through four life periods including up until 6 months prior to admission: childhood (C), early adolescence (EA), late adolescence (LA), and adulthood (A). The reliability and validity of the PAS have been well established.

2. Modified Scale for the Assessment of Negative Symptoms (SANS) (Andreasen, 1984): The SANS is a set of rating scales for the assessment of the severity of negative symptoms. As described above, negative symptoms fall into different classes consisting of affective flattening and decreased affective tone, asociality, and anhedonia. The SANS is made up of 23 separate symptom severity rating scales that are grouped under five classes: alogia, avolition–apathy, attention, asociality–anhedonia, and affective flattening and blunting. The reliability and validity of this measure have been reported by Andreasen and Olsen (1982).

The parents in the study were assessed with the following instruments:

1. The Camberwell Family Interview (CFI) (Vaughn & Leff, 1976): The CFI is an audiotaped, semistructured interview that covers the history of present illness and specific symptomatology providing the basis for the making of EE ratings. The interview is conducted by an interviewer trained specifically in the CFI interview and rating procedures with the relative of the schizophrenic patient, and it assesses the relative's attitudes about and relationship with the patient. The latest and shortest version of the CFI (duration: 45 minutes) has been shown to have high reliability for the CC and EOI components of EE (.93 and .95, respectively). The validity of the CFI has largely been established through its ability to predict relapse in schizophrenic and depressed subjects on follow-up (Miklowitz, Goldstein, Falloon, & Doane, 1984; Miklowitz et al., 1986; Valone, Norton, Goldstein, & Doane, 1983).

2. The Gottschalk Task (GT): The GT has been adapted for use with the Camberwell Family Interview. The instructions for the GT portion of the CFI instruct the relative of the patient to discuss, for a 5-minute period, their relationship to the patient and "what kind of

person (the patient) is." During the time that the relative is speaking, the interviewer sits with the patient and relative and listens attentively or takes notes but does not comment in any way. The narrative sample provided by the parent during the GT provided the data for the EARS ratings. The ratings of these dimensions were made by an expert rater.

Pearson product–moment correlations between EARS dimensions and PAS total and age summary scores appear in Table 3.11. EARS dimensions Empathy and Personal Agency are significantly correlated with the PAS total score (Empathy: $r = -.28$, $p < .05$; Personal Agency: $r = -42$, $p < .01$). Significant correlations are found between these same two EARS dimensions and poor premorbid adjustment during the childhood period (Empathy: $r = -.26$, $p < .05$; Personal Agency: $r = -.38$, $p < .01$). For the early adolescent period, significant correlations are found solely between PAS scores and EARS dimension Personal Agency ($r = -.34$, $p < .01$).

Pearson product–moment correlations between parent EARS dimensions and patient SANS ratings appear in Table 3.12. As can be seen, significant and trend-level negative correlations are found between EARS dimensions Affect Tolerance ($r = -.37$, $p < .01$), Affect Expression ($r = -.27$, $p < .05$), Empathy ($r = -.22$, $p < .10$), and Uses of an Object ($r = -.27$, $p < .05$) and the total negative symptom score of the SANS. EARS dimension Empathy is significantly correlated with the global rating of avolition–apathy ($r = -.19$, $p < .10$) at the trend-level of significance. EARS dimension Uses of an Object is significantly correlated with the global rating of avolition ($r = -.32$, $p < .01$). EARS dimension Personal Agency is not correlated with the global ratings of avolition.

Multiple regression analyses were performed to examine the

TABLE 3.11. Correlations between EPI-LOG Variables and Premorbid Adjustment Scale (PAS) Total and Age Period Scores

EPI-LOG variables	PAS total and age period scores				
	Total PAS	Child-hood	Early adolescence	Late adolescence	Adult-hood
Affect Tolerance	−.04	.03	−.04	−.07	−.05
Affect Expression	−.02	.04	−.03	−.11	−.03
Empathy	−.28[a]	−.26[b]	−.16	−.18	−.12
Use of an Object	−.14	−.11	−.04	−.08	−.17
Personal Agency	−.42[b]	−.38[b]	−.34[b]	−.28[a]	−.44[b]

[a]$p < .05$. [b]$p < .01$.

TABLE 3.12. Correlations between EPI-LOG Variables and Scale for the Assessment of Negative Symptoms (SANS) Total Score and Global Ratings

| | SANS total and global ratings | | |
EPI-LOG variables	Total SANS	Anhedonia–asociality	Avolition–apathy
Affect Tolerance	$-.37^c$	$-.20^a$	$-.32^c$
Affect Expression	$-.27^b$	$-.17^a$	$-.26^b$
Empathy	$-.22^a$	$-.08$	$-.19^a$
Use of an Object	$-.27^b$	$-.09$	$-.32^c$
Personal Agency	$-.10$	$-.02$	$-.07$

[a] $p < .10$. [b] $p < .05$. [c] $p < .01$.

relationships between EARS dimensions, EE variable emotional overinvolvement (EOI), premorbid adjustment, and negative symptoms. The first two of these analyses concern the prediction of poor premorbid adjustment in the earliest periods in the patients' lives — childhood and early adolescence. In each case, the relative contributions of EE-EOI and EARS dimensions Empathy, Use of the Object, and Personal Agency were examined.

In the first analysis, the PAS score representing poor premorbid adjustment in the childhood period (PAS-C) is used as the dependent variable. SES was entered into the equation on the first step. EE-EOI was entered into the equation in the second step, followed by EARS dimensions Empathy, Use of an Object, and Personal Agency entered as a block on step three. The results of this multiple regression analysis appear in Table 3.13. Please note that significance in this statistical test is gauged by the beta weight, not the R^2 change.

In the second analysis, the PAS score representing poor premorbid adjustment in the early adolescent period (PAS-EA) is used as the dependent variable. SES was entered into the equation on the first step. EE-EOI was entered into the equation in the second step, followed by EARS dimensions Empathy, Uses of an Object, and Personal Agency entered as a block on step three. The results of this multiple regression analysis appear in Table 3.14.

The results of these two hierarchical multiple regression analyses suggest that the best parental predictors of poor premorbid adjustment during childhood are a low level of speaker Personal Agency and SES, while the best predictors of poor premorbid adjustment during the early adolescent period are low levels of speaker Personal Agency. Emotionally overinvolved speaker attitudes as tapped by EE-EOI scores do not emerge as a significant predictor of poor premorbid adjustment early in the patient's life. The inclusion of

TABLE 3.13. Regression Analysis of Poor Premorbid Adjustment in Childhood

Variables entered	r	Beta	R^2 change	F (df)
Step 1				
Speaker's SES	.20	.20[a]	.04	$F = 2.11$ (1,48)
Step 2				
EE-EOI	− .06	− .03	.00	$F = .06$ (2,47)
Step 3				
Empathy	− .26	− .16		
Uses of an Object	− .11	− .21		
Personal Agency	− .38	− .35[a]	.13[a]	$F = 2.44$ (5,44)[a]

NOTE: Empathy, Uses of an Object, and Personal Agency entered as block; R^2 change is for block.
  When all variables were entered into the equation the overall multiple $R = .42$, $F = 1.93$, $df = 5$, $p = .10$.
  [a]$p < .10$.

TABLE 3.14. Regression Analysis of Poor Premorbid Adjustment in Early Adolescence

Variables entered	r	Beta	R^2 change	F (df)
Step 1				
Speaker's SES	.19	.19	.03	$F = 1.97$ (1,48)
Step 2				
EE-EOI	− .05	− .02	.008	$F = .04$ (2,47)
Step 3				
Empathy	− .16	− .03		
Uses of an Object	− .04	.25		
Personal Agency	− .34	− .41[b]	.12[a]	$F = 2.12$ (5.44)[a]

NOTE: Empathy, Uses of an Object, and Personal Agency entered as block; R^2 change is for block.
  When all variables were entered into the equation the overall multiple $R = .40$, $F = 1.69$, $df = 5,44$, $p = .15$.
  [a]$p < .10$; [b]$p < .05$.

EE-EOI, therefore, does not aid in predicting these particular patterns of maladjustment.

A multiple linear regression analysis was also performed to examine the relative contributions of EARS dimensions Empathy, Uses of an Object, and Personal Agency and EE variable EOI on negative symptom avolition–apathy. The global rating of avolition–apathy serves as the dependent variable. Again, SES is entered into the equation on the first step. In this particular multiple regression analysis, gender of patient is dummy-coded and entered into the

TABLE 3.15. Regression Analysis of Avolition–Apathy

Variables entered	r	Beta	R^2 change	F (df)
Step 1				
Speaker's SES	$-.06$	$-.06$		
Gender of patient	$-.19$	.002	.004	$F = .10$ (2,47)
Step 2				
EE-EOI	.22	.20	.04	$F = 1.98$ (3,46)
Step 3				
Empathy	$-.20$	$-.03$		
Use of an Object	$-.35$	$-.41^b$		
Personal Agency	$-.07$	.11	$.13^a$	$F = 2.31$ $(6,43)^a$

NOTE: Speaker's SES and gender of patient entered as block; R^2 change is for block. When all variables were entered into the equation the overall multiple $R = .42$, $F = 1.55$, $df = 6,43$, $p = .18$.
$^a p < .10$; $^b p < .05$.

equation along with SES on step one. This was due to the significant difference in EARS dimension Uses of the Object for speakers in relationship to male and female patients. EE-EOI was entered into the equation in the second step, followed by EARS dimensions Empathy, Uses of an Object, and Personal Agency entered as a block on step three.

The results of this hierarchical multiple regression analysis appear in Table 3.15. The results indicate that the best parental predictor of patient negative symptom avolition–apathy is a low level of speaker use of object. The inclusion of emotionally overinvolved parental attitudes as tapped by EE-EOI scores does not aid in predicting these particular negative symptoms in patients.

Passik's dissertation research has helped to further validate the epigenetic narrative scoring system. Additionally, he demonstrated a link between the syndromal characteristics of the patient's illness and the parent's empathic understanding of the patient. The results also indicate the degree to which their relationship is rooted in a predominantly regulatory mode (see Wilson et al., 1990). The EARS has great value as a way to apply an epigenetic perspective to schizophrenia to generate and test hypotheses about patients and their families and prescribe treatments tailored to their individual needs.

CONCLUSION

The experiments described in our second generation of EARS research are demonstrations of the type of studies on a variety of clinical factors and psychopathological phenomena that can be conducted using our instrument. Both employ only a few of the EARS dimensions in order to explore particular hypotheses, and they link these dimensions with more established measures. Further, the psychoanalytic hierarchical approach consistently emerges as possessing significant predictive power. In both studies, we learn a great deal not only about the measures but also the clinical phenomenon as well.

In introducing the EARS, we have relied upon a between-groups analysis of the data, to the exclusion of a within-group analysis or even longitudinal repeated measures studies that examine changes in EARS scores over time within individuals. A profile analysis using subjects as their own controls and the EARS dimensions as a repeated measure over time will yield quite different information from using this instrument for between-groups studies. Important individual differences will be amplified rather than washed out as error variance. Future studies are planned that will do exactly this.

We conclude with a brief comment on our method, which we think serves as a complement to clinical description and theoretical elaboration. Promising future directions for our approach to psychoanalytic research are presaged by the work on addicts and parents of schizophrenic patients, which builds a bridge between psychoanalytic theory and other perspectives. This bridging is made possible by the hierarchical conception, which does not assume a "great divide" between data gathered from within and without the clinical situation, and by the empirically defined nature of the modes, which emphasizes the utilization of the classical scientific method for promoting the evolution of psychoanalytic propositions.

NOTES

1. A manual explaining and suggesting scoring and training procedures, providing detailed scoring examples, and supplying response protocols is available from the senior author. Expanded and specific descriptions of the 10-dimension, 5-mode profile is also contained in the EARS manual. Please note that in this chapter we do not describe in detail how we theoretically conceive of the 10 dimensions, nor how we operationalize the manifestations of each dimension scaled at 5 modal levels. This is all explained in depth in the manual.
2. For critiques of research aimed to illuminate psychoanalytic operations using nonpsychoanalytic process and outcome measures, see Wilson, et al.'s (1990) discussion of the "presence–absence" and "recognition" problems, and Strupp, Schacht, and Henry's (1988) discussion of "problem–treatment– outcome (P-T-O) congruence."

3. For an elaborate discussion of the multiple problems of establishing forms of reliability on the TAT with psychometric precision, and of the validity claims possible, see Murstein (1973).
4. It should be noted that even when treated as continuous variables, the EARS modal levels do not clearly possess characteristics of an equal interval scale.
5. This research was carried out by Dr. Daniel S. Keller under the supervision of Dr. Arnold Wilson as part of Dr. Keller's dissertation requirements at the New School for Social Research. See Keller and Wilson (1992) for a complete discussion of the rationale for the hypotheses of the study.
6. The research in this study was carried out by Dr. Steven Passik under the supervision of Dr. Arnold Wilson as part of Dr. Passik's dissertation requirements at the New School for Social Research. See Passik (1990) for detailed discussion of the rationale for the hypotheses of the study.

REFERENCES

Allison, J., Blatt, S., & Zimet, C. (1968). *The interpretation of psychological tests.* New York: Harper and Row.

American Psychiatric Association (1987). *Diagnostic and statistical manual of mental disorders* (3rd ed., rev.). Washington, DC: Author.

Andreason, N. (1984). *The scale for the assessment of positive symptoms.* Iowa City: University of Iowa Press.

Andreason, N. (1985). Positive versus negative schizophrenia: A critical evaluation. *Schizophrenia Bulletin, 11,* 380–389.

Andreason, N., & Olsen, S. (1982). Negative versus positive schizophrenia: Definition and validation. *Archives of General Psychiatry, 39,* 789–794.

Atkinson, J. (1980). Thematic apperceptive measurement of motivation in 1950 and 1980. In G. d'Ydewalle & W. Lens (Eds.), *Cognition, human motivation and learning.* Hillsdale, NJ: Lawrence Erlbaum.

Bartko, J. J., & Carpenter, W. T. (1976). On the methods and theory of reliability. *Journal of Nervous and Mental Disease, 163,* 307–317.

Block, J. (1965). *The challenge of response sets: Unconfounding meaning, acquiesence, and social desireability in the MMPI.* New York: Appleton–Century–Crofts.

Bruner, J. (1964). The course of cognitive growth. *American Psychologist, 19,* 1–15.

Bruner, J. (1986). *Actual minds, possible worlds.* Cambridge, MA: Harvard University Press.

Campbell, D. T., & Fiske, D. W. (1959) Convergent and discriminant validation by the multitrait-multimethod matrix. *Psychological Bulletin, 56*(2), 81–105.

Cannon-Spoor, H., Potkin, S., & Wyatt, R. (1982). Measurement of premorbid adjustment in chronic schizophrenia. *Schizophrenia Bulletin, 8,* 470–484.

Carpenter, W., Heinrichs, D., & Wagman, A. (1988). Deficit and nondeficit forms of schizophrenia: The concept. *American Journal of Psychiatry, 145,* 578–583.

Chafe, W. (1980). *The pear stories: Cognitive, cultural, and linguistic aspects of narrative production.* Norwood, NJ: Ablex.

Ehrenreich, J. (1989). *Psychodynamic aspects of personality and sociocultural identity.* Unpublished doctoral dissertation, New School for Social Research, New York, NY.

Erikson, E. (1959). *Childhood and society.* New York: Norton.

Faude, J. (1991). *Epigenetic variables in major depression and their relationship to narrative themes, pervasiveness of conflicts, symptomatology, and maintenance of gains in short-term psychotherapy.* Unpublished doctoral dissertation, New School for Social Research, New York, NY.

Freedman, N. (1985). The concept of transformation in psychoanalysis. *Psychoanalytic Psychology, 2,* 317–339.

Gedo, J. (1979). *Beyond interpretation: Towards a revised theory for psychoanalysis.* New York: International Universities Press.

Gedo, J. (1981). *Advances in clinical psychoanalysis.* New York: International Universities Press.

Gedo, J. (1984). *Psychoanalysis and its discontents.* New York: Guilford Press.

Gedo, J. (1986). *Conceptual issues in psychoanalysis: Essays in history and method.* Hillsdale, NJ: Analytic Press.

Gedo, J. (1988). *The mind in disorder.* Hillsdale, NJ: Analytic Press.

Gedo, J., & Goldberg, A. (1973). *Models of the mind: A psychoanalytic theory.* Chicago: University of Chicago Press.

Greenspan, S. (1977). Substance abuse: An understanding from psychoanalytic developmental and learning perspectives. In J. D. Blain & D. A. Julius (Eds.), *Psychodynamics of drug dependence* (pp. 73–87). NIDA Research Monograph 12. Rockville, MD: National Institute on Drug Abuse.

Greenspan, S. (1979). *Intelligence and adaptation: An integration of psychoanalytic and Piagetian developmental psychology.* Psychological Issues, Monograph No. 47/48. New York: International Universities Press.

Grotstein, J. (1977). The psychoanalytic concept of schizophrenia: I. The dilemma. *International Journal of Psycho-Analysis, 58,* 403–425.

Grotstein, J. (1989). Self-regulation in schizophrenia. *Psychoanalytic Psychology, 9,* 239–268.

Hollingshead, A. B., & Redlich, F. C. (1958). *Social class and mental illness.* New York: Wiley.

Holt, R. (1978). *Methods in clinical psychology.* New York: Plenum Press.

Keller, D., & Wilson, A. (1992). *Affectivity in cocaine and opiate abusers.* Unpublished manuscript.

Kernberg, O. (1975). *Borderline conditions and pathological narcissism.* New York: Aronson.

Khantzian, E. (1978). The ego, the self, and opiate addiction: Theoretical and treatment considerations. *International Review of Psycho-Analysis, 5:* 189–198.

Kitchener, R. (1978). Epigenesis: The role of biological models in developmental psychology. *Human Development, 21,* 141–160.

Klein, G. (1976). *Psychoanalytic theory: An exploration of essentials.* New York: International Universities Press.

Kraemer, H. C. (1981). Coping strategies in psychiatric clinical research. *Journal of Consulting and Clinical Psychology, 49,* 309–319.

Krystal, H. (1975). Affect tolerance. *The Annual of Psychoanalysis, 3,* 179–219.

Krystal, H. (1987) *Integration and self-healing: Affect, trauma, and alexithymia.* Hillsdale, NJ: Analytic Press.

Krystal, H., & Raskin, H. A. (1970). *Drug dependence: Aspects of ego function.* Detroit: Wayne State University Press.

Malatesta, C., & Wilson, A. (1988). Emotion/cognition interaction in personality development: A discrete emotions, functionalist approach. *British Journal of Social Psychology, 27,* 91–112.

Mandler, M., & Johnson, N. (1977). Remembrance of things parsed: Story structure and recall. *Cognitive Psychology, 9,* 111–151.

Miklowitz, D., Goldstein, M., Falloon, I., & Doane, J. (1984). Interactional correlates of expressed emotion in the families of schizophrenics. *British Journal of Psychiatry, 144,* 482– 487.

Miklowitz, D., Strachen, A., Goldstein, M., Doane, J., Snyder, K., Hogarty, G., & Falloon, I. (1986). Expressed emotion and communicational deviance in the families of schizophrenics. *Journal of Abnormal Psychology, 95,* 60–66.

Milkman, H. A., & Frosch, W. (1973). On the preferential abuse of heroin and amphetamines. *Journal of Nervous and Mental Disease, 156*(4), 242–248.

Murstein, B. (1973). *Theory and research in projective techniques, emphasizing the TAT.* New York: Wiley.

Parducci, A. (1974). Contextual effects: A range frequency analysis. In E. C. Carterette & M. A. Friedman (Eds.), *Handbook of perception* (Vol. 2, pp. 130–131). New York: Academic Press.

Passik, S. (1990). *An investigation of parents' of schizophrenics expressed emotion, empathy, and affectivity and their childrens' premorbid adjustment and symptatology: An epigenetic and psychoanalytic perspective on object relations in schizophrenia.* Unpublished doctoral dissertation, New School for Social Research, New York.

Peterfreund, E. (1978). Some critical comments on psychoanalytic conceptions of fantasy. *International Journal of Psycho-Analysis, 59,* 427–442.

Pine, F. (1981). In the beginning: Contributions to a psychoanalytic developmental psychology. *International Review of Psycho-Analysis, 8,* 15–33.

Rapaport, D., & Gill, M. (1959). The points of view and assumptions of metapsychology. *International Journal of Psycho-Analysis, 40,* 153–162.

Rapaport, D., Gill, M., & Schafer, R. (1968). *Diagnostic psychological testing.* New York: International Universities Press.

Ricoeur, P. (1977). The question of proof in Freud's psychoanalytic writings. *Journal of the American Psychoanalytic Association, 25,* 835–872.

Sander, L. (1964). Adaptive relationships in early mother–child interactions. *Journal of the American Academy of Child Psychiatry, 3,* 131–164.

Sander, L. (1980). New knowledge about the infant from current research:

Implications for psychoanalysis. *Journal of the American Psychoanalytic Association, 28,* 181–198.

Schachtel, E. (1945). Subjective definitions of the Rorschach test situation and their effect on test performance. *Psychiatry, 8,* 419–448.

Schafer, R. (1954). *Psychoanalytic interpretation in Rorschach testing.* New York: Grune and Stratton.

Schafer, R. (1967). How was this story told? In *Projective testing and psychoanalysis* (pp. 114–169). New York: International Universities Press.

Schafer, R. (1983). *The analytic attitude.* New York: Basic Books.

Spence, D. (1982). *Narrative and historical truth.* New York: Norton.

Spence, D. (1987). *The Freudian metaphor.* New York: Norton.

Stern, D. (1985). *The interpersonal world of the infant: A view from psychoanalysis and developmental psychology.* New York: Basic Books.

Strupp, H., Schacht, T., & Henry, W. (1988). Problem–treatment–outcome congruence: A principle whose time has come. In H. Dahl, H. Kachele, & H. Thomae (Eds.), *Psychoanalytic process research strategies* (pp. 1–14). New York: Springer-Verlag.

Taylor, G. (1987). *Psychosomatic medicine and contemporary psychoanalysis.* Madison, CT: International Universities Press.

Taylor, G., Ryan D., & Bagby, R. M. (1985). Toward the development of a new self-report alexithymia scale. *Psychotherapy and Psychosomatics, 44,* 191–199.

Treece, C. (1984). Assessment of ego functioning in studies of narcotic addiction. In L. Bellak & L. A. Goldsmith (Eds.), *The broad scope of ego function assessment* (pp. 47–69). New York: Wiley.

Valone, K., Norton, J., Goldstein, M., & Doane, J. (1983). Parental expressed emotion and affective style in an adolescent sample at risk for schizophrenia spectrum disorders. *Journal of Abnormal Psychology, 92,* 399–407.

Vaughn, C., & Leff, J. (1976). The influence of family and social factors on the course of psychiatric illness. *British Journal of Psychiatry, 129,* 125–137.

Vygotsky, L. (1956). *Selected psychological investigations.* Moscow: Izdatel'stvo Akademii Pedagogicheskikh Nauk.

Werner, H. (1948). *The comparative psychology of human development.* New York: International Universities Press.

Werner, H., & Kaplan, B. (1963). *Symbol formation: An organismic-developmental approach to language and expression of thought.* New York: Wiley.

Wertsch, J. (1991). *Voices of the mind.* Cambridge, MA: Harvard University Press.

Wieder, H., & Kaplan, E. H. (1969). Drug use in adolescents: psychodynamic meaning and pharmacogenic effect. *Psychoanalytic Study of the Child, 24,* 399–431.

Wilson, A. (1986). Archaic transference and anaclitic depression: Psychoanalytic perspectives on the treatment of severely disturbed patients. *Psychoanalytic Psychology, 3,* 237–256.

Wilson, A. (1989). Levels of adaptation and narcissistic psychopathology. *Psychiatry, 52,* 218–236.

Wilson, A., & Malatesta, C. (1989). Affect and the compulsion to repeat: Freud's repetition compulsion revisited. *Psychoanalysis and Contemporary Thought, 12,* 243–290.

Wilson, A., Passik, S., & Faude, J. (1990). Self-regulation and its failures. In J. Masling (Ed.), *Empirical studies of psychoanalytic theory* (Vol. 3, pp. 149–211). Hillsdale, NJ: Aronson.

Wilson, A., & Weinstein, L. (1992a). An investigation into some implications for psychoanalysis of the Vygotskian view on the origins of mind. *Journal of the American Psychoanalytic Association, 40* 357–387.

Wilson, A., & Weinstein, L. (1992b). Language and the clinical process. *Journal of the American Psychoanalytic Association, 40,* 725–759.

Winnicott, D. W. (1956). Primary maternal preoccupation. In *Maturational processes and the facilitating environment* (pp. 300–305). New York: Basic Books, 1958.

Wurmser, L. (1974). Psychoanalytic considerations of the etiology of compulsive drug use. *Journal of the American Psychoanalytic Association, 22,* 820–843.

Wurmser, L. (1978). *The hidden dimension.* New York: Aronson.

II

Theoretical/Historical Contributions

4

The Hierarchical Model of Mental Functioning: Sources and Applications

JOHN E. GEDO

A PERSONAL HISTORY

In the 1950s, when I first turned to the serious study of psycho-analysis, the theoretical revolution Freud brought to the discipline through his great conceptual works of the 1920s (S. Freud, 1920, 1923, 1926) had occurred within the professional lifetimes of my teachers. Indeed, less time had elapsed since the promulgation of this "structural theory" (summed up in Freud's "tripartite" model of the mind) than I have spent in our professional domain since those years of apprenticeship. From the vantage point of 1992, it may be difficult to realize that in the years following World War II the structural theory was still encountering some conservative resistance on the part of survivors of a previous generation, brought up in the intoxicating atmosphere of early psychoanalysis and its conceptual simplicities. The most progressive theoretical work on the contemporary scene was that of Hartmann and his collaborators (Hartmann, 1939, 1964; Hartmann, Kris, & Loewenstein, 1964), then regarded as bold revisionists.

In the pluralistic ambience of the 1990s, my generation looks back on the unthinking enthusiasm that characterized our entry into psychoanalysis with a mixture of embarrassment and wry amuse-ment. Therapeutic optimism was at its height—be it in experimenta-tion with brief therapy (Alexander, 1956; Alexander & French, 1946), with the hospital treatment of psychotic patients (Fromm-Reichmann, 1950; Sullivan, 1940, 1956), or with broadening the scope of psychoanalysis proper to groups of patients Freud regarded as unanalyzable (see M. Klein, 1984, for her publications of the 1930s and 1940s). The triumphant incursions of psychoanalysts into American psychiatry encouraged the application of an accepted theoretical system to the challenge of contiguous fields, such as psychosomatic medicine or inpatient treatment, without too much inquiry into the adequacy of that traditional conceptual schema.

Yet the pioneers who conducted these "colonial ventures" (Freud's description of Carl Jung's analogous activities ca. 1912) had a disquieting tendency to break the psychoanalytic consensus by systematizing their findings within theoretical frameworks that could not be reconciled with any of Freud's schemata. Within the quasi-religious atmosphere that then prevailed, such proposals led to numerous schisms and secessions and considerable dissension within organized psychoanalysis. Elsewhere, I have attempted to explore the dynamics of such disputes (Gedo, 1986), using among my illustrative cases the controversies aroused by the work of Sandor Ferenczi in the 1920s and 1930s and that of Melanie Klein in the 1940s and 1950s. It would have been just as cogent to use the example of the American interpersonal school that grew out of the work of Harry Stack Sullivan or the object relations theories put forward by the British "middle group," which tried to remain neutral in the civil war between Freudian traditionalists and Kleinian radicals (see Fairbairn, 1954; Winnicott, 1958).

In Chicago, Franz Alexander led the exciting enterprise of developing alternative models of psychoanalytic therapy, and Roy Grinker established a first-rate psychoanalytic hospital within a comprehensive medical center. At the same time, the Institute for Psychoanalysis gave my cohort of candidates an impeccably traditional education. As a result, I found it impossible to dismiss any of the competing points of view. Although I was baffled about how some of these might be reconciled, I found all of them to be overly reductionistic, including the most sophisticated efforts to conceptualize the gamut of psychoanalytic findings under the aegis of the structural theory (Arlow & Brenner, 1964). I became convinced that lasting controversies within psychoanalysis are caused by seemingly reasonable conclusions, based on unrepresentative population samples, adhered to with excessive rigidity. This view was strengthened by the major scholarly project I undertook in the mid-1960s, a thorough review of Ferenczi's total contribution to psychoanalysis (Gedo, 1967; commissioned by *Psyche* on the occasion of the reissue of Ferenczi's four-volume corpus of writings in German [Ferenczi, 1908–1933]).

Serendipitously, the next significant assignment that came my way was a request from the *Psychoanalytic Quarterly* to assess the *Collected Papers* of David Rapaport (1967) in some detail. I took this responsibility most seriously (see Gedo, 1973; 1986, chap. 5), for I regarded Rapaport to have been the only psychoanalytic author of the postwar era who approached the subject matter of our discipline in an ecumenical spirit. In his monograph of 1960, Rapaport had made "a systematizing attempt" to map out the conceptual terrain of psycho-analysis and the nature of the evidence on which those concepts were based. I believed his effort had been largely successful. In order to make it so, however, Rapaport was forced to keep to a level of abstraction so far removed from clinical observations that it remained extremely difficult to correlate the theories competing for our atten-tion with his general propositions.

At any rate, I decided to approach the project for the *Quarterly* by studying all of Rapaport's psychoanalytic writings in the sequence of their publication—the methodology I had already used for my work on Ferenczi. This effort brought to my attention Rapaport's scholarly compilation of 1951, *The Organization and Pathology of Thought*, where I encountered Rapaport's insistence that developmental psychology must be understood as an epigenetic sequence organized in a hierarchical manner[1] (e.g., pp. 721–722) a concept already employed by Jean Piaget in his work on the development of cognition (summa-rized in Piaget, 1971) and, much earlier, by Hughlings Jackson (1884) in his description of brain functioning. It occurred to me that the various parts of the psychoanalytic elephant described by our quar-reling sages might well be capable of correlation into an internally consistent schema by being arranged in a *developmental* sequence. And the manner in which such a sequence could be arranged hierarchically was suggested to me by the models employed in Erikson's 1959 monograph, *Identity and the Life Cycle*, a work that was lent its conceptual rigor through an introductory essay provided by Rapaport![2]

When I decided to embark on this theoretical exploration, in the late 1960s, I had barely transcended the status of a psychoanalytic beginner, and the task of writing a book of any kind seemed overwhelming to me. Consequently, I shared my idea with a col-league, Arnold Goldberg, whose critical intelligence and epistemo-logical sophistication promised to complement my assets and limita-tions in the service of this project. Goldberg approved of my idea and agreed to coauthor the book. In retrospect, his agreement with my viewpoint must have been provisional, for he has never written about these matters again, and his subsequent writings have espoused and promoted self psychology—a school of thought that I have come to view as antithetical to an ecumenical position in psychoanalysis (see Gedo, 1991, chap. 11). Goldberg and I ended our collaboration shortly after *Models of the Mind* (Gedo & Goldberg, 1973) was published because I disagreed with the views Kohut began to share with us around 1974.

To be sure, while we were writing *Models of the Mind*, self psychology did not yet exist, and my coauthor and I were about equally interested in and influenced by the work of our preeminent teacher, Heinz Kohut. At the time we started research for our book, Kohut had published three major papers (1959, 1966, 1968) that seemed to open the door to the understanding and rational psychoanalytic treatment of various syndromes that I later proposed to name "archaic" (Gedo, 1977a). In my view (see Gedo, 1981a, section II; 1986, chaps. 7 & 8), Kohut's work through 1972—that is, the preliminary papers mentioned, his 1971 book, and his 1972 paper on aggression—offered a provisional and reasonable alternative to the less-than-satisfactory proposals of predecessors such as Ferenczi and M. Klein concerning the problems of the archaic psyche. Consequently, in *Models of the Mind*, we concentrated on Kohut's earlier formulations about these matters to the neglect of various alternatives. Today it may be difficult to believe that in following this option we earned the appreciative concurrence of Anna Freud, who was kind enough to read our earliest drafts.

TOWARD A DEVELOPMENTAL PSYCHOANALYSIS

The conceptual tool used by psychoanalysis to lend order to its propositions concerning the maturation of personality is that of "developmental lines" (see Ferenczi, 1913; A. Freud, 1965; S. Freud, 1905). The most familiar of these sequences is the succession of libidinal phases (see Abraham, 1924): oral, anal, phallic, and so forth. The lines of development are to be understood as listings describing successive conditions that *predominate* within defined spans of time. In other words, the advent of the anal phase must not be conceptualized as a cessation of orality; it only signals a shift of emphasis from one libidinal zone to another. Alerted to the theoretical flexibility afforded by this concept through the then-recent work of Anna Freud (1965), *Normality and Pathology in Childhood*, I determined to attempt to coordinate as many as possible of the lines of development widely regarded as significant in terms of adaptation to form one coherent schema.

Goldberg and I were pleasantly surprised to find that most psychoanalytic authors had postulated five significant phases for whichever lines of development they happened to be outlining. When, on occasion, someone proposed a sequence of more than five phases (as Abraham tried to do for libidinal development in 1924), common usage tended to elide some of them. There seemed to be consensus that the libidinal phases that matter are those named oral, anal, phallic, oedipal, and postoedipal. (I here use this most familiar of examples, although Goldberg and I decided not to include this line of development in our schema because we felt that libidinal interests are so ubiquitous and changeable that they cannot be used for diagnostic purposes.) At any rate, it was the nature of much of the preexisting literature that dictated our choice of a five-phase schema. Although we stressed that one could only make an arbitrary decision in this regard, we also found this number of variables to be most convenient in terms of an appropriate balance between differentiating cogent phasic units and avoiding unmanageable complexity.

In *Models of the Mind*, the developmental lines chosen for the effort of correlation were those of the most prominent (or "typical") situations of danger, of the predominant (or "typical") mechanisms of defense used to deal with dangers, of the expectable nature of the prevailing object relationships, of reality testing, and of the state of "narcissism." We leaned on the correlation previously noted by Modell (1968) between the secure achievement of reality testing and viewing objects as whole and differentiated from the self. It also became apparent that, for phases that follow the attainment of these maturational steps, these developmental lines had been poorly elaborated, so that so-called object relations theories would prove to be no more serviceable as a basic framework for psychoanalytic psychology than was the libido theory. To put this another way, drive theories and object relations theories, which had never been properly recon- ciled, seemed to be most applicable to different phases of the developmental sequence and their subsequent psychological derivatives.

Despite the foregoing exception to a neat five-phase sequence for all these lines of development, we found that existent theories postulated essentially contemporaneous transitions from each earlier phase within the lines to a later one. We decided to call these transitional eras "nodal points." In other words, we found that the developmental hypotheses of psychoanalysis appeared to posit well-defined phases of maturation, organized into characteristic modes of functioning (to which we simply gave numerical designations, I through V). We hypothesized, in turn, that these modes of organi-

zation become available as a hierarchically arranged set of potential-
ities, as each of them is added to the psychological repertory in the
course of development. (The nodal events at these points of transition
are the acquisition of a series of essential psychological structures,
such as the consolidation of a cohesive self-organization or the
formation of a repression barrier.) We believed at the time that this
conceptualization amounted to the introduction of systems theory
into psychoanalytic discourse.

It proved to be relatively easy to make the argument that each of
the five modes of mental functioning we had discerned as implicit
features of existing psychoanalytic hypotheses about development
corresponded to one of the (competing) clinical theories then extant in
the psychoanalytic arena. Mode V is explicated by Freud's topographic theory of 1900; Mode IV is explicated by his structural theory
of 1923; Modes III and II are explicated by theories of object relations
dealing with whole objects and part objects; and Mode I is explicated
by the hypotheses about primitive mentation, also put forward by
Freud (1900) in *The Interpretation of Dreams*.

Freud had drawn graphic "models of the mind" to represent
three theories he had devised: the topographic model, the tripartite
model, and that of the reflex arc. Goldberg and I (1973) made a
somewhat feeble effort to draw models representing the more recent
theories of object relations. Thus, although each mode within the
overall hierarchy of psychic functioning could still be conceptualized
in terms of theories and models previously introduced, we offered a
novel articulation of these conceptual fragments into an integrated
whole. We chose to call this view the "hierarchical model."

As this model is drawn, it forms a layered edifice or grid of the
functional modes; the passage of time is represented by movement
from left to right that adds successive new modes to the repertory,
drawn one on top of the other. Figure 4.1 represents the most recent
version of the model, elaborated in *The Mind in Disorder* (Gedo, 1988).
Thus, the fully differentiated psyche consists of a hierarchy of five
modes; functional regression is represented by downward movement
from more mature to more primitive alternatives—progress by ascent
in the opposite direction. We made provision for the possibility of the
regression-proof maturation of specific functions by permitting them
to be represented as leaving the area of the grid (upward) into an
implied area of "secondary autonomy" (Hartmann, 1939). This possibility is made more explicit in the 1988 version of the model shown
here.

The clinical significance of this hierarchical view of development
was spelled out in both nosological and therapeutic terms. The

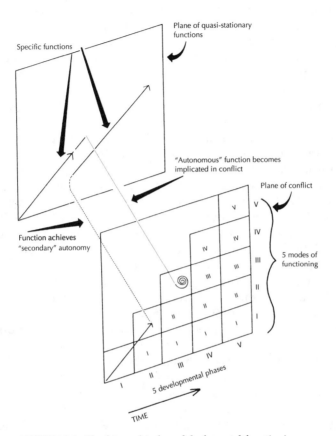

FIGURE 4.1. The hierarchical model of mental functioning

schema treats clinical syndromes not as disease entities but as adaptive responses to particular inner and outer demands. Such a response consists of selecting that mode from the repertory of functional alternatives that promises to attain as many of the person's goals, in conformity with his or her ideals, as is possible. Although everyone is capable of making use of all of the functional modes in the repertory, as dictated by rapidly shifting requirements, predominant use of one or another mode will lend the personality a more or less characteristic flavor that corresponds to one of the major diagnostic categories of psychopathology. In other words, expectable adult functioning implies a predominance of Mode V; if Mode IV is the one selected most of the time, personality functioning is in the "neurotic" realm; if Mode III is predominant, the adaptation will have the characteristics of "narcissistic" disturbances; the prevalence of Mode II is the hallmark of "psychotic" adjustment, and that of Mode I betokens the advent of an acute traumatic state. If, on the other hand, one or more of the more advanced modes are simply unavailable to an individual, this failure to mature may be conceived as an *arrest* of development.[3]

To avoid confusion with a putative schema of disease entities, it is actually preferable to lay stress on the differing principles of behavior regulation prevalent in each mode. Thus Mode I is ruled by the principle of (avoidance of) unpleasure, Mode II by that of organismic integration, Mode III by the pleasure principle, Mode IV by that of reality; I proposed that Mode V is governed by a principle of creativity. (In 1983, I explored the last mode in my monograph, *Portraits of the Artist: Psychoanalysis of Creativity and Its Vicissitudes*.)

As corollaries of the clusters of maladaptation, there are different therapeutic requirements at each level of regression from optimal adult functioning, wherein introspection is sufficient to achieve most conflict resolution. The modality of treatment appropriate to deal with the unconscious intrapsychic conflicts characteristic of Mode IV is the traditional interpretive technique of psychoanalysis. In states of deeper regression, measures "beyond interpretation" are required—a phrase I selected as the title of my 1979 book, in which I tried to spell out these noninterpretive techniques. In *Models of the Mind*, Goldberg and I contented ourselves with listing these modalities of treatment: Regression to Mode III necessitates dealing with a variety of (narcissistic) illusions by means of nontraumatic (i.e., "optimal") disillusionment; the disorganization characteristic of Mode II must be remedied through measures promoting reintegration, that is, "unification" of the total personality; the disturbances of tension regulation encountered in Mode I require techniques of "pacification." In a psychoanalytic context, these measures are considered to be the "parameters" of technique Eissler (1953) advocated in cases of impaired ego functioning. In nonanalytic therapies, the same measures may constitute the principal tools of relatively brief treatment programs (see Gustafson, 1984, 1986).

CLINICAL EXPERIENCE WITH THE HIERARCHICAL MODEL

For most of the decade from 1969 to 1978, I was deeply immersed in the clinical practice of psychoanalysis, conducted mostly on a schedule of five sessions per week—a clinical laboratory where I attempted to put the propositions put forward in *Models of the Mind* to clinical trial. I was doubly determined to test my ideas because the book, despite uniformly favorable reviews, was largely received as a clever conceptual exercise without practical significance. From my vantage point, by contrast, these conceptual clarifications seemed immensely helpful in pinpointing when and why particular classes of interventions should be resorted to in psychoanalytic work. Although any decrease of an analyst's bewilderment is bound to increase his or her effectiveness and, therefore, cannot serve as evidence for the validity of the hypotheses that produced it, the magnitude of the improvement in my therapeutic results encouraged me to *hope* that I had found an effective conceptual tool. I have reported these promising results on more than one occasion (Gedo, 1979b; 1984, chap. 2; 1991, chap. 10) and have also published extensive case reports illustrating my analytic techniques (Gedo [1979a, chaps. 4, 6, & 8; 1984, chaps. 4 & 5] contains the most detailed presentations of individual cases).

In the course of these clinical experiments, I gradually became convinced that the hierarchical model could be greatly improved through more careful consideration of certain issues within psychoanalytic psychology that Goldberg and I had consciously decided *not* to address in *Models of the Mind*. Specifically, we had avoided the controversy that was gathering steam in the late 1960s about the epistemological status of Freud's metapsychology—a clash of opinions that was to produce a cluster of important theoretical statements during the next decade (see Gill & Holzman, 1976; G. Klein, 1976; Rosenblatt & Thickstun, 1977; Schafer, 1976). We took cognizance of these unresolved issues by constructing our model in such a way that its validity and usefulness would remain unimpaired no matter how the metapsychological controversy was eventually decided: we made no reference to the concept of psychic energy and tried, as much as possible, to take for granted that psychoanalytic psychology is built around a tenable theory of motivation. (The major exception to this policy was our inclusion of the line of development of "narcissism" within the schema. It is true that, unlike Kohut in his works prior to 1973, Goldberg and I did not use this term in its narrower—and technically more correct!—sense of denoting vicissitudes of narcissistic libido; by the same token, however, we had covertly distorted its original meaning.)

When, in the early 1970s, Kohut was persuaded by some of his followers (notably Goldberg and Michael Basch) to abandon his adherence to traditional metapsychology—or, if you will, to give up his effort to assume the mantle of Heinz Hartmann as the savior of the paradigm of psychic energy—much of the controversy about that tradition became confused with the entirely separate issue of the adequacy of the system Kohut (1977, 1984) proposed to substitute for it. To prevent my own work from being wrongly subsumed within this new controversy, I published a series of papers clarifying my position vis-à-vis Kohut's clinical findings and theoretical propositions (Gedo, 1975; 1977a; 1980; see also Gedo, 1986, chaps. 7 & 8; 1989).

The crux of the matter was that, seduced by my conviction that Kohut had accurately pinpointed a number of hitherto neglected transference constellations, I had reached a false consensus with him on his other theoretical propositions as well. To be more precise, when Kohut began to write about a "psychology of the self," I mistakenly assumed that he was adumbrating a theory focused on the organization of the total personality, whereas (as the subsequent history of self psychology has made clear) he actually had in mind an object relations theory dealing only with what he called "self-selfobject relations"—a matter that in the hierarchical model is dealt with in terms of our Mode II. When, in *Models of the Mind*, I insisted on summarizing Kohut's work under the heading of an "emerging psychology of the self," I was predicting not the course of his future work (despite his appropriation of that name for it) but that of my own.

To return to the major theoretical debate of the 1970s, my own convictions were shaped by numerous discussions with one of the leading theoretical revisionists, George Klein. He encouraged me to tackle the project that resulted in *Models of the Mind*, rightly regarding it as a potential demonstration of the *irrelevance* of traditional metapsychology for the clinical theories in everyday use. By the time I got the privilege of reviewing (Gedo, 1977b) Klein's posthumous book (1976) in tandem with the monograph Gill and Holzman (1976) edited in his memory, I greeted these revolutionary works by comparing them to the fall of the Bastille, although I did not endorse their specific programs for a New Regime—in Klein's case largely because it was left unfinished at his death. In the work of other hermeneuticists, I was dissatisfied by total neglect of the preverbal phases of development (i.e., the failure to adopt a hierarchical model) in the adoption of this newly fashionable epistemology. (For a critique of hermeneutics as a psychoanalytic methodology, see Gedo, 1986, chap. 13.)

Unlike Schafer (1976) or, later, Kohut (1984), I remain committed to psychoanalysis as a discipline grounded in biology. Indeed, the hierarchical model embraces an initial phase of postnatal existence wherein behavior regulation is governed entirely by inborn neu-rophysiological mechanisms that operate automatically (i.e., without prior learning through deliberate instruction or the interposition of symbolic systems). As I wrote in the Preface to *Beyond Interpretation*:

> The central concept around which my tentative revision of psycho-analytic psychology is built is that of human personality as a hierarchy of personal aims. The infant's biological needs constitute the earliest of these goals; by the end of the second year of life, these have been supplemented by a variety of subjective wishes; the entire hierarchy, in both conscious and unconscious aspects, will form the person's primary identity, or, as I would prefer to call it, the "self-organization." The formation of the self-organization and its later transformations, especially through the acquisition of systems of values, should be viewed in epigenetic terms as the core of personality development. (1979a, p. xi)

Given these convictions, it became necessary to reconsider the details of the hierarchical model of 1973. As the motto of my renewed effort, I chose Danton's revolutionary slogan, "Toujours de l'audace!"

THE HIERARCHICAL MODEL REVISED

In *Beyond Interpretation*, I began to advocate abandonment of the traditional theories and models of psychoanalysis in favor of the hierarchical schema, now understood as the delineation of the epigenesis of self-organization, that is, of the hierarchical arrange-ments of the sum of personal goals. This change permits us, at the same time, to dispense with the entire set of metaphors Freud borrowed from 19th century physics. Apparatus, forces, and energies can be replaced with concepts that refer to the actual functions performed by the brain as an information-processing—and, therefore, meaning-generating—organ. I credited Lichtenstein (1964, 1965) with being the first to propose a conception of self, which he called a "primary identity," as the organizer of subsequent psychic life. This view is utterly different from that of self as a content of the mind (i.e., merely a representation). My conception of self as a mental structure implies a hierarchy of potentials for action, ipso facto laden with affect and extending beyond the realm of subjective intentionality into a nonexperiential one involving constitutionally given, physiological capacities for satisfying organismic needs.[4] Incidentally, these no-tions support the contention of Rubinstein (1976) that, when psychoanalysis postulates a realm of unconscious mental life, it is focused on matters in part beyond the reach of subjectivity and introspection.

The self-organization is gradually formed in the course of Phases I and II of development. When discrete personal goals have been ordered within a unified hierarchy of motivations, this achievement may be called the attainment of a cohesive self. That is to say that the principal task of Phase II is the achievement of motivational integration, and the "typical" problem encountered whenever there is regression into Mode II is the disruption of self-cohesion. Cohesiveness means the relatively stable structuring of goals and values into potentials for action, a process we might also call "self-definition." Following this achievement (in Mode III), it becomes possible to view behavior as regulated by the pleasure principle—that is, in terms of seeking satisfactions on the basis of purposeful choices. When Freud (1920) postulated a realm of behavior "beyond the pleasure principle," he was referring to the derivatives of what I call Modes I and II, which manifest themselves in adulthood as an overriding, unverbalizable need to restore self-cohesion, at whatever cost. Hence Freud was fully justified in attributing these behaviors to a "repetition compulsion."

The second major revision of the hierarchical model I offered in 1979 concerned Phase I in development and consisted in an effort to substitute more plausible hypotheses for Freud's untenable suggestion that the essential challenge of mentation in the infant is the discharge of quanta of psychic energy. In this regard, I borrowed from the prior work of Basch (1975a, 1975b, 1975c, 1976a, 1976b, 1976c), who postulated that the principal issue of this phase is the ordering of experience (i.e., novel stimuli). Through the continuous monitoring of environmental signals, stable representations of patterned transactions with the milieu are formed. This process is facilitated by a system of communication with the caregivers through preprogrammed patterns of expressive signals that accompany affective reactions.

In these terms, the traditional notion that the newborn's behavior is regulated in accordance with the need to avoid unpleasure should be understood as the need to forestall progressive disorganization (trauma). Thus, the characteristics of Mode I can best be described in terms of a model we might call "sensorimotor," because it portrays behavior that does not involve the operation of the cerebral cortex.

The last revision in the model necessitated by repudiation of the concept of psychic energy concerned the line of development of "narcissism," which is rendered hollow by such a deformation of drive theory. In its place, I suggested considering (in parallel with the development of object relations) the evolution of attitudes about one's own person—from the earliest phases in which there is no self-awareness, through various illusory wish-fulfilling views of oneself, to the attainment of realistic self-esteem.[5] Clearly, the maturation of these functions depends on the development of more precise perception and cognition; consequently, I also suggested that the developmental line of reality testing might preferably be broadened to encompass perceptual and cognitive functions in their entirety. However, it is only in the most recent past that I have begun to reconsider this issue in greater detail, particularly as a consequence of Levin's (1991) work. (For a representation of the foregoing revision of the hierarchical model, see Gedo [1979a, p. 195].)

I concluded the theoretical section of *Beyond Interpretation* with a chapter on the disarray of psychoanalytic metapsychology. I tried to show that since the general rejection of Freud's hypothesis of a "death instinct," no alternative had been offered that would have brought the phenomena of the repetition compulsion into the realm of explanation provided by drive theory. Because my latest proposals for a hierarchical model eschewed dealing in satisfactory detail with the problem of motivation, the theoretical system I outlined was still incomplete, and it remained to be seen whether it would eventually gain true coherence through appropriate linkage with consistent, biologically valid propositions about the functioning of the brain.

Shortly after its publication, *Beyond Interpretation* was the subject of a 1981 symposium in the journal *Psychoanalytic Inquiry* (vol. 1, no. 2). A distinguished roster of commentators responded, for the most part, to the theory of psychoanalytic technique contained in the book—a bias I had promoted by my choice of a title that focused attention on that issue. Only Gill (1981) had the discernment—while reserving overall judgment on the theories proposed—to pinpoint the seeming inadequacy of the hypothesis I had offered to link the biological sources of motivation with subjective intentionality. He called the concept of repetition compulsion (on which my explanation was based) a "slender reed" for the purpose of providing such a connection.[6]

In my attempt to answer the objections of my critics (Gedo, 1981b), I responded to Gill's challenge as follows:

I continue to adhere to the conclusion Freud reached in 1920: that our clinical work fails to unearth subjective wishes to account for a variety of maladaptive behaviors. I have added the hypothesis that the realm of subjectivity also fails to account for other behaviors, both useful and pleasurable, which are compulsively repetitive.

Such phenomena have tended not to elicit psychoanalytic scrutiny because they are not pathological. Gill is correct in discerning that this idea is the biological bedrock of my overall proposal. (pp. 300–301)

Further, I asserted that my hypotheses lay within the boundaries of natural science because I conceived of the self-organization "as the sum of those psychobiological patterns that become obligatory components of the compulsion to repeat" (p. 309). One prominent class of patterns of this kind is the need actively to repeat archaic affective states. Another way to put these points is that a theory of self-organization consists of an inclusive hierarchy of personal aims. Hence the task of the hierarchical model is to portray "the manner in which the regulation of behavior at prepsychological (i.e., presymbolic), psychological (symbolic), and transitional levels [may] be conceptualized in one inclusive and consistent theory" (p. 312).

The concept of repetition compulsion "explains that early biological experiences which, from our usual psychological perspective, are passively endured, affect later action through automatic repetition in the active mode." Hence, the unconscious is ultimately unknowable because whatever we need to repeat has no mental (i.e., symbolic) representation (pp. 314–315). I concluded by noting that we need to understand better how "stable patterns of stimulation and affective response [are maintained] through active mechanisms seeking to restore previous equilibria" (p. 315)—a question to which answers have to be provided by future research into the functions of the brain.

It may be relevant to repeat at this point that the pertinent neurophysiological data were recently summarized by June Hadley (1989). In her view, these findings are generally congruent with the contentions of Joseph Lichtenberg (1989) (see also Chapter 7, this volume), who postulates five distinct preprogrammed biological patterns of motivation. Lichtenberg calls these motivational systems attachment, sensuality/sexuality, aversion, active exploration, and the maintenance of physiological equilibria. It remains to be seen whether this list is complete and definitive.

As I see this issue, such blueprints for action operate in pure culture only during Phase I (i.e., in Mode I). Depending on the affective coloring they acquire at that time, the individual will seek to repeat a hierarchy of *experiential* patterns. This is why the various preprogrammed motivational alternatives play such different roles in the psychic lives of different individuals. At the same time, action in subsequent modes continues to be classifiable only according to a schema of biologically programmed motivations—one cannot live life divorced from a body. But these basic blueprints are assimilated through the mediation of affectivity into a need to repeat a set of concrete experiential states. As G. Klein (1976, pp. 114–115) put this, the memories of previous sensual experiences are organized into cognitive schemata. (For a more detailed examination of these principles and their applicability to a view of sexuality within the hierarchical schema, see Gedo [1979a, pp. 183–184].)

FURTHER CLINICAL APPLICATIONS

Through the 1980s, I tried to document the clinical usefulness of the hierarchical model in a series of reports focused on specific topics. Perhaps the most significant of these was an effort to apply this conceptual tool to the problem of "choice of symptom" (Gedo, 1981a, chap. 12). By means of a case illustration, I suggested that, as a result of developmental progress, addictive behaviors may spontaneously turn into fetishistic perversion (and in stressful circumstances this evolution may be reversed). I tried to highlight that the choice between these alternative symptom clusters was determined by the specific mode of functioning to which the analysand regressed (in the illustrative case, from a tenuous adaptation generally maintained in Mode IV whenever human assistance was steadily available).

Yet the identification of the symptom's adaptive function is not sufficient by itself to explain the *specific* configuration the symptom comes to assume. In order to understand the manner in which this configuration is reached, other developmental issues must be considered—specifically, those of the particular meanings the behavior that becomes a symptom had in the historical context in which it arose. To illustrate, an addiction is generally regarded as extremely archaic from a functional viewpoint; yet, in the case I presented, it began relatively late in the course of development, and it happened to represent a neurotic compromise formation. The archaic mechanisms that were brought into operation were regressive adaptations in the service of compromise formation. When, in this case, maturation rendered the pacifying function of the addictive behavior superfluous, it acquired a variety of symbolic meanings once again referable to the historical context of this altered situation—mostly meanings that could buttress self-esteem through fantasies of perfection in the phallic sphere and, at the same time, avoid guilt-provoking clashes with essential objects. These intersecting influences leading to particular symptomatic behaviors are best understood in terms of the availability of the full range of functional modes (Modes I to V) in the phase of development when the symptom arose—and when it changed in function.

Another distinction that is greatly facilitated by the hierarchical model is that between an arrest of development and functional regression from developmentally more advanced positions—a matter also taken up in *Advances in Clinical Psychoanalysis* (Gedo, 1981a, chap. 13). As for the etiology of arrestation, I suggested (on the basis of clinical material) that development could not proceed whenever a child confronts the challenges of the present with psychological dispositions that reflect unsuccessful solutions from those of previous developmental phases. In particular, the demands of the oedipal period (Phase IV) are usually insurmountable if the child, upon entry into this new arena, is still struggling with unfinished problems from his or her past—in other words, if his or her current behavior is for the most part organized in the more archaic modes (see also Gedo, 1981a, chap. 14). Another way to put this is that "most of the ego defenses which serve to ward off oedipal strivings consist of behaviors that constitute, at the same time, adaptive solutions to the psychological vicissitudes of still earlier phases of development" (Gedo, 1984, p. 6).

A few years later, I attempted to reassess the place of the hierarchical view of mental life within the evolution of psychoanalytic ideas (Gedo, 1984, chap. 1) by putting forward the claim that it constitutes an insistence on the import of the structural (i.e., biological) viewpoint, in contrast to the emphasis on mental contents that had characterized psychoanalysis for several decades. In particular, the

> hierarchical model stresses the fact that psychological maturation involves the acquisition of competence with respect to a progressively expanding list of specific mental and behavioral skills. . . . Competence in the domain of certain crucial mental capacities enables an individual to confront the challenges of subsequent developmental phases. If . . . an individual is deficient with respect to certain requisite skills, this deficiency . . . may have to be patched over through external assistance. The need to find symbiotic partners who can render such aid leads to the manifold behavioral potentialities . . . labeled "archaic transferences" in the analytic setting. (Gedo, 1984, p. 8)[7]

At this time, I catalogued the adaptive solutions available in the various modes of structuralization as follows:

> [In] mode I [there is only] resort to the biological resources of the organism; from a strictly "psychological" viewpoint . . . experience

in this mode is endured passively. The child has acquired the capacities [of] mode II when, as a matter of routine, he or she can actively recreate a subset of subjective experiences. Similarly, mode III is attained when the child's characteristic response has changed from the automatic repetition of specific experiences to a holistic program of action. . . . Mode IV, in turn, signifies that the individual need no longer process typical experiences through concrete enactments; instead [they] can [be] mediate[d] . . . through the channel of fantasies. . . . Finally, in mode V, people characteristically make use of their nuclear fantasies in a creative manner as blueprints for constructive activities. (Gedo, 1984, p. 15)

It should be noted that the transitions between modes are attributed to new cognitive achievements that had not at this point been incorporated into the model's 1979 version.

It was Lichtenberg (1983) who first published specific examples of various regulatory or cognitive deficits that proved to be severe enough to interfere with expectable structuralization of the self. In a commentary on his work, I noted once again that a child impaired in this manner must inevitably rely on external assistance to adapt to the escalating demands of life (Gedo, 1986, chap. 12). Hence, a persisting need for symbiosis is the general end result of such a condition. A symbiotic adaptation is often accompanied by illusions of grandiosity to compensate for the attendant humiliations. My essential agreement with Lichtenberg's clinical observations, therefore, also compelled me to reconsider the developmental line of the cognitive functions in the hierarchical model, which were not sufficiently elaborated to deal with the kind of data he chose to highlight. As an example of the kind of concepts needed to illuminate this domain, one might cite the manner in which certain bodily processes of toddlers in the sensorimotor phase might be linked to the emergent capacities to symbolize—usually in terms of verbal codes—or fail to gain this potential for cortical regulation. There are, of course, many other types of cognitive deficit to be considered. (For a clinical example of one of these, see Gedo [1986, pp. 182–184].) Robbins (1987) soon joined in calling for careful attention to this aspect of development.[8]

THE CURRENT POSITION

Over the years, I gradually realized that one obstacle to ease of utilization of the hierarchical model is that it portrays only expectable developments, whereas clinicians must continually deal with maladaptive derailments of those same processes. To mitigate this problem, I decided to outline a psychoanalytic nosology based entirely on the hierarchical view of mental life—a project that culminated in *The Mind in Disorder* (Gedo, 1988). In order to accommodate the complexities of perceptual/cognitive development in the schema, I proposed a conception of processes taking place on parallel planes, one devoted to the sphere of conflicts, the other to the "quasi-stationary functions" (Rapaport, 1951) that usually develop in a conflict free manner. Whenever a specific function changes from one of these conditions to the other, this alteration can be noted by means of arrows between the two planes. (For a diagram of these relationships, see Figure 4.1.) Functions that fail to mature give rise to deficiencies in skills that I termed "apraxias." (In a discussion of this idea, Robbins [1988] made the fine suggestion that, in contrast, the patterning of maladaptive behaviors might be called "dyspraxias." These are manifestations of the need to repeat established properties of the personality.)[9] Until the 1988 modification, the hierarchical model was equipped to show only three specific types of apraxia: problems in tension regulation ("typical" for Mode I), difficulties in organizing a coherent program of action ("typical" for Mode II), and the inability to renounce illusions (referable to Mode III). The latest version of the model has the scope to accommodate an infinite variety of these deficiencies: disorders of thought, communication, learning, planning, affectivity, encoding of bodily signals, and so on (see Gedo, 1988, chaps. 13 & 14).

The developmental theory I espouse involves a combination of cognitive maturation and learning as a result of appropriate nurture. Thus, psychological deficits (apraxias) are merely consequences of the failure to learn. Other maladaptive behaviors consist in the automatized repetition of behavioral patterns learned earlier in life, patterns that have proved to be inappropriate in novel circumstances and are therefore dyspraxic. Progression and regression around nodal points that delimit significant phases are implicit in the very concept of development; the epigenetic model universally accepted within psychoanalysis involves, in addition, the idea of a gradually expanding repertory of modes of organization, all of which remain forever available whenever they might once again prove to be advantageous. This aspect of the conceptual schema makes use of general biological principles, without adding any specifically psychoanalytic propositions. Psychological constructs have to be invoked only for that particular portion of the theory that deals with the processing of symbolic thought.

The foregoing consideration brings us back to the realms of

neuroscience. As I noted elsewhere (Gedo, 1991, chap. 1), it is the development of neural structures that leads to behavioral regulation by means of symbolization, and it is the acquisition of language that seems to lead to a new mode of neural organization. Hence the most pressing question about the hierarchical model concerns the manner in which it should incorporate the role of language acquisition in personality development. This is the most promising avenue of inquiry into the ways in which biology and the world of the psyche overlap, a decisive expansion of the "slender reed" of connecting them exclusively by way of affectivity. As Levin (1991; Chapter 5, this volume) has suggested, the developmental line of human communicative skills fits well into the five-phase sequence of the hierarchical schema. We might postulate that the typical communicative channels added to the individual's repertory are: gestural in Mode I, sonic in Mode II, verbal in Mode III, syntactical in Mode IV, and (perhaps) capable of constructing narratives in Mode V. It would, however, be premature to arrive at any closure on this score.

NOTES

1. For a more detailed discussion of Rapaport's contributions to hierarchical conceptualization in psychoanalysis, see Gedo (1986, chap. 5).
2. Grossman (Chapter 6, this volume) has demonstrated that the concept of hierarchically structured subsets of mental organization was implicit in Freud's theorizing all along. This insight was not consciously available to me until I read Grossman's essay.
3. From the vantage point of an alternative nosological system, one might call Mode II functioning "borderline" and that of Mode I "psychotic." In 1973, however, Goldberg and I adhered to the nosology proposed by Kohut (1971), wherein there was no room for a "borderline" category, that is, the propensity to lapse into disorganized states was seen as evidence for a covert psychosis. In terms of such a schema, only the episodes of acute disorganization in the course of psychoses amount to regression to Mode I. The syndromes most often called "borderline" are those in which functioning oscillates between Modes II and III.
4. I first presented the concept of self as structure in May 1975 at the Panel on "New Horizons in Metapsychology" of the American Psychoanalytic Association (Panel, 1976).
5. This line of development corresponds to the concept of self used by a number of authors (e.g., Lichtenberg, 1983; Stern, 1985)—one focused on the subjective experience of one's own person.
6. It is the repetition of the patterns of affectivity established in early life that links the realms of neurophysiology and subjectivity.

7. To illustrate the utility of the hierarchical model in delineating varied states of structuralizatiɔn, I made use at this time of the illustrative case of differing phenomenology of a "masochistic" and "depressive" nature as correlated with functioning in the various modes, I through V (see Gedo, 1984, p. 14).

8. Previously, Robbins (1983) had endorsed the hierarchical conception of ordering psychoanalytic data. Because much of his clinical experience was with personalities arrested in (or regressed to) primitive modes, including some schizophrenics, Robbins feels that the more archaic end of the developmental scale needs to be refined into a greater number of subsidiary categories. Grand, Freedman, Feiner, and Kiersky (1988) have proposed a modification along these lines. Chapter 2, this volume, provides and elaboration of their views.

9. For a thorough discussion of the role of such repetitions in development, see also Malatesta and Wilson (1988).

REFERENCES

Abraham, K. (1924). A short study of the development of the libido viewed in the light of mental disorders. In *Selected papers on psycho-analysis* (pp. 418–449). London: Hogarth Press, 1942.

Alexander, F. (1956). *Psychoanalysis and psychotherapy*. New York: Norton.

Alexander, F., & French, T. (1946). *Psychoanalytic therapy*. New York: Ronald Press.

Arlow, J., & Brenner, C. (1964). *Psychoanalytic concepts and the structural theory*. New York: International Universities Press.

Basch, M. (1975a). Perception, consciousness, and Freud's "Project." *The Annual of Psychoanalysis, 3,* 3–19.

Basch, M. (1975b). *Psychic determinism and freedom of will*. Paper presented to the Chicago Institute for Psychoanalysis, Chicago.

Basch, M. (1975c). Toward a theory that encompasses depression: A revision of existing causal hypotheses in psychoanalysis. In E. Anthony & T. Benedek (Eds.), *Depression and human existence* (pp. 483–534). Boston: Little Brown.

Basch, M. (1976a). The concept of affect: A re-examination. *Journal of the American Psychoanalytic Association, 24,* 759–777.

Basch, M. (1976b). Psychoanalysis and communication science. *The Annual of Psychoanalysis, 4,* 385–422.

Basch, M. (1976c). Theory formation in chapter VII: A critique. *Journal of the American Psychoanalytic Association, 24,* 61–100.

Eissler, K. (1953). The effect of the structure of the ego on psychoanalytic technique. *Journal of the American Psychoanalytic Association, 1,* 104–143.

Erikson, E. (1959). *Identity and the life cycle*. Psychological Issues, Monograph 1. New York: International Universities Press.

Fairbairn, W. (1954). *An object relations theory of personality*. New York: Basic Books.

Ferenczi, S. (1913). Stages in the development of the sense of reality. In *Selected papers of Sandor Ferenczi* (Vol. 1, pp. 213–239). New York: Basic Books, 1950–1955.

Ferenczi, S. (1908–1933). *Bausteine zur Psychoanalyse.* Vols. 1 & 2. Leipzig: Internationaler Psychoanalytischer Verlag, 1927; Vols. 3 & 4. Bern: Hans Huber, 1939.

Freud, A. (1965). *Normality and pathology in childhood.* New York: International Universities Press.

Freud, S. (1900). The interpretation of dreams. *Standard Edition* (Vols. 4 & 5). London: Hogarth, 1953.

Freud, S. (1905). Three essays on the theory of sexuality. *Standard Edition* (Vol. 7,pp. 130–243). London: Hogarth, 1953.

Freud, S. (1920). Beyond the pleasure principle. *Standard Edition* (Vol. 18, pp. 7–64). London: Hogarth, 1955.

Freud, S. (1923). The ego and the id. *Standard Edition* (Vol. 19, pp. 12–59). London: Hogarth, 1961.

Freud, S. (1926). Inhibitions, symptoms, and anxiety. *Standard Edition* (Vol. 20, pp. 87–172). London: Hogarth, 1959.

Fromm-Reichmann, F. (1950). *Principles of intensive psychotherapy.* Chicago: University of Chicago Press.

Gedo, J. (1967). Noch einmal der gelehrte Säugling. *Psyche, 22,* 301–309.

Gedo, J. (1973). Kant's way: The psychoanalytic contribution of David Rapaport. *Psychoanalytic Quarterly, 42,* 409–434.

Gedo, J. (1975). Forms of idealization in the analytic transference. *Journal of the American Psychoanalytic Association, 23,* 485–505.

Gedo, J. (1977a). Notes on the psychoanalytic management of archaic transferences. *Journal of the American Psychoanalytic Association, 25,* 787–803.

Gedo, J. (1977b). Review of George S. Klein's *Psychoanalytic theory: An exploration of essentials* and Merton M. Gill and Philip S. Holzman's *Psychology versus metapsychology: Psychoanalytic essays in memory of George S. Klein. Psychoanalytic Quarterly, 46,* 319–325.

Gedo, J. (1979a). *Beyond interpretation.* New York: International Universities Press.

Gedo, J. (1979b). A psychoanalyst reports at mid career. *American Journal of Psychiatry, 136,* 646–649.

Gedo, J. (1980). Reflections on some current controversies in psychoanalysis. *Journal of the American Psychoanalytic Association, 28,* 363–383.

Gedo, J. (1981a). *Advances in clinical psychoanalysis.* New York: International Universities Press.

Gedo, J. (1981b). Measure for measure: A response. *Psychoanalytic Inquiry, 1,* 289–316.

Gedo, J. (1983). *Portraits of the artist.* Hillsdale, NJ: Analytic Press, 1989.

Gedo, J. (1984). *Psychoanalysis and its discontents.* New York: Guilford Press.

Gedo, J. (1986). *Conceptual issues in psychoanalysis.* Hillsdale, NJ: Analytic Press.

Gedo, J. (1988). *The mind in disorder.* Hillsdale, NJ: Analytic Press.

Gedo, J. (1989). Self psychology: A post Kohutian view. In D. Detrick & S. Detrick (Eds.), *Self psychology—comparisons and contrasts* (pp. 415–428). Hillsdale, NJ: Analytic Press.

Gedo, J. (1991). *The biology of clinical encounters.* Hillsdale, NJ: Analytic Press.

Gedo, J., & Goldberg, A. (1973). *Models of the mind.* Chicago: University of Chicago Press.

Gill, M. (1981). The boundaries of psychoanalytic data and technique: A critique of Gedo's *Beyond interpretation. Psychoanalytic Inquiry, 1,* 205–232.

Gill, M., & Holzman, P. (Eds.) (1976). *Psychology versus metapsychology: Psychoanalytic essays in memory of George S. Klein.* Psychological Issues, Monograph 36. New York: International Universities Press.

Grand, S., Freedman, N., Feiner, K., & Kiersky, S. (1988). Notes on the progressive and regressive shifts in levels of integrative failure. *Psychoanalysis and Contemporary Thought, 11,* 705–740.

Gustafson, J. (1984). An integration of brief dynamic psychotherapy. *American Journal of Psychiatry, 141,* 935–944.

Gustafson, J. (1986). *The complex secret of brief psychotherapy.* New York: Norton.

Hadley, J. (1989). The neurobiology of motivational systems. In J. Lichtenberg, *Psychoanalysis and motivation* (pp. 337–372). Hillsdale, NJ: Analytic Press.

Hartmann, H. (1939). *Ego psychology and the problem of adaptation.* New York: International Universities Press, 1958.

Hartmann, H. (1964). *Essays in ego psychology.* New York: International Universities Press.

Hartmann, H., Kris, E., & Loewenstein, R. (1964). *Papers on psychoanalytic psychology.* Psychological Issues, Monograph 14. New York: International Universities Press.

Jackson, H. (1884). Evolution and dissolution of the nervous system. In J. Taylor (Ed.), *Selected writings of Hughlings Jackson.* New York: Basic Books, 1958.

Klein, G. (1976). *Psychoanalytic theory: An exploration of essentials.* New York: International Universities Press.

Klein, M. (1984). *Writings* (4 Vols.). New York: Free Press.

Kohut, H. (1959). Introspection, empathy, and psychoanalysis: An examination of the relationship between mode of observation and theory. In P. H. Ornstein (Ed.), *The search for the self* (Vol. 1, pp. 205–232). New York: International Universities Press, 1978.

Kohut, H. (1966). Forms and transformations of narcissism. In P. H. Ornstein (Ed.), *The search for the self* (Vol. 1, pp. 427–460). New York: International Universities Press, 1978.

Kohut, H. (1968). The psychoanalytic treatment of narcissistic personality disorders: Outline of a systematic approach. In P. H. Ornstein (Ed.), *The search for the self* (Vol. 1, pp. 477–509). New York: International Universities Press, 1978.

Kohut, H. (1971). *The analysis of the self.* New York: International Universities Press.

Kohut, H. (1972). Thoughts on narcissism and narcissistic rage. In P. H. Ornstein (Ed.), *The search for the self* (Vol. 2, pp. 615–658). New York: International Universities Press, 1978.

Kohut, H. (1977). *The restoration of the self.* New York: International Universities Press.

Kohut, H. (1984). *How does analysis cure?* Chicago: University of Chicago Press.

Levin, F. (1991). *Mapping the mind.* Hillsdale, NJ: Analytic Press.

Lichtenberg, J. (1983). *Psychoanalysis and infant research.* Hillsdale, NJ: Analytic Press.

Lichtenberg, J. (1989). *Psychoanalysis and motivation.* Hillsdale, NJ: Analytic Press.

Lichtenstein, H. (1964). The role of narcissism in the emergence and maintenance of primary identity. *International Journal of Psycho-Analysis, 45,* 49–56.

Lichtenstein, H. (1965). Towards a metapsychological definition of the concept of self. *International Journal of Psycho-Analysis, 46,* 117–128.

Malatesta, C., & Wilson, A. (1988). Emotion/cognition interaction in personality development: A discrete emotions, functionalistic analysis. *British Journal of Social Psychology, 27,* 91–112.

Modell, A. (1968). *Object love and reality.* New York: International Universities Press.

Panel (1976). New horizons in metapsychology (W. Meissner, reporter). *Journal of the American Psychoanalytic Association, 24,* 161–180.

Piaget, J. (1971). *Biology and knowledge.* Chicago: University of Chicago Press.

Rapaport, D. (1951). *The organization and pathology of thought.* New York: Columbia University Press.

Rapaport, D. (1960). *The structure of psychoanalytic theory: A systematizing attempt.* Psychological Issues, Monograph 6. New York: International Universities Press.

Rapaport, D. (1967). *The collected papers of David Rapaport* (M. Gill, Ed.). New York: Basic Books.

Robbins, M. (1983). Toward a new mind model for the primitive personalities. *International Journal of Psycho-Analysis, 64,* 127–148.

Robbins, M. (1987, May). *Broadening the scope of psychoanalysis to include more seriously disturbed individuals.* Paper presented to the American Academy of Psychoanalysis, Chicago, IL.

Robbins, M. (1988, October). *Discussion of John Gedo's The mind in disorder.* Paper presented to the Boston Psychoanalytic Society, Boston.

Rosenblatt, A., & Thickstun, J. (1977). *Modern psychoanalytic concepts in a general psychology.* Psychological Issues, Monograph 42/43. New York: International Universities Press.

Rubinstein, B. (1976). On the possibility of a strictly clinical psychoanalytic theory: An essay in the philosophy of psychoanalysis. In M. Gill & P. Holzman (Eds.), *Psychology versus metapsychology: Psychoanalytic essays in memory of George S. Klein.* Psychological Issues, Monograph 36 (pp. 229–264). New York: International Universities Press.

Schafer, R. (1976). *A new language for psychoanalysis*. New Haven: Yale University Press.

Stern, D. (1985). *The interpersonal world of the infant*. New York: Basic Books.

Sullivan, H. (1940). *Conceptions of modern psychiatry*. Washington: W. A. White Psychiatric Foundation.

Sullivan, H. (1956). *Clinical studies in psychiatry*. New York: Norton.

Winnicott, D. (1958). *Collected papers*. London: Tavistock.

5

The Hierarchical Developmental Model: Neural Control, Natural Language, and the Recurrent Organization of the Brain

FRED LEVIN

In many scholarly works, first with Arnold Goldberg (Gedo & Goldberg, 1973) and then alone (Gedo, 1979, 1981, 1984a, 1986), John Gedo has elaborated a model of psychological development that is both elegant in its simplicity and yet in keeping with the veritable explosion of knowledge within the neurosciences. A mere handful of psychoanalysts (including Reiser, 1985; Schwartz, 1987; and Lichtenberg, 1988) have engaged the difficult task of balancing the insights among different fields rather than deciding in favor of paradigms of a single science. In what follows I describe first what I consider the core of Gedo's hierarchical model and then two fundamental phenomena: neural control and the languages of mind and brain. The reader may then more deeply appreciate how the Gedo model cuts across disciplines by identifying the importance of hierarchies in the brain and mind, and by highlighting the criticality of language, in general, and psychoanalytic interpretations, in particular, in decisively altering man's inner (hierarchical) organization.

It may be helpful to begin by briefly locating Gedo's theorizing within psychoanalysis. One might arbitrarily divide post-Freudian psychoanalysis into four major theoretical camps: drive–defense, self psychological, hermeneutic/philosophical (linguistic), and a systems or interdisciplinary (eclectic) approach. Drive–defense theory focuses primarily on conflict and its resolution and is based on work with neurotic people. This school is most often assumed to be representative of the field of psychoanalysis (at least so far as analysts describe their work in writing). Anna Freud and Heinz Hartmann were the two pioneers most connected with this school, and the evidence is that they saw themselves more as preserving, rather than revitalizing or modifying, Sigmund Freud's original theorizing.

Self psychology can be traced from Freud's (1914) "On Narcissism," through the dissidence of Carl Jung and Alfred Adler, to Freud's later interest in the application of psychoanalysis beyond the realm of adult neurosis: first to children and then to a heterogeneous cluster that has included psychotics, those who today would be called borderline or narcissistic personalities, and such other kinds of characterologically disturbed individuals as addicts and perverts. Self psychology draws on the work of Melanie Klein, Anna Freud, W. R. D. Fairbairn, D. W. Winnicott, and the rest of the British object relations school, as well as on the contributions of such Americans as Harry Stack Sullivan, Otto Will, and Ping Nie Pao.

The hermeneutic (or philosophical) school propounds sensitivity to the meaning of the patient's personal sense of history and communicative style. Freud was interested in language as a deep structure of the brain (e.g., consider his *On Aphasia*), and his lead has been followed by Saussure, Jakobson, Rosen, Derrida, Lacan, Ricouer, Ornston, Mahony, and others.

I have saved the systems (or eclectic) school for last because it is to this branch of psychoanalysis that I assign Gedo. Of course, the division of psychoanalysis just outlined is arbitrary to some significant degree; for example, Gedo is clearly also interested in language. The different schools seem to merely express their personal preferences among the multiple factors that Freud felt contribute to mental life: sexuality, aggression, and conflict; disturbed narcissism; language and personal history; and neuroscience. It is probably fair to say that the formal descriptions of the tenets of the various schools are more likely to differ from each other than the actual practice of such views. Thus, seasoned and talented clinicians will at different times make use of the insights of each of the perspectives, depending on what is appropriate or expedient. How even subtle theoretical differences might affect therapeutic outcome remains to be studied systematically.

Of what does the eclectic, or systems, approach consist? Gedo presents what he considers to be the core of a credible, internally consistent psychoanalytic theory supported by three distinctly different sorts of evidence: clinical psychoanalysis; infant and child observation studies; and contemporary neuroscience. At the core of the neuroscience contribution, as I interpret it, is the work of John Hughlings Jackson of a century ago, demonstrating clinically the fundamental hierarchical organization of the brain.

Dispensing with libido theory, ego psychology, dual-instinct theory, and object relations theory as such, Gedo builds on the following sources:

1. Anna Freud's conceptualization of multiple lines of development (an extension of her father's simpler concept of the developmental sequence of autoerotism to narcissism to object love), which represents a unique organization of psychoanalytic data in the direction of a systems approach and is fundamentally included in Gedo and Goldberg's (1973, p. 7) hierarchical model. Ludwig von Bertalanffy and Roy Grinker, Sr., must also be mentioned for the former's development of his general systems theory and for their joint effort in employing this framework to psychiatry. Credit goes as well to Erik Erikson (1959) for pioneering epigenetic models.

2. Jean Piaget's epistemology of knowledge described by Rapaport as "a hierarchical series of thought organizations [which] arises, in the courses of maturation and development, culminating in reality-adequate thinking" (quoted in Gedo, 1986, p. 65).

3. Melanie Klein's recognition of the role in neurosogenesis of the failure to integrate ego/self nuclei, which is also adumbrated in Gedo's model (see the discussion of Klein in Gedo, 1986, pp. 82–98).

4. Ferenczi's description—which according to Gedo (1986, pp. 40–41) was years ahead of his time—of narcissistically injured or borderline individuals, their fluctuating ego states, and the role in their lives of failures in good enough mothering. (Gedo has noted that subsequent research in self psychology—including most prominently Heinz Kohut's contributions—has moved psychoanalytic theorizing, without derogating oedipal-level pathological mechanisms, toward the kind of integration of interactional and intrapsychic approaches contained in the hierarchical model).

5. The work of Michael Basch, which has been decisive for Gedo, especially for its integration of vast numbers of infant observations and neuroscientific and philosophical knowledge into the corpus of psychoanalysis. (Other contributions, for the interested reader, are reviewed in greater detail in Levin [1989, 1990, 1991])

THE HIERARCHICAL MODEL: ITS CORE

Gedo's (1986) current model, in contrast to the original version, developed with Goldberg (Gedo & Goldberg, 1973), strips the hierarchical model of its formal linkage to the five older models of which it was an amalgam. What remains are multiple, linked nodal points of development in which the organizational axis changes as a function of time. In this hybrid model, one passes through the following stages: a stage of ego nuclei needing unification (i.e., a stage of nuclear or cohesive-self formation delineated as self-definition, or Mode I); the establishment of self-awareness with the ability to formulate wishes and establish priorities among them (self-organization, or Mode II); a stage characterized by the ability to keep in mind differing (potentially competing) wishes and to deal adaptively with such conflicts and their associated affects (what Gedo calls self-regulation, or Mode III); the establishment of the ability to renounce wishes that threaten adaptive equilibrium (Mode IV, which coincides most closely with oedipal-level problems); and the achievement of a significant level of symbolic capacities (Mode V); and so on. (Note here that "and so on" indicates the possibility of adding nodal points to the hierarchy, i.e., the model is an open system.)

What is the essence of such a hierarchical model? Clearly, this will vary with one's theoretical perspective. As for me, the model's essence (aside from the arrangement of elements into a hierarchy that allows for progressive or regressive movements) is its conception of the changing fulcrum or motive around which development is seen to organize at each stage. These motives include the need to avoid overstimulation; the need for self-integration; the need to organize around real object relationships (with the focus on awareness of self and other and attunement concerns); id–ego–superego concerns; and focus on adjustment of one's hierarchy of goals and values. Levey (1984/1985) has cogently described this developmental view and its implications for psychoanalytic metatheory in a paper on the concept of structure in psychoanalysis.

The implicit reason for the changes in underlying motive or structure in such a model of development is that the genetic blueprint for human beings is so written. Within genetics there has been the discovery of the "homebox" (see DeRobertis, Oliver, & Wright 1990), that part of the genetic material that is conserved over a large number or phyla and that is the DNA master control for the general order in which development (gene activation) proceeds. What differs between phyla with respect to this general order of gene activation involves the nature of the structure that develops; for example, in an insect the plan specifies that wings are added to the step following body formation, whereas in humans, limbs are the next addition. Of course, it remains to be learned how environmental experience may alter the expression of such a genetic blueprint. That such sequences are influenced by both biological (i.e., built-in) plans and experience (accidental or intended factors) is a crucial point that will be considered toward the end of this chapter.

THE HIERARCHICAL MODEL
AND NEURAL CONTROL

Research on the brain is proceeding so rapidly that it is becoming extremely difficult to write about the subject with any certainty that what is said today will hold for tomorrow. In this sense, I value the opportunity to elaborate on some aspects of adaptation within the framework of Gedo's model that I have written about elsewhere, since new information is now available that helps us better understand the relationship between adaptation as a psychological construct and adaptive change in a neuroscientific sense (Levin, 1991).

Adaptation and adaptive change are complex subjects. Gedo (1989) has described adaptation as "the attempt to fulfill as many as possible of [a] person's lasting motivations by means of selecting from a repertory of patterned modes of behavior those particular alternatives that have the best chance to attain the desired goals in the context of current circumstances" (p. 5). Yet the question remains: How do we accomplish such a task? More specifically, how can we combine what we intuitively and introspectively know about adaptation with what is known about how the brain works so as to understand the fundamental mechanisms of such a psychological function?

Elsewhere (Levin, 1991, chaps. 2, 3, 5, & 6), I describe ways in which the brain might facilitate adaptive decisions. I focus primarily on two basic mechanisms: (1) an adaptive integration of the two cerebral hemispheres in which a strategy is employed such that (a) interhemispheric communication blocks can at times serve as psychological defenses and (b) the matching of the brain subsystem best suited for the task with the problem at hand involves critical decision making; and (2) the provision by the cerebellum (more exactly, the vestibulocerebellar system) of decisive input to the cortex in carrying out many tasks, allowing adaptation to occur by means of either real or imagined actions (i.e., through what might be called "gedanken experiments" by way of manipulation of a cerebellar-based "self-in-the-world model").[1] Left unanswered in this earlier work, however, was how (i.e., where in the brain) such complex internal decisions are regulated.

Significant progress has, however, occurred. I shall briefly summarize some of the conclusions here, since they bear on our understanding of Gedo's hierarchical model. This discussion is divided into three sections: The first describes some of the evidence related to the connection between neural control and the prefrontal cortex. The second considers evidence relating neural control to the brain's

temporal (serial) organization. The third speculates about the hierarchical organization of the brain's "operating system" and the role of
natural (native) language in modifying the rules of this system.

First, however, I provide a word about the hierarchical model
and neural control. Gedo's model assumes that various mental
functions and the memories of the situations out of which they arise
are organized in hierarchical form. This hierarchical organization is
what allows progressive and regressive swings along the developmental axis of the model (as Jackson [1958] understood such change).
In other words, new developments usually, but not invariably,
become superordinate; they come to represent preferred values,
goals, or methods for achieving goals. I say not invariably because
Gedo has stated that some development occurs outside the usual
order; for instance, creativity requires this kind of "splitting" (see
Gedo, 1989). This aspect of Gedo's model appears to be the least
detailed, though it could turn out to be crucial for the model.[2] There
is an ambiguity regarding the rules governing the shift between
modes within the model. One problem is Gedo's emphasis on
individual control over the arrangement of elements within the
various hierarchies, and control over the time sequence for their
unfolding. But nowhere in Gedo's writings is there an explanation for
the mechanisms of such control. One possible mechanism, discussed
later in this chapter, as well as in Levin (1989, 1990, 1991), is that the
brain's operating-system instructions for the unfolding developmental sequence are capable of being readjusted decisively on the
basis of input from one's natural language. Of course, the possibility
of individual control over the developmental trajectory does not mean
that genetics has now been overruled. It only means that we need to
think of the ways in which the genetic machinery is activated (or
inactivated) by environmental factors.

Some clinical material may clarify what is meant by the concept
of language decisively changing neural organization. Let us first
consider briefly the situation of those who are born deaf. Some deaf
persons grow up to be intellectually and emotionally advanced
adults, fully on a par with the healthiest hearing people. But others
suffer from a critical linguistic–cognitive deficiency that significantly
limits their ability both to conceptualize and to communicate, even
by sign language. The advanced group of deaf persons can abstract,
that is, "shift to categorical, definition-based lexical organization"
(Sacks, 1989, p. 108); the latter or "slow" group are limited to
perceptually based organization and will show what experts in the
field call "low language ability" (i.e., they may become functionally

retarded). Sacks (1989) has cogently described these differences and has offered an explanation. His suggestion is that deaf children who are not exposed early to good language or communication may suffer "a delay (even an arrest) of cerebral maturation, with a continuing predominance of right hemisphere processes and a lag in hemispheric 'shift'" (p. 110). In other words, without exposure to signing or meaningful language input before puberty, these children will not experience the normal shift to left-hemisphere dominance, with its superior syntactical and abstracting abilities (Collins, 1990). Clearly, language acquisition can decisively alter neural organization.

This experience of some deaf persons who have suffered because of a lack of proper and timely language input is a very real and poignant problem, of which I am well aware since I have been a consultant to a psychiatric clinic for the deaf since 1974. For this discussion, however, what appears crucial is that the experience of language deprivation in the deaf population supports the view that the establishment of one's natural (formal) language early in life is a developmental step that can be decisively organizing for the brain.

Although the emphasis here is on the possible releasing role of language exposure, development of advanced or abstract cognitive abilities is more complex by far than mere language input. Shallice (1988) describes a patient (Mr. R), an accountant who had a large orbitofrontal meningioma removed. Six years after surgery his IQ was over 130, and he did well on a variety of other psychological tests. However, his ability "to organize his life was disastrously impaired" (p. 336). He drifted through a series of jobs, fleeing from each; unable to manage his financial affairs or his marriage, he suffered bankruptcy and divorce. He could not be punctual or organized, nor listen to advice. Decision making became extraordinarily difficult, and he would take hours reviewing the details of such trivial issues as the relative merits of various restaurants so that he could decide where to eat. Shallice sees Mr. R as lacking a supervisory organizational function. Without this capability, Mr. R is trapped in a sea of irrelevant details within which he endlessly perseverates. "The primary function of the supervisory system is that of producing a response to novelty that is planned rather than one that is routine or impulsive" (p. 345). Thus, there is evidence that under normal circumstances the frontal cortex provides decisive organization by way of selective attention and selectivity of response. For this reason it will help to return to a review research on the frontal part of the brain, as promised earlier.

NEURAL CONTROL
AND THE PREFRONTAL CORTEX[3]

Several converging lines of evidence suggest that the prefrontal cortex regulates the brain's system for neural control, or what might be called (analogous to computers) the brain's operating system. This subject has been reviewed elsewhere (Benson & Stuss, 1989; Levin, 1989, 1990, 1991) but will be summarized here briefly. One line of evidence deals with the experience of persons who have undergone prefrontal cortical injury. This group suffers from a spectrum of difficulties, which may include concreteness, impaired attention, difficulty abstracting, problems excluding what is irrelevant, diminished spontaneity of speech, perseverative behavior, apathy, indifference, shallowness, and a kind of inappropriate jocularity called *Witzelsucht* (Andreasen, 1989). The prefrontal cortex is also required for the coding and encoding of speech and language (Ingvar, 1987). Experiments with animals confirm that with injury to the prefrontal cortex there is a general difficulty in forming problem-solving strategies, especially using "selective attention"[4] (Kent, 1981, p. 208). Memory per se is not the problem, but rather there is an apparent disturbance in the ability of the animal to act on the memory of an object in the absence of its appearance (Goldman-Rakic, Isserhoff, Schwartz, & Bugbee, 1983; Kent, 1981; Reiser, 1985). Most critical perhaps is poor "recency memory," that is, the memory for the time order of experience (Kolb & Winshaw, 1980). Ingvar (1987) reports the same time sense or seriality as a critical function provided by the frontal cortex, without which the language or speech function deteriorates.

Studies of schizophrenia, which has been associated with several brain abnormalities on scanning, provide a second line of evidence suggesting that the prefrontal cortex regulates the brain's system for neural control. A group of right-handed schizophrenics showed diminution of the left temporal pole of the brain, as seen on computed tomography (CT) scans. (See Levin [1988] and Levin [1991, chap. 10] for a review of this work by T. J. Crow.) A second finding that has proven reliable in schizophrenics is prefrontal hypoactivity, as seen on magnetic resonance imaging (MRI) and in studies of regional cerebral blood flow (rCBF) and of regional cerebral metabolic rate (rCMR) (see Levin [1991] for detailed references to the work of Andreasen, Ingvar, and others). The conclusion to be drawn from these studies is that the cognitive and language disturbances of schizophrenia are most likely the result of diminished prefrontal cortical functioning.

Studies of schizophrenia have also demonstrated alterations in reaction time (RT) and evoked response potential (ERP), the latter finding being reversible by an encouragement paradigm. Such work, in the United States and in Japan, has led to the speculation that the key pathogenic factor in schizophrenia, as indicated by the massive input–output processing (stimulus set–response set) problems, is likely the loss of prefrontal cortical control over the machine language (operating system) of the brain (Niwa, 1989).

A third line of research relates to the work on the cerebellum by Itoh (1988), which I have reported elsewhere (Levin, 1991, chap. 3). Itoh's (1988) research as well as that of Kent (1981), Ingvar (1987), and Decety and Ingvar (1988) suggest that the prefrontal cortical system for neural control is primarily a feedforward system with adaptive mechanisms (see Figure 1 in Levin, 1991, p. 85) in which the crucial element coordinating the exercise of judgment and insight in decision making is the prefrontal cortex. The other elements of the system are the cerebellum and the basal ganglia, and the prefrontal cortex maintains this control by "sculpting out" (activating or recruiting) those other parts of the brain whose arousal is critical to the decision-making process. Note that the prefrontal cortex also hastens decision making by controlling selective attention by means of its influence over the frontal eyefields (i.e., we gaze on what we need to facilitate the decision). Research on the cerebellum is complemented by work in the field of artificial intelligence, which seeks to investigate by still different means the mechanisms of neural control (see Kent, 1981; Levin, 1991).

NEURAL CONTROL AND SERIALITY (TEMPORALITY)

As noted earlier, Ingvar (1987) has reported that the prefrontal cortex is necessary for speech and language encoding and decoding. Although language is usually thought to be mediated by Broca's and Wernicke's areas in the left hemisphere, Ingvar (1987) reports that studies of rCMR and rCBF demonstrate unequivocally that these areas are not activated in all language activity, whereas the prefrontal cortex is! What is of special interest to this discussion, however, is the role of seriality (temporality), since the arrangement of elements into a hierarchy within the brain would appear to require the ability to organize memories according to time or some other similar function. Now, it might be that the brain does not employ a time tag as a basis for distinguishing recent from remote memory, but this seems unlikely. That is, it seems probable that the brain's ability to distinguish memories in a time sequence (recency) is required for the hierarchical organization of virtually anything. Otherwise, recent solutions and old solutions would be indistinguishable from each other and would be randomly employed. Whatever we decide about hierarchies, therefore, should take into account the probability that this function requires an intact prefrontal cortex.

THE BRAIN'S OPERATING SYSTEM AND THE ROLE OF NATURAL LANGUAGE

Mention has been made of the work of Niwa (1989), who suggests that the language of the brain and that of mind (i.e., our natural language) share a common grammar and that the latter influences the former. Put differently, our natural language provides us with an adaptive means of modifying the operating instructions of the brain (i.e., the operating system itself). We have also mentioned Sack's (1989) account of the world of the deaf, where language stimulation and acquisition seem decisive in modifying brain organization. But to appreciate fully the complex role of language, we must also mention the work of Tsunoda (1987), who studied lateralization of sounds using dichotic listening tasks. Tsunoda has shown that Japanese people, unlike Westerners, hear vowel sounds, human affective sounds (laughter, crying, humming), and the sounds of nature (crickets, for example) with the left, not the right, hemisphere. The most interesting of his findings, however, is that Westerners who are fluent in the Japanese language also lateralize these listening activities to the left hemisphere! (Tsunoda has also studied Polynesians and Koreans, but these groups, unlike Japanese speakers, lateralize sound in the same manner that Westerners do.) Tsunoda's research seems to provide us with the first convincing evidence of Niwa's speculation that one's natural language is capable of serving as a vehicle for altering the brain's operating instructions (i.e., altering brain organization for a specific task).

Tsunoda's research is important, suggesting as it does something about the language-based determinants of the brain's hierarchical rules of operation. But it is also vital to keep in mind that his research would be much less interesting if it were not for the findings of Niwa, Ingvar, Kent, Itoh, and their collaborators, who have helped generate important pieces of the brain operating system puzzle. Further, we owe a debt to Gedo and those who inspired his work, because these largely psychoanalytic efforts begin to place the basic research cited here in a meaningful psychological context, namely, that of human adaptation as a hierarchy of self-in-the-world potentials.

At this point it is worth speculating further on the nature of the adaptive process.

SOME ADDITIONAL SPECULATIONS

We cannot be sure how much of what humans are able to accomplish is actually "hard wired" into the brain and how much is the product of learning. Bharucha, studying musical discrimination, has demonstrated that much of what was considered innate musical "grammar" is really the consequence of repeated experience within a specific culture (cited in Heinrichs & Endicott, 1988). This finding should caution those who would make premature theoretical leaps about brain mechanisms. However, there does seem to be enough reliable empirical evidence to conclude that learning itself involves multiple systems and multiple mechanisms. At the system level, there are the corticolimbic, corticostriatal, and corticovestibulocerebellar systems, which complement each other and provide for the processing of the complex, cognitive discriminative kind of "declarative" learning, habit–pattern learning, and self-related episodic memory ("procedural") learning, respectively (see Levin, 1991, chaps. 3 & 10). At the subsystems level, individual neurons are best understood in terms of the chemical cascade involving neurotransmitter(s) including 3',5'-AMP (cyclic AMP), calcium channels, and activation of the operator gene. And although we do not yet understand the basis of long-term memory, there seems to be a consensus that it relates to changes in nucleic acid or related DNA compounds. The changes within each of these hierarchically organized, interconnected levels associated with experience constitute a comprehensive operational definition of learning. That is, learning is a characteristic of large populations of connected neurons, such as the hundred billion or so neurons (and their trillions of synapses) that constitute our brain.

But what more might be said about the relationship between natural language, learning, and the operating system of the brain (neural control)?[5] A question comes to mind. Is it possible that what we call natural language might be a design component within the brain with fractal-like quality?[6] This would mean that the different modules (or levels) of knowledge within the brain[7] are interdigitated with each other by means of a recurring hierarchical arrangement of instructions that might be a shared property of both one's native (natural) language and also of the operating system of the brain. Put differently, if, as with the "homebox," there is a set of operating instructions for each knowledge system of the brain that specifies the "default" settings that obtain under ordinary circumstances, then there must also be a way of altering these settings when circumstances warrant adaptive change. Perhaps language evolved to fulfill this task.

It may be helpful to describe the hierarchical nature of each level of brain organization. At the level of organization usually designated physicochemical, that of the DNA (mostly) in the nucleus of neurons, a clear hierarchical organization is demonstrated by structures like the "homeobox," which determines the order in which the various parts of the DNA blueprint are activated during development. At the next higher level of organization, which is usually called physiological, the brain is clearly arranged hierarchically in the form of multiple feedforward and feedback loops (see Levin, 1991, chaps. 2 & 3; Levin, 1989). And finally, at the highest level of abstraction, that of neural control, at which level phenomena are usually labeled psychological, hierarchical systems in the form of the formal "languages" of the mind (native languages) and of the brain (its so-called machine language) once again serve as fundamental regulatory units. Therefore, hierarchies are one of the key recurrent patterns inscribed into the brain. From the neuroscientific perspective, Shallice (1988) (following Luria) notes that "the triggering of schemata is frequently mediated by language in humans" (p. 333). Conventionally in psychoanalysis, formal language is the level at which interventions are usually made in order to potentially alter the entire interlocking organization of the brain; as reported in the research paradigm of Tsunoda (1987) noted earlier, the language of mind and brain are related to each other. In addition, I have suggested that one's natural language, once assimilated, permanently and decisively alters brain organization. Language may thus not only facilitate the development of the genetic plan for psychological organization but it may also allow for adaptive reorganization as a solution to problems requiring novelty and for the manipulation of modules of knowledge.[8]

I have suggested (Levin, 1991, chap. 1) that metaphors in transference interpretations appear to contain coded elements that appeal to the three primary sensory modalities of touch, vision, and, hearing and that these cortical areas might become activated simultaneously (rather than serially), thus unlocking critical memories and opening the way for insights. Over the past decade I have continued to focus in particular on parts of the central nervous system that are involved with cross-modal synthesis, for I believe intuitively that these sensory integration zones are likely to be the leading part of the brain's system for coding experience in abstract format. As suggested by the studies of Ingvar, Itoh, Niwa, and others noted earlier, it is possible that our natural language also contains recurrent hierarchical elements that can be decoded as instructions to the brain's operating system, the function of which is to rearrange the operating instructions in a manner that is conducive to the processing of particular input (i.e., to change the "default" settings, as noted earlier). In this regard, Tsunoda (1987) seems to have hit upon an important piece of the puzzle related to how the brain might communicate with itself. Apparently, the Japanese language (unlike other languages studied by Tsunoda) has within it a structural/functional unit that the brain interprets as an instruction to rearrange the pattern of hemispheric localization or activation (from right to the left hemisphere) for certain sounds.

It is anyone's guess what the nature of the linguistic code consists of. Two possibilities are suggested by Tsunoda's research. Since many Japanese words have onomatopoeic significance to Japanese listeners (my own impression quite subjective, to be sure), one mechanism behind the unexpected left-side localization phenomenon described by Tsunoda might be a linguistic reliance on the bridging of various sensory experiences, such as I observed nearly a decade ago playing a role in the insights following some psychoanalytic interpretations that had made special use of vivid metaphors. That is, the Japanese language may have become over years of evolution a special vehicle for the processing of certain kinds of (in this case, onomatopoeic) qualities in the auditory realm that have assumed a "logic" of their own (in this case, a left-sided localization).

Another possibility is that Japanese speakers first use the left hemisphere, rather than the right, to process the sounds mentioned earlier (emotional expressions, such as crying and laughing, and the sounds of natural objects, such as the chirping of crickets), because Japanese culture seems to place higher relative value (more perhaps than in the West) on decoding the "texture" of various emotional experiences, while at the same time not reacting overly to the emotional content implicit or explicit within the message. Thus, it would make sense for the prefrontal cortex in Japanese speakers to attend selectively to voice sounds with the relatively emotionless syntactic power of the left hemisphere first. As is known, the right hemisphere has some language-processing ability but almost no ability in the syntactical area. Its forte is analyzing affect.

Beyond these speculations, however, we need to admit our ignorance. Only careful clinical observations of how the brain accomplishes its tasks will provide answers to the questions that we are raising regarding neural control and adaptive decision making. But, in reviewing the evidence, one is struck by the likely importance (in such adaptive processes) of the prefrontal cortex. Specifically, it seems likely that it is the prefrontal cortex (with its special ability with language and serial organization) that controls brain organization decisively, once natural (native) language is assimilated during development. In fact, the true importance of language, in an evolutionary sense, might be this ability it provides for adaptive, individual control over brain organization.[9]

NOTES

1. The reader may better appreciate the significance of such models by reading Bower and Morrow (1990), who state: "We build mental models that represent significant aspects of our physical and social world, and we manipulate elements of those models when we think, plan, and try to explain events of that world. The ability to construct and manipulate valid models of reality provides humans with our distinctive adaptive advantage; it must be considered one of the crowning achievements of the human intellect" (p. 44; see also Boden, 1988). From the perspective of psychoanalytic theory, the cerebellar self-in-the-world model is the equivalent of what Gedo has called self-organization. In Gedo's Mode I, this model is rudimentary; that is, the nuclei of self are inadequately coordinated. Coordination of percepts improves in Gedo's Mode II. Finally, in his Mode III "characteristic motivations and/or affective patterns are also included in a coordinated gestalt" (Gedo, personal communication, July 3, 1990).
2. A similar point appears in the essay by Robbins (Chapter 8, this volume).
3. For a similar discussion of the role of the prefrontal cortex, see Lichtenberg (Chapter 7, this volume).
4. For other discussions on the important topic of "attention," the reader is referred to Lichtenberg (Chapter 7, this volume) and Levin (1991, chap. 4).
5. Also see Grossman (Chapter 6, this volume).
6. From the point of view of Mandelbrot's concept of fractal geometry, certain larger patterns in nature can be generated from the reproduction of smaller and smaller units of the same original shape. As an example of a fractal, consider a snowflake. Its six-sided symmetry has been shown to exist within a high-power magnification of its component parts. Moreover, still higher-power magnification of these parts shows that these microscopic snowflake components are made up of still smaller elements with the same six-sided snowflake symmetry. This recurrent quality is what defines fractals.
7. Nadel and Wexler (1984) describe in detail what is meant by "modules," or knowledge-acquisition systems of the brain. The shift from associationist

perceptions and narrow anatomical localizations for memory to the concept of subsystems specialized for specific tasks (facial recognition, spatial perception, language, etc.) makes a great deal of sense to me, and a paper is in progress on this important perspective.

8. Gedo's model can also be examined from a language perspective: "Mode I is prelinguistic, Mode II is organized around the protolanguages studied by Fonagy . . . , and Mode III concerns the lexicality of the natural language" (Gedo, personal communication, 1990).

9. Some readers will object to my speculations on the ground that it is culture, and not biology, that is the decisive factor in the evolution of language. I think, however, this is an open question (see Levin, 1991, chap. 11). It is also interesting to speculate whether the different languages (rather than one international language) evolved because there were selective advantages provided by the different languages, such as, for example, their adaptiveness in solving specific problems in the realm of different life contingencies (cultural contexts). For those interested in pursuing more about the subject of human language and cognition from an evolutionary perspective, I suggest Lieberman (1984). His central premise is that "human linguistic ability is based on rather general neural mechanisms that structure the cognitive behavior of human beings as well as that of other animals, plus a limited set of language-specific mechanisms that differentiate the particular manner in which we transmit information" (p. 1). My interest here is in expanding our understanding of exactly this relationship between neural control mechanisms and cognition, particularly the relationship between the language of the brain and that of the "mind" (see Levin, 1991, chap. 4).

REFERENCES

Andreasen, N. C. (Ed.). (1989). *Brain imaging: Applications in psychiatry.* Washington, DC: American Psychiatric Press.

Benson, D. F., & Stuss, D. T. (1989). Theories of frontal lobe function. In J. Meller (Ed.), *Neurology and psychiatry* (pp. 266–283). Basel: Karger.

Boden, M. A. (1988). *Computer models of the mind.* Cambridge, England: Cambridge University Press.

Bower, G. H., & Marrow, D. G. (1990). Mental models in narrative comprehension. *Science, 5,* 45–58.

Collins, N. (1990). Psychotherapy and minimum language skills: Mutual exclusion? In D. Watson (Ed.), *At the crossroads: A celebration of diversity* (pp. 1–10). Little Rock, AR: American Deafness and Rehabilitation Association.

Decety, J., & Ingvar, D. (1988, October). *The principles and operation of the brain.* Paper presented to the Pontifical Academy Symposium Rome, Italy.

DeRobertis, E. M., Oliver, G., & Wright, C. E. V. (1990). Homeobox genes and the vertebrate body plan. *Scientific American, 263* 46–53.

Erikson, E. (1959). *Identity and the life cycle*. Psychological Issues, Monograph 1. New York: International Universities Press.

Freud, S. (1914). On narcissism: An introduction. *Standard Edition* (Vol. 14, pp 73–102). London: Hogarth Press, 1966.

Gedo, J. (1979). *Beyond interpretation*, New York: International Universities Press.

Gedo, J. (1981). *Advances in clinical psychoanalysis*. New York: International Universities Press.

Gedo, J. (1984a). *Psychoanalysis and its discontents*. New York: Guilford Press.

Gedo, J. (1984b). Discussion of Joseph Lichtenberg's "The empathic mode of perception and alternative vantage points for psychoanalysis," In: J. Lichtenberg, M. Bernstein, and D. Silver (Eds.), *Empathy II* (pp. 137–142). Hillsdale, NJ: Analytic Press.

Gedo, J. (1986). *Conceptual issues in psychoanalysis: Essays in history and method*. Hillsdale, NJ: Analytic Press.

Gedo, J., & Goldberg, A. (1973). *Models of the mind*. Chicago: University of Chicago Press.

Gedo, J. (1989, October). *Psychoanalysis and Occam's razor*. Paper presented to the Chicago Psychoanalytic Society.

Goldman-Rakic, P. S., Isserhoff, A., Schwartz, M. L., and Bugbee, N. M. (1983). Neurology of cognitive development in nonhuman primates. In P. Mussen (Ed.), *Handbook of child psychology: Biology and infant development* (pp. 281–344). New York: Wiley.

Heinrichs, J. & Endicott, K. (1988). Music of the mind: Modelling the brain. *Dartmouth Alumni Magazine*, 82(1), 18–23.

Ingvar, D. (1987). *Serial aspects of language and speech related to prefrontal cortical activity: A selective review*. Unpublished manuscript.

Itoh, M. (1988, October). *Neural control as a major aspect of high order brain function*. Paper presented to the Pontifical Academy Symposium on Principles of Design and Operation of the Brain, Rome, Italy.

Jackson, J. H. (1958). *Selected writings* (J. Taylor, Ed.). New York: Basic Books.

Kent, E. W. (1981). *The brains of men and machines*. Peterborough, NH: Byte.

Kolb, B., & Winshaw, I. Q. (1980). The frontal lobes. In *Fundamentals of Human Neuropsychology* (pp. 277–307). San Francisco: Freeman.

Levey, M. (1984/1985). The concept of structure in psychoanalysis. *The annual of psychoanalysis* (Vol. 12/13, pp. 137–154). New York: International Universities Press.

Levin, F.M. (1980). Metaphor, affect and arousal: How interpretations might work. *The annual of psychoanalysis* (Vol. 8, pp. 231–248). New York: International Universities Press.

Levin, F. M. (1988, October). *Recent advances in understanding mentation and affect*. Paper presented to the 44th Annual Regional Midwest Conference of the Chicago Medical Society, Chicago.

Levin, F. M. (1989, October). *Discussion of J. Gedo's paper on psychoanalytic theory and Occam's razor*. Paper presented to the Chicago Psychoanalytic Society, Chicago.

Levin, F. M. (1990). Psychological development and the changing organization of the brain. *The annual of psychoanalysis* (Vol. 18, pp. 45–72). Hillsdale, NJ: Analytic Press.

Levin, F. M. (1991). *Mapping the mind: The intersection of psychoanalysis and neuroscience*. Hillsdale, NJ: Analytic Press.

Lichtenberg, J. (1988). A theory of motivational-functional systems as psychic structures. *Journal of the American Psychoanalytic Association, 36,* 57–72.

Lieberman, P. (1984). *The biology and evolution of language.* Cambridge, MA: Harvard University Press.

Nadel, L., & Wexler, K. (1984). Neurobiology, representations, and memory. In G. Lynch, J. L. McGaugh, & N. M. Weinberger (Eds.), *Neurobiology of learning and memory* (pp. 125–133). New York: Guilford Press.

Niwa, S. (1989). Schizophrenic symptoms, pathogenic cognitive and behavioral features: Discussion of the language of brain and of mind. In M. Namba & H. Kaiya (Eds.), *Main currents in schizophrenia research.* Tokyo: Hesco International. (Japanese)

Reiser, M. (1985). Converging sectors of psychoanalysis and neurobiology: Mutual challenges and opportunities. *Journal of the American Psychoanalytic Association, 33,* 11–34.

Sacks, O. (1989). *Seeing voices: A journey into the world of the deaf.* Berkeley: University of California Press.

Schwartz, A. (1987). Drives, affects, behavior and learning: Approaches to a psychobiology of emotion and to an integration of psychoanalytic and neurobiologic thought. *Journal of the American Psychoanalytic Association, 35,* 467–506.

Shallice, T. (1988). *From neuropsychology to mental structure.* Cambridge, England: Cambridge University Press.

Tsunoda, T. (1987). *The Japanese brain: The workings of the brain and the cultures of east and west.* Tokyo: Daishu Shoten. (Japanese)

6

Hierarchies, Boundaries, and Representation in a Freudian Model of Mental Organization

WILLIAM I. GROSSMAN

> We know two kinds of things about what we call our
> psyche (or mental life): firstly, its bodily organ and scene
> of action, the brain (or nervous system) and, on the other
> hand, our acts of consciousness, which are immediate
> data and cannot be further explained by any sort of
> description. Everything that lies between is unknown to
> us, and the data do not include any direct relation
> between these two terminal points of our knowledge.
> —S. Freud (1940, p. 144)

> There is a straight ladder from the atom to the grain of
> sand, and the only real mystery in physics is the missing
> rung. Below it, particle physics; above it, classical physics;
> but in between, metaphysics. All the mystery in life turns
> out to be this same mystery, the join between things
> which are distinct and yet continuous, body and mind,
> free will and fate, living cells and life itself; the moment
> before the foetus.
> —T. Stoppard (1989, p. 37)

It is well known that Freud's topographical theory in *The Interpretation of Dreams* (1900) shows the influence of his neurological background. Less familiar until recently is the fact that many of his later clinical formulations retain both the structure and, at times, the language of his early work, *On Aphasia* (1891). (See also Edelheit, 1969, 1978, and Stengel, 1954.) In that monograph, Freud discussed the way the periphery of the body is represented in the brain. He then elaborated and extended this idea to provide a complex picture of the formation of words, objects, and their associations. In this way, he created a model derived from the spatial or topographical arrangements of the nervous system, which he used as one of the organizing frameworks of psychoanalytic theory. The schematic spatial arrangements of the nervous system were the source of Freud's spatial images of the mental apparatus, occasional diagrams, and his diagrammable descriptions of mental relationships.

Although Freud used other models and organizing concepts (see Grossman, 1986), and although there are aspects of psychoanalytic theory that do not fit neatly into this model, it seems to me to be a particularly important one. This model provides a thread of recurrently recognizable organization leading through a labyrinth of diverse conceptualizations. The fact that a basic model, with some variations, can be used to organize at least some aspects of mental function and phenomena, some aspects of interpersonal and social phenomena, and some kinds of biological phenomena gives the theory cohesion and flexibility over a wide and complex range.

In the discussion to follow, I shall try to show how the organization of mental function called "metapsychology" is derived from the basic aphasia/nervous system model. In Freud's *On Aphasia*, the model served to explain how sensory information is organized in the brain and then in mental functions. This framework provided the template for a later picture of mental organization that could be used eventually to fit the clinical theories about the minds of analyst and patient in the analytic situation.

Freud's use of a single model was reflected in the use of the same term to refer to a series of related phenomena. This is one reason that Freud's terminology is imprecise, as critics have observed. Terms such as identification, narcissism, masochism, and repression require the specifications of primary and secondary in an effort to deal with the ambiguities. The point is that the use of the same imprecise term for related, though different, concepts is one key to the system Freud was constructing. It indicates that essential properties were present in a number of different contexts. The meaning of general or ambiguous terms became more specific in each context. The use of a single term, like the use of metaphors and analogies, shows the inner relationship between different meanings in a domain of related phenomena.

The term "transference" (*Übertragung*), for example, is used in a number of different senses, first in *On Aphasia*, then in *The Interpretation of Dreams*, and still later for different clinical phenomena. In all these cases, Freud's usage of a "transference" concept retained the idea of the substitution of one object for another (though not always in the psychoanalytic sense of object), the creation of a representative or representation, and a displacement of meaning and value.

Substitutions of objects and displacements of meaning and value are, of course, necessarily related. Freud emphasized one or another of these elements when describing the relationship between conscious and unconscious fantasies and the way the mental apparatus develops. Although we naturally attempt to restrict our clinical concept of transference to distinguish it from other related processes, Freud used the same (German) term for many different processes involving the substitution of representations and shifts of meaning and value. In this way, he created a picture of the mind as a hierarchical structure of agencies, functions, and fantasy organizations in which complexity resulted from the combination of relatively simple relationships and operations.

This chapter considers some aspects of Freud's theoretical accounts of metapsychology and clinical theory from the point of view of the core model first used in *On Aphasia*. The purpose of examining Freud's way of developing his imaginative description of the mind, based on this model, is to discover some essential features of the structure of the mind in the picture he presented. Even though there have been obvious changes in psychoanalytic theory over time, his picture of the mind and ours are still closely related to a significant extent because of this underlying model.

Exploring the way Freud constructs his account of the mind leads readily to considering the relation between the structure of the mind that Freud discloses and the structure of his way of explaining it. In many respects, the two structures are the same, so that, in effect, he both describes and demonstrates the mind as he sees it. Other authors have shown that various formal properties of Freud's texts, as well as his metaphors and rhetoric, are important vehicles for conveying his image of the mind (e.g., Derrida, 1978; Mahony, 1986, 1987). My purpose is to show that Freud presented a model by the use of rhetoric, analogies, metaphors, imprecise terminology, and his reflections on theory formation. Moreover, this model unifies the more abstract aspects of the theory and its clinical applications more than is generally appreciated. However, I do not intend to examine or argue the question of whether it is a good, adequate, or desirable model. The aim is, first, to show convincingly that there is a latent model and, second, that when this model is recognized in Freud's work, the theory and the various stages of its development show a greater coherence. At the least, awareness of this basic model helps us in reading Freud and may, therefore, add clarity to discussions of Freud's ideas.

This line of thought implies, too, that Freud's theory about mental life was also a description of the way he thought as a scientist, his creative process. For this reason, Freud's ideas about theory formation are also of interest, since theory formation is a model of thinking about experience as analysts and patients do it. Therefore, it is at least plausible to think of Freud's version of psychoanalytic theory as a picture or an account of a person observing his own mental processes and arriving at a picture of his mind and his world. That is, the mind described by Freud's psychoanalysis is the self-reflecting mind and the mental activity of an analyst and a patient in analysis. One of the goals of psychoanalytic theory is to explain how one person's mind can be used to understand another person's.

For the purposes of this discussion, it is useful to think of Freud as trying to understand the workings of human irrationality and its relationship to reason in the context of ideas about adaptation and epigenesis. To this end, he was concerned with the way a person understands experiences as meaningful, how and in what form a person remembers and reexperiences what is meaningful, and how and in what form a person conveys this to another person, as in analysis. All of this may be conscious or unconscious. I am suggesting that this concern of Freud's and our thinking unifies the various aspects of psychoanalytic theory. This way of thinking about Freud's work is intended as a version of, not an alternative to, motivational and drive theories, structural theory, and the role of adaptation and biology in Freud's thought.

Taking the idea of this organizing concern further, for the purposes of this discussion, conveying and understanding the meanings from "person" to "person" could include from unconscious to conscious, from patient to analyst, and from oneself as a child to oneself as an adult, that is, as a genetic process. In this way, the central issue is found in the different contexts explored by the theory.

ON APHASIA: THE LANGUAGE OF NEUROLOGY
AND THE NEUROLOGY OF LANGUAGE

When Freud addressed the problems of aphasia (1891), he was interested in the way speech is learned, the way sounds and associations make up words in the brain, and the way object images and their associations are recorded and associated with words. Freud placed these problems in a chain that begins with the surface of the body and ends with the organization of mental functions and their expressions. The result was a hierarchical series of systems within which are clusters of elements. The systems are separated by boundaries. The contents of one system are transferred, translated, and transformed as they are represented in another system. Neither the contents of the systems nor the hierarchy itself are linear in their organization. Altogether, we have systems of hierarchies, boundaries and representations that derive from processes of transference, translation, and transformation.

At the beginning of his monograph, Freud attributed to Meynert the view that the periphery of the body is "projected" point for point onto the cerebral cortex, and then he argued against it. He suggested:

> If the way in which the periphery is reflected in the spinal cord is called a "projection," its counterpart in the cerebral cortex might suitably be called a "representation," which implies that the periphery of the body is contained in the cerebral cortex not point by point, but through selected fibres. (1891, p. 51)

He added that the nerve fibers did not remain unchanged from the periphery to the cortex. They did not pass through the gray matter, as Meynert had said. Freud thought that the fiber going into the gray matter terminates in a ganglion and that other fibers exit after making associative connections with other sources of stimuli. Consequently, each time a fiber emerged from a nucleus, it had changed its "functional significance" (1891, pp. 52–53).

He concluded that

> the fibre tracts, which reach the cerebral cortex after their passage through other grey masses . . . no longer reflect a topographically exact image of it [the periphery]. They contain the body periphery in the same way as—to borrow an example from the subject with which we are concerned here—a poem contains the alphabet, i.e., in a completely different arrangement serving other purposes, in manifold associations of the individual elements, whereby some may be represented several times, others not at all. (1891, p. 53)

Freud also contrasted the idea of a topographical projection of the periphery onto the cortex with the functional organization in which the periphery was "contained," that is, "represented," in the cortex. Consistent with this idea, there could be two types of representation in the brain. Freud (1893) called the organic paralyses of cerebral origin "representation paralyses," and remarked "Hysterical paralysis is also a representational paralysis, but with a special kind of representation whose characteristics remain to be discovered" (p. 163).

The relationship between the periphery and the cortex, to which

Freud gave the name "representation" in the aphasia monograph, is a static, spatial preliminary version of "overdetermination"—a term used in his monograph. More generally, overdetermination provides a picture of two organizations in which a second system revises the organization of the first according to some other functional schema. Aspects of each system may be multiply represented in the other, or not represented at all.

Now one of the interesting things about Freud's carefully argued presentation is that, even in this treatise on neuropathology, it is a preliminary to a refutation of the idea of a one-to-one correlation (analogous to a projection) between mental and physiological processes in the brain. Freud insisted that even the "simple sensory impression" or "simple idea" was simple only from the psychological point of view, but not from the standpoint of physiology.[1] He asserted that terms like "association" and "perception" were psychological abstractions that had no simple, differentiated anatomical or physiological counterparts. He then reminded his readers not to confuse the physical with the psychic:

> But shall we not be making the same mistake in principle whether what we are trying to localize is a complicated concept, a whole mental activity, or a psychical element? Is it justifiable to take a nerve fibre, which for the whole length of its course has been a purely physiological structure and has been subject to purely physiological modifications, and to plunge its end into the sphere of the mind and to fit this end out with a presentation or a mnemic image? (1891, p. 55)[2]

He added:

> The physiological events do not cease as soon as the psychological ones begin; on the contrary, the physiological chain continues. What happens is simply that, after a certain point of time, each (or some) of its links has a psychical phenomenon corresponding to it. Accordingly, the psychical is a process parallel to the physiological—"a dependent concomitant." (1891, p. 55)[3]

Freud had now described first the relation between the periphery and the brain, and then the relation between the brain and psychic processes. Using almost the same language in both cases, he had described each level as consisting of two systems whose contents are not correlated one-to-one but rather related by inexact parallelism. These are two levels of organization of sensory input on its way to becoming the idea of a word.[4]

With this model, Freud avoided a point-for-point reduction of psychology to physiology. In fact, the real problem was to find the physiology to fit what was understood of the psychology of language and association (Marx, 1967). Freud noted that those who speak of localizing presentations in cells "can say a great deal more about presentations than about the modifications [in nerve cells], of which no physiological characterization whatever has yet been reached." (1915c, p. 207). The relationship between simultaneous events described psychologically and physiologically—in Hughlings Jackson's words, "dependent concomitance"—could be explored in terms of representation and translation instead of anatomical or physiological localization.[5] In this way, Freud argued for, and tried to give, a careful psychological description before attempting reduction to physiology or anatomy.

Freud's critique of the neurology of speech included his own ideas on analyzing language and its development. He was looking for a new way to picture brain organization, combined with a different way of thinking about the speech/language functions. In Freud's conception of speech development, words are learned by being heard and spoken in multiple contexts. Freud insisted that there is no separation of the word from its associations since the sensory material of the word and its contextual associations together create the presentation of the word in the brain. When each of the auditory and visual sensory contributions reaches the cortex, it sends out radiating fibers that form a variety of nodes with the fibers of other sensory inputs. In this way, interconnected chains of associations are created. We shall see later that Freud pictured the organization of memory in hysteria in precisely the same way.

Thus far, we can discern some elements of the model to be traced in Freud's later work. First, there are the two topographies of the body surface and the cerebral cortex, joined by branching fibers with nodal interconnections. Second, the system formed by the periphery, the pathways, and the cortex is one part of another system whose second member is the system of psychic phenomena. We now have: periphery, pathways, cortex, and psyche. The psychic system, or speech apparatus, has in turn its own organization, based on Freud's version of association psychology and the contemporary theories of language. The elements of this psychic system are various kinds of sensory impressions, motor images and their interconnections that go to make up the word presentations. Their connections can be represented diagrammatically, but they have no known material basis.[6] That is, as Freud often said in later works, the newly constructed mental topography of images and presentations could not be reduced to an anatomical topography.

The processes of the brain have only some counterparts, or we might say, representations, in mental phenomena, just as the points on the periphery have only some representation in the cortex. If we now imagine a diagram of the systems, we can see that it is hierarchical and that each half of the brain–mind system is made up of components connected by pathways. In the cortex, these are nerve pathways, in the psyche, association pathways.

The speech apparatus contains various speech and language functions having their own nodes and pathways. The system of word presentations is then placed in a relationship with another system, the system of object presentations. Each of these systems, too, has its own organization.

An essential feature of the description I have just given is a hierarchy of systems separated by boundaries. Any two separate organizations are often related to one another as representations. Within each of the systems, a similar structure of chains of elements is repeated.

A model of this kind, in which a number of systems having similar structure are combined to form a larger system having the same structure as the smaller systems, is called a recursive model. A set of identical Russian dolls nested one inside the other gives a rough idea of what this model looks like. Recursive models often involve feedback, as does Freud's.

THE BOUNDARIES AND TRANSFORMATIONS OF THE ANATOMICAL MODEL

Until recently, *On Aphasia* and, in particular, Freud's "Project" (1895) were considered to be primarily neurophysiological treatises. Now, it is widely accepted that these works employed the vocabulary of neurophysiology to clothe Freud's ideas on psychology, philology, philosophy, and his experiences with hysterical patients (see Forrester, 1980; Kanzer, 1973; Levin, 1978; Mancia, 1983; Marshall, 1974; Marx, 1967; Rizzuto, 1989, 1990; Solms & Saling, 1986). According to this current viewpoint, Freud cannot really be said to have abandoned physiological for psychological explanation since his theories of language and consciousness were not primarily neurophysiological in the first place. Because of this fact, Freud could change his terminology, apply his model to description of psychological issues, and bequeath to the future the task of correlating or reducing psychological organizations to brain physiology.[7]

In Freud's occasional discussions of the relationship between the mental apparatus and the brain, he noted the problems of reduction. His alternative was to describe the spatial character of his model and to outline the hierarchy of systems he constructed in the context of his later theories.

One of Freud's earliest and most elaborate uses of the spatial model turned from the organizations of word and object associations in the brain to the organization of associations in the clinical study of hysteria. In his psychotherapy chapter of *Studies on Hysteria* (Breuer & Freud, 1895), he hoped to contribute to the understanding of the dynamics of ideation. The complex organization of clinical phenomena required spatial similes and was difficult to translate into verbal description. The problem of giving a verbal description of the nonverbal spatial model in presenting the theory was, therefore, similar to the problem of the psychotherapy of hysteria. In the case of psychotherapy, the task was to translate the symptomatic images and perceptions into verbal interpretations.

Here is a brief summary of his account: In every case of hysteria there are collections of memories, or themes, as Freud called them. Each theme is arranged linearly and is also stratified concentrically around a pathogenic nucleus. This nucleus consists of "memories of events or trains of thought in which the traumatic factor has culminated or the pathogenic idea has found its purest manifestation." A third arrangement according to thought content is dynamic. This is, Freud tells us, the linkage made by a logical thread or chain following a roundabout path "from the periphery to the central nucleus." It is a ramifying and converging system of lines. "It contains nodal points at which two or more threads meet and thereafter proceed as one. . . . Several threads which run independently, or which are connected at various points by sidepaths, debouch into [einmünden] the nucleus. To put this in other words, . . . a symptom . . . is 'overdetermined'" (Breuer & Freud, 1895, pp. 288–290).

Thus elaborated, the anatomical model of the periphery and the cortex has become multidimensional, made up of concentrically organized, stratified units of associated memories.[8] Utilized to describe memory and association, this hierarchical, recursive model became a central organizing structure for psychoanalytic theory—at least as Freud wrote it. The spatial diagram of chains of associations was taken as a picture of mental organization and is taken for granted by analysts today.

In a letter to Fliess on December 6, 1896, Freud (1887–1904) discussed the developmental significance of his account of memory. He wrote:

> Our psychic mechanism has come into being by a process of stratification: the material present in the form of memory traces being subjected from time to time to a rearrangement . . . —to a retranscription. . . . Memory is present not once but several times over . . . (I postulated a similar kind of rearrangement some time ago (Aphasia) for the paths leading from the periphery. . .). (p. 207)

Further on, he added that

> the successive registrations represent the psychic achievement of successive epochs of life. At the boundary between two such epochs a translation of the psychic material [takes] place. I explain the peculiarities of the psychoneuroses by supposing that this translation has not taken place in the case of some of the material. (p. 208)

He went on to conclude that repression is a failure of translation. This way of looking at the process provides a rationale for the idea that clinical interpretation is a type of translation leading to reorganization, or "rearrangement" and "retranscription," in a manner similar to the developmental reorganization of successive epochs.

Freud's letter anticipated many later conceptualizations. The idea of a stratification, based on the relationship to consciousness and characterized by translation, gives the form of the topographical model of the mind. Freud's use of the model in a description of development expanded the picture of successive reorganizations, translations, and transcriptions.

The idea of boundaries between levels in a hierarchy is an important concept in this letter and throughout Freud's work. Here we see that translation is one of the relationships defining the boundary. That is, the boundary is a conceptual boundary characterized by the different organizations of the systems so that one must be translated into the other. (See Kaplan [1988, 1990] for illuminating discussions of boundary issues in psychoanalysis, in general, and in applied analysis, in particular.)

Although the spatial model is obviously suitable for static translation and representation relationships, it was, as noted earlier, both clinically and developmentally applicable. The dynamic factors animating the spatial model are supplied by concepts like maturation, development, and the force of wishes. Developmentally and clinically, the effort to replace lost or abandoned infantile objects via transference, that is, to satisfy infantile wishes with symbolic substitutes, can be conceptualized in terms of translation, representation, and dynamic factors. The task, as we all know, is endless. The reason is that no new person provides an identity of the infantile perception or an exact translation of the infantile satisfaction (Freud, 1910b, 1912).[9]

When Freud (1900) turned to the theory of dream formation, he described the overdetermination in the various relationships of dream content and dream thoughts in a way that recalls the earlier models of aphasia and hysteria. That is, there is a close resemblance between the language describing the multiple and incomplete representations arising from condensation and displacement in the dream work and the formulations describing the relations between brain and periphery, and between the elements of memory content.[10] These applications of the model provide a dramatic picture of the way the idea of "dependent concomitance" conveys the extent and limitation of expression of one system in the content of the other.

The translation aspect of the model is seen still more clearly in Freud's accounts of dream interpretation. During dreaming, thoughts are translated into images. In telling the dream, images are translated into verbal thoughts. In effect, the dreamer's narrative is an interpretation of the recalled image. The analyst then interprets the dream narrative. Freud treated dream analysis as a new translation that reverses the process of dream formation. Reconstruction can be conceptualized in the same way.

The clinical process of association and interpretation is thus treated as the same process that is going on in the mind—with the addition of another person or one's own conscious mind as interpreter. We have just seen this construction of the mind on the basis of the clinical activity in Freud's equation of association chains with memory chains in hysteria. Now we can see that the picture of the self-interpreting mind is similar to the picture of the clinical dialogue. Only the participants are different.

Like the theories of memory and dreams, the theory of instinctual drives also involves the ideas of "dependent concomitance," parallelism, and boundaries associated with representation.[11] In a well-known passage in "Instincts and Their Vicissitudes," Freud (1915a) described the relationship between mental functions and peripheral body-functions—sexual zones and chemistry—as follows:

> Considering mental life from a biological point of view, an "instinct" appears to us as a concept on the frontier between the mental and the somatic, as the psychical representative of the stimuli originating from within the organism and reaching the mind, as a measure of the demand made upon the mind for work in consequence of its connection with the body. (pp. 121–122)[12]

Freud is saying that the influence of peripheral sexual functions on the mind can be expressed by a boundary concept. In this statement, the idea that the instinct is a "concept on the frontier" or boundary refers to the idea that there is an intimate functional connection between peripheral soma and mind. This connection is analogous to the function of the nerve fibers in connecting the body surface with the brain. These formulations make explicit both the representation of the body in the mental life, in some form, and the role of the body in stimulating mental activity.

The concept of instinctual drives is often taken to be an "ultimate" biological explanation of motives, as though the forces driving motives rendered the content and occasions of motives insignificant. Although loose formulations of explanations in terms of drives (including Freud's) may often be read in this way, I believe that the drive concept in Freud's work is the expression of a need for correlations and connections (Freud, 1920). Drives are, therefore, concepts defining a boundary: The content of the concept is to be found either in the derivatives that are their psychological content or in the biological events, for example, of sex hormones, central nervous system organization, neurotransmitters, and so on. Thus, the instinctual drive represents two different kinds of events and two different kinds of research interests, with their appropriate methods of study. As Freud (1913) said, "We cannot help regarding the term 'instinct' as a concept on the frontier between the spheres of psychology and biology" (p. 182). The ideas of the driving force of wishes and the range of sexual and aggressive interests characterize the mental side of the boundary.

The concept of drives provides, in this definition, something dynamic to account for mental activity and the representation of bodily urges and needs. The somatic factor introduced in this way into the analysis of mental activities has long been a focus of controversy. It suggests that Freud believed that a system of interpretation alone could not account for change and development. Nor was he content to leave the problem entirely out of consideration. For this reason, the specification of the boundary and some statement about the boundary conditions noted were important.

At times, Freud acknowledged the problem by reflecting on theory construction. He provided a justification for the introduction of concepts from other fields and demonstrated his method of taking multiple viewpoints toward his material to delineate the specifically psychoanalytic issues.

DYNAMIC ASPECTS OF THE MODEL: FREUD ON THEORY CONSTRUCTION

The function of the model as the organizer of many different levels of mental and interpersonal function has been emphasized so far. Understanding that the relationships among systems and levels can be treated as representation and translation is the basis for interpretation. The problem now is to see how the processes of change from level to level were formulated, that is, how translation occurs. Freud dealt with the problem by looking elsewhere for concepts and analogues that would help to conceptualize development and change in mental life. The result was a picture of the development of mental life, of analysis, and of scientific thinking as processes of adaptation to reality. Our consideration of the problem leads to discussion of the relations (conflict) among preconception (disposition), reality testing (trial action), and creative or constructive mental activity (compromise formation). For Freud, reality testing—in common sense and in science—is an important boundary process that animates the hierarchical organizations whose parts are related by translation.

Apparently, Freud thought he needed to explain why he borrowed ideas from other fields like biology. At various times throughout his work, he reflected on his own difficulties of description, his own way of working, and his theory construction. These self-descriptions were an aspect of his self-analyzing, part of his effort to achieve objectivity, and often a dramatization or enactment of the processes he was trying to describe. Clearly, he knew that restatements of his model and demonstrations of his thinking and results were not equivalent to a systematic proof of his ideas. Yet he also wanted to show that psychoanalysis was a science. To do this, he dismissed the idealized and overly rational accounts of the scientific method. Instead, like a growing number of scientific philosophers and psychologists, he described the way scientists think, the way ideas develop in science. When he did this, for example, in his paper on drives (discussed earlier), Freud (1915a) described theory construction in terms that are equally appropriate for finding an interpretation for clinical material. Here we see Freud the clinician examining science, while Freud the scientist examines psychoanalysis.

According to this approach, the development of scientific ideas was not an impersonal and logically unfolding march of progress. Science was, like clinical psychoanalytic exploration, the creative mental process of someone searching for understanding of "reality," a matter of interpretation. This means that a person interpreting engages in the same mental processes, whatever the data. The issue is the activity of the thinker—the scientist, the analyst, the patient—and how the thinker goes about formulating ideas about what he observes, his experience. The principles by which the data can be organized, that is the model to be used, have to be invented, discovered, or borrowed, as in the case of the drives.

Both scientific method and psychoanalysis were described as adaptive processes of approaching an understanding of reality through the overcoming of infantile fantasies and prejudice. Modern consideration of the way sciences develop has abandoned rigid ideas about the advances of scientific discovery by the application of the scientific method. Instead, more students of scientific thought have addressed the role of scientists' thinking processes and the influence of social attitudes and values in the development of knowledge. Freud's approach brought psychology into this orientation to the philosophy of science.

Was this a question of Freud having shifted his level of consideration because his description alone does not fit a systematic format of proof? The only thing he could do, in considering science as the activity of thinkers, was to use a psychoanalytic approach and to consider scientific thinking in terms of his model. Since analysis is distinguished by its interpretive stance, Freud as the analyst examining science could only interpret.

Freud had taken a new viewpoint from which he could compare the way analysts deal with data and concepts with the way other scientists do this. His position was that of a "metascientist," looking at both the study of the mind and the study of the world, in an effort to compare them neutrally or objectively. When he did this, he used the same model. He placed scientific thinking and science, alongside psychoanalysis, into the model of thought constructed of hierarchies and boundaries.

In this way, Freud used his model of the mind for the analysis of how science, in general, and his science of the mind, in particular, work. The process is thus reflexive. First, he used available theory to observe and understand how the mind works. Then, he gave an analysis of how the mind uses theory to understand itself and the external world. This method describes the process of self-analysis in a formal sense. Although unconscious motives are not included, it would be possible to include them. This approach also had the effect of treating the growth of scientific knowledge as a growth process like the development of an individual's knowledge. In effect, the result is an expansion of the levels of his model. Scientific investigation of the world is a higher level in the hierarchy, a further development of common sense, "a refinement of everyday thinking" (Einstein, 1936).

Freud focused on the way psychoanalytic process, psychoanalytic theory, and science in general overcome the intrusions of irrationality—infantile thinking— in the construction of reality. What Freud says about theory construction was for this reason an application of his psychoanalytic theory of mental activity to the kinds of theory construction and testing we do as analysts. The self-analysis of countertransference is the clinical counterpart of the scientist's overcoming of irrationality and prejudice.

These processes are seen still more clearly in a late work, *An Outline of Psychoanalysis* (Freud, 1940, pp. 196–197), which addressed these issues directly. Freud's argument goes something like this: Since both inner reality and external reality are "foreign territory" to the ego (Freud, 1933), the mind exploring inner reality is like the mind exploring external reality. Both the mind and the external world must be constructed in the language of perception. We infer the unconscious processes and fantasies from our observations of clinical data. We "translate" material of observation into the language of conscious fantasies. As he had said long before (Freud, 1917), we do not really know the Unconscious. Freud (1925) had also said that the Unconscious "had to be inferred like some fact in the external world" and added that "this was only treating one's own mental life as one had always treated other people's" (p. 32) since it is only an inference that other people have mental processes like our own. The essentially unknowable unconscious processes are placed in the picture of the spatial mental apparatus by the translation into the language of experience. We can discuss this map of the unconscious mind in perceptual terms in the way we do the invisible entities inferred by physics.[13] In analysis, the picture of the mental apparatus is a map of mental functions, of "external reality" and of object relations.

The idea of a model with two topographies, an inner and an outer world allowed Freud, the theoretician, to look in either direction at both worlds. In his comments on inferring the Unconscious, Freud, the clinician placed himself on the boundary between two minds, his own and another person's. System Conscious has two faces as does the ego. The theoretician, the clinician, the ego, and the

Conscious are all translators and "boundary creatures [*Grenzwesen*]." As a boundary science, "psychoanalysis acts as an intermediary between biology and psychology" (Freud, 1913b, p. 182; see Kaplan, 1988, 1990).[14]

Notice that with the spatial model, Freud was constructing an analogue. He once wrote in his notes, perhaps mischievously: "Space may be the projection of the extension of the psychical apparatus" (Freud, 1941). The usual view is the reverse: *space* is extended and serves as the model for a spatial conception of the mental apparatus. In other words, he was saying that the idea of physical space is like animism and like the development of the object world in that it is a mental construction, an interpretation, based on projection. The distortions introduced by this constructive projection have to be progressively corrected by psychoanalysts in their work and by scientists in theirs (Freud, 1940) and, of course, by the developing child.

In brief, this view says that both the internal and external worlds are known only as mental creations, that is, as interpretations, translations, and constructions. To arrive at our constructions, Freud says, we need provisional ideas that come from outside the field of observation and the experiences to be organized (1915a). The organization and meaning of the data are not self-evident. The provisional ideas must be chosen, discovered, or "invented" and may be conscious or unconscious. (cf. Einstein, 1914.)

Freud's (1915a) prelude to the discussion of the instinctual drives provides one statement of this point of view:

> The true beginning of scientific activity consists . . . in describing phenomena and then in proceeding to group, classify and correlate them. Even at the stage of description it is not possible to avoid applying certain abstract ideas to the material in hand, ideas derived from somewhere or other but certainly not from the new observations alone. . . . We come to an understanding about their meaning by making repeated references to the material of observation . . . upon which, in fact, they have been imposed. Thus, strictly speaking, they are in the nature of conventions—although everything depends on their not being arbitrarily chosen but determined by their having significant relations to the empirical material, relations that we seem to sense before we can clearly recognize and demonstrate them. (p. 117)[15]

It is significant that other thinkers of that time had begun to think about scientific theory construction in a similar way. For example, Einstein (1914), presented his views on theory construction in terms remarkably like Freud's, despite some important differences. Both men emphasized the need for introducing concepts to organize observations. Whereas Einstein discussed the use of a mathematical model, Freud indicated that the ideas that are chosen at the beginning may be indefinite. Freud's remarks could be used to describe the psychoanalytic situation as well. In the clinical situation, the theory provides provisional concepts for use in formulating interpretations from the beginning. In the case of theory building, a concept like "instincts" is chosen as a biological model and acquires its meaning through repeated clarification of its use with observations. As such concepts take on more specific meaning through their application to the data, they fit into the conceptual structure of the developing theory.

Freud's and Einstein's accounts of their creative processes can be extended so that the organizing principles themselves, at any particular step, can be seen to have been derived from the interplay of "free inventions of the human intellect" (Einstein, 1934) and experience—a version of the model of adaptation. (For a critique of Einstein's views on creativity in science, see Feyerabend [1987].)

The idea that organizing concepts must be imposed on, or projected onto, the data is one step in the development of a dynamic viewpoint that equates theory construction with the growing child's construction of a picture of reality. At the same time, formulations provided by theory are the provisional ideas that the analyst brings to clinical data to organize his or her theory about a particular patient.

One of the advantages of the recursive representational model is that the chains and layers of systems can be of different kinds while the overall schema of organization remains the same. Although the functions and relations may differ in many respects from system to system, those aspects that can be conceptualized in terms of representation, communication, and interaction can be organized on this model. It is this unity of conceptual organization that makes the model useful in applying theoretical concepts in clinical thinking. For instance, Freud (1924) tells us that the relationship between the moral masochist and his father is repeated in the relationship of his ego and superego. In this concrete example, the formation of the superego splits the ego into two systems that together make a new system. This intrapsychic pair (ego and superego) constitutes one mind of the interpersonal pair (father and child). Likewise, when the self-analyzing analyst is interpreting the productions of the patient in conflict, both subjects are at least double systems whose relationships are a function of representation and translation. In this way, impersonally or organismically conceived mental agencies can be thought to be in interaction or dialogue (Freud 1910a, 1916–1917). Freud (1910a, 1916–1917) uses the analogy of a person at a door letting only some people in as a model of repression, resistance, and censorship. In addition, he comments on his own use of analogies (1916–1917, pp. 295–296).

As I have tried to demonstrate thus far, the spatial model from *On Aphasia* is itself a provisional idea with considerable organizing power. It allowed Freud, for better or worse, to think of organism, mind, person, and society as having some fundamental organization in common. This facilitated a notion of development in which early modes of experience could be retained in later organizations but shaped to later content.

For Freud, theory construction in both physical science and psychoanalysis, on one side, and the activities of the clinician, on the other, all involve the forming and testing of hypotheses about reality. He, therefore, wrote about them all in the same language. His comments about the way we arrive at clinical interpretations resembled his descriptions of the way we arrive at psychoanalytic theoretical formulations. In effect, he used the same approach in constructing the theory that he did when applying it to particular clinical problems.

The method I refer to as the "multiple viewpoint method" is well known to clinicians in the form of free association. I noted earlier that Freud's picture of memory organization was a spatial representation of free association. They were both conceptualized along the lines of the recursive spatial model. The principle underlying the multiple viewpoint method follows from the nodes and interconnections of that model. The method is simply to start from any one of the nodes and follow the thread for a while, then start over from another point. In free association, the patient picks the starting point or else the analyst's question or interpretation is a starting point. In theory building, the organizing ideas the theorist brings to the data may be the starting point.

The analysis of a dream serves here as a clinical example of the application of the method of beginning with individual elements and arriving at their multiple meanings by association. Accordingly, Freud (1911) tells us the interpretation of a dream is "the same as with the elucidation of a single symptom . . . one must endeavor to lay hold first of this, then of that, fragment of the symptom's meaning, . . . until they can all be pieced together" (p. 93).

In parallel fashion, Freud presented his method of theory construction as a similar process of starting from different points of view and developing a picture of mental contents and functions from each point of view. I mentioned earlier, discussing drive theory, that the starting points or provisional ideas may be taken from other fields and other points of view. The resulting picture of the mind is constructed from these suborganizations centered on individual points of view. In a similar way, the mind constructed by each dream interpretation is similar in organization to the mind constructed by that analysis as a whole from many interpretations. The mind constructed by this particular analysis is in turn similar to the generalized mind constructed piecemeal by the analyses collected by many analysts.

The same idea is repeated when Freud (1915c) writes that psychic processes must be described according to the points of view of metapsychology. The points of view of metapsychology are separate loci for organizing observations, ideas, and so on. In his "Autobiographical Study" (1925), he wrote: "Later on I made an attempt to produce a 'Metapsychology'. By this I meant a method of approach according to which every mental process is considered in relation to three co-ordinates, which I described as *dynamic, topographical,* and *economical* respectively" (pp. 58–59). Once again, in describing the way we arrive at understanding of phenomena, Freud (1915d) says we have to start from many different points of view and follow each for a while, deferring a final synthesis[16] — a description that sounds like free association.

The same multiple viewpoint method was applied in the same way to only a part of the theory. Discussing object relations, Freud (1915d) discussed three polarities that he said govern the mental life: ego–external world, pleasure–unpleasure, and active–passive. The relations among the three polarities are complex since the polarities do not coincide. They are, in fact, organizers along three dimensions that come into prominence successively in development. Freud names them the real, the economic, and the biological, respectively. In this way, the description of development also follows the multiple viewpoint method. In this case, the provisional ideas that are the starting points of view come from the popular image of the mind, since it is evident that people do commonly classify their experiences along the lines of the polarities. This is an indication that Freud's model includes in its picture of the mind some significant organizations that are pictured in everyday conceptions of the mind by introspection.

Thus, we can see that Freud's method of theory construction is similar to the application of the theory to any particular problem of interpretation. It is this approach to interpretation that permits the elaboration of meanings and differentiation within the levels of the hierarchy. The theory itself is a generalized map or model of the relationship among the elements of mental activity of whatever complexity. Of course, it may be that theories of the mind do not have to be of this kind, but Freud's is.

METAPHOR AND ANALOGY IN MENTAL ACTIVITY AND IN THEORY

The model that has been explored here has been inferred from Freud's rhetorical devices, analogies, metaphors, imprecise terminology, and so on, as well as from the ideas about theory formation throughout his work, including some of his explicit descriptions. It is possible to do this because, as already mentioned, Freud's accounts of the theory demonstrate the processes he described. This means that in some respects the narratives follow a path of the same form that he described.[17] Insofar as the narrative itself takes the form of the picture of the mind that it is describing, we might think of it as a rhetorical model with spatial properties (like a calligram).[18]

Freud's rich narratives of psychoanalytic theory and the theory of the development of theory are consistent with Schafer's (1980) view that theories have the properties of narratives. Freud sometimes added diagrams to supplement the narrative accounts of mental relations as spatial relations. Some examples are the forgetting of the name Signorelli (Freud, 1898), transformations of instincts (1917) and "complemental series" (1916–1917).

We can use the text itself as an example of thought processes, a kind of specimen of mental constructions in both narrative and visual forms. A number of authors have used the text in this way for various purposes. Mahony (1986, 1987), in particular, has closely examined the structure of Freud's texts and his various rhetorical devices, including his use of figurative language. He points to the importance of rhetoric in the development of Freud's concepts, and he considers its role in theory building. My purpose, though closely related, is somewhat different. The point here is to show how the texts, taken together, are an illustration of some features of the model. In fact, it is by means of the consistent use of a set of metaphors that Freud assembles a recognizable model. Examples of Freud's use of analogy and metaphor, and his allusive use of repetitive words and formulations, cannot be given here, but they are readily found throughout his work.

In the recent past, the risks of using metaphors in science were frequently noted. Although metaphors might have some potential value in the first steps of theorizing, the ease with which they could provide a comforting illusion of knowledge required constant vigilance. Exploring this problem, a number of authors, such as Canning (1966), Schafer (1968, 1976), and Holt (1964, 1972), among others, discussed observations similar to those I shall mention. Their objective was to show some of the problems created by the use of reified metaphors in psychoanalysis. Grossman and Simon (1969) examined Freud's use of anthropomorphic metaphors with somewhat greater acceptance, questioning the value and success of efforts to replace them (e.g., by Hartmann, Kris, & Loewenstein, 1946).

Recently, however, there is a growing appreciation of the importance of analogies and metaphors in science and in everyday thinking. Metaphors are currently explored as the bearers of encoded relationships that are transferred to different kinds or levels of mental organization from biological organizations of the brain, to linguistic organizations, to systems of imagery, and so on. This appreciation comes from a variety of sources such as linguistics (e.g., Eco, 1986; Jakobson & Pomorska, 1983; Kittay, 1987), philosophy (e.g., Boyd, 1979; Davidson, 1978; Johnson, 1981; Miller, 1979; Ortony, 1979), psychoanalysis (e.g., Arlow, 1979; Kaplan, 1988; Rubinstein, 1972; Wurmser, 1977), and cognitive psychology (e.g., Erdelyi, 1985).

Analogy and metaphor are not only essential steps in the elaboration of thought but in the elaboration of theory. They are certainly not the desired end stage of scientific thought—because there is no end stage—but their presence does not disqualify thought as scientific. Analogies and metaphors are tools in the processes elaborating thoughts. (See also Schafer, 1977.)

The role of metaphor and analogy is essential in the elaboration of thought because the way some relationships are learned is first in the modalities that are not verbal. They must then be reedited, in Freud's terms, or undergo accommodation, in Piaget's. They must be translated to verbal schemata. Metaphor and analogy thus play a role developmentally. They play a similar role in the adult when there is a question of shifting from the nonverbal to the verbal modes of expression and the reverse.

Spatial metaphors are useful in constructing a model or picture of the mind as it is experienced because spatial representations are a fundamental form of mental activity on which more refined abstractions are constructed. Metaphors, too, are a type of abstraction. It may be that one does not need the spatial model and metaphors to represent the mind, but if one is to have a model of mental activity at all, it will have to be derived from some manifest or covert metaphor (Freud, 1920, p. 60).

Rather than being methods of reduction, metaphor and analogies construct new ideas. Creating a metaphor or an analogy is one way to shift one's point of view. Metaphors are, in a sense, an example of the multiple view point method insofar as they actually abstract properties from one context and discover them in another. The abstract language of psychoanalytic theory, as I've tried to show, has concrete referents in the organization of clinical concepts. Multiplicity of metaphors means multiplicity of viewpoints. The common properties alluded to by different metaphors and analogies point to an underlying model, a kind of "deep structure" of implied theory.

Freud was explicit in his repeated use of the spatial model, and, in addition, used spatial imagery at other times. The repeated use of the same imagery, metaphors, and analogies in different contexts points to connections among various aspects of mental functioning as described by the model. By repeating particular words, phrases, forms of argument and exposition, spatial imagery, and metaphors, Freud both constructed a model and evokes it in the mind of the reader. Perhaps, at the present time, an unrecognized danger in the use of metaphor is that our recognition of Freud's evocative use of rhetoric may obscure the model it creates.

When Freud described "verbal bridges" (1900) and "switch words" (1905b) in dreams and neurosis, he was referring to something similar to his own repetition of certain key words, phrases and so on in different kinds of theoretical formulations. That is, the repeated elements are similar to the nodal points in the model of memory organization and free association. Used in theory construction, these verbal devices impart to Freud's narrative the observed similarity to the organization of mind that they describe. Where propositions of differing content are given similar form, and identical words are used in different descriptions, the elements of language may function as "thing representations" in addition to conveying their ordinary meanings (cf. Jakobson & Pomorska, 1983). The words themselves—apart from their meaning—and the form—apart from its content—thus become concrete representatives of one formulation in another.[19] In this way, two descriptions or explanations become analogues created on the same fundamental model and connected by their similar principles of organization. The two narratives are joined and anchored, like the links in a chain of associations of the model itself.

An essential aspect of the point of view presented here is that the function of Freud's model is to transcend the limitations of conventional distinctions—including mind and body. Utilizing the concept of boundaries, the model unites the multiple modalities of perception and modes of expression, verbal and nonverbal, within a single framework, not limited to the requirements of any particular mode. Speaking metaphorically, it creates its own conceptual space within which the relationships among disparate modes can be explored. Formal similarities in action and thought, such as the similarities between compulsive acts and obsessional thoughts, can be considered to be related by translation (cf. Mahony's [1986, pp. 206–208] discussion of a passage from the Rat Man case [Freud, 1909]).

Freud's use of metaphors and analogies has long been disparaged as a rhetorical device masquerading as theory. I have emphasized instead the role of these rhetorical devices in constructing a model dealing with thought, behavior and self-reflection.

SUMMARY AND CONCLUSIONS

In this chapter, I have tried to show that Freud constructed a hierarchical recursive model of the mind as it is explored in psychoanalysis by a self-analyzing analyst and a freely associating patient. Within this model, both the metapsychology, that is, the general formulations of mind, and some aspects of clinical interaction and of development are organized by the same model. I have not discussed the further possibilities of psychoanalytic theory beyond this model nor other parts of the theory that do and do not fit within this model. Other advantages and limitations imposed by using this model, either alone or simultaneously with other models, remain to be explored.

Freud attempted to present a theory of the mind that was supported by observation. He wanted it to be a special theory of the mind that could make a contribution to other fields and take its place alongside other sciences. In doing this, Freud had a great deal to say about other fields of inquiry as he tried to articulate them with psychoanalytic observation. In addition, he needed a theory that would account for the findings of the psychoanalytic method for studying inner experience. However, in view of the vulnerability of the psychoanalytic method to the intrusion of the analyst's subjectivity, his theory had to account for the way this subjective factor could at least be modified by analysis and self-analysis.

Thus, although Freud and analysts since Freud have included many kinds of issues and interests in psychoanalytic psychology, we might speak of the psychoanalytic method and theory as addressing a core issue. This issue is the effort to describe the analyst's use of his or her self-observation as a tool in the study of his or her patients and their self-observations. Clinical interpretation tests the picture of the mind that is created. Psychoanalysis, in this sense, is about the way people try to understand one another in ordinary interaction as distinguished from laboratory experiments.

Freud's development of a method that systematically treated one's own mental life as one treated that of others was unique as a way of arriving at a picture of the mind. I emphasize "systematically" because according to Freud's theory, this process, acting automatically and unconsciously, is the usual way that ideas of one's own and others' mental life develop. Therefore, there is also something unique in the way we as analysts learn about this picture of the mind and go about modifying it, so long as we use the same method. This method and the picture of mental organization that it presents (our theory) find their special relevance in relation to the processes involved in self-exploration through analytic dialogue, whatever other value they may have.

Freud's writings describe his mind creating psychoanalytic theory. We might think of the metapsychology of "chapter 7" (Freud, 1900) as a representation of the *process* of Freud's self-analysis, a complement to the way the contents of *The Interpretation of Dreams* (Freud, 1900) present the *contents* of his self-analysis.

Freud's extensive use of the model described here, the issues of its integration with other models, and its close connection with self-reflection in the foundations of psychoanalytic theory may contribute to some problems within and at the boundaries of psychoanalysis. These factors may account for some of the difficulty of formulating hypotheses for testing outside analysis, and for the special ways analysts use data from outside their field.

NOTES

Earlier versions of this chapter were presented to The Michigan Psychoanalytic Society, March 12, 1988; to the Columbia Psychoanalytic Clinic for Training and Research and the Association for Psychoanalytic Medicine as the Sandor Rado Lecture, June 7, 1988; and to The Psychoanalytic Institute at New York University as the Maurice R. Friend Lecture, October 12, 1989. The author wishes to express his gratitude to the many thoughtful colleagues who have given discussions, criticisms, and suggestions on earlier versions of this chapter. I am especially grateful to Drs. Gerald I. Fogel, Donald M. Kaplan, and Roy Schafer for their patient, challenging, and detailed responses to various drafts. In addition to his comments on the chapter, Dr. Otto Kernberg helped to clarify the German texts.

1. For a modern echo of Freud (1891, pp. 53–56), see Kosslyn (1988):

Perhaps the most fundamental insight of contemporary cognitive science is the discovery that mental faculties can be decomposed into multicomponent information-processing systems. Although mental faculties such as "memory," "thinking," "imagery," and so on intuitively may seem to be single abilities, they are not. . . . Visual mental imagery is being analyzed into distinct processing components and . . . these functionally characterized components are coming to be identified with brain structures. (p. 1621)

The point being made here is not that Freud was right, since his comments certainly do not do justice to the problem. However, they support the principle that carefully describing a functional organization is a prerequisite to correlation.

2. Compare this with a quote from H. Lotze, a philosopher admired by Meynert, from Lotze's 1856 work, *Microcosmus*:

However far we pursue the course of the sense-excitation through the nerve, in however many ways we suppose its form changed and converted into ever finer and more delicate movements, we can never prove that it is in the nature of any movement so produced to cease as movement of its own accord, and to reappear as a bright color, a tone, as a sweet taste. The chasm is never bridged over between the last state of the material elements within our reach and the first rise of the sensation. (quoted in Ladd, 1895)

3. This description of the relationship between the physiological and the psychical is repeated in similar language for unconscious and conscious in Freud (1940, pp. 196–197).

4. Compare this with Freud (1915c, pp. 174–175), where the systems Ucs. and Cs. can be thought of as belonging to the series of systems just mentioned. On those pages, Freud considers the question of whether the transposition of an idea from the Ucs. to the Cs. involves a second registration. He returns to the question of the relationship between the mental apparatus and anatomy, stating that such relations exist. However, he adds that the different parts of the brain have unequal importance in relation to different parts of the body and to different mental activities, so that the localization of ideas, mental processes, excitations, and consciousness is not possible. His discussion is a slightly altered echo of his words in *On Aphasia*. He adds that "Our psychical topography . . . has reference not to anatomical localities, but to regions in the mental apparatus" (1915c p. 175). Moreover, "our hypotheses set out to be no more than graphic illustrations" (p. 175). His final conclusion on the double registration problem is important for my later discussion: The relationship between the Ucs. and the Cs. involves the introduction of words to the idea of the object in the second system (1915c, p. 201).

5. The historian of science Robert M. Young (1970) says, speaking of Herbert Spencer's influence:

His theory of psychophysical parallelism, through Jackson's "Law of Concomitance," provided the form of Freud's psychoanalytic theory and provided the position which Freud held on the mind-body problem from his first work (*On Aphasia*, 1891) to his last (*Outline of Psychoanalysis*, 1940). This aspect of relations among Spencer, Jackson, and Freud should be pursued as part of a more general study of the central role psychophysical parallelism has played in the history of neurology, psychiatry, and psychoanalysis. (p. 196)

6. Many of the writers on aphasia at that time used spatial diagrams resembling flow charts to describe the interruption of postulated brain pathways. Freud used similar diagrams to illustrate the idea of mental topography and to picture mental functions, both concurrent (synchronic) and temporally ordered (diachronic), as having the same overall organization, despite changing conditions and content, symbolic or concrete. This mode of conceptualization allowed for the pictorial representation of mental function along the lines of the hierarchical organization proposed by H. Jackson for the nervous system and by Spencer for all biological systems.

7. Freud's occasional statements regarding the relationship between his spatial model of the mental apparatus and physiological space show instructive uses of representation as a replacement for mechanism.

   Freud (1905a) says that "cathexis of psychical paths"—with displacement of energy and persistence of traces of psychic processes—is not the same thing as cells and neurons but would have to be represented in them. This important statement suggests that at least one relationship of the organization of the mind to the organization of the brain is representation. It is evident that "what is represented in what" is a question of point of view. In this case, reduction and representation coincide (pp. 147–148).

   Freud (1915c) asserts: "Our psychical topography has for the present nothing to do with anatomy, it has reference not to anatomical localities, but to regions in the mental apparatus, wherever they may be situated in the body" (p. 175).

   Freud (1939) states: "The psychical topography that I have developed here has nothing to do with the anatomy of the brain, and actually only touches it at one point. . . . Of the phenomenon of consciousness we can at least say that it was originally attached to perception" (p. 97). The remainder of this paragraph and the next show Freud working out his outline of the hierarchy, beginning with sensation, adding the sensory contents of seen and spoken words to unconscious processes to arrive at preconscious and conscious thought, proceeding to speculation on the "translations" between systems occurring with very early trauma, conditions in animals, and finally the way innate factors—"elements with a phylogenetic origin"—operate.

8. A similar, though less elaborate, account of memory and association can be found in "The Aetiology of Hysteria" (1896, pp. 198–199). The memories in cross-linked chains of associations, with their convergence and divergence through nodal points were compared to a genealogical tree that includes intermarriages. Freud offers, in addition, an elaborate archeological analogy, to which he returned on other occasions (i.e., 1901, 1930).

   Freud's description on the pages 288 to 290 of *Studies on Hysteria* (Breuer & Freud, 1895) resembles Hofstadter's (1979) description of "recursive transition networks" (pp. 131ff).

9. Freud asserted:

As a result of the diphasic onset of object-choice, and the interposition of the barrier against incest, the final object of the sexual instinct is never any longer the original object but only a surrogate for it. Psychoanalysis has shown that when the original object of a wishful impulse has been lost as a result of repression, it is frequently represented (*vertreten*) by an endless series of substitutive objects (*Ersatzobjekten*) none of which, however, brings full satisfaction. (1912, p. 189; cf. 1910d, pp. 168, 169–170. Freud [1920, p. 42] adds a quantitative dimension.)

10. The following passages from Freud (1900) are close to the language of their source: Freud (1891). They display the transformation appropriate to the "new transcription" of a "new epoch" of theory formation:

Each of the elements of the dream's content turns out to have been "overdetermined" – to have been represented in the dream-thoughts many times over. (1900, p. 283)

Not only are the elements of a dream determined by the dream-thoughts many times over, but the individual dream-thoughts are represented in the dream by several elements. Associative paths lead from one element of the dream to several dream thoughts, and from one dream thought to several elements of the dream. (1900, p. 284)

The elements which stand out as the principal components of the manifest content of the dream are far from playing the same part in the dream thoughts. And . . . what is clearly the essence of the dream thoughts need not be represented in the dream at all. (1900, p. 305)

Here and elsewhere in the same work, we can hear the echo of his earlier words:

The periphery of the body is contained in the cerebral cortex not point by point, but through selected fibres. (1891, p. 51)

They contain the body periphery . . . in a completely different arrangement . . . in manifold associations of the individual elements, whereby some may be represented several times, others not at all. (1891, p. 53)

11. A complete account of Freud's continuing use of his model would have to include a review of his papers on anxiety neurosis. Those papers discussed the relationship between the somatic and the mental libido in ways that retained a number of features of the earlier body–brain–mind model. These precursors of the later formulations of drive theory already involved the mental control of bodily functions. Mental activity had the function of "working over" the excitation generated somatically.

Even Freud's formulation of the dual instinctual drive theory (1920) can be shown to be conceptualized according to the same ideas. The concept of the repetition compulsion addresses the biological aspect of the impulsion of the drives and their attachment to objects and their representations. Later, in summarizing the dual drive theory, Freud (1940) added to the hierarchy: "The analogy of our two basic instincts extends from the sphere of living things to the pair of opposing forces— attraction and repulsion—which rule in the inorganic world" (p. 149). The hierarchy now extends from the atom to the instinctual drives.

12. In other places, Freud spoke of the instinct as a "psychical representative of organic forces" and as "the psychical representative of an endosomatic, continuously flowing source of stimulation." (See editor's note to Freud, 1915a, p. 112)

13. There is an important issue that coannot be discussed here. The *theory* is constructed by translating things experienced into the language of perception. In a parallel fashion, the resulting theory conceptualizes *development and experience* as processes of translation.

14. The following quotations give the hierarchy and boundary relationships: body–id–symptoms–ego–external world–that is, external to the person.

> Psychoanalysis acts as an intermediary between biology and psychology. (1913, p. 182)

> As a frontier creature [*Grenzwesen*], the ego tries to mediate between the world and the id. . . . In point of fact it behaves like the physician during an analytic treatment. (1923, p. 56)

> We picture it [the id] as being open at its end to somatic influences, and as there taking up into itself instinctual needs which find their psychical expression in it. (1933, p. 73)

> The transference thus creates an intermediate region between illness and real life through which the transition from one to the other is made. (1914b, p. 154)

> Symptoms are derived from the repressed, they are, as it were, its representatives [*Vertreter*] before the ego; but the repressed is foreign territory to the ego–internal foreign territory–just as reality (if you will forgive the expression) is external foreign territory. (1933, p. 57)

15. A similar statement is found in Freud (1925):

> Clear basic concepts and sharply drawn definitions are only possible in the mental sciences in so far as the latter seek to fit a region of facts into the frame of a logical system. In the natural sciences, of which psychology is one, such clear-cut general concepts are superfluous and indeed impossible. Zoology and Botany did not start from correct and adequate definitions of an animal and a plant; to this very day biology has been unable to give any certain meaning to the concept of life. Physics itself, indeed, would never have made any advance if it had had to wait until its concepts of matter, force, gravitation, and so on, had reached the desirable degree of clarity and precision. The basic ideas or most general concepts in any of the disciplines of science are always left indeterminate at first and are only explained to begin with by reference to the realm of phenomena from which they were derived; it is only by means of a progressive analysis of the material of observation that they can be made clear and can find a significant and consistent meaning.

See Freud (1900, p. 536) for a similar account of models and provisional ideas in theory construction.

16. Freud (1915b) asserted:

> The extraordinary intricacy of all the factors to be taken into consideration leaves only one way of presenting them open to us. We must select first one and then another point of view, and follow it up through the material as long as the application of it seems to yield results. Each separate treatment of the subject will be incomplete in itself, and there cannot fail to be obscurities where it touches upon material that has not yet been treated; but we may hope that a final synthesis will lead to a proper understanding. (pp. 157-158)

17. Many writers have discussed related ideas in a somewhat different way. The phenomenon is also familiar in clinical situations where a patient describing a situation may enact what is being described or tell it in a form that carries some of the features of the events described. This is an impressive aspect of the redundancy of modalities and representations in communication.

18. A calligram is a poem written in a form that gives a picture of its subject. Foucault (1982) writes:

> The calligram has a triple role: to augment the alphabet, to repeat something without the aid of rhetoric, to trap things in a double cipher. . . . It lodges statements in the space of a shape, and makes the text say what the drawing represents. On the one hand, it alphabetizes the ideogram, populates it with discontinuous letters, and thus interrogates the silence of uninterrupted lines. (pp. 20–21)

It seems that some aspects of the form of Freud's propositions about the mental apparatus provide a map of the organization within which the words describing it are contained, as a description of the alphabet would contain the alphabet.

Words have two functions, at least. One is to offer linear logical scrutiny of experience. This is a commonplace descriptive use. Another use is to convey meaning also by the way thoughts are organized verbally—rhetorical devices, embedded stories and clauses such as this one—or the way the argument or conception is organized, and the choice of particular words for their evocative quality rather than their denotative value alone. These ways of using words are a type of indirect representation in which the concrete aspects of words and organization serve as icons because the perceptual aspects of words and organization are added to the formulation. This enriches the meaning. From the combination of the various ways of using language we can extract a picture of the organization of mind that the words' literal meaning alone can only awkwardly express. The purpose of words used in this iconic way is to represent something that is more easily expressed in a spatial form (cf. Foucault, 1970).

19. A deliberate literary use of the same method is found in James Joyce's *Ulysses*. In the section often referred to as "The Sirens," Joyce presents a series of subepisodes within the main narrative. In each subepisode, phrases appear that belong to other episodes, not to the main narrative. These jarring, inappropriate phrases belong to the action of the other episodes and thus indicate the simultaneity of two events. The whole section is in fact preceded by a presentation of these phrases, the whole list serving as an overture to the section in deliberate analogy to a piece of music.

REFERENCES

Arlow, J. A. (1979). Metaphor and the psychoanalytic situation. *Psychoanalytic Quarterly, 48*, 363–385.

Boyd, R. (1979). Metaphor and theory change: What is "metaphor" a metaphor for? In A. Ortony (Ed.), *Metaphor and thought* (pp. 136–408). Cambridge, England: Cambridge University Press.

Breuer, J., & Freud, S. (1895). Studies on hysteria. *Standard Edition* (Vol. 2, pp. 1–309). London: Hogarth Press.

Canning, J. W. (1966). *A logical analysis of criticisms directed at Freudian psychoanalytic theory*. Unpublished doctoral dissertation, University of Michigan Dissertation Information Service, Ann Arbor, MI.

Davidson, D. (1978). What metaphors mean. In M. Johnson (Ed.), *Philosophical perspectives on metaphor* (pp. 200–220). Minneapolis: University of Minnesota Press, 1981.

Derrida, J. (1978). Legs de Freud. *Études Freudiennes*, nos. 13–14, 87–125.

Eco, U. (1986). *Semiotics and the philosophy of language*. Bloomington: Indiana University Press.

Edelheit, H. (1969). Speech and psychic structure. *Journal of the American Psychoanalytic Association, 17*, 381–412.

Edelheit, H. (1978). On the biology of language: Darwinian/Lamarckian homology in human inheritance (with some thoughts about the Lamarckianism of Freud). *Psychiatry and the Humanities, 3*, 45–74.

Einstein, A. (1914). Inaugural address to the Prussian Academy of Sciences. In *Essays in science* (A. Harris, Trans, pp. 6–10). New York: Philosophical Library, 1934.

Einstein, A. (1934). On the method of theoretical physics. In *Essays in science* (A. Harris, Trans.). New York: Philosophical Library.

Einstein, A. (1936). Physics and reality. In *Out of my later years* (pp. 59–97). Secaucus: The Citadel Press, 1956.

Erdelyi, M. H. (1985). *Psychoanalysis: Freud's cognitive psychology*. New York: Freeman.

Feyerabend, P. (1987). Creativity—a dangerous myth. *Critical Inquiry, 13*(4), 700–711.

Forrester, J. (1980). *Language and the origins of psychoanalysis*. New York: Columbia University Press.

Foucault, M. (1970). *The order of things*. New York: Pantheon.

Foucault, M. (1982). *This is not a pipe*. Berkeley: University of California Press.

Freud, S. (1887–1904). Letter of December 6, 1896. In J. M. Masson (Ed.), *The Complete letters of Sigmund Freud to Wilhelm Fliess, 1887–1904* (pp. 207–208). Cambridge, MA: Belknap Press, 1985.

Freud, S. (1891). *On aphasia* (E. Stengel, Trans.). New York: International Universities Press, 1953.

Freud, S. (1893). Some points for a comparative study of organic and hysterical motor paralyses. *Standard Edition* (Vol. 1, pp.155–172). London: Hogarth Press, 1966.

Freud, S. (1895). Psychology for neurologists. *Standard Edition* (Vol. 1, pp. 283–387). London: Hogarth Press, 1966.

Freud, S. (1896). The aetiology of hysteria. *Standard Edition* (Vol. 3, pp. 191–221). London: Hogarth Press, 1962.

Freud, S. (1898). The psychical mechanism of forgetfulness. *Standard Edition* (Vol. 3, pp. 289–297). London: Hogarth Press, 1962.

Freud, S. (1900). The interpretation of dreams. *Standard Edition* (Vols. 4 & 5, pp. 1–338, 339–625). London: Hogarth Press, 1958.

Freud, S. (1901). The psychopathology of everyday life. *Standard Edition* (Vol. 6, pp. 1–290). London: Hogarth Press, 1960.

Freud, S. (1905a). Fragment of an analysis of a case of hysteria. *Standard Edition* (Vol. 7, pp. 1–122). London: Hogarth Press, 1953.

Freud, S. (1905b). Jokes and their relation to the unconscious. *Standard Edition* (Vol. 8 pp. 9–236). London: Hogarth Press, 1960.

Freud, S. (1909). Notes on a case of obsessional neurosis. *Standard Edition* (Vol. 10, pp. 155–318). London: Hogarth Press, 1955.

Freud, S. (1910a). Five lectures on psycho-analysis. *Standard Edition* (Vol. 11, pp. 9–55). London: Hogarth Press, 1957.

Freud, S. (1910b). A special type of object choice made by men. *Standard Edition* (Vol. 11, pp. 165–175). London: Hogarth Press, 1957.

Freud, S. (1911). The handling of dream-interpretation in psycho-analysis. *Standard Edition* (Vol. 12, pp. 91–96). London: Hogarth Press, 1958.

Freud, S. (1912). On the universal tendency to debasement in the sphere of love. *Standard Edition* (Vol. 11, pp. 179–190). London: Hogarth Press, 1957.

Freud, S. (1913). The claims of psycho-analysis to scientific interest. *Standard Edition* (Vol. 13, pp. 165–190). London: Hogarth Press, 1955.

Freud, S. (1914). Remembering, repeating and working through. *Standard Edition* (Vol. 12, pp. 145–156). London: Hogarth Press, 1958.

Freud, S. (1915a). Instincts and their vicissitudes. *Standard Edition* (Vol. 14, pp. 109–140). London: Hogarth Press, 1957.

Freud, S. (1915b). Repression. *Standard Edition* (Vol. 14, pp. 141–158). London: Hogarth Press, 1957.

Freud, S. (1915c). The Unconscious. *Standard Edition* (Vol. 14, pp. 159–204). London: Hogarth Press, 1957.

Freud, S. (1916–1917). Introductory lectures on psycho-analysis. *Standard Edition* (Vols. 15 & 16, pp. 9–239, 243–463). London: Hogarth Press, 1963.

Freud, S. (1917). On transformations of instinct as exemplified in anal erotism. *Standard Edition* (Vol. 17, pp. 127–133). London: Hogarth Press, 1955.

Freud, S. (1920). Beyond the pleasure principle. *Standard Edition* (Vol. 18, pp. 7–64). London: Hogarth Press, 1955.

Freud, S. (1923). The ego and the id. *Standard Edition* (Vol. 19, 12–66). London: Hogarth Press, 1961.

Freud, S. (1924). The economic problem of masochism. *Standard Edition* (Vol. 19, pp. 159–170). London: Hogarth Press, 1961.

Freud, S. (1925). An autobiographical study. *Standard Edition* (Vol. 20, pp. 7–74). London: Hogarth Press, 1959.

Freud, S. (1930). Civilization and its discontents. *Standard Edition* (Vol. 21, pp. 64–145). London: Hogarth Press, 1961.

Freud, S. (1933). New introductory lectures on psychoanalysis. *Standard Edition* (Vol. 22, pp. 5–182). London: Hogarth Press, 1964.

Freud, S. (1939). Moses and monotheism. *Standard Edition* (Vol. 23, pp. 7–137). London: Hogarth Press, 1964.

Freud, S. (1940). An outline of psychoanalysis. *Standard Edition* (Vol. 23, pp. 144–207). London: Hogarth Press, 1964.

Freud, S. (1941). Findings, ideas, problems. *Standard Edition* (Vol. 23, pp. 299–300). London: Hogarth Press, 1964.

Grossman, W. I. (1986). Freud and Horney: A study of psychoanalytic models via the analysis of a controversy. In A. D. Richards & M. S. Willick (Eds.), *Psychoanalysis: The science of mental conflict* (pp. 65–87). Hillsdale, NJ: Analytic Press.

Grossman, W. I., & Simon, B. (1969). Anthropomorphism: Motive, meaning, and causality in psychoanalytic theory. *Psychoanalytic Study of the Child, 24,* 78–111.

Hartmann, H., Kris, E., & Loewenstein, R. M. (1946). Comments on the formation of psychic structure. *Psychoanalytic Study of the Child, 2,* 11–38.

Hofstadter, D. R. (1979). *Goedel, Escher, Bach: An eternal golden braid.* New York: Vintage, 1980.

Holt, R. R. (1964). A review of some of Freud's biological assumptions and their influence on his theories. In N. S. Greenfield & W. C. Lewis (Eds.), *Psychoanalysis and current biological thought* (pp. 93–124). Madison: University of Wisconsin Press.

Holt, R. R. (1972). Freud's mechanistic and humanistic images of man. *Psychoanalysis and Contemporary Science, 1,* 3–24.

Jakobson, R., & Pomorska, K. (1983). *Dialogues.* Cambridge, MA: MIT Press.

Johnson, M. (1981). *Philosophical perspectives on metaphor.* Minneapolis: University Minnesota Press.

Kanzer, M. (1973). Two prevalent misconceptions about Freud's "Project" (1895). *Annual of Psychoanalysis, 1,* 88–103.

Kaplan, D. M. (1988). The psychoanalysis of art: Some ends, some means. *Journal of the American Psychoanalytic Association, 36,* 258–293.

Kaplan, D. M. (1990). Some theoretical and technical aspects of gender and social reality in clinical psychoanalysis. *Psychoanalytic Study of the Child, 45,* 3–24.

Kittay, E. F. (1987). *Metaphor: Its cognitive force and linguistic structure.* Oxford: Clarendon Library of Logic and Philosophy. Oxford University Press.

Kosslyn, S. M. (1988). Aspects of a cognitive neuroscience of mental imagery. *Science, 240,* 1621–1626.

Ladd, G. T. (1895). *Philosophy of mind: An essay in the metaphysics of psychology.* New York: Scribner's. Reprint. New York: AMS Press, 1983.

Levin, K. (1978). *Freud's early psychology of the neuroses: A historical perspective.* Pittsburgh: University of Pittsburgh Press.

Mahony, P. J. (1986). *Freud and the rat man.* New Haven: Yale University Press.

Mahony, P. J. (1987). *Freud as a writer.* New Haven: Yale University Press.

Mancia, M. (1983). Archaeology of Freudian thought and the history of neurophysiology. *International Review of Psycho-Analysis, 10*(2), 185–192.

Marshall, J. C. (1974). Freud's psychology of language. In R. Wollheim (Ed.), *Philosophers on Freud: New evaluations* (pp. 349–365). New York: Aronson.

Marx, O. M. (1967). Freud and aphasia: An historical analysis. *American Journal of Psychiatry, 124,* 815–825.

Miller, G. A. (1979). Images and models, similes and metaphors. In A. Ortney (Ed.), *Metaphor and thought* (pp. 202–250). Cambridge, England: Cambridge University Press.

Ortony, A. (1979). *Metaphor and thought.* Cambridge, England: Cambridge University Press.

Rizzuto, A.-M. (1989). A hypothesis about Freud's motive for writing the monograph "On Aphasia." *International Journal of Psycho-Analysis, 16,* 111–118.

Rizzuto, A.-M. (1990). The origins of Freud's concept of object representation ("Objektvorstellung") in his monograph "On Aphasia": Its theoretical and technical importance. *International Journal of Psycho-Analysis, 71,* 241–248.

Rubinstein, B. B. (1972). On metaphor and related phenomena. *Psychoanalytic Contemporary Science, 1,* 70–108.

Schafer, R. (1968). *Aspects of internalization.* New York: International Universities Press.

Schafer, R. (1976). *A new language for psychoanalysis.* New Haven: Yale University Press.

Schafer, R. (1977). The interpretation of transference and the conditions for loving. *Journal of the American Psychoanalytic Association, 25,* 335–362.

Schafer, R. (1980). Narration in the psychoanalytic dialogue. *Critical Inquiry, 7*(1), 21–53.

Solms, M. and Saling, M. (1986). On psychoanalysis and neuroscience: Freud's attitude to the localizationist tradition. *International Journal of Psycho-Analysis, 67*(4), 397–416.

Stengel, E. (1954). A re-evaluation of Freud's book "On Aphasia": Its significance for psycho-analysis. *International Journal of Psycho-Analysis, 35*(2), 85–89.

Stoppard, T. (1989). Double agents: Espionage and the uncertainty principle. *The Sciences, 29*(5), 36–37.

Wurmser, L. (1977). A defense of the use of metaphor in psychoanalytic theory construction. *Psychoanalytic Quarterly, 46,* 466–498.

Young, R. M. (1970). *Mind, brain and adaptation in the nineteenth century: Cerebral localization and its biological context from Gall to Ferrier.* Clarendon Library of Logic and Philosophy. Oxford: Oxford University Press.

7

Human Development and Organizing Principles

JOSEPH D. LICHTENBERG

Mr. T had attained high scores on his LSATs but was in danger of failing law school. After graduating from college he had spent two years living with his family while he daydreamed about being a rock music star. He knew the name of every popular rock band, the musicians in each, who had switched from one to another, and the gossip about their lives. He had problems in a variety of areas and was diagnosed as borderline. After a period of treatment in his home city, he was accepted to law school and began treatment with me. During one hour I asked him to give me details about a law school problem with which he was having difficulty. He told me the fact pattern—a man had an automobile accident in a state in which he was not a resident, and so on. The problem was to determine what laws applied to the case. The decision about the law depended on the jurisdiction in which the case would be tried. That in turn depended on a particular principle of law governing interstate matters. When he provided me with all this information in response to my questions, I summarized the problem through a sequence of governing principles. He instantly comprehended and was furious. How could I, who knew nothing about law, solve the problem while he couldn't. This was a repeat of narcissistic in-juries he had received all his life when others no smarter than he, often clearly less smart, could learn and he couldn't. After he became calm, I suggested that maybe he had a serious learning difficulty, an inability to arrange information in hierarchies of in-creasing or decreasing significance. He acknowledged that while he could absorb huge quantities of linear information—narratives about people—he could never make a successful outline. With these organizers, he could compensate for his learning deficit.

I relate this vignette to indicate the enormous handicap for an individual (or a science) to be unable to conceptualize a hierarchical order of significance. But where does hierarchical ordering lie in the multitude of factors that govern human development? That is the theme of this chapter.

To conceptualize the development of human experience and motivation, I have advocated the use of a system approach (see also Rosenblatt, 1984; Rosenblatt & Thickstun, 1977; Stern, 1985). Following Sameroff (1983) I regard a developmental system as evidencing four attributes or properties: self-organizing, self-stabilizing, dialectic tension, and hierarchical arrangement. Guided by information gleaned from infant research and observation and from clinical experience, I have identified five motivational systems, each developing in response to a basic need: the need for psychic regulation of physiological requirements, the need for attachment and later affiliation, the need for exploration and assertion, the need to respond aversively through antagonism and/or withdrawal, and the need for sensual enjoyment and sexual excitement. Each motivational system would have as *one* of its properties a hierarchical arrangement of its components or modes of operating. But what about the relationships between systems? I will indicate that between motivational systems we can easily observe dialectic tensions and shifting dominance, that is hierarchical arrangements and rearrangements. And as if that is not enough complexity, we must answer the question: Does a higher level of integration exist, one that continually works to organize and stabilize dialectic tensions and hierarchical shifts between the five motivational systems? Such an integrative capacity, for which I borrow the concept of self (Kohut, 1971, 1977) or self-organization (Gedo, 1979, 1984, 1986), would constitute another hierarchical organizer.

To illustrate the complex relationships between hierarchies and other organizing principles, I will select one motivational system, the exploratory–assertive system. I will describe in detail the formation and properties of the exploratory–assertive system as it self-organizes, self-stabilizes, responds to dialectic tensions, and forms hierarchical alignments. I will only refer to the other motivational systems.

THE EXPLORATORY–ASSERTIVE MOTIVATIONAL SYSTEM

Self-organizing

Sander (1975, 1980) tracked infants through 24-hour cycles, noting their state changes from crying to alert wakeful to quiet wakeful to fussy to REM and non-REM sleep. He noted an "open space" that occurred when physiological requirements were satisfied (that is, the babies were neither hungry, eliminating, cold, or needing sleep) and their mothers were not engaged with them in attachment play (for example, eye contact or vocalization). Babies fill these open spaces in the daily cycles with spontaneously occurring exploratory activities. They eye scan and appear to work to bring objects into focus. They attempt to grasp objects near at hand. They use their mouth as an organ of exploration. These observations support the contention that exploration of the environment is spontaneous, that is, it is an activation of an innate neurophysiological system. Other observations lend further support. It was found empirically that of all the positions in which one can hold a somewhat fussy infant, the position that seemed most effective for calming is the front of the baby's body pressed against the adult's shoulder, the baby's head held firmly above the shoulder. Why? Is it a matter of equilibrium? Or of body closeness? The answer seems to lie in the baby's eyes. The infants use the propped position to scan and thus to "turn on" exploratory motivation. As another example, babies in the midst of feeding may become fussy because of gas. The baby is propped, patted, and burped, the fussiness disappearing because of the physiological relief of the air bubble. But often babies stop fussing before the air bubble is released. Again the answer is that in the propped position the infant undergoes a brief shift of state from physiological distress to exploratory interest via eye scanning. Parents intuitively will try to calm distressed infants by offering them a rattle, toy, or finger to "distract" them, actually to use the object to activate exploratory activity and the calming effect that is triggered by it.

The triggering for a self-organizing motivation may arise internally or from an external stimulus. Frequently an internally evoked exploratory pattern will activate spontaneously when conditions are opportune, when an "open space" exists. An externally evoked exploratory pattern will be activated by any object that arouses interest (in Dr. Seuss's words, "A shovel is to dig"). The experiential side of self-organizing lies in a remarkable double aspect of emergence. One aspect lies in the emergence of perceptual clarity as the infant's sensory skills (visual, auditory, tactile) and their cross-modal information processing form a perception of a face, a hand crossing the midline, or a mobile. This emergence is akin in very simplified form to the sense one has in awakening in a strange place such as a foreign hotel room, and gradually focusing on some object in the room as one pulls together the where and when and how of one's situation. The second aspect of emergence lies in the recognition that the baby's own activity brings about the perception. This recognition comes, of course, not from reflective awareness but from feedback information. Proprioceptive feedback tells infants that their moving their head, focusing their eyes, putting an object in their mouth, or grasping is a part of the perceptual event. Further, the activity is innately monitored for consequence. Infants work with the coordination of their muscular, visual, tactile, and proprioceptive mechanisms to get their fingers in their mouth. Fetuses suck for soothing, often sucking their fingers so the experience of that sensual sensation precedes birth. The task after birth of approximating finger and mouth differs because of the lack of resistance of air in comparison to fluid. The arm movements, body hunching, and mouth protrusion are at first discoordinated and overly rapid and flailing. But often within 10 to 11 days babies will accomplish the task. To do so they must track the contingent effect of their sensorimotor activity, learning the needed coordinations and control. Thus, infants' monitoring a contingent effect adds to their sense of agency. They develop awareness of their part in the exploration and assertion of an innate preformed intent (to suck one's fingers). This relatively simple feedback contingent awareness helps to self-organize the exploratory-assertive motivational system at an elementary level. The affect that is triggered by the earliest innate and learned patterns of exploration and assertion is a mood state of interest. The linking of exploratory-assertive activity and the triggered interest is I believe "hard-wired" (Hadley, 1989), but, once experienced, interest becomes a target mood state to be reexperienced, each reexperience consolidating through memory the desirability of the increasingly familiar percep-tual–action–affect state.

Self-stabilizing

While self-organizing of the exploratory–assertive motivational system in the earliest weeks and months originates with the affect state of interest, self-stabilizing occurs with the development of a pattern that triggers the pleasurable affects of efficacy and compe-tence. Self-stabilizing can be illustrated by the Papouseks' (1975) classic experiment in which 4-month-old infants were exposed to 5 seconds of bursts of multicolored light. They oriented themselves toward the stimulus with interest, and then, typical of responses to unvaried stimuli, their orientation diminished after repetition. The experiment was arranged so that when the infants in the course of their movements rotated their head 30 degrees to a predetermined side three times successively within a time interval, the light display was switched on. As soon as the infants turned on the light presentation by their own head movements, their behavior changed dramatically. Their orientation reactions increased in intensity, and they continuously made all kinds of movements to try to switch on the visual stimulation again. To this point, the experiment might have been simply a proof of classic conditioning of stimulus–reward response. But the Papouseks then made a significant observation. They found that the infants, after a few successes, would leave their heads turned 90 degrees even though the lights were to be seen in midline. Furthermore, the infants did not seem to be watching. Nonetheless, they continued to turn on the display and responded to their success with smiles and happy bubbling.

What was the source of the pleasure? The source of pleasure lay not in problem solving alone (for example, the discovery of a contingency between two external events) but in the pleasure derived from the infant's awareness that he himself or she herself had produced the result. A sense of efficacy and pleasure is experienced when the infant recognizes "a contingent relationship between one's own initially spontaneous behavior and an event in the external world and the subsequent ability to produce at will the external event through repetition of the antecedent act" (Broucek, 1979, p. 312). The infant in these experiments was motivated not by exploration alone (that is, by the discovery of the connection between two external events) nor by assertion alone (that is, random then purposefully directed movements) but by a combination of the two. Problem solving by exploration and assertion together triggers the pleasure that comes from a sense of efficacy and competence.

In moments of disengagement from physiological need and attachment activities, "the conditions are optimal for infants to differentiate effects contingent on their own initiative. The experience of contingent effects has a profound impact on the alerting and focusing of infant attention" (Sander, 1983, pp. 98–99). Sander attributed the profound and highly personal impact of these developments to the richness of individual selectivity or option that occurs. By virtue of the self-organization of the exploratory-assertive motivational system, the infants are able to initiate new behavioral organizations that have "the qualities of 'real' and of 'own'" (p. 99). The affective marker for this experience lies in competence and efficacy pleasure. Expressed in the language of later life, this might be: I can recognize it, I can match it, I make it go on or off; I have discovered it, I have altered it; and so on, exploration being closer to the "Aha!" of insight and assertion being closer to power and mastery.

A sense of competence would appear to result from the infants' being able to reproduce the experience of a desired state. Innate and quickly learned patterns of response to preferred stimuli trigger affects of interest and surprise. Novelty and detection of contingent effects prolong states of attentive arousal. As the state of aroused attentive alertness consolidates, infants can be inferred to experience, along with interest and surprise, a quality of "aliveness" quite different from their affective experience during states of physiological need, crying, fussiness, sleepiness, or sleep. Looked at in this way, the exploratory and assertive activity of infants would not be to seek stimuli as such, but to experience the particular affective sense of aliveness of the aroused exploratory state. Competence would then be a measure of infants' ability to organize and regulate their activity to produce a new version of the desired state.

Let me restate this complicated idea more simply. Success is twofold: having a desired "reward," the preferred stimulus of the lights, and having the sense of success at having produced the desire state. This concept presumes that infants have a complex capacity for matching. One matching capacity permits infants to recognize that the external stimulus of the flashing light coincides with an internal criterion for a preferred stimulus. An additional matching capacity employs feedback information and contingency tracking for recognizing that the light display has been activated as a consequence of the infant's own activity. But Sander (1986) proposes another matching capacity, by which infants compare an experiential state they are in with an experiential state that past experience has marked as desired. Recognizing their ability to create the match successfully conveys a sense of competence and pleasure. This conception establishes three sources of motivation: the pleasure to be derived from a preferred stimulus, the pleasure to be derived from being the source of a preferred stimulus, and the pleasure of recreating a previously experienced desired affective experiential state.

The exploratory–assertive motivational system can be said to have become self-stabilized when a basic schema has become established: a need and/or opportunity for exploration and assertion → interest and perceptual–action activity patterns → a sense of pleasure from efficiency and competence. Once stabilized, this schema forms a fundamental motivational pattern that persists throughout life and underlies the infant and toddler activities of practicing (Mahler, 1968) and play, the latency child's learning, the adolescent's experimentation with ideas and careers, the adult's exploration and assertion at work and in recreation, and a host of problem-solving activities including those in dreams.

Throughout life, competence as an outcome of a person's exploratory–assertive motivations is commonly experienced as concordant with the actual, assumed, or fantasied confirmation and approval of others. The sense of competence rapidly becomes entwined with the encouragement and values of caregivers, family and, culture. For example, research studies (Bornstein, 1985) indicate that cognitive competence is the result of not only the infant's information-processing capabilities and maternal encouragement but also the infant and mother's mutual influence of one another. Infants who process information well at 4 months pull their mothers into encouraging them to note more and more properties, objects, and events; mothers who give encouragement stimulate more active interest and provide more opportunity to practice processing. The cogwheel effect at 4 months influences the children's later success at verbal comprehension and the acquisition of vocabulary. Self-stabilizing of the exploratory–assertive system thus involves an intrapsychic schema solidly embedded in the contextual world of relationships with others who provide opportunities for disengaged exploration, who participate in and encourage learning, and who thereby further enliven the sense of efficiency and competence.

Dialectic Tension

Three sources of dialectic tension within the exploratory–assertive motivational system can be identified. (1) Tensions arise in response to choices and preferences, the making and carrying out of plans of a purely personal nature. These are the tensions of achieving internal regulation. (2) Tensions arise when personal choices and preferences collide with the choices and preferences of others. These are the tensions of achieving mutual internal–external regulation. The tensions of internal (self) regulation and of internal–external (self–other) regulation of exploration and assertion may occur at any time throughout life when the exploratory–assertive system is activated. (3) Another source of tension is most apparent when a maturational transition occurs. During periods of important maturational transitions that affect exploration and assertion, tensions arise as the person is torn between maintaining the continuity of one mode of exploratory–assertive activity and beginning to institute an entirely new form of seeking and processing information.

When we consider the genetic programs that contribute to individuality, we can cite innate preferences for sensory modalities for exploring the world around. Infants vary in their predilection for visual, auditory, and tactile processing, that is, for looking at, listening to, grasping, and mouthing. The degree of internal tension stimulated by competing sensory modes is probably relatively minor, especially since the information from each source is processed intermodally. The nature of these small variations in infants can be appreciated when observed in their more dramatic polarities. At one pole are creative types who process visually (artists such as Picasso) and auditorially (musicians such as Mozart). At the other pole are infants whose hypersensitivity to light, sound, or touch may render them unable to tolerate ordinary stimuli. Innate preferences also involve types of stimuli—for example, visual patterns that contain the outline of the human face and others that are abstract but regular, sounds in the higher range, singsong rhythms, textures that are soft and smooth. The tension of choice can be demonstrated experimentally by confronting infants with alternatives in each of these modes and forms. Further minor tensions arise in response to the mode of presentation. If a preferred pattern is repeated at fixed intervals, interest wanes. If a new pattern is introduced, interest reawakens; but if infants have a choice between a familiar pattern and an unfamiliar pattern of equal stimulus potential, they will attend to the familiar. A stimulus too unfamiliar may lead to an aversive reaction. Viewed overall, the innate and learned preferences and the rules about familiarity and novelty that trigger minor dialectic tension make infants prone to explore their own particular environments, that is, the objects and people present become sources of continuing interest.

More dialectic tension in exploration and assertion inevitably arises when the intentions and plans of infants and caregivers must be coordinated. Often their intentions will coincide as when each can play and work separately or when playing together. Inevitably infants will want to explore electric plugs, earrings, and many other items to which parents will object. Infants will not wish to play with toys offered or at times when parents prefer. These situations can generally be managed with only temporary antagonism.

These regulatory exchanges between parents and children utilize inherent dialectic tensions for adaptive learning. Possibly the most significant parent–child exchange is the intuitive feel by a caregiver with a particular child of the need for disengagement to create an "open space" during which optimal self exploratory–assertive activities can progress to competence. Winnicott's (1958) description of the child's ability to be alone in the presence of the other characterizes this state—alone but not lonely, with another but free to be following one's own interest. Caregivers take cognizance of childrens' needing an open space in which to explore on their own and thus develop increased awareness of self-agency, as well as needing the active participation of another. How parents interact intuitively to promote learning has been the subject of many studies (Bornstein, 1985; Papousek, 1986; Stern, 1985). These studies indicate that mothers demonstrate with gesture, facial expression, and through a verbal flow of dialectic instructions what they want their babies to learn to do. Long before the words have conceptual meaning, infants and young toddlers are bathed in a gestural and verbal flow of communication that guides and limits their exploration and assertion. As babies act independently, mothers give responses of rhythmic attunement that encourage the activity and ensure its liveliness. Parents adjust their approach to the maturing child in keeping with changes in the child's potential to master tasks. Often parents stay just a bit ahead of the infant or toddler, encouraging the child to move forward. At the same time, they will monitor the degree of frustration—helping when necessary but not overanticipating and interfering with self-assertion of solutions. Many parents marvel that the solution the child comes to is one they would not have thought of. The point of these observations is that the dialectic tension inherent in choice making and match–mismatch experiences for children, and the tension between the approach and level of cognitive capacity of parents and children, become the dynamic "playground" in which learning takes place through continuing episodes of exploring and asserting of individual preferences.

Hornik, Risenhoover, and Gunnar (1987) investigated the dynamic interplay between children's inclination to explore a toy and assert their preference and the influence of their mother to instruct them. Three groups of 12-month-old children were tested with toys when their mothers displayed by face, voice, and gestures, positive affect, negative disgust, or neutrality and silence. One toy used was a musical Ferris wheel that attracts children. A second toy was a stationary robot that recited facts about outer space in a machine-like voice, which elicited neither strong approach nor avoidance. The third toy was a mechanical, cymbal-clanging monkey that children tend to avoid. The mothers, training to convey negative affect, were told to imagine that the toys were crawling with horrid bugs and to talk about how "yucky" they were. The researchers found that, regardless of the infant's inclination toward the toy itself, if the mother signaled negative disgust, the child treated the toy as aversive.

The researchers asked three questions: Did the child recognize the message as specific to the toy? Are the children more sensitive to negative or positive communications? Did the effect carry over time? Since the infants, given an opportunity for free play after the maternal instruction, did so without an alteration in mood, the researchers reasoned that the children regarded their mothers as delivering specific messages about particular objects and not about play or toys in general. Second, since the infants were more influenced by mothers' registering disgust about otherwise attractive toys than by mothers' registering positive affect (go ahead, it's fun) about the ambiguous robot or the unappealing clanging monkey, the researchers concluded that, in the test situation, infants responded more immediately to being warned off than to being encouraged. Third, the infants were retested with the same toys after a 3-minute break. The mothers were now instructed to be silent and neutral. The infants maintained their aversion to the toys that had been singled out by the mothers as "yucky."

The findings of Hornik et al. indicate that the dynamic tension for children between interest in exploring and asserting preferences or aversive responses can be influenced by maternal reactions, but not evenly. Mothers telling children a toy they might prefer to explore is bad warns them off, but telling the children a toy they don't want to explore is good does not create interest. Interest is an internally self-stabilized affective response.

Dialectic tension becomes painfully apparent when the interactions between infant and parent are persistently misattuned, oppositional, and competitive. Videotapes are painful to watch when caregivers push toys at infants at rates to which the babies can't possibly respond or punish a young toddler for "letting" a ball roll under a couch where she can't get to it by refusing to help retrieve it, or insist an older toddler play with a toy the mother prefers—a puppet she wants to manipulate, rather than the toy with which the child is engaged. We empathetically sense the conflictual tension of the child trying to respond to the stimuli and retain a positively toned affect of interest while aversive anger and an inclination to withdraw mounts.

The last example of dialectic tension at work during development refers to instances in which seemingly self-stabilized interest in exploration and assertion is lost. These puzzling occurrences have been of particular interest to psychoanalysts. One example is the familiar observation that infants at about 9 months will suddenly become frightened in the presence of nonhousehold members for whom they previously would have shown interest. A number of explanations have been offered for this so-called "stranger anxiety" (Spitz, 1957, 1959). The child has been seen as making a differentiation between its mother, a primary libidinal object, and others, "strangers" onto whom it projects aggressive urges. This explanation is opposed by two findings. From birth, infants can be shown experimentally to respond with clear indications of differentiation to their mother and father as compared to others. Recognition of familiar and unfamiliar and exploration of both constitute an important daily activity in the lives of infants, thus 9-month-olds have a clear capacity to distinguish between familiar people (the household members) and others — including grandparents, to whom they may suddenly react with fear rather than interest. A second reason the libidinal object differentiation hypothesis is unlikely is that the fear response does not occur when the nonhousehold member attempts to engage 9-month-olds in attachment activities — holding, cuddling, or loving play. The response occurs when the person approaches more rapidly than infants can seem to adjust. Previously the same or similar people were subject for exploratory interest, regardless of whether attachment experiences did or didn't follow.

Another explanation is the maturation of fear as a category of affect. The reasoning is that only at 9 months could infants organize their responses to strange situations in response to fear because previously that affect was unavailable. The opposing argument is that infants have been organizing responses in the form of aversive withdrawal since birth, and many observers believe a fear response, especially to trauma, occurs much earlier than at 9 months.

An explanation I offered (Lichtenberg, 1983) is that a major cognitive development, which I call the imaging capacity, occurs beginning at about 8 months. Perception during the early months has a kaleidoscopic quality, as motivational dominance shifts and self and object are involved in the actions and affects characteristic of one system or another. Recognition is highly developed but is action bound; that is, what is recognized is not the object per se but the whole action sequence connected with the object — a bottle is to put in the mouth, a ring is to grab, a smiling mother is to smile back at. As the action dissolves, so presumably does the "image." The properties of the object and its independent existence have not become abstracted out of an action sequence. What the imaging capacity does is to create what Werner and Kaplan (1963) call "things-of-contemplation, that is, objects that one regards out there, rather than things upon which one merely acts" (p. 67). The properties of the image (its appearance, attributes, and the information it conveys) are conceived as having an existence independent of the perceiver's presence: "My mother is there whether I see her or not." "My room is there whether I am in it or not." (Of course, the symbolic representation involved in the language I am using for illustrative purposes does not apply to the initial experience of the imaging capacity.) In 1983 I stated that

> the most developmentally normal response to the not-mother person (often no "stranger") is one of wary exploratory interest; that is the approaching person becomes in Werner and Kaplan's

(1963) phrase an object of contemplation—a problem to be puzzled through. My thesis is that the approaching not-mother person may be the first of a group of objects that is responded to as an image that has become objectified. Put another way, the response to the stranger may be the first example of the functioning of the imaging capacity.

What is the basis of the need to exercise this capacity? As the infant's attachment to mother intensifies, each approaching person is scanned to see if that person raises or lowers the infant's sense of security, the central pivot of which lies in the mother's presence. It is not the presence of the relatively familiar grandmother or the totally unknown visiting aunt that determines the response, but the status of the mother's security providing support, measured against other factors such as the startle pressure exerted by the stranger. Thus infants in their homes, with their mothers available for physical contact, will react to the not-mother person in a way that indicates that it is important that he or she is not mother. This person is lifted out of the surround and regarded as an object in his or her own right. (pp. 102–104)

My 1983 explanation remains accurate I believe but inadequate. To say mother represents security is to present a truism; she has since birth. What I failed to recognize and cite was that infants at 8 or 9 months utilize a different means to elicit that sense of security: They read the affect state of the mother from rapid scanning of her facial expression. Mother's smile conveys the information I am pleased or this person is our friend; mother's frown indicates I am displeased or this person's presence arouses annoyance; mother's fear expression means I am frightened or this person's presence arouses alarm. From this time on, infants are guided by the subjective interplay of the emotions of others and of themselves. But as yet they are only practiced at "reading" the affective facial expressions of those most familiar to them. Following this line of reasoning, the "stranger," who often is not at all an unknown person, is one whose affect state cannot be read and whose friendly intent cannot be instantly incorporated into the infant's security system. The fact that this particular response of "stranger anxiety" involves people, not inanimate objects, suggests that a response applicable to people only—the subjective reading of an affect state—is involved. The imaging capacity is the cognitive precursor for affect referencing, not the cause of the anxiety response.

Infants at about 9 months are thus between two markedly different methods of processing information. An aversive state of wary or fearful avoidance of people who previously were a source of interested exploration results from the dialectic tension between an old approach that provided security and a new maturational advance not yet absorbed adequately into the infant's repertoire. The almost universal inclination toward distrust of the stranger/foreigner (such as the presumably "inscrutable Oriental") whose affect state we cannot easily assess suggests that this dialectic tension may never be fully resolved.

Between 18 and 22 months, another period of heightened dialectic tension arises from the simultaneous presence of an earlier and a later method of processing information. Toddlers of this period have long been observed to be "difficult." Many toddlers will seem to want to be close to their mothers, only to resent any attempt to be held or helped, and then demanding the very closeness or help they rejected. Their displeasure is often indicated by tantrums or other forms of antagonism or by withdrawal, shyness, or sad pensiveness. Almost all children at some moments during this period do not seem to know what to do with themselves, and parents often feel equally uncertain and helpless. Early analysts explained these phenomena as a psychic reflection of an anal erotogenic zone conflict between retention and expulsion. Mahler, Pine, and Bergman (1975) explain the occurrences of this period on the basis of the relationship between child and mother. In the prior months children are captivated by the opportunities for play with toys and practicing their skills while coming to mother for occasional "refueling." Gradually the child becomes more aware of himself or herself "as a relatively helpless, small, and separate individual, unable to command relief or assistance merely by feeling the need for it, or even by giving voice to that need" (p. 78). Toddlers are thus pulled between their rapidly developing individuation and their fear of separateness (helplessness). They turn toward their mother, shadowing her and involving her more in all their activities. But they are also confronted with their limitations and the call of their personal interests. Mahler et al. conclude that the crossroads they term the "rapprochement crisis" lies in the painful relinquishment of the delusion of parental omnipotence and the toddler's own grandeur. The toddler is thus vulnerable to abrupt deflation of self-esteem.

In 1983 I noted that

> toddlers are under pressure from competing high-intensity sensations from the mouth, skin, bowels, bladder, perineum, and genitals. They are under pressure from the upsurge of assertiveness associated with their developing but fragile sense of themselves as directors. They show a heightened responsiveness of reactive aggressiveness and resentment to any frustration or frustrator. The strain on the parental support system from the move toward greater autonomy, body exploration, intentionality, and

privacy stirs up confrontations in the foreground, and sometimes
threatens the background ambience of basic support and trust as
well . . . . The total effect of the moment-to-moment swings of
experience creates the pulling and tugging, dysphoric states Mahler
has characterized as the rapprochement crisis. (p. 143)

I should like to suggest that an unrecognized source of dialectic
tension arises from the developing toddlers having to shift from one
method of processing and communicating information to another—
that is, from one based on sign–signal communication to one utilizing
symbolic representation in the dual modes of primary and secondary
process (see Lichtenberg, 1983, pp. 132–147). When viewed from the
perspective of the exploratory–assertive motivational system, toddlers must make the transition from a method of solving problems
from which they have learned to derive efficacy and competence to
another that is at first far less reliable. Younger toddlers have worked
out whole areas of their life with a high degree of efficacy. They know
where the items of their daily needs are placed and the timing of most
events. They know the meaning of such signs as mother taking only
her coat or taking her coat and theirs. They know how to negotiate
many intentions by taking their parents by the hand and leading
them, by pointing and vocalizing, by rapid reading of facial expressions, and most of all by what "works" with each parent in the form
of the right mix of insistence and compliance. Suddenly two things
happen to them. Because of myelination of the frontal cortex and the
associational pathways, processing of information in each frontal lobe
comes "on line," providing greatly enhanced complexity. The toddler
suddenly has verbal comprehension and a flow of communicative
words that seem to spring up in bursts. He or she also has a whole
new—previously impossible—way to play with toys and people,
giving them symbolic meaning as expressions of wishes and fantasies. Concurrently, a second vicissitude confronts toddlers. Parents
now regard them as becoming capable of more adult-like symbolic
functioning, and parents intuitively pull on their toddlers to express
their often puzzling wishes and demands in words, that is, through
a symbolic language as yet too uncertain for the child to grasp with a
feeling of efficacy and competence. Thus, sources of the dialectic
tension of the rapprochement crisis arise from the cognitive transition
to symbolic representation and the effects on the parent–toddler
relationship.

Exploring a later phase of development, Wolf (1982) called
attention to the impact of the transition point in cognitive development that occurs at age 12 to 14 when formal operations (Piaget, 1969)

replace concrete operations. "This newfound capacity to combine propositions to isolate variables in order to confirm or dispose of hypotheses, and to carry out these operations with symbols rather than only with objects or concrete events has a great impact on the adolescent self" (Wolf, 1982, p. 178). Adolescents can now create a more personal system of values, ideals, and ethics. Wolf noted the inevitable disappointment (deidealization) that accompanies the greatly increased cognitive capacity. "The adolescent can no longer hide from himself the inevitable discrepancies between who he has imagined his parents to be and who the parents really are" (p. 179). This transition places a burden on both parents and the early adolescent. The parents must accept with relatively good grace the loss of the prior more consistent idealization as they provide support for their offspring's new adventures in exploration and assertion, especially their glee at finding their parents' feet of clay. The adolescent must seek affirmation and support from elsewhere, commonly turning to peer groups, older adolescents, teachers, and fictional heroes. The interim period during which the adolescent's cognitive capacity for formal operations develops is, thus, often one of great dialectic tension. When the reciprocal expectations of parents and adolescent are in phase with each other, the potential for consolidation of these advances in the exploratory–assertive motivational system is enhanced.

Hierarchies of the Exploratory–Assertive Motivational System

The hierarchical arrangement of a developmental sequence is a fundamental conception of every psychoanalytic theory. Stages in psychosexual development (Freud, 1905), successive "positions" (M. Klein, 1952), epigenetic stages (Erikson, 1959; Spitz, 1959), stages within lines of development (A. Freud, 1965), successive models (Gedo & Goldberg, 1973), stages of separation–individuation (Mahler et al., 1975), and self developmental stages (Stern, 1985) are well known examples. In each of these examples some combination of drive or other general motivation and object relationship (Greenberg & Mitchell, 1983) is given precedence.

A problem that has long been recognized with hierarchical concepts of development is the nature of the relationship between early and later stages. Do later stages totally or for the most part transform and thereby essentially replace earlier stages? The transformational concept is illustrated by the belief that at the completion of the oedipal phase (and/or adolescence) genitality transforms pregenital configurations (Arlow, 1963). I noted the transformation that takes place in the perceptual life of the infant when the properties of physical objects become subjects of contemplation and when the emotions of humans become guides for sharing and security. I emphasized the major change that occurs in perception, cognition, and problem solving when at 18 months the myelinization of associational pathways and the frontal cortex ushers in symbolic representation in the dual modes of primary and secondary process. I compare the dynamics of this momentous development to Pirandello's "Six Characters in Search of an Author." Each character has a story to tell but needs a way to give his or her life representation in the play. Episodic memories of the events of the toddler's prior life, especially those in each motivational system that are given significance by strong or persisting emotion, are available for or, in a sense, call for the new form of representation. All emotionally significant trends that occur in the present and activate associative memory to those of the past can now be formed into the contents of play, of fantasy, of dreams, and of increasingly organized intentions. Clearly the transformation is very widespread, but considerable evidence indicates it is not complete. Numerous clinical examples indicate the persistence of residues of early traumatic events in the form of behavior patterns (Anthi, 1983; Lichtenberg, 1983, 1989), character traits (Gedo, 1979), and pathogenic beliefs (Weiss & Sampson, 1986). Evidence of continuity rather than transformation can also be deduced for both adaptive and maladaptive residues of procedural memory in the manner in which parents "intuitively" respond to their infants and older children (Lichtenberg, 1989). While most discussions of the fate of earlier hierarchical levels contrast continuities and transformations, Horowitz (1972) noted that the sequence of modes of representation from enactive to imagic to lexical suggests a more dynamic integrative formulation: "the early forms of representation . . . do not disappear as the new lexical capacity is gained. They do not remain at primitive organizational levels. They probably continue epigenetic development because the acquisition of lexical capacities increases the availability of schemata for organization of information in any mode" (p. 805). I understand Horowitz's proposal to mean that when lexical capacities can enhance an earlier form of representation, some degree of integration will occur. In many interactional gestural activities, words further define the situation and make it more flexible. Alternatively, in many activities guided by procedural memory (for example many athletic skills), representation of an enactive nature may be more effective without the ambiguity or discursiveness of verbal representation.

The theoretical formulations of hierarchies I have referenced are efforts to account for developments in the functioning of the individual as a whole, whether construed as tripartite structure, self, or self-organization. In contrast, Piagetian theory provides a hierarchical conception of cognitive development, or, in my terms, an accounting of significant features of the exploratory–assertive motivational system. The intricate presentation of developments leading to and from formal operations constitutes a standard against which all other presentations of exploratory–assertive motivation may be measured. A contemporary view adds the effect of cross-modal processing of early perceptual information (Stern, 1985) and the essential role of affects as sources of motivation (Lichtenberg, 1989). The sense of efficacy and competence that motivates child and adult alike can be inferred in Piaget's schema. The subtle relationship of pleasure in intimacy and competence pleasure that motivates play and helps to explain the emotional difference between work (efficacy and competence alone) and play (efficacy and competence plus intimacy) is less clear in the structuralist–epistemological theory of Piaget. Evaluated overall, the Piagetian schema serves well as the basis for an hierarchical account of stages of dominance of exploratory–assertive endeavors by denoting a level and method of information processing available at different ages.

A developmental account of the form of cognition, for example operational thinking, that dominates at a given age helps us to formulate a normal hierarchical sequence. However, I believe dominance is equally well conceptualized as meaning the choice within alternative possibilities allowed by the prevailing mode of cognition that a particular individual makes to approach exploration and problem solving at any given moment, or, more commonly, repeatedly over time. I will examine studies suggest that an individual's cognitive style reflects his or her giving ascendance to one or another mode of information processing.

In 1959, Gardner, Holtzman, G. Klein, Linton, and Spence, a group of psychologists well versed in psychoanalytic theory, reported a study of individual consistencies in cognitive control. A central finding of their study is to confirm their premise that individual differences in controlling perception and cognition do not imply distortion but exist as alternative ways to explore the external world. Under conditions in which individuals are free to direct their attention, some will scan extensively, others relatively little. Scanning refers to the *breadth* of attention in situations of perceived incongruity. Extensive scanners will note properties of objects relevant to both their intentions and fringe properties. They have the advantage of forming stable concepts of the objects they explore, but, because they deploy attention to relatively many aspects of external and internal fields, they are slow to make decisions and prone to doubt. In contrast, those who are not extensive scanners have the ability to concentrate when required on relevant aspects of stimuli, focusing on certain aspects while avoiding or withholding attention from other aspects, which enables them to cope well with incongruities. Those who lack these capacities organize along simpler lines and are less able to resolve an incongruity. Another capacity studied by Gardner et al. (1959) was modes of organizing behavior in respect to experiences that violate normal assumptions of reality. One group, who could be spoken of as intolerant of unreality, engaged in continual efforts to make their experience conform to the actual state of affairs in the external world. Another group, those tolerant of unreality, while in equally adequate contact with external reality, were much more relaxed in their acceptance of both ideas and perceptual organizations that called for deviation from the conventional. They displayed "more direct evidence of the influence of momentary feeling states on their experiencing of the external world" (p. 94). Another dichotomy of cognitive control, leveling versus sharpening, is relevant to situations involving the temporal patterning of stimuli. Levelers tend to blend together a current percept with a memory of a past percept so that the elements lose their individuality. Sharpeners differ in that both memories and current percepts are more differentiated, less assimilated. Another cognitive difference occurred in the way people make judgments about equivalences between perceptual objects. One group emphasized disparities, responding to the inherent properties of objects rather than to their conative implications. The other group emphasized similarities, responding not to differences in details of physical properties but to associated meanings. This group linked objects because of similarities in where they were seen or because of their relevance to a personal activity.

What are the hierarchical implications of these cognitive approaches to exploration and assertion? First, each cognitive-control tendency represents an unconscious preferential choice, the alternative being possible at another time. But the relative consistency of the same tendency indicates that a dominance of hierarchical arrangement has occurred. Second, several cognitive tendencies work in combinations that the Gardner and his colleagues call cognitive styles. They offer as an example that a person whose style is to be passive in exploration would be inclined to *leveling* (that is, to easily assimilating a present percept with a memory by ignoring differentiating factors), *low field-articulation* (that is, directing little attention to differentiating features that reveal incongruities), and *low scanning* (that is, when regarding a visual field to paying attention to a narrower field and to fewer details of properties). People with this cognitive style would be easily satisfied that they have explored a problem. They are apt to be satisfied with an understanding that might seem simplistic to someone with a different cognitive style.

I described (Lichtenberg, 1983) two well-defined markedly different cognitive styles of talented 6-year-olds—James and David. James is a fictional version of the analyst-to-be Adrian Stephen, described in *To the Lighthouse* (1927) by his exquisitely observant sister, Virginia Woolf:

> Since he belonged, even at the age of six, to that great clan which cannot keep this feeling separate from that, but must let future prospects, with their joys and sorrows, cloud what is actually at hand, since to such people even in earliest childhood any turn in the wheel of sensation has the power to crystallize and transfix the moment upon which its gloom or radiance rests, James Ramsay, sitting on the floor cutting out pictures from the illustrated catalogue of the Army and Navy Stores, endowed the picture of a refrigerator, as his mother spoke, with heavenly bliss. It was fringed with joy. The wheelbarrow, the lawnmower, the sound of poplar trees, leaves whitening before rain, rooks cawing, brooms knocking, dresses rustling—all these were so colored and distinguished in his mind that he had already his private code, his secret language, though he appeared the image of stark and uncompromisingly severity. (pp. 9–10)

David, another 6-year-old, had a different approach to exploration. Frequently playing alone with his soldiers, he constructed forts for them and had elaborate but distinct battle plans, both offensive and defensive. Although he had a number of friends with whom he played outside games, he only enjoyed playing soldiers with Jack, because only Jack, among his friends, shared his passion for accuracy. David, who already at 6 read at a fourth-grade level, had his soldiers organized in units—foot soldiers, cavalry, and artillery. He knew how far the rifles and the cannons would fire; how large the squads, platoons, and companies would be; how fast and how far the cavalry and horses could travel. The floor on which he played was, in his imagination, carefully scaled from inches to miles. When Jack and he argued about the validity of a plan, he would consult one of his books, or, if necessary, wait for his father to supply the needed information. Although he enjoyed the fantasied charges and the battles as a whole, his real satisfaction came from the categorizing of information and the simulation of objective reality that his carefully made distinctions gave him. To add a new fact from a book or from his father to his catalogue of knowledge gave him as much joy as the whoop of victory when the walls of the fort were breached in a successful assault.

These examples of James and David illustrate the manner in which differing hierarchical arrangements of cognitive control tendencies combine to produce a wide variety of individual approaches to exploration and assertion. The creative potential of both hierarchical arrangements can be easily appreciated, James's possibly more suited for aesthetic pursuits, David's for scientific exploration, but both possibly flexible enough to do either.

HIERARCHICAL RELATIONS BETWEEN MOTIVATIONAL SYSTEMS

The form or style the exploratory–assertive system takes has innate proclivities, often recognized as mixtures of family predispositions plus identifications, but all systems develop in dialectic tension with the other systems. The interplay between attachment and exploratory–assertive motivations are particularly delicate. Parents who can sensitively provide children with the opportunity (time and tools) to play on their own help to establish a solid base for exploration and assertion. Alternatively, parents whose loneliness or isolation forces them to use the child for their own attachment needs will interfere with this development, and parents whose attentional focus is drawn inward or away from the child may provide "time and tools" but the child's exploration is apt to have a desultory, lonely quality. A child and mother ideally can comfortably shift between the child's fingering mother's earring while engaged with mother and the child's exploring the earring that happens to be on mother. Such moments, plus those of mutual exploration with toys and books, give place its special quality of exploration and assertion combined with intimacy, even if done alone.

A struggle for hierarchical dominance between the need for psychic regulation of physiological requirements and the desire for exploration and assertion are daily experiences. This struggle can be typified by the child who persists in building his or her blocks or playing ball while straining and squirming to hold back his urine or feces, or by the diver who prolongs submerged snorkeling to the point of discomfort to see a bit more. Likewise, the psychic regulatory motive inevitably utilizes the exploratory–assertive system to explore new approaches to eating, eliminating, sleep patterns, and exercise while asserting preferences – often against those of others. Alternatively, the phenomenon of physiological requirement regulation is a source of interest. Ingestion, excretion, sleep (and by extension death), health, illness, and injury are a universal trigger for exploration, from an older toddler who connects the mysteries of bodily functions with the toilet flushing to an adult physician who has made a career choice of this exploratory interest.

At first glance, the relationship between the sensual–sexual motivational system and the exploratory–assertive system could seem to be simply that the mysteries of creation and gender differences are *primary* sources of curiosity. In this view, perception and cognition are low-tension, neutralized, conflict-free functions (Hartmann, 1964) unless taken over by sexual (libidinous) drive urgency. Any observation of the intensity with which infants pursue their exploratory interests and struggle against restraints to assert their preferences in nonsexual or sexual areas disproves the "neutralized" contention (Parens, 1979). Thus, exploratory–assertive motivations do not depend on sensual–sexual motives to be intense. Interest, efficacy, and competence pleasure are powerful affective motivators. Paradoxically, it is the other way around, sexual motivation often depends on exploratory–assertive motivations (as well as antagonism) (Stoller, 1975) for successful potency to occur. To understand this paradox, we must compare the premise of libido theory with clinical psychoanalytic observations. According to libido theory, a drive for orgastic satisfaction drives the individual more or less persistently, requiring defensive measures to prevent (socialize) coital urgency. Unlike animals whose estrus cycles govern rises and falls of sexual phases, the human's hormonal levels are relatively constant. However, although biologic factors are responsible for upsurges in genital sensation at periods such as at 18 months and in early puberty, potency, responsiveness, and orgastic expression are essentially psychically triggered. Clinical observation confirms the dependence of sexual arousal on conscious and unconscious fantasy, exploratory–assertive activity in the form of looking and display, and illusions of mysterious discovery, novelty and variation. Thus, a sizable segment of the film, magazine, lingerie, swimsuit, and all of the pornography and topless nightclub industries are designed to titillate curiosity and stimulate or reinforce fantasies that ensure potency. The hierarchical arrangement is that the search for sexual excitement as dominant motive recruits the exploratory–assertive system as a subset reinforcement.

The aversive motivational system and the exploratory–assertive system are complexly interrelated and often conflated by psychoanalytic theoreticians. A child who is frustrated in an exploratory activity may become angry, exerting thereby an additional thrust enabling the assertive effort to be effective. The sequence of assertion augmented by anger then conveys a sense of power. The hierarchical arrangement would be a dominant exploratory–assertive motive mixed with or briefly supplanted by an aversive motive; but, with success, competence pleasure becomes dominant and the anger quickly recedes. Especially with toddlers, if the exploratory–assertive task is too complex or the child is prone to rapid acceleration of frustration/anger, a temper tantrum may ensue with aversive motivation totally superceding exploration and assertion. Dominance of aversive motivation may also occur if becoming angry when frustrated is regarded as unacceptable. Then the frustration of an exploratory–assertive effort may lead, not to an instrumental augmenting by the vigor of anger, but to shame and/or guilt. The outcome will not be competence pleasure with exploratory–assertive success and the rapid fading of anger, but a prolongation of aversion, often characterized by withdrawal, disinterest, or even the grudge holding of a narcissistic injury.

Alternatively, fear, as well as shame and guilt, are the affects parents most commonly evoke to erect prohibitions against exploratory–assertive activities they regard as dangerous or damaging: climbing on tiltable chairs, running after a ball into a street, grabbing a toy away from another child, pulling on mother's earring or glasses to inspect them. A subtle but important interplay exists in the parent's perception of the child's motive. Parents who recognize their child's activity as exploratory, self-assertive, and playful in nature, will, after effectively prohibiting a dangerous pursuit, help the child to switch to another exploratory–assertive goal—including exploring the nature of the source of the danger when appropriate. Parents who regard their child's exploratory–assertive activity as aversive, that is, as antagonistic and rebellious because they don't like it, will, after prohibiting the dangerous pursuit, shame the child as foolish, malicious, and bad. Consequently, the child will confuse assertion with antagonism and will come to view the persistent carrying out of a self-conceived agenda as shameful and evil. The subsequent permutations of this confusion of assertion and antagonism will be pathogenic beliefs (Weiss & Sampson, 1986) that others are hostile suppressors to whom one must be compliant and/or that the self is faulty and bad and that self-exploratory motives are not to be trusted.

The final relationship between the exploratory–assertive and aversive systems that I will discuss deals with the psychoanalytic discovery of the mechanisms of defense. This relationship might seem to require no comment. Each phase of psychoanalytic theorizing would place the mechanisms of defense as functional capacities responsive to aversive needs. Ideation unacceptable to the dominant mass of ideas, to the censor guarding the preconscious and conscious realms, to the ego and superego are subject to denial, disavowal, projection, introjection, repression, isolation, reversal, identification, intellectualization, and other similar means of regulatory distortion. Most discussions of defense mechanisms have tended to follow two trends. A. Freud (1936) and Lichtenberg and Slap (1971, 1972) considered the relationship between normal (adaptional) and patho-logic (conflictual) aspects of defensive functional. Theoreticians as diverse as Kernberg (1975) and Gedo and Goldberg (1973) grouped mechanisms developmentally into those earlier or later in origin, the earlier being associated with more severe pathologic entities, the later with the psychoneuroses. The point I wish to make here is one Slap and I made earlier: many of the so-called mechanisms of defense are identical with the means of controlling and regulating cognition used by the exploratory–assertive system. Gardner et al. (1959) stated: "It is . . . doubted that two sets of controls are involved, each invoking different mediating structures. It seems more likely that defenses and cognitive controls involve the same signal and action apparatuses" (p. 12). These authors assert that the crucial vantage point lies in *the motivational conditions* present, an assertion to which I shall return. First, I will summarize the examples they present or what their findings suggest.

1. Levelers and repression: Freud (1915) described repression as the removal of a potentially dangerous idea from consciousness by assimilating the current idea to something previously repressed. Since levelers during exploratory activities emphasize similarities at the expense of distinctions and have memory organizations in which fine shadings are lost, their memory organization is congenial to the kind of easy assimilative clearing of consciousness performed in repression. The five authors experimentally confirmed that subjects who relied on repression as their principal means of dealing with conflictual ideas were predominantly levelers.

2. Extensive scanners and isolation: Extensive scanners are those who deploy their attention very broadly across a perceptual field. In this broad scanning, expressive attributes and emotional reverbera-tions are apt to be deemphasized. Extensive scanners indicated an active dislike of stimuli with sexual and emotional connotations. The defense of isolation operates by full focus on ideas from which affects are separated. By this means, isolation increases the breadth of

consciously accessible ideas, including perverse, murderous, and incestuous thoughts. Experimentally subjects for whom isolation was a conspicuous defense had significantly high scorings as extensive scanners.

3. Extensive scanners and obsessional doubt: Extensive scanning slows decision making since attention may be deflected back and forth from external and internal stimuli. Because of the emphasis of scanners on factors and properties, the affective side of preferences may be neglected so that emotion as an essential guide to choice is relatively absent. Obsessive doubting operates to slow down decision making when the emotional urgency that might underlie the decision is aversive and must be denied conscious awareness.

4. Broad equivalence ranges and displacement: When asked to judge the similarity of disparate stimuli, subjects with broad equivalence ranges dismissed differences in detail and linked objects because of their associated meanings, such as visual impressions of the places in which they were seen. The defense of displacement functions by allowing a source of a troubling problem to be regarded as equivalent to another source that bears even a loose resemblance, thus disguising the real source.

What can we conclude from the preceding review of the relationship of cognitive controls to the defense mechanisms of repression, isolation, obsessional doubting, and displacement? First, the development of the cognitive-control capacity is a precondition for the use of the same regulatory approach for aversive (defensive) purposes. This places each defense mechanism along a time continuum of cognitive development and lends support to the contention that groups of defenses are arranged hierarchically. Second, the term defense mechanism is a label having historical significance and thereby conveniently designates a function, but it may be misleading. If we fail to recognize that neither aversive responses nor cognitive exploration are mediated by a separate group of "mechanisms," we can easily become involved in unproductive argument about whether a response is adaptive (a cognitive control) or conflictual and maladaptive. The means should not be the main point of our focus, but rather the motivation that the means have been recruited to serve. I recommend that we give precedence to the motivation that dominants an experience we have under consideration. Thus, motivational system dominance and the affects that serve as the goals of that system receive precedence as hierarchical organizations.

SELF AS HIERARCHICAL SUPERORDINATE

If an acceptable explanation for mental functioning lies in the postulate of motivational systems, each having a hierarchical arrangement within and each capable of being the dominant governor for experience at any moment, do we require a conception of capacities hierarchically superordinate to the systems? Two observable phenomena argue for such a hierarchical conception, which I will call self after Kohut or self-organization after Gedo.

The first phenomenon is the relatively seamless manner in which most people are able to shift from the dominance of one motivational system to another without a sense of disruption. We can easily take this experiential sense of self-sameness for granted and ignore the remarkable psychological feat it represents. At all ages, transitions of state—from sleep to awake, from happy to sad, from tantrum-like anger and rage to friendly and pacified, from feeling separate to feeling as one with another, from sexually aroused to relaxation, from postmenstrual to premenstrual to menstrual—exert a continuous strain on an individual's sense of unity. At different stages of life an individual may function with remarkable variances of compliance and rebellion, of risk taking and conservatism, of sociability and reclusiveness, which present a challenge to the maintenance of a sense of continuity. Moreover, gaps in memory ranging from instrumental nonretentiveness to prevent information overload to defensive repression and the distorting of denial and disavowal inevitably occur and must be bridged. Because of this remarkable capacity for unity, I have recommended amending Kohut's definition of self (an independent center of initiative and perception) to an independent center for the initiating, organizing, and integrating of experience and motivation.

The second type of phenomenon that compels us to recognize the organizing and integrative capacities of the self are failures in unity of experience. For many years, failures in unity were recognized primarily in the "splits" of cognitive experiencing that gave schizophrenia its name and in the markedly altered affective states of manic–depressive psychosis. Increasingly, under the close scrutiny of intensive treatment, pattern disorders of "personality" and "character" have revealed clear discontinuities of experience. These include the exuberant grandiosity and fragmentation and depletion of narcissistic personality disorders, the entrenched hostile depreciatory states and awe-filled compliant states of borderline disorders (Lichtenberg, 1987), the blackouts attendant on alcohol and drug addictions, and the dramatic discrepant dissociative organizations of those with multiple personality disorders. From these clinical findings we have learned that the organizing and integrating capacities of the self can be adversely affected. The factors are varied and complex. On one side are the individual's experiences of subtle and gross instances of empathic failure: coldness, physical and sexual abuse, smothered individuality, unreasonable demands for success without adequate support, a hostile home environment. Severe disruptive traumata may occur at any age, as evidenced by many victims of the Holocaust and the Vietnam war and others with posttraumatic syndromes. On the other side are factors that make a child less able to respond to an ordinarily responsive nurturant environment—faulty genetic predispositions, prematurity, drug toxicity at birth, sensory deficits, severe hypo- and hyperactivity. Individuals with learning disorders, such as Mr. T with whom I opened this chapter, are at risk for disruptive personal and interpersonal experiences.

As clinicians we are drawn to an investigative interest in failures of integration, but I believe that our study of hierarchies indicates that the integrative–organizing capacity itself needs to be a central focus for future research. At present the self as an independent center for initiative, organizing, and integrating is easier to define than to specify. We can recognize correlations to the integrative centers of the brain. The enormously rich associational pathways in the prefrontal and frontal cortex, the interplay of right and left hemispheres, and the great redundancy and overlap of function assure the brain's overall capacities for integration and cohesion of experience once maturity has occurred. Even in the brain of the infant and small child, stimulating and inhibiting centers assure complex regulation and dense feedback loops assure integration. The findings of infant research point to memory representations based on the ability to abstract core elements of experiences in each motivational system and generalize their properties (RIGs, in Stern's 1985 term). Thus we begin life with the capacity to organize and integrate experiences central to regulation under conditions of empathic support. The self or self-organization develops from this core to take its eventual superordinate hierarchical position. We can recognize its functioning in the 5-year-old's narratives of early identity themes, which build and change through life while maintaining the remarkable sense of continuity that characterizes the uniqueness of the human.

SUMMARY

I have attempted to illustrate that an account of human development requires an understanding of organizing principles. By making the development of motivational systems central to my account of human development and by selecting for illustration one system, the exploratory–assertive, I indicated the relevance of the organizing principles of self-organizing, self-stabilizing, dialectic tension, and hierarchical arrangement for the formation and functioning of each system. When the relationship between systems is considered, dialectic tension and hierarchical dominance are central to our understanding. When the remarkable sense of unity and self-awareness of experience and its continuity over the life cycle are considered, the hierarchical superordinance of self or self-organization is conceptualized as the initiator, organizer, and integrator of experience and motivation.

REFERENCES

Anthi, P. (1983). Reconstruction of preverbal experiences. *Journal of the American Psychoanalytic Association, 3,* 33–58.

Arlow, J. (1963). Conflict, regression, and symptom formation. *International Journal of Psycho-Analysis, 44,* 12–22.

Bornstein, M. (1985). How infant and mother jointly contribute to developing cognitive competence in the child. *Proceedings of the National Academy of Science, 82,* 7470–7473.

Broucek, F. (1979). Efficacy in infancy: A review of some experimental studies and their possible implications for clinical theory. *International Journal of Psycho-Analysis, 60,* 311–316.

Erikson, E. (1959). *Identity and the life cycle.* New York: Norton, 1980.

Freud, A. (1936). *The ego and the mechanisms of defense.* New York: International Universities Press, 1966.

Freud, A. (1965). *Normality and pathology in childhood.* New York: International Universities Press.

Freud, S. (1905). Three essays on the theory of sexuality. *Standard Edition* (Vol. 7, pp. 125–243). London: Hogarth Press, 1953.

Freud, S. (1915). Repression. *Standard Edition* (Vol. 14, pp. 146–158). London: Hogarth Press, 1957.

Gardner, R. W., Holzman, P. S., Klein, G. S., Linton, H. S., & Spence, D. P. (1959). *Cognitive behavior.* Psychological Issues, Monograph 4. New York: International Universities Press.

Gedo, J. E. (1979). *Beyond interpretation.* New York: International Universities Press.

Gedo, J. E. (1984). *Psychoanalysis and its discontents.* New York: Guilford Press.

Gedo, J. E. (1986). *Conceptual issues in psychoanalysis.* Hillsdale, NJ: Analytic Press.

Gedo, J. E., & Goldberg, A. (1973). *Models of the mind.* Chicago: University of Chicago Press.

Greenberg, J., & Mitchell, S. A. (1983). *Object relations in psychoanalytic theory.* Cambridge, MA: Harvard University Press.

Hadley, J. (1989). The neurobiology of motivational systems. In J. Lichtenberg (Ed.), *Psychoanalysis and motivation* (pp. 337–372). Hillsdale, NJ: Analytic Press.

Hartmann, H. (1964). *Essays on ego psychology.* New York: International Universities Press.

Hornik, R., Risenhoover, M., & Gunnar, M. (1987). The effects of maternal positive, neutral, and negative affective communications on infant responses to new toys. *Child Development, 58,* 937–944.

Horowitz, M. (1972). Modes of representation of thought. *Journal of the American Psychoanalytic Association, 20,* 793–819.

Kernberg, O. F. (1975). *Borderline conditions and pathological narcissism.* New York: Aronson.

Klein, M. (1952). *Development in psycho-analysis* (J. Riviere, Ed.). London: Hogarth Press.

Kohut, H. (1971). *The analysis of the self.* New York: International Universities Press.

Kohut, H. (1977). *The restoration of the self.* New York: International Universities Press.

Lichtenberg, J. (1983). *Psychoanalysis and infant research.* Hillsdale, NJ: Analytic Press.

Lichtenberg, J. (1987). An experiential approach to narcissistic and borderline conditions. In J. Grotstein, M. Solomon, & J. Lang (Eds.), *The borderline patient* (Vol. 2, pp. 127–149). Hillsdale, NJ: Analytic Press.

Lichtenberg, J. (1989). *Psychoanalysis and motivation.* Hillsdale, NJ: Analytic Press.

Lichtenberg, J., & Slap, J. (1971). On the defensive organization. *International Journal of Psycho-Analysis, 52,* 451–457.

Lichtenberg, J., & Slap, J. (1972). On the defense mechanism: A survey and synthesis. *Journal of the American Psychoanalytic Association, 20,* 776–792.

Mahler, M. S. (1968). *On human symbiosis and the vicissitudes of individuation.* New York: International Universities Press.

Mahler, M. S., Pine, F., & Bergman, A. (1975). *The psychological birth of the human infant.* New York: Basic Books.

Papousek, H. (1986). Intuitive parenting: A didactic counterpart to the infant's precocity in integrative capacities. In J. D. Osofsky (Ed.), *Handbook of infant development* (2nd ed., pp. 669–720). New York: Wiley.

Papousek, H., & Papousek, M. (1975). Cognitive aspects of preverbal social interaction between human infant and adults. In *Parent–infant interaction* (Ciba Foundation Symposium). New York: Associated Scientific Publishers.

Parens, H. (1979). *The development of aggression in early childhood.* New York: Aronson.

Piaget, J. (1969). The intellectual development of the adolescent. In G. Kaplan & S. Lebovici (Eds.), *Adolescence: Psychosocial perspectives.* New York: Basic Books.

Rosenblatt, A. (1984). The psychoanalytic process: systems and information processing model. *Psychoanalytic Inquiry, 4*, 9–86.

Rosenblatt, A., & Thickstun, J. (1977). *Modern psychoanalytic concepts in a general psychology*. Psychological Issues, Monograph 42/43. New York: International Universities Press.

Sameroff, A. (1983). Developmental systems: Context and evolution. In W. Kessen (Ed.), *Mussen's handbook of childbook of child psychology* (Vol. 1). New York: Wiley.

Sander, L. (1975). Infant and caretaking environment: Investigation and conceptualization of adaptive behavior in a system of increasing complexity. In E. J. Anthony (Ed.), *Explorations in child psychiatry* (pp. 129–166). New York: Plenum Press.

Sander, L. (1980). Investigation of the infant and its caregiving environment as a biological system. In S. I. Greenspan & G. Pollock (Eds.), *The course of life* (Vol. 1, pp. 177–202). Rockville, MD: National Institute of Mental Health.

Sander, L. (1983). To begin with—reflections on ontogeny. In J. Lichtenberg & S. Kaplan (Eds.), *Reflections on self psychology* (pp. 85–104). Hillsdale, NJ: Analytic Press.

Sander, L. (1986, May). *The inner experience of the infant: A framework for inference relevant to development of the sense of self.* Paper presented to Mahler Symposium, Paris.

Spitz, R. (1957). *No and yes.* New York: International Universities Press.

Spitz, R. (1959). *A genetic field theory of ego formation.* New York: International Universities Press.

Stern, D. (1985). *The interpersonal world of the infant.* New York: Basic Books.

Stoller, R., (1975). *Perversion.* New York: Pantheon.

Weiss J., & Sampson, H. (1986). *The psychoanalytic process.* New York: Guilford Press.

Werner, H., & Kaplan, B. (1963). *Symbol formation.* New York: Wiley.

Winnicott, D. (1958). The capacity to be alone. In *The maturational processes and the facilitating environment* (pp. 29–36). New York: International Universities Press, 1965.

Wolf, E. (1982). Adolescence: Psychology of the self and selfobjects. *Adolescent Psychiatry, 10*, 171–181.

Woolf, V. (1927). *To the lighthouse.* New York: Harcourt, Brace, 1955.

III

Clinical Contributions

8

Disturbances of Affect Representation in Primitive Personalities

MICHAEL ROBBINS

One of the most fundamental changes affecting psychoanalysis during the past half century is the apparent disappearance of symptomatic neurotic patients from our consulting rooms and their replacement with persons with more or less severe disturbances of character and personality in which the traditional neurotic configuration of conflict, defense, symptom, and character constriction is not so evident. Some believe there has been an actual shift in modal psychopathology, while others maintain that what has changed is our clinical and conceptual power to look beneath the surface and to be more concerned with the person who presents the problems and less mesmerized by symptoms per se. Whichever of these explanations may be true, adherents of single-model theories of the mind, such as the neurosis model of conflict, defense, and symptom or character formation, have been increasing hard put to account for the entire spectrum of pathology or for the full range of infant and child development and behavior beyond those phenomena for which the model was originally designed. The response of clinicians committed to the neurosis model has in some instances been to exclude clearly nonneurotic patients from the scope of analysis as they define it and in other cases to search for ways to rationalize that their model is sufficiently elastic to account for the range of psychopathology.

While it is easy in instances of phenomena that do not seem readily analyzable in terms of intrapsychic conflict and defense to assert that the patients' drives are too strong and their ego is too weak and, therefore, their conflicts too fixed and their tendency to repeat too deeply ingrained to permit of analytic treatment, or to maintain that the analyst is incapable of perceiving the presence and nature of relevant intrapsychic conflicts because the analyst is blinded by his or her adherence to one of the upstart theoretical systems, not everyone is satisfied with such explanations. Kohut's response to encountering seemingly nonneurotic analysands (narcissistic personalities) was to propose an alternative model of the mind. But Kohut's alternative self psychology has proven to be at least as limited as neurosis theory. It has little place for nonnarcissistic object relations; it holds that the events of the first year and a half of life, prior to the dawn of the cohesive self, are psychologically meaningless (Kohut & Wolff, 1978); and it dismisses the psychoses and borderline personalities and their treatment from the realms both of meaningfulness and psychoanalysis because of the self-fragmentation characteristic of those conditions. Other skeptics have been reluctant to abandon the neurosis model for, though it may be limited, it has proven itself to be of extraordinary value. In search of more creative ways to understand the clinical heterogeneity among the various psychopathological conditions, Gedo has raised important questions about the development of some of the basic mental capacities we take for granted in normal and neurotic individuals, and he has conceptualized the existence of forms of pathology characterized not by defense against intrapsychic conflict but by qualitatively different modes of thinking that emerge as a consequence of arrested and deviant development. He has proposed (Gedo, 1981, 1988; Gedo & Goldberg, 1973) a multiple model hierarchy, which is for the most part consistent with the broader biopsychosocial model hierarchy that Weiss (1969, 1977) and Engel (1977, 1980) have outlined. In fact, Gedo's multiple model hierarchy, located between organic scientific theories and social or interpersonal theories, fills the place in the biopsychosocial model designated as self or person.

In this chapter I shall describe one phenomenon characteristic of some personalities who do not appear to be neurotic. In this group, which I refer to as primitive personalities, I include patients from the borderline, narcissistic, paranoid and schizoid groups, which I believe share common characteristics (Robbins, 1983, 1989; Chapter 10, this volume). The phenomenon to which I refer is a pervasive lack of emotional awareness and control, and I shall hypothesize that it may best be accounted for not as the result of repression and other defenses against intrapsychic conflict, but by a fundamental, epigenetically antecedent disturbance in affect representation. I have commented about this disturbance elsewhere (1989) and its existence is implicit in some of my earlier writing (particularly 1981, 1983).

The patients to whom I refer are on the surface a varied lot. In some instances they fail to exhibit contextually expectable affect; in others they are overwhelmed with what an observer would define as amorphous dysphoria and rage. Typically they are anhedonic. They may manifest signs and symptoms of depression without experiencing emotions of sadness or despair. Though they may be manifestly rageful and hostile without apparent provocation, they do not own these emotions as disturbed characterological predispositions. Even when we may infer from improvements in their life during the course of analysis that they have experienced the analyst as helpful, expectable feelings of satisfaction, pleasure, and loving attachment are conspiciously absent, not simply withheld. They are not satisfied by the analyst's empathic "mirroring" and the provision of a "holding environment," and they may respond in a hostile–paranoid or phobic–avoidant way to the analyst's attentions.

Efforts to comprehend our difficulties with such patients by invoking classical neurosis concepts, for example, insatiable drives, unrealistic wishes, intractable primitive defenses, or repetition compulsion, may be thinly disguised judgmental efforts to rationalize our failures of comprehension and treatment. I believe a more useful hypothesis may be that these patients are unable to represent affect. That is, they cannot name, reflect upon, and learn to control their emotions. They experience analytic attention as distressing and even harmful because they are discomforted by (but not necessarily unconsciously conflicted about) the beginnings of awareness of the feelings implicit in their affective behavior, and they are unable to differentiate these states as internal events from their perceptions of and responses to the analyst.

If our vantage point is that of the more mature mental apparatus and the neurosis theory that accounts for it, particularly ego psychology, we may consider that these cognitive, affective, and adaptive difficulties are crippling "defects." Freud assumed as a basic given of mental functioning the binding of ideas with instinctual cathexis in the form of affect, and classical theory, stemming from his contributions, assumes that the capacity to represent affect falls within what Hartmann (1958) refers to as the conflict-free sphere of mental functioning. In other words, it is not considered disruptable by pathological processes in childhood. Freud attempted to account for instances of ideation without accompanying affect, or of seemingly inappropriate affect, by using concepts of repression and unconscious conflict (1911, 1926). Contemporary theorists who retain the classical model may attempt to explain phenomena such as I shall describe using the defense concept of splitting and projective identification. It did not occur to Freud that the capacity to represent and regulate affect might be learned in the caregiver–infant dyad, and that such learning might be fundamentally compromised in situations in which this dyad was disturbed. The point of view I am suggesting, in contrast to the classical model, is epigenetic and adaptive and embraces a mental organization that, though less mature and differently organized than the neurotic, is meaningful in its own right and not simply a hole or defect in the psyche, or a defense against intrapsychic conflict.

DEFINITIONS

According to Knapp (1963), *emotion* is a general term that encompasses three distinct phenomena: biological processes; expressive, communicative behaviors; and subjective phenomenological experiences. We shall consider the behavioral and subjective phenomena. The term *affect* denotes innate expressive facial, gestural, and vocal behaviors such as Darwin (1872) first observed in neonates. But the presence of affect is no guarantee of reflective awareness of an underlying feeling, regardless of the complexity of underlying cerebral structuralization or the capacity, which Stern (1985) is the latest to portray vividly in his vignettes of infants and their mothers, for sophisticated human interactions. A term such as mood, or perhaps *emotion*, might be appropriate to designate subjective experience. *Affect representation* is a mental construct intervening between affective behavior or expression and the subjective experience and conscious or secondarily unconscious manipulation of emotion.

Affect expression is, for the most part, a social phenomenon. With the possible exception of expressions of organic discomfort, it originates and develops only in the presence of other persons. As Loewald (1971) asserts, affect representation develops from innate affect expression within the undifferentiated self–object matrix and is probably never entirely differentiated from object representation. Yet I believe that a deficit in affect representation such as I am postulating is not simply another description of failure to achieve object constancy, although the capacity to represent affect must be an essential component of that more complex cognitive achievement. In the course of development of the capacity to differentiate subject from object, there is a considerable separation between the more subjective awareness of feeling states and the more objective awareness of another person. Affect representation also differs from object representation insofar as it implies the capacity to abstract a common emotional element from otherwise disparate experiences. Object constancy requires, in addition to the capacity to represent and sustain affect, the capacity to integrate discrepant emotional experiences as belonging to the same object, that is, representations of the object experienced under a variety of subjective states or conditions.

ALEXITHYMIA

Observations similar to my hypothesis of defective affect representation have previously been made with psychosomatic patients. In two 1963 papers, one co-authored with David, Marty and de M'Uzan noted that patients with psychosomatic disorders demonstrate a paucity of libidinal attachment affect as well as a kind of thinking that they term "operational," that is, lacking in affect and object references. In 1967 Sifneos coined the term "alexithymia" (no words for emotion). Nemiah and Sifneos (1970) could not conceptualize these psychosomatic disturbances in traditional neurotic conflict–defense terms because the patients seemed unable to wish and to symbolize. Because it did not occur to these authors to seek another psychoanalytic explanatory model, they turned instead to neurophysiology and postulated the influence of chronic autonomic arousal without mental representation. More recently McDougall (1974, 1982a, 1982b) and Krystal (1982) have written that alexithymia in psychosomatic patients is the result of developmental arrest in the capacity to represent affect and instinct. But as both McDougall and Krystal also emphasize the central role played by primitive conflicts and defenses against affect awareness, there is confusion about whether they believe that affect has been repressed or has never been represented to begin with. Taylor (1987) has begun to consider some of these psychosomatic phenomena in the broader context of object relations theory and the biopsychosocial model hierarchy of Engel and Weiss. Khantzian and Wilson (Chapter 9, this volume) employ the alexithymia concept to comprehend addictive pathology.

CLINICAL DESCRIPTION

Patients with the affect disturbance about which I write do not all seem alike. While some may appear to be deficient in emotional repertory (for example, narcissistic and schizoid individuals), others (particularly those diagnosed as borderline), have a characteristic propensity to emote with volatility and to experience chronic feelings of dysphoria, although the specific emotions that comprise their feeling state are typically impossible to identify. Because they tend to emote and complain angrily, and often pursue pleasure with relatively little restraint, members of this latter group are not, at first glance, individuals one might think of as deficient in the experience of emotion. However, more intensive acquaintance reveals that they know very little about the feelings they are enacting and, in some instances, are hardly aware of having feelings at all, beyond their endlessly reiterated complaint of undifferentiated dysphoria.

The patient who acts chronically and sporadically enraged is a good example. Noting the prominence of rage and envy in the treatment of such individuals, authorities including M. Klein (1935), who was convinced of the centrality of a death instinct, and Kernberg (1975) concluded that they suffer from a quantitative excess of anger. In contrast, I am suggesting that there may be a qualitative defect in its representation, integration, and control. In primitive perceptual–enactive thinking (Robbins, 1983, 1989), the subject does not recognize that he or she is, by temperamental disposition, an angry person who needs to exercise some control so as not to be indiscriminately destructive. Instead, such individuals view their behavior as an unremarkable and appropriate reaction to the way they perceive they are being treated. They cannot control what they have not mentally represented, but they characteristically try to attack and control the object in whom they perceive it. Moreover, they have not integrated the part of their personality that expresses extraordinary and seemingly inappropriate hostility with an equally inappropriate propensity to respond with docility and compliance under circumstances in which anger and aggressiveness might ordinarily be expectable. Those individuals tend to accept actual abuse, be it mistreatment or hostile attribution, as though it were normal and appropriate attention, and comply with it without experiencing anger or instituting an appropriately adaptive aggressive or self-protective response. It would seem that an element of anger toward the self, perhaps a hostile introject, is not consciously recognized but enacted for the patient by those who mistreat him. Part of the goal of treatment of such patients is to help them become aware of their hostility toward themselves. Until that is accomplished, their "masochistic" acceptance of mistreatment probably fuels and keeps "alive" the segment of the personality that continues to need to enact hostility toward more benign objects in their lives.

These patients also do not seem to experience warm, positive feelings about other people, no matter how caring or attentive they may be, or how (objectively) important the relationship seems to their well-being. Consequently, they cannot experience, much less sustain, such pleasurable object-related adaptations as healthy dependency, orgastic pleasure, loving commitment, and normal, prideful exhibition of accomplishments. While they may be quite capable of the physical experience of orgasm, the concomitant experience of object-related emotional satisfaction is absent. This deficiency in pleasure experience may be masked by the functioning of a false self. Or the insatiable, often sexualized quest for gratification may lead the observer to the mistaken conclusion that they are hedonists, overinvested in pleasure.

I shall present several cases that illustrate the affect disturbance (Cases I–III), and one (Case IV) that illustrates some issues of treatment, particularly the dynamic and structural process associated with improvement. I have written about technical issues elsewhere (Robbins, 1989). I have edited the vignettes in the first group to highlight the affect problem, so that material illustrative of transference issues and the conduct of the treatment has deliberately been omitted.

Case I

Brian, a mild-mannered, polite young man, consulted me because of lack of interest in living, including suicidal preoccupation, and a passivity and withdrawal so pervasive that he was barely functional. He lived reclusively with his girlfriend, supported by a large inheritance. Brian was very compliant and never engaged in conflict or asserted himself in any way. He found nothing remarkable in his descriptions of his girlfriend's critical and ungiving behavior toward him or her feeling of entitlement to be supported by him in style, without having to work. Another person Brian believed to be his friend often "borrowed" large sums of money from him and failed to return them. Alongside his gullibility, my patient harbored an almost paranoid feeling that others outside his circle of "friends" were critical and threatening toward him, aware of his "badness," and not to be trusted. Brian was hardly aware of an inner life of thoughts or feelings other than the aforementioned sense of being criticized and an experience of joylessness and wish to withdraw from the world. These feelings had led a psychiatrist with whom he consulted prior to seeing me to tell him that he was depressed and to treat him without success with antidepressant medication.

Brian's family had been unable to communicate verbally

about feelings and instead enacted dramatic emotional scenarios. His mother was a reclusive, phobic alcoholic, who had prowled the house on drunken, destructive nocturnal binges during his childhood. She would invade his bedroom and launch sexual and aggressive assaults on him that were mostly, but not entirely, verbal. His father was a businessman who, until Brian's early adolescence, maintained a successful facade in the outside world while isolating himself from his family. At that time he became intractably depressed, and despite several hospitalizations and various somatic treatments, he committed suicide by shooting himself in the head.

After six years of intensive therapeutic work Brian's situation had improved rather dramatically. He was much more optimistic and productive. He had several more or less successful work experiences. And he had negotiated a reasonably gratifying relationship with a seemingly mature young woman. But he remained unable to focus his talents and pursue his career interests. It was particularly difficult for him to recognize and communicate feelings. For the first time in his memory, Brian was now aware of feelings of caring about others and pleasure in their company, although he could not sustain awareness of such feelings. He usually spoke sparsely, in an affectless voice that tended to make me sleepy. Although we eventually understood this phenomenon as a childhood effort to play dead in hopes that his drunken mother who had invaded his room might leave, and we learned about some of its transference aspects, to which I shall return in a moment, interpretation of the conflictual significance of this aspect of his behavior made Brian no more able to identify and communicate affect. I learned that when he was angry but unaware of it Brian would begin to puff rhythmically, like a steam engine. Very gradually, over a period of years, he accepted that he was a very angry person, and it was this rage, which he could not contain in mental images, reflect on, and communicate in words, that led him to destroy any constructive endeavor he undertook. His chronic vacancy that made me sleepy turned out to be an enactment of the wish to communicate the experience of hopelessness and rejection he was as yet unable to verbalize as memory. After additional years of work he realized his action was motivated by rage, but he experienced this as a novel revelation, not as the recovery of a memory. He treasured his new awareness of being a very angry man; rage became the core of the first authentic sense of identity he had ever experienced. At first Brian was hardly able to feel and contemplate the rage except when he was with me, and then only inconstantly. Initially he feared knowing more about his rage, as well as his sadness, because he believed that if he should experience these feelings outside my presence, he would not be able to survive.

In the first hour I shall summarize he talked about his renewed efforts to relate to his mother, whom he had come to realize he cared about and had unrequited wishes toward, despite her proven inability to care about him. He reported that when he tried to talk to her about something meaningful, she either withdrew or else provoked a fight. With mounting frustration but no awareness he was having a specific emotional experience, Brian described to me the futility of attempting to communicate with her, and he concluded, quite literally, "the only way to make an impact on her would be to kill her!"

In the next hour he talked about his isolation and difficulties pursuing the career of his choice. He was sure that if he ventured outside and committed himself to work or to school, he would become enraged at authority figures, not because of a propensity for anger, but because he experienced them as hostile and ridiculing, and that this would lead him to destroy what he was doing.

In the third of these hours he talked, in a voice devoid of affect, about the urge to explode. He was hardly aware of anger. There was an affectless burst of anal expletives (his mother's binges had been accompanied by much mess-making). He had the urge to throw a chair in my office out the window, and "smash someone in the face." He despaired that he could ever know what the underlying feeling was, and communicate it in words.

In the final hour of this sequence he reported having discovered in the course of driving his car, to his surprise, that he was hitting himself. This made him realize he must be angry. Somehow it felt satisfying, for it made his feeling seem real to him. He associated the urge to hit himself with feeling he was to blame for his mother's attacks on him when he was a child. Simultaneously I noted that he was beginning to interpret all my comments as blame or criticism. Then he began to talk about the frightening prospect of becoming less withdrawn and perhaps murderous. As he talked he began to feel increasingly frustrated with what he perceived as my silence. Again, however, he had no idea that he was becoming aware of his own anger.

The traditional construction of this material would probably be that there were conflicts involving rage and sexuality, fears of retaliation from his parents, and conflicting identifications with his withdrawn, destructively internalizing father and his destructively expressive mother. While it is easy to infer the existence of these from Brian's behavior, what impressed me more was that even after six years of treatment had made him much more aware of the significance of his emotional life, he remained unable to contemplate, sustain, and communicate awareness of rage, sadness, or loving feelings, and he tended instead toward an action mode of thinking in which destructiveness was expressed toward himself or toward the environment in an introjective or projective (sensorimotor) manner. Moreover, his eventual acquisition, after many years of therapeutic work, of the ability to recognize conflicts with regard to impulses and parental identifications and imagos did not, of itself, result in any greater awareness of, or capacity to sustain and bear, his feelings. This suggests that they were not already represented in the dynamic unconscious.

During a vacation separation from me, after we had made some progress in his ability to identify and control his emotions and use them to help orient himself, and long after the hours just summarized, Brian dreamed that he was possessed by the devil. In the dream, Brian had a powerful urge to vomit or convulse; he felt an urgent need to see me, but my door was closed. His associations were to the feelings of disappointment and rage he carried with him, more or less unaware, and to his choices—to see me and recognize and deal with them as emotions or to blindly and destructively enact them.

Case II

Carl (also described in Robbins, 1989) had been in analytic therapy for 18 years at the time of the events I am about to relate. He was a withdrawn, isolated person, generally unaware of feelings. It had taken him years of treatment to acknowledge that he needed other human beings. Previously human contact only caused him to become aware of intense discomfort and a sour sense of grievance. He had sustained himself with a hallucinatory-like fantasy life involving music, parts of objects, perverse ideas, and masturbation or its equivalents, which seemed to represent his pitiful efforts to construct out of parts a mother he had never experienced. We had worked over a period of many years on his tendency to withdraw from me, to perceive me as hostile and ridiculing toward him, and to have action fantasies of commiting mayhem on my person, and gradually he had come to realize that these phenomena represented his perceptual recognition of his own anger. Slowly he realized that he felt more oriented and had more of a sense of potency and control in his daily life when he was aware of his anger and that he required my mirroring of his enactments in order to do so. These developments, in turn, had been made possible by acquisition of the capacity not only to acknowledge his dependency on me but also to experience an intermittent sense of pleasure in seeing me, as he came to realize I helped him to attend to and identify aspects of himself he could not keep track of without assistance. Gradually he had become able to differentiate this childlike sense of pleasure in my attentions from the painful emotions he invariably experienced in my presence, which he had begun to acknowledge were his own and not inflicted upon him by me. Not long before the sessions I am about to describe he had become intermittently aware of an overwhelming sense of despair and hopelessness that occurred only during his hours with me. I hasten to state my opinion that this was not a regression, for this previously isolated, anhedonic, chronically aggrieved man now had a very full and satisfying life. He had achieved some prominence in his scientific career, which was now richly interwoven with family relationships. He had married and become a father, an experience he found enormously satisfying.

During one of his hours with me his feelings began to emerge in somatic form as heartburn and stomach pain. Considering the general context of his associations, I suggested he might be experiencing heartache. He acknowledged that it must be an emotion, for he could observe other signs, such as that he was beginning to cry. He was also aware of his wish to flee into a compensatory fantasy of gratification, as was his lifelong wont. Suddenly he realized that he was experiencing a sense of despair and rage related to his childhood so intense that he could neither conceptualize nor bear it without my sustaining presence. Moreover, he realized that, lacking such a presence in his childhood, had he not turned away from awareness of these feelings entirely and into fantasy, he would almost certainly have tried to kill himself. Concurrent dreams and memories, direct and disguised, of wishes and fears about jumping from windows, which he associated to the apartment he had lived in with his parents during his early childhood, seemed to confirm his insight. It was not as though the repressed had emerged into consciousness, however. Not only could Carl not recall experiencing these feelings in childhood, but it took much therapeutic work before he was able to sustain the feelings more than transiently and begin to reflect on their meaning.

One might certainly postulate that Carl's lack of emotional awareness was a defensive response to intrapsychic conflict involving threatening parental imagos, between life preservative and suicidal wishes. And indeed, after many years, Carl was able to perceive and work on such conflicts. However, I was much more impressed, first, by his global inability to experience, sustain, and contemplate emotional states or to be aware of internally conflicting states of mind and, second, by the presence instead of perceptual and somatic precursors such as I have described. At one point Carl referred to these transference enactments and new discoveries in the course of therapy as "feelings that never had a chance to happen." He could not experience conflict until he learned to integrate experiences; he could not sustain awareness of conflict until he could sustain awareness of the conflicting affects and a constant sense of the relevant objects.

DISCUSSION

As I have suggested, I doubt that the missing emotional awareness in these patients is fully represented in the unconscious to begin with, much less repressed or projected as a solution to intrapsychic conflict. It does not appear that these primitive personalities are in fact capable of holding polar aspects of a complex issue simultaneously in mind and of experiencing intrapsychic conflict or ambivalence (Robbins, 1983, 1989). Consciousness tends to be dominated by extreme positions that these personalities perceive to be the totality of their thoughts and feelings on the subject, even though, to the observer, these positions may blatantly contradict or conflict with equally extreme positions held at other times. Interpretation of these gross self-contradictions as indications of unconscious conflict may reflect our own wishful thinking.

It is important, of course, to recognize that we infer the existence of intrapsychic conflict from behavior, verbal and nonverbal, and that two other phenomena which are conceptually distinct may present behavioral manifestations superficially indistinguishable from those of intrapsychic conflict: lack of psychic integration, and external (person–environment) conflict. In other words, conflictual or defensive *behavior* does not necessarily imply the existence of intrapsychic conflict or unconscious mental representation. There is no disputing that primitive personalities are grossly inconsistent and even contradictory, are often in conflict with their interpersonal environment, are at odds with their own well-being, and behave defensively (and offensively). In our efforts to account for this, we must consider the evidence (Fairbairn, 1952; Gedo & Goldberg, 1973; Kohut, 1971; Robbins, 1983, 1989) that their personalities are simply unintegrated. In addition, patients I have studied seem to have grown up in an environment where they were neither assisted to learn about nor held responsible for the consequences of their feelings, and it is understandable that they might feel overstimulation and aversion when called upon as adults to bear emotion. The capacity for aversive response to overstimulation is characteristic of the most primitive organisms, and it is clearly evident in neonates, in whom, unless we are of Kleinian persuasion, we have no reason to postulate the existence of intrapsychic conflict and defense. Finally, the fact that the inability to bear and sustain object-related emotions seems to be global rather than specific to particular emotions, situations, and conflicts also mitigates against the notion of unconscious representation, conflict, and defense, as we ordinarily employ these terms.

The transcript of a portion of a session with Carl (Case II), provides further evidence for the existence of a representational defect rather than repression in these cases. Carl had recently begun to tape-record his sessions, to assist himself to remain oriented between appointments. He seemed ambivalent about the process and came to his sessions with a large quantity of recording equipment, which took him an inordinate amount of time to set up. At the start of one hour he complained bitterly about losing a bit of his therapy hour because he had been late. I expressed surprise in light of his apparent equanimity with regard to all the time he spent setting up his recording equipment. He began the next hour, from which I quote, by saying that he had been thinking about what I had said and had decided the taping was valuable to him and worth the time he spent deploying his equipment, though perhaps he could be more efficient about it. In reading the dialogue to follow, remember that it took many years of work for Carl to develop any awareness of being angry, and he was only able to sustain such an awareness briefly.

CARL: I'll back up a bit (*sheepish laugh*). I'm feeling angry. I have this feeling like my discovery this is important, and the time it takes to set it up is worth it. . . . I feel resentment as if you challenged the value of it and I have to defend it (*pause*). You questioned the time I spent setting things up. I guess one way to look at it is you *questioned* it and I *thought* about it and decided it was *worth* it. So I don't know where my feeling of being challenged in a negative way comes from (*pause*). I suspect my mother challenged everything I did in a negative way, and I didn't have the resources to give it any thought and decide what I was doing was worth it and important (*pause*). Now, having come to that conclusion, I guess I have room (*chuckle*) to feel angry and to experience the feeling I was unfairly criticized for doing the things I did. So that's what I'm feeling angry about. Not really *remembering* being angry. It's remembering the experience that I didn't even have the ability to feel a sense of self to know that I was angry. So it's not really memory. You talk about memory. I think there is some kind of delay; a delayed experience of something I wasn't able to experience.

M.R.: I think that's why these feelings have such a force of immediacy in our relationship. It's as though you're feeling them for the first time, and they have no sense of belonging to the past.

Carl: It also has some connection with my resistance to your suggestion about memory, because I don't see these things as remembering, or even the possibility that I felt this way when I was young and I'm not admitting it, so sometimes when you suggest I'm not allowing myself to remember I feel put upon to admit something I don't really know about. . . . There *are* some things I honestly feel are memories, but some things are not!

Let us return to the question of how the affect representation hypothesis may help to account for other phenomena typical of primitive personalities. We have already examined the absence of pleasurable attachment to objects, the perceptual experience of dysphoric affects in their objects and their consequent enactive or behavioral responses, the diffusion of unrepresented rage toward the self, and the formation of relationships in which a hostile symbiotic object enacts such anger for and toward the subject.

Knowledge of emotions and body feelings is the compass and beacon of mental life. Primitive personalities live in a chronic subtle state of disorientation. Analytic hours with such patients tend to differ from those typical of neurotics. The neurotic analysand may explore why he feels what he reports or how to resolve conflicting feelings. Although the primitive personality often has convictions about such matters, his hour more frequently is a voyage of emotional discovery. He needs the analyst in order to know what he is feeling. The result, including the eventual emotional orientation toward the analyst, is often a surprise, akin to the surprise of uncovering unconscious motivation in the neurotic and tends to be as quickly forgotten as it was discovered. Part of the intense attachment the successfully treated primitive personality comes to develop toward the analyst is based on his experience that achievement of emotional orientation leads to more effective functioning and on the recognition that the analyst's attentions are essential in order that he attain and sustain this orientation (see Gedo's 1988 contribution on apraxia and symbiosis for a similar discussion).

Inability to sustain affect representations underlies some of the peculiarities and deficiencies in the fantasy lives of primitive personalities, as well as a defect in their memory function. Because a representational world has not developed separate from perception of and action on an object, to imagine a thing is to do it; these people are terrified of the action potential of their minds and may go to great lengths to avoid affect-laden fantasy making. This leads to a condition that resembles the absence of fantasy noted in psychosomatic patients. Paradoxically, the fear of a fantasy life lest it lead to action is associated with their embroilment in that precise predicament; they often "mindlessly" enact what more maturely ought to be fantasy or reflection, hence their reputation as impulsive individuals who "act out." As I believe I am describing a developmental arrest, it follows that I differ from Kleinian analysts, who seem to believe that in infants and primitive adults fantasy is present from the very start. It seems to me that one of the tasks of the analyst of primitive personality is to help the patient elevate mental processes from the perceptual–enactive level that characterizes Piaget's sensorimotor infant to the more mature level characterized by fantasy and symbol.

Enactment occurs in lieu both of fantasy and of memory. Emotion is central to remembering. The hypothesis that a sensorimotor-affective precursor mode of thinking is present instead of affect-laden memory representations may account, at least in part, for my observation that, in an emotional sense, these individuals are nonhistorical. They are not parent blamers who are obsessed with the past, as Arlow (1981), for example, asserts. Rather, they tend to blame current objects and to view their family histories in an emotionally desiccated manner as inconsequential to their current experience and to view their parents either as ideal or as objects of indifference.

The evanescent, unintegrated, and affectively contradictory self and object representations encountered in primitive personalities, which underly their lack of object constancy, may also reflect, in part, their inability to maintain affect representations, although, as I suggested earlier, object constancy is a more complex cognitive achievement. So long as they do not have to deal with emotion, most patients present at least a mechanical simulation of object constancy, for they have achieved "thing constancy" in Piaget's sense of the term, as well as a variety of compensatory social skills. They preserve the constancy of inanimate aspects of the object, things such as name, physical characteristics, and demographic attributes. In an emotional sense, however, the object is repeatedly forgotten, discovered, and transformed by subjective distortion. This is not the same as the transference distortions of a constant object. The analyst tends to be absent from the mind of the patient between hours, and there is a related absence of awareness of emotions of longing, sadness, and anger, which would indicate that the separation is being experienced. The reunion feels like an encounter with a stranger, though most patients dissimulate this experience so that it is not casually apparent. The analyst becomes "alive" not as an object of stable emotional predispositions but as an unassimilated mirror of aspects of the patient, a projection screen for his or her noninternalized emotions.

The presence of wish-fulfilling fantasies in which aspects of the analyst's appearance or manner play a part may also deceive the analyst into believing that his or her patient has achieved object constancy. In fact, the objects in these fantasies bear more resemblance to creatures of dreams or hallucinations than to the missing person, and the fantasies seem to function as anodynes against the emotional representation of separation experience. Case III illustrates some of these phenomena.

Case III

Paul, a skilled and popular professional person whom I have described elsewhere (1989), managed quite successfully in a field in which the cultivation and maintenance of relationships was very important. He had never been intimate with anyone, however. When he married a woman who turned out to be less impressed by his very effective show of involvement and functioning than by his emotional vacancy, and she began to challenge and criticize him about this, he became panicked and sought treatment. There it became apparent that most of the time he was hardly aware of having any feelings or of his wife as a separate person. He viewed people uniformly as nonhuman and frightening, though he was most astute at intuiting social rules and expectations and performing as though he was at ease and involved. After seven years of analytic therapy he had become much more conscious of his emotional predispositions toward others, particularly during his sessions. But he experienced these as entirely novel at best and more often as shocking and disruptive to his equilibrium, certainly not as the return to consciousness of repressed, previously experienced states of mind. In fact, it took a long time before he abandoned his belief that experiencing feelings about others was abnormal and traumatic, so that he might begin to accept the idea that by assisting him in such self-awareness I was not in fact harming him. On occasion he still returned from even a brief separation in a state of vagueness and absence of feeling, apprehensive about encountering me because I seemed to him like a threatening stranger.

DEVELOPMENT OF THE CAPACITY
TO REPRESENT AFFECT

In order to understand the origin and developmental significance of a defect in affect representation, we must first understand something about how affect becomes represented, structured, "internalized" as part of the mind. In 1911 Freud defined affect as motor discharge bound by the mental apparatus in the form of thought. In 1926 he suggested that this binding is an ego function and that the ego's capacity to "sample" affects and use these samples as signals is an important part of its defense function. This contribution paved the way for an epigenetic view of affect.

The intellectual precocity Kernberg and his Kleinian predecessors attribute to infants is based on a failure to distinguish between the biological phenomenon of primal affect expression and the mentational process that enables reflective awareness of emotion. Darwin (1872) was the first of many to note that newborns experience and express discrete affects. But the presence from birth of a functioning affect system by no means implies the kind of representation and conscious or unconscious processing of emotion the analyst assumes in normal and neurotic mental functioning. Wolff (1966) notes that, in observing infants, one must "distinguish between an affect expression and the emotional significance which the adult observer may attribute to it" (p. 76). Zajonc (1980) makes the case that affect precedes cognition and that the two are in fact separate systems. In other words, affect must be represented by a mental apparatus that, through a process of biological maturation and psychological development, has become capable of symbolization, fantasy, and reflective self-awareness. Wilson and Malatesta (1989) believe this process may occur in the second year of life, as part of language acquisition and the development of defense mechanisms.

Piaget's model of cognitive development may provide a framework for understanding the development of affect representation. Efforts in this direction have been made by several authors (Basch, 1976; Greenspan, 1979; Lane & Schwartz, 1987; Wilson & Malatesta, 1989; Wolff, 1960, 1966). Greenspan (1979) asserts that the "split [between Piaget and psychoanalysis] may be reversed by consideration of a more general model in which a developmentally determined set of cognitive structures interacts with external and internal stimuli" (p. 168). Lane and Schwartz (1987) propose five levels of emotional awareness that parallel Piaget's stages of cognitive development, as well as structural transformations of emotion at each stage.

It is my impression that, by 3 to 5 years of age, having had much assistance in doing so from parents, most children are able to recognize and label the emotions underlying basic nonsuperego affects (such as sadness, anger, happiness or joy, and disgust). But it is remarkable how flat and affectless their volitional speech remains. The capacities to emotionally modulate speech and to consciously evoke and enact affect, which are hallmarks of evocative mental representational constancy, are relatively late in development, perhaps occurring at the end of latency or early in adolescence. This suggests that affect recognition and representation occurs early in childhood as a result of mirroring feedback, but representational constancy and evocative capacity are not achieved until later, at which time mental process can be employed in the absence of an external stimulus to evoke an affective experience.

If we attempt to view affect development within a hierarchical schema such as Gedo's, then it would appear to be a complex, multilevel process that commences at Level I, with the beginning of state regulation and ability to maintain affective equilibrium. At Level II the process of psychic integration begins. This is the level of sensorimotor–affective thinking and symbiotic object relations. Psychic differentiation and integration occur not simply at the macroscopic level of self development and cohesion of aims and goals but at the microscopic level of psychic structuralization and mental representation. While a degree of affect representation is obviously necessary for successful progression to Level III (fantasy that is susceptible to gradual reality testing and modification) and Level IV (intrapsychic conflict and defense), affect representational development continues beyond Level II, for example, in the volitional capacity to emote, which requires evocative memory capacity. Development of the capacity to evoke affect is probably a complex evolving process that relates to the taming of fantasy at Level III, to the capacity for emotional ambivalence, which, along with the experience of intrapsychic conflict and defense, is acquired at least in part at Level IV, and to the more genuinely creative uses of emotionality that characterize Level V.

With regard to the question of affect pathology, Freud believed that affect is a quantifiable instinctual cathexis that does not necessarily have to remain bound to an idea (represented), but may, under certain conditions, become separated. He asserted that neurosis develops when repression dissolves the "instinctual representative" into its component ideational and affective aspects (1915, p. 152). This phenomenon, which Freud referred to as "repression," we nowadays might describe as a regressive transformation of affect representation. He went on to describe how pathological separation of affect from idea may produce the emotionally indifferent hysteric whose affect has been converted into physical symptomatology or the obsessive-compulsive whose affect has been isolated and displaced. It is important to note that because Freud did not concern himself with the process of development of mental representation of affect, he could not consider the possibility of pathological miscarriage of that process. For Freud, as well as for the heirs to classical theory, affect pathology is the result of conflict and defense. Freud came closest to suggesting pathology of the representational process in his efforts to comprehend repetition compulsion phenomena, when he observed that the destructive process is not accompanied by an unconsciously represented wish. To account for this, however, he invoked the controversial death instinct concept (1920).

Gedo (1979, 1981) and Cohen and Kinston (1983, 1986) have considered the possibility that behavior patterns of which an individual is unconscious persist because of a archaic mode of thinking in which the relevant aims and needs have not been dynamically repressed as the result of intrapsychic conflict and defense but have never gained symbolic (wish) expression and been the subject of intrapsychic conflict to begin with. But they conceive of islands of trauma-induced failure to represent experience in otherwise normal or neurotic individuals, whereas I hypothesize the possibility of a more general failure to develop the capacity to represent affects.

How may we account for this failure of development? First, let me reiterate that the development of affect representation is a complex process that continues in its various aspects throughout childhood. This means that disturbances in affect representation encountered in adults may be qualitatively different from one another and may stem from trauma, disruption, neglect, and the like that occured at a variety of different periods during childhood. Second, reconstructions from analyses of adults lead me to believe that the origin of affect representational disturbances may be either conflictual or adaptive. After emphasizing that the relevant contemporary dynamic in these cases of affect disturbance is not that of conflict and defense, I hope it will not seem confusing or contradictory to suggest that, in some instances, the genesis of the disturbance may well have involved defense against a primal intrapsychic conflict over the continuing awareness of a state of dependency (that is, emotional ties to an object) that has become intolerably painful for the infant. In these instances of intrapsychic conflictual origin, Modell's (1985) equation of nonrecognition of affect with defense against feelings of dependency may be relevant. In other instances it may be part of a preconflictual adaptation to a particular kind of parenting that has systematically rejected, attacked, and invalidated emotional awareness and expression and then infantilized the affectively crippled individual so that he or she has never had to learn to identify and sustain awareness of the emotions that underly his affective expressions. In these instances where the origin is adaptive rather than conflictual, the seemingly maladaptive symbiotic relationships formed by the adult primitive personality, with their associated dysphoria and nonrecognition of affect, are probably efforts to repeat a primary relationship rather than examples of defense against feelings of dependency. Even in instances of intrapsychic conflictual origin, analysis of the conflict over emotions of human attachment will not, of itself, lead to awareness of and capability to bear emotions. This is because the solution to the infantile conflict was not repression of emotion but avoidance of development of the nascent capacity to represent affect. Whether the original precipitant is defensive or adaptive may depend on the age of the infant when the major burden of pathological parenting is encountered. This is consistent with Stern's (1985) assertion that early infant development involves adaptation to reality, whereas later development involves symbolization, conflict, and defense. Of course, none of this precludes the possibility of an underlying genetically determined organic susceptibility.

The capacity to represent affect may be acquired during the course of analytic treatment. Piaget (Wolff, 1987) has noted five behavior patterns in young children that accompany the development of mental representational capability. These include deferred imitation, symbolic play or pretending, drawing or graphic imagery, internalized mental imagery, and verbal evocation of past events. These are illustrated in the case of Ann.

Case IV

Ann was in her mid-forties when she sought treatment because of overwhelming anxiety and dysphoria. She was unable to make an important decision about the direction of her very successful career, which was the consuming interest of her life, and she felt helpless to leave a sadomasochistic lesbian relationship she said she no longer wanted. She did not consider herself a lesbian, although she had never been able to achieve emotional or physical intimacy with a man. The lesbian relationship was a thinly disguised repetition of her unresolved and consuming dependency on her mother.

In fact, Ann was more attracted to males than to females. But the attraction involved distant idealization and envy rather than sexuality, which both terrified and repelled her. She loathed her body and refused to look at herself in the mirror. She expressed wishes to amputate her breasts and tried to maintain a seemingly delusional belief that she had a penis. In this manner, which turned out to be an effort to identify with her father's fantasized phallic aggression, she attempted to ward off more basic dysphoric images of herself as a helpless victim of incipient abuse or as a toilet, either empty of anything good or filled with feces. These images were derived from her relationship with her mother. But, perhaps most fundamentally, as it took many years to discover, both her self-abusive attitudes and avoidance of sexually stimulating contact related to her terror of incipient sexual feelings and her inability to tolerate them without disruption for more than a few moments.

Although she was known as an academic, Ann was extremely action oriented; indeed, she could not "sit with" emotion of any kind. She avoided intimate relationships and awareness of her body because for she seemed unable to deal with the feelings that were involved. Ann might get diffusely anxious or upset, and at such times she often experienced cramps and diarrhea, but she had little awareness of specific emotions and bent all her efforts to remove the source of the disturbance or her awareness of it. It shocked her when I suggested that she was chronically depressed, although she gradually accepted the truth of my observation and found it orienting. Her contact with me did not make her feel better, however, for she experienced me as critical, and any hint of sexual feelings about me was followed immediately by disruption or avoidance. During the first several years of our work she was unaware of being an angry person, and her rationale for two things that we gradually learned about—her disgust with herself and her terror of involvement with me—was the anger and rejection she was convinced she perceived in me.

Ann had not been seeing me for long when she began to experience a sense of terror at any separation. From this we gradually inferred that she experienced me as vital to her life, even though she remained unaware of much actual good feeling during our encounters. In fact, her hours were filled with recitations of her suffering, of which I felt myself to be a necessary but inadequate container. She began to keep track of my comings and goings from my office as well as she was able. She worked nearby, and she would sit outside the building and look up at my window, because she discovered this would alleviate feelings of distress. Doing so incidentally made her uncomfortably sexually aroused. She would call me on the telephone to find out whether I was there (that is, whether I existed). She felt reassured on hearing my voice on my answering machine. She gave me various small items that, she said, represented the positive feelings she was beginning to have for me and that she hoped might help me to remember her when she was not with me.

Ann refused to consider even the smallest alterations in our schedule. Any disruption, real or imagined, was the occasion for anxiety, depression, efforts to control and possess me, and rage, which she became aware of for the first time. Signs of my autonomy such as interests, activities, or relationships that did not include her aroused a kind of idealization and envy, associated with intense rage. Ann was amazed to discover her rage; hitherto she had hardly ever been aware of anger. Her image in her work and social relationships was that of an active and cheerful person who pleased others and lived up to the highest of expectations. However, there had been a childhood history of tantrums, and she had been told she was an angry (or, as she experienced it, a bad) child.

The possessiveness was not entirely related to rage, however. She believed that I was perfect and had everything and that I experienced no pain, whereas she was excrement and had nothing to hold onto except her suffering. The meaning of her idealization turned out to involve a deep-seated fantasy, derived from observing her "perfect" mother, that one should not have to bear any emotional pain or distress or do any emotionally taxing work in life. This was what she imagined the relationships of "perfect people" like me were like.

Gradually Ann began to articulate wishes to possess, control, and consume me and to take on my identity, and as we worked on this, other, more constructive motivations began to emerge. But she continued to believe that if she could become me, and have what I had, then she would feel the unadulterated good feeling (or perhaps absence of feeling) she imagined I experienced.

By the third year, Ann would, during our separations, recall softness in my voice along with things I had said and done that she experienced as caring and that evoked positive images of our relationship. She engaged in activities that she connected to our relationship because they tended to evoke images and good feelings about it. She started keeping a journal in order to remember her feelings, which she had begun to realize were important. She also liked to wear an amulet, which signified me as well as previously unsustainable sexual feelings and erotogenic body parts she had difficulty owning.

In the fourth year of our work, two strikingly similar incidents occurred in the space of several months. Each incident involved an interruption in the treatment during which Ann read a book or saw a movie with the theme of women with small daughters who were deserted by their husbands. Her own father had had an affair, eventually left her mother when she was 5, and initiated little subsequent contact with Ann, although he was affectionate enough when they did meet. Eventually we believed his behavior must have been at least in part a response to her mother's sexual coldness, but at the time her mother subtly poisoned Ann's mind against him by referring to his need for another relationship and his erotic proclivities as evidence of his infantile, undependable nature. This had prevented Ann from counteracting her mother's cold, anhedonic approach to life with his sensual vitality. During each interruption she became extremely upset. Although she knew she could reach me by phone if need be, she felt driven to act on impulse. The first time she had discovered I was out of town, and she went to my house at night, prowled the grounds, and entered and explored an outbuilding she found unlocked. The second time she decided to medicate herself with an antidepressant without waiting to discuss the matter with me. She was especially troubled by the first incident, as she had felt "crazy" and out of control. In retrospect she realized that feelings of sadness and rage, and wishes to possess and control me, which she imagined would alleviate her distress, had been involved. However, she was hardly aware of these feelings at the time, and even in retrospect they remained vague to her. She lamented that she had not tried to contain herself and talk with someone who might have helped her to bear the feelings, instead of acting. Concluding her discussion of the second incident she exclaimed, "I just realized what's the matter with me; I never learned to deal with feelings!" After another two years of treatment she realized she had been reenacting an early adolescent pattern of hiding in dark, cold places, which symbolized her relationship with her mother, when troubled by disturbing feelings she could neither identify nor understand.

Ann began to experience more feeling, which was accompanied by dread of explosion or catastrophe and sometimes by severe headaches and even nosebleeds. She reported transient, completely novel experiences of sensual and loving thoughts involving her body, me, and our relationship. She could recall no precedent for these in her life. Her positive memories and related pleasurable fantasies about me became a source of autonomous energy for her during our separations, as well as fuel for her first forays toward new relationships. She realized her rage at any separation or frustration would lead her to destroy these positive feelings and images, so she began to struggle to recognize, articulate, and control the rage and to understand its origins in her contemporary thought process and in her personal history. Nevertheless, she was unable to recognize this issue as an intrapsychic conflict until about 5 years of treatment had elapsed. Prior to this time, she either liked me or hated me; when she hated me there was no leavening element; when she liked me we both came to realize the state was untrustworthy because her rage, which she could by then recall intellectually if not actually experience, was missing. The experience of conflict and ambivalence was unfamiliar. Moreover, the first times she experienced an ambivalent state in which good feelings predominated, she felt confused; something seemed abnormal.

In her efforts to sustain pleasurable feelings, Ann developed an avid interest in life drawing and painting. This was quite out of keeping with her previous scientific background and expressive inhibition. She drew and painted extensively, attempting to capture images of the female and male body, which she associated to her good feelings about herself and me. During one of my ensuing vacations she dreamed she was trying to draw a loving mother and child, but she did not know what they looked like and in frustration drew two parallel lines instead.

As she developed the capacity to sustain positive images of our relationship, Ann's concrete need to control and possess me, with its concomitant rage and envy, diminished, and she became calmer, more productive, and more self-sustaining. She felt she had not hitherto been a person, and she was amazed to discover expressive, creative aspects of herself grounded in her new somatic and emotional awareness, with which she gradually began to elaborate an emotionally satisfying identity, first in fantasy, and then, gradually and selectively, in action as well. She became increasingly capable of sustaining and elaborating loving and sensual feelings and fantasies about me characterized by enteroceptive wishes and related to uterine contractions she was convinced she could sense. But, characteristically and repeatedly, these feelings were disrupted by a self-critical, self-devouring part, which at times functioned as an introject and at other times was projected and which she associated with memories of her mother's subtle criticisms. Loving feelings also frightened her because of their association with the unknown and with change, particularly separation from mother, that is, from her cherished dysphoria and the special attention it had gained her as a "problem child." As her efforts gradually bore fruit, it was both amazing and disconcerting to her to discover that she could feel good and function effectively in settings where her colleagues were feeling stressed and miserable; somehow it just didn't seem right!

CONCLUSION

When primitive personalities gain emotional competence in the course of successful analysis they report an experience that is utterly novel to them, like that of a congenitally blind person who suddenly can see. This suggests that they have truly developed a new capability.

I have begun to address issues of treatment of patients with affect disturbance and related cognitive impairments (Robbins, 1989), and Gedo has addressed similar problems in his most recent (1988) book. I do not believe that these patients are unanalysable because their pathology originates from a death instinct or because relevant pathogenic experiences occurred prior to acquisition of symbolic function and are therefore analytically inaccessible. The somatic substrate of early experience remains alive and enactable as an aspect of core identity and is therefore potentially available for mental representation as well as construction of fantasy, transference, and history in the analytic situation. While treatment of primitive personalities by classical analysis is frequently unsuccessful because its underlying assumptions of cognitive and affective intactness and the existence of unconscious conflict over emotion-saturated thoughts from childhood keep the analyst from addressing the pathology I have described, analysts who believe they are adhering to the neurosis model and classical technique sometimes enjoy success treating these difficult cases. This may be because, alongside more classical methodology, instinctively and without conceptualizing what they are doing, they employ techniques that address the cognitive and affective pathology.

NOTE

Abbreviated versions of this chapter were presented to the Boston Psychoanalytic Society, September 30, 1987, and at the 78th annual meeting of the American Psychoanalytic Association, May 6, 1989.

REFERENCES

Arlow, J. (1981). Theories of pathogenesis. *Psychoanalytic Quarterly, 50,* 488–514.
Basch, M. (1976). The concept of affect: A re-examination. *Journal of the American Psychoanalytic Association, 24,* 759–777.
Cohen, J., & Kinston, W. (1983). Repression theory: A new look at the cornerstone. *International Journal of Psycho-Analysis, 65,* 411–422.
Cohen, J., & Kinston, W. (1986). Primal repression: Clinical and theoretical aspects. *International Journal of Psycho-Analysis, 67,* 337–355.
Darwin, C. (1872). *The expression of the emotions in man and animals.* Chicago: University of Chicago Press. 1965.
Engel, G. L. (1977). The need for a new medical model: A challenge for biomedicine. *Science, 196,* 129–136.
Engel, G. L. (1980). The clinical application of the biopsychosocial model. *American Journal of Psychiatry, 137,* 535–544.
Fairbairn, W. (1952). *Psychoanalytic studies of the personality.* London: Routledge & Kegan Paul.
Freud, S. (1911). Formulations on the two principles of mental functioning. *Standard Edition* (Vol. 12, pp. 215–226). London: Hogarth Press, 1966.

Freud, S. (1915). Repression. *Standard Edition* (Vol. 14, pp. 141–158). London: Hogarth Press, 1966.

Freud, S. (1920). Beyond the pleasure principle. *Standard Edition* (Vol. 18, pp. 3–66). London: Hogarth Press, 1966.

Freud, S. (1926). Inhibitions, symptoms and anxiety. *Standard Edition* (Vol. 20, pp. 77–178). London: Hogarth Press.

Gedo, J. (1979). *Beyond interpretation.* New York: International Universities Press.

Gedo, J. (1981). Measure for measure: a response. *Psychoanalytic Inquiry, 1,* 289–316.

Gedo, J. (1988). *The mind in disorder.* Hillsdale, NJ: Analytic Press.

Gedo, J., & Goldberg, A. (1973). *Models of the mind.* Chicago: University of Chicago Press.

Greenspan, S. (1979). *Intelligence and adaptation.* Psychological Issues, Monograph 47/48. New York: International Universities Press.

Hartmann, H. (1958). *Ego psychology and the problem of adaptation.* New York: International Universities Press.

Kernberg, O. (1975). *Borderline conditions and pathological narcissism.* New York: Aronson.

Klein, M. (1935). A contribution to the psycho-genesis of manic–depressive states. In *Contributions to psycho-analysis, 1921–1945.* London: Hogarth Press, 1948.

Knapp, P. (Ed.). (1963). *Expression of the emotions in man.* New York: International Universities Press.

Kohut, H., & Wolff, E. (1978). The disorders of the self and their treatment: an outline. *International Journal of Psycho-Analysis, 59,* 413–425.

Krystal, H. (1982). Alexithymia and the effectiveness of psychoanalytic treatment. *International Journal of Psycho-Analysis, 9,* 353–378.

Lane, R., & Schwartz, G. (1987). Levels of emotional awareness: A cognitive-developmental theory and its application to psychopathology. *American Journal of Psychiatry, 144,* 133–143.

Loewald, H. (1971). On motivation and instinct theory. *Psychoanalytic Study of the Child, 26,* 91–128.

Marty, P., & de M'Uzan, M. (1963). La pensée operatoire. *Revue Francaise de Psychoanalyse, 27* (Suppl.), 1345–1356.

Marty, P., de M'Uzan, M., & David, C. (1963). *L'investigation psychosomatique.* Paris: Presses Universitaires de France.

McDougall, J. (1974). The psychosoma and the psychoanalytic process. *International Review of Psycho-Analysis, 1,* 437–459.

McDougall, J. (1982a). Alexithymia: A psychoanalytic viewpoint. *Psychotherapy and Psychosomatics, 38,* 81–90.

McDougall, J. (1982b). Alexithymia, psychosomatosis, and psychosis. *International Journal of Psychoanalytic Psychotherapy, 9,* 379–388.

Modell, A. (1975). A narcissistic defense against affects and the illusion of self-sufficiency. *International Journal of Psycho-Analysis, 56,* 275–282.

Nemiah, J., & Sifneos, P. (1970). Affect and fantasy in patients with psychosomatic disorders. In O. Hill (Ed.), *Modern trends in psychosomatic medicine* (Vol. 2, pp. 430–439). London: Butterworth.

Robbins, M. (1981). The symbiosis concept and the commencement of normal and pathological ego functioning and object relations, II: Developments subsequent to infancy and pathological processes. *International Review of Psycho-Analysis, 8,* 379–391.

Robbins, M. (1983). Toward a new mind model for the primitive personalities. *International Journal of Psycho-Analysis, 64,* 127–148.

Robbins, M. (1989). Primitive personality organization as an interpersonally adaptive modification of cognition and affect. *International Journal of Psycho-Analysis, 70,* 443–459.

Sifneos, P. (1967). Clinical observations on some patients suffering from a variety of psychosomatic diseases. In *Acta Medica Psychosomatica, Proceedings of the Seventh European Conference on Psychosomatic Research* (pp. 452–458). Basel: S. Karger.

Stern, D. (1985). *The interpersonal world of the infant.* New York: Basic Books.

Taylor, G. (1987). *Psychosomatic medicine and contemporary psychoanalysis.* Madison, CT: International Universities Press.

Weiss, P. (1969). The living system: Determinism stratified. In A. Koestler & J. Smythies, (Eds.), *Beyond reductionism* (pp. 3–55). New York: Macmillan.

Weiss, P. (1977). The system of nature and the nature of systems: Empirical wholism and practical reductionism harmonized. In K. Schaefer, H. Hensel, & R. Brady (Eds.), *Toward a man-centered medical science* (pp. 17–64). Mt. Kisco, NY: Futura.

Wilson, A., & Malatesta, C. (1989). Affect and the compulsion to repeat: Freud's repetition compulsion revisited. *Psychoanalysis and Contemporary Thought, 12,* 243–290.

Wolff, P. (1960). *The developmental psychologies of Jean Piaget and psychoanalysis.* Psychological Issues, Monograph 5. New York: International Universities Press.

Wolff, P. (1966). *The causes, controls, and organization of behavior in the neonate.* Psychological Issues, Monograph 17. New York: International Universities Press.

Wolff, P. (1987). *The development of behavioral states and the expression of emotions in early infancy.* Chicago: University of Chicago Press.

Zajonc, R. (1980). Feeling and thinking: Preferences need no inferences. *American Psychologist, 35,* 151–175.

9

Substance Abuse, Repetition, and the Nature of Addictive Suffering

EDWARD J. KHANTZIAN AND ARNOLD WILSON

Our aim in this chapter is to reconcile two seemingly disparate aspects of drug dependence. On the one hand, reliance on addictive drugs involves attempts to relieve psychological suffering; on the other hand, suffering becomes a prominent invariable consequence of such a reliance on drugs. In order to reconcile this seeming contradiction, we will invoke a hierarchical conception of personality organization, and we will depict how a higher-level form of suffering can be preferred or invoked as a "trade-off" for a lower-level form of suffering that is more distressing because it is immersed in failures of self-regulation. In and of itself, this pattern of avoiding while embracing suffering certainly is not unique to substance dependence; symptom choice in most psychopathology often has the dual aspect of relieving distress at the same time that the symptom causes suffering in its own right. An exhaustive review of the psychodynamics of this exchange or trade-off in understanding the conflicted nature of psychological defenses in general would go beyond the scope of this paper. We believe that an exploration and clarification of this dual aspect of addiction has important theoretical and treatment implications for the addictions. When it comes to the particular instance of the addictions, most explanations in the literature of the processes involved in the relief and perpetuation of suffering are insufficiently detailed; addictions are thus poorly understood, oversimplified, and often reduced to mutually exclusive psychological or physiologic/addictive mechanisms. Fyodor Dostoyevsky, himself gifted with marvelous insight into the dynamics of masochism, once observed, "Man is sometimes extraordinarily, passionately, in love with suffering." While this is certainly so for many individuals, in this chapter we will explore how this is particularly the case for addicts.

Many contemporary psychodynamic formulations of addicts' vulnerabilities have sought to explain, on the adaptive side of this schism, how the effects of addictive drugs relieve suffering. However, such theories have been less clear in explaining the maladaptive, repetitious suffering that also occurs. In this chapter, we will first address recent psychodynamic formulations that explain the adaptive basis for substance dependence. We will then explore a possible relationship between recent psychoanalytic formulations on affect deficits and repetition and the painful and self-perpetuating nature of addictive suffering. We will attempt to show that substance dependence cannot be reduced to such simplistic explanations involving addictive mechanisms as pleasure seeking, self destruction, or relief of pain alone. Rather, we understand substance dependence as related to attempts to self-regulate human suffering, that is, as related to the overriding principle of self-regulation and its complex branches in psychological life (Wilson, Passik, & Faude, 1990).

AFFECT DEFENSE AND THE ADDICTIVE PROCESS

Before specifying what the special nature of the attachment to suffering is all about in addicts, we would like to briefly consider and recapitulate some of the more obvious reasons why individuals rely on drugs. Gaining a refined and balanced understanding of substance dependence is hindered by some new and old psychiatric and psychological tautologies. The recent hegemony of "the disease concept" of alcoholism and addiction, bolstered by the meteoric rise of etiologic explanations involving neurotransmitters and cortical mechanisms, has tended to reduce substance dependence to problems with biological disequilibrium. These formulations can help explain the cyclical, repetitive nature of substance dependence on the basis of feedback loops in which the exogenous substance disrupts internal homeostatic mechanisms, which in turn produce neurochemical alterations whereby constant or increasing amounts of the substance are required to maintain equilibrium. These mechanisms are implicit and/or explicit in such phrases as "loss of control" or "an addiction takes on a life of its own," often heard when researchers try to describe the compelling nature of addiction. Psychoanalysts who report on the addictions have not done much better in avoiding their own tautologies, often reducing the motive behind the repetitive and self-destructive aspects of addiction to the "pleasure" or "death" instincts. The tendency to reduce and polarize addictions into simplistic biologic/pharmacodynamic versus psychological/psychodynamic mechanisms can be seen to result, in part, from a failure to specify and differentiate the *predisposing, evolving,* and *advanced* phases of addictive disorders. This reluctance to look past one's own theoretical borders also deters investigators from adopting a multietiologic approach, which we hold is necessary in order to unravel the biological and psychological complexities of addictive suffering. A contemporary psychodynamic and clinical understanding of the addictions is totally consistent with and complements the evolving understanding of the biological underpinnings of substance dependence. It is to the credit of the hierarchical model first advanced by Gedo (1979) and Gedo and Goldberg (1973) that the biological and psychological can come together in a confluence of understanding within the jurisdiction of psychoanalytic theory. This adds greatly to the explanatory power of psychoanalysis and allows for the potential integration of much relevant data in the case of the addict.

We will now examine some recent psychodynamic formulations on addicts' vulnerabilities that emphasize problems with affect tolerance associated with the addictive process. In the subsequent sections we will explore how these vulnerabilities of affect tolerance interact with the addictive process. We will emphasize how such vulnerabilities in the personality organization of addicts, the nature of their distress, and the effects of drug intake make for a virtually compulsory and repetitive interaction that can be understood from a hierarchical perspective.

Affect Defense and Self-medication

Corresponding to advances in psychoanalysis in general over the past 50 years, psychoanalytic explorations of substance dependence and compulsive drug use have shifted from a focus on drive theory, topographic factors, and the symbolic meanings attached to drugs to a greater emphasis on affects, human development, and structural factors (Khantzian, 1974; Khantzian & Treece, 1977). Beginning around 1970, a number of psychoanalytic investigators began to report on the general and specific properties of addictive drugs that afforded users "protection" from internal and external chaos. Wurmser (1974), for example, placed the "defect of affect defense" at the heart of the addict's problem. Others who worked closely with increasing numbers of substance dependent people in psychotherapy and psychoanalysis also observed and described how such patients rely on these drugs to protect against painful affect states. There was a rather quick consensus that these drugs served as correctives or prosthetics for developmental (structural) impairments to compensate for a defective stimulus barrier (Krystal & Raskin, 1970; Weider & Kaplan, 1969). Khantzian (1974, 1978, 1979) emphasized defects in affect and drive defense, dysphoria, and how addicts seek to produce not euphoria but rather relief from dysphoria. Relief from dysphoria is necessary for addicts because defenses against affects during the addictive process become overdrawn, rigid, defective, or absent. With the failure of defensive operations comes an early form of depression that focuses on experiences of emptiness, depletion, impulsivity, and helplessness.

Beyond drugs serving as a general prosthetic that protects against painful affect states, a number of investigators from a psychodynamic perspective attempted to formulate why and how individuals experimenting with different classes of drugs come to prefer the specific effects of one as opposed to another particular class of drugs. The views of these investigators have in common an emphasis on the adaptive value of drug effects, but they have differed in stressing both regressive and progressive adaptations in order to explain why each class of drugs has its particular appeal. For example, Weider and Kaplan (1969) proposed that with their "drug-of-choice," narcotic addicts sought to induce a regressed state of "blissful satiation" corresponding to the first year of life as described by Mahler (1968). Others suggested that the calming and dampening effects of barbiturates and opiates against intense affect fostered a tendency for withdrawal and isolation (Hendin, 1974; Milkman & Frosch, 1973). Thus, affects themselves are transformed along developmental pathways (as recognized by Krystal's [1974] dedifferentiation hypothesis) and can be located within specific structures that correspond to modal organizations. In the terms of Gedo's hierarchical model, narcotic addicts are struggling with Mode II structural problems, and barbiturate and cocaine addicts are struggling with Mode III structural problems. This hypothesis has received experimental support in the research of Keller (1989), which is also presented in Chapter 3 of this volume.

To be sure, our observations of the psychodynamics of addiction lead us to be less impressed that the drug-of-choice corresponds to static factors of a specific developmental phase or hallmark and to be more impressed with states of pervasive dysphoria and related negative affects. We think that these negative affects stem from very early origins, preverbal and presymbolic, which through repetition are linked to all phases of the life cycle and interact with later experiences of trauma, abuse, and neglect. One of us (Edward Khantzian) has tried to specify how individuals attempt to differentially "self-medicate," with the various classes of drugs, the affect states associated with varying distortions and deficits in defenses and personality organization. Opiates, sedatives, and stimulants are conceived of as separate classes of drugs. It has been proposed that narcotic addicts use the anti-aggression/rage action of opiates progressively to compensate for and reverse these intensely threatening affects that are associated with defects in drive and affect defense. Sedative-dependent people, including alcoholics, counter feelings of emptiness, coldness, and isolation through the softening–dissolving effects of these drugs on overdrawn and rigid defensive organizations. Stimulant abusers counter affect states of depletion, anergia, and hyperactivity associated with the inflated–deflated ego ideal structures of depressive and narcissistic characters (Khantzian, 1972, 1974, 1975, 1979, 1982, 1985).

The Addictive Process

We believe that what psychoanalysis has uncovered about self-medication motives are important, especially when individuals first use drugs and discover the relief-producing properties of drugs. However, it is also a truism in the addiction field that the initial reasons a person takes drugs are different from those that subsequently occur once the person becomes addicted or physically dependent on the drug. This truism is all too often invoked to explain how the main perpetuating factor in middle and advanced phases of drug dependency is the motive of remaining "normal" by avoiding withdrawal symptoms. This motive or explanation, of course, is valid, but, again, is excessively simplistic and reductionistic.

The painful affects associated with withdrawal are real, but they are compounded by the now-addicted individual's preexistent intolerance to painful affect. In fact, one of the most striking features seen with addicted individuals is how much the subjective feeling states associated with physical withdrawal from each class of addictive drugs (i.e., opiates, stimulants, and sedatives) resemble the preexisting painful affects that were originally relieved by their drug-of-choice. Martin (Martin, Haertzen, & Hewett, 1978; Martin, Hewett, Baker, & Haertzen, 1978), using empirical methods, has concluded that the withdrawal feelings (he calls them "hypohoria") that are part of the "protracted withdrawal syndrome" are much like the feeling states that first predisposed addicts and alcoholics to rely on substances. Hence the inner horror of withdrawal during the evolving phases of addiction. The return of the aversive early affect states are defended against vigorously, in new and changing ways. Furthermore, it should also be mentioned here that the course of addictive illness and the feeling states associated with such a course are highly variable in an individual's natural history with drugs, such that at different times different physiological or psychological factors may predominate (Wilson, Passik, Faude, Gordon, & Abrams, 1989). For example, in addition to the predisposing and resulting mechanisms of drug dependency, drugs can be used short term adaptively or "instrumentally" (McAuliffe et al., 1984) to solve problems, augment performance, or contain behavior (e.g., use of stimulants for wakefulness and improved attention). Conversely, drugs can be used maladaptively and regressively to avoid and withdraw from challenges.

WITHIN THE BORDERLANDS OF AFFECT, REPETITION, AND ADDICTION

Addicts are clearly vulnerable in their inability to self-regulate their emotional lives. Each has had the powerful discovery that particular drugs relieve the suffering associated with overwhelming painful affects. Their desperation might seem to be the main and only factor necessary to explain addicts' repeated and continual return to drugs, even after long periods of abstinence and despite the invariable deleterious consequences of long-term drug use. Of course, one need not treat addicts too long to be aware of the high price they pay for their attempts at self-treatment. Observing narcotic addicts first coming to a methadone clinic, it is quickly evident how much they suffer as a consequence of their drug use. They are physically deteriorated, manifesting nutritional deficiencies, unkempt appearances, poor grooming, and a variety of skin lesions and scars; psychological regression is evident in hypochondriacal complaints, paranoid mistrust, irrational demands, and aggressive use of obscenities; an internal world of emotional chaos is thinly veiled by cool posturing and/or contemptuous requests for methadone alone (Khantzian & Kates, 1978).

One might argue, as did Rado (1933), that the "pleasure" is worth the pain. We note that if one reads Rado carefully, it seems clear that he did not mean pleasure but the relief from dysphoria and painful affect states, given the presence of a predisposing "tense depression," which he observed to be present in most addicts. The behavioral and psychological deterioration and/or regression might then be explained as a function of artificial psychological and biological drive cycles of addiction that are beyond the person's intention or control. Once again, our patients have instructed us differently. A number of them have indicated that often they are compelled to use drugs when they are not necessarily experiencing or aware of overwhelming painful feelings. In fact, they might simply be feeling bored or vaguely uncomfortable, or yet still they might be feeling or doing well and know that taking drugs will make them feel worse. Yet they revert to drug use. Charles, a 33-year-old narcotic patient whom one of us (Edward Khantzian) had been treating for 10 years, was in a phase of recovery in which he was using drugs only intermittently. He described this more subtle compulsion to use drugs. He had recently sprained his ankle (an all-too-common type of occurrence seen with addicts), and he was fighting his impulse to obtain and use a narcotic analgesic. He complained, "I can't bear it anymore. I'm bored with doing so good. If I take the drug it'll make me feel very shitty, but it'll be more bearable. Tomorrow I will be okay, because I'll feel shitty but I'll know why I feel shitty." He emphasized that he did not want to "obliterate" himself the way he did before, and he would not; he just wanted to change how he felt. In the terms of the hierarchical model, the conscious suffering that is under control characteristic of the higher modes is preferred to the presubjective failures of self-control characteristic of the lower modes. Whereas in classical analysis pre-oedipal pathology has long been seen as a regressive defense against oedipal anxieties, we also note that the opposite can be seen—higher-level pathology can be used as a progressive defense against pre-oedipal pathology. There is a preference for the more conscious mentation, and along with it, the maladaptive ravages of addiction than the more vague, obscure, oceanic distress of Modes I and II. This formulation runs counter to the dichotomy in the pleasure–reality principle as a primary motivational explanation. We wish to emphasize the stark power of the above motive for ingesting drugs, seen over and over again in our clinical work. Thus, the suffering of one level can serve as a defense against the suffering of another, more primitive (presubjective) level. The suffering of Modes III, IV, and V can be used as a trade-off to defend against the more self-destructive (and presubjective, i.e., beyond memorial access) sufferings of Modes I and II. Why this is the case with certain addicts is an individual question having largely to do with their affect tolerance and affect defenses, as well as with other factors related to their particular personality organizations.

There is a great deal of paradox and contradiction in what addicts "achieve" with their drug use. Most descriptions of the adaptive and maladaptive aspects of drug reliance do not do justice to the experience of addicts. An articulate and gifted lawyer, who was also an addict, provided reactions to his drug use in group therapy that underscore some of the seemingly antithetical motives involved in drug use. The group members were discussing the relief they obtained from drugs, but they were also lamenting how much pain and discomfort resulted from their reliance on and withdrawal from drugs. In this context, he stated that he and the other members were as drawn to "misery" as a result of drug use as they were with drugs for the relief they offered—if not more so. He added, "At least it was a misery I produced and I could control, whereas the misery that caused my drug use I could not control." Here again we see the trade-off of the postsubjective suffering for the presubjective suffering. Variations on this kind of statement from our patients in psychotherapy and psychoanalysis are not atypical. Some of them, knowing about the "self-medication" hypothesis (they see reprints and/or read our papers) have gratuitously offered comments about the proportion of relief to misery by such comments as, "Doc, that's only part of the story; sure, I get relief, but it's 10% relief and 90% misery." As we have become more alert to such responses, our patients have forced us to consider, from a psychodynamic perspective, that the negative consequences (including dysphoric affects) that drug dependency entails might be as important a determinant of compulsive drug use as the relief it provides. An explanation of these seemingly contradictory motives can be garnered from considering that way such patients are different in the ways they experience affects and in the special way repetition of both the pain and relief associated with drugs and related behaviors serves them adaptively. That is, a more inclusive explanation of addiction needs to account for more than the suffering associated with unmanageable, painful affects that make drug use compelling. Addicts suffer as much because their affects are absent and fail them. Modes I and II affects are not just overwhelming; they can be absent, split, not linked to the verbal system (alexithymia), and so on. Addicts are also just as often confused, impoverished, and cut off from their feelings as they are overwhelmed by them, as the lawyer's keen description reveals or as Charles's case demonstrates.

Thus, we will proceed to explore recent clarifications on the theory of affect deficits and motives for repetition in general, which bear on the problems addicts display with confusion and dysfunction around affects. We will provide evidence in support of the idea that addicts might be as involved in efforts to control their bewilderment around their feeling life as they are involved with relieving their painful feeling states. Much of the literature on which we will draw comes from work with special populations, not necessarily addicts, but interestingly and significantly many of these reports use addictive metaphors and references to substance use in describing affect pathology and the dynamics of repetitious suffering.

Affect Deficits and Dysfunction

There is a modest yet growing and important literature that has appeared over the past 25 years that describes how certain patients experience their feelings in unusual or atypical ways. These reports have largely involved work with the addictions but have also grown out of work with patients whose problems lie on the borders of neurotic, psychosomatic, and characterologic pathology. Terms such as "alexithymia," "dysphoria," "dis-affected," "affect deficit," "hypophoria," and "non-feeling response" have been coined or adopted to capture or convey how certain patients have very different experiences and/or dysfunction in relation to their feeling life. What characterizes most of these descriptions is their presubjective, ineffable, uncontrollable quality, which in our opinion places them in the realm of self-regulatory concerns. Sashin (1985, 1986) has recently provided a useful description of how such "abnormal affect response(s)" manifest themselves. These may include apparent non-reactions to experiences that would be expected to produce feelings, a rapid conversion of experience into action, somatic dysfunction, cognitive disorganization, rapid shifts from seeming to have no reaction to violent motor reaction, peculiar delays in reaction, and other extreme patterns. He quotes Fenichel's story of a patient who responded to the news of his mother's death by saying, "Oh, what a shock this will be in the morning." These terms and characterizations share in common an appreciation that, in addition to patients being overwhelmed with painful affect and feeling too much, they also suffer because they often do not feel enough, or do not feel at all, or their feelings are distorted and confusing.

Although addicts display a wide range of emotional responses, we have been repeatedly impressed that addicts are, as a group, strikingly different in the way they experience their internal feeling life. In order to account for their pain and suffering, a number of clinicians have emphasized the extremely traumatizing and hurtful environments that they have endured. We agree, but note that in the literature there has not been a sufficient appreciation of how much their developmental backgrounds and experiences have distorted and significantly altered their feeling responses. Although many addicts appear to be verbally facile and superficially engaging, many others are neither verbal nor engaging, and it often seems difficult to empathically relate to them, especially around affects. Invariably, almost all the addicts with whom we have worked clinically demonstrate to some degree major constrictions and/or peculiarities in describing or expressing their affects. Often, despite circumstances and experiences that would ordinarily evoke strong feelings, addicted patients seem devoid of them, as Sashin has described, or revert to action and activity and describe instead, in great detail, the circumstances of what they did. Much of the time they appear to function at an enactive/action rather than lexical/reflective level. The most available and easiest emotion to express, however, seems to be anger, often expressed in a paranoid style, in bursts and using projection to demonstrate persecution. When we have presented patients with this observation, they have agreed that "it is easier to fight than to feel." Countertransference reactions to such patients at times lead the therapist to experience them as vacuous and devoid of affects, that is, as if affects just were not there. At other times, the therapist can better experience and identify tension, fear, if not terror, distortions, and intense transference reactions, which suggest more primitive and/or massive defensive attempts to avoid feelings.

Krystal and Raskin (1970) whose observations derive from their work with alchoholics and victims of massive trauma, have provided important theoretical building blocks for understanding what might be the basis for the distortions and dysfunction in affect experience we describe here. They have proposed that affects have a normal developmental line in which there is progressive differentiation but, as a consequence of developmental vicissitudes or subsequent trauma, are subject to arrest or regression in function. Optimal development of affects serves to maintain the stimulus barrier.

More recently, Krystal (1982) has adopted the term "alexithymia," coined by Sifneos (1967) and Nemiah (1970) from their work with psychosomatic patients, to capture the quality of this deficit in the patients with whom he has worked. He emphasizes that patients with alexithymia show a minimal capacity to verbalize their feelings and that separate and identifiable feelings such as anxiety and depression cannot be articulated and are often expressed somatically. He observes that they often cannot tell or distinguish whether they are sad, tired, hungry, or ill. Similarly, Nemiah (1975) has observed,

> Many psychosomatic patients, although they use words like "sad," "angry" and "nervous," are unable to describe their feelings; further, they appear to be at a loss for language to convey their experience of them to others, and frequently when pressed by the interviewer for a response assert that they "just can't put it into words." (p. 43)

On the other hand, Krystal underscores that such patients may also briefly display intense outbursts of feelings, including feelings of rage and violence. The deficit is also evident in the cognitive realm. Krystal cites the work of the French analysts Marty and de M'Uzan (1963) on operational thinking (*pensée opératoire*) in which patients show flashes of brilliant thinking, but these flashes are ultimately revealed to be bound to facts and external stimuli with little connection to the patients' inner lives.

Along similar lines, McDougall (1984) has described certain patients seen in her psychoanalytic practice as "dis-affected." These patients seem to be generally out of touch with their feelings, and in the treatment relationship they produce a sense of paralysis in the analyst as well as a mutually experienced stagnation and boredom. She characterizes these patients as pragmatic, unimaginative, factual, and unemotional in spite of significant emotional events in their lives. Instead, they immediately disperse any emotional arousal in action. Like Krystal, Sifneos, Nemiah, and Marty and de M'Uzan, with whom she links her observations, she stresses how unaware these patients are of their affective reactions. Instead, they drown strong emotion through alcohol use, bulimic bouts, or drug abuse; furthermore, some of these patients engage frenetically in perverse or compulsive sexual activity, which appears addictive to her. She believes that all these responses are a means to avoid affective flooding. She goes on to speculate that narcissistic defenses, relationships, and addictive-action patterns, albeit painful, might serve to protect against psychosomatic regression.

A number of other clinicians have noted findings in patients that are similar or related to the deficits seen with alexithymia, operational thinking, and dis-affected patients. Wurmser (1974) has adopted the term "hyposymbolization" to describe addicts' inability to describe their inner life and their impoverishment of emotions, sense of self, and fantasies, and Sashin (1985) has linked the inability to fantasize and verbalize about one's inner life to major disturbances in affect tolerance and has termed such problems "non-feeling response(s)." Gedo (1986) and Lichtenberg (1983) have both attempted to link and correlate their experiences as psychoanalysts working with adults, with observations and findings from infant research and to provide a basis to understand why and how affects can be so bewildering. The problem is that often what is most meaningful in life "is not necessarily encoded in words" (Gedo, 1986, p. 206), and that so much of what is affectively charged, distorted, and expressed somatically is due to the fact that some of the most lasting emotional experiences derive from preverbal, psychobiological, presymbolic phases of development. These presubjective phenomena, according to Gedo, can be understood as within the domain of the repetition compulsion, swept up by the urge to repeat that which cannot be put into words, in bewildering ways and in endless permutations. Gedo concurs with Lichtenberg that very often early emotional experiences are not coded into subjectively accessible memories and are without symbolic representation, but they remain and extend into adult life as "perceptual–action–affect" responses. We are in agreement that the affective experiences of the addict from early phases of development significantly shape and influence certain adult tendencies to repeat distressful experiences and that such vulnerabilities can also become linked in painfully repetitious ways to much of the suffering entailed in addictive disorders.

Repetition

Given the centrality of the repetitious nature of human suffering in all the varied forms it takes in severe and "everyday" psychopathology, it is impressive, with some notable exceptions, how little we have moved beyond Freud's (1920) observations about the repetition compulsion to explain the human tendency to perpetuate psychological pain. This is especially so with character pathology and behavioral disturbances. Many analytic formulations about behavioral and impulse disorders, especially the addictions are often still more influenced than is realized by notions about "life" (pleasure) and "death" (aggressive) instincts. We do not observe or consider often enough and clearly enough (especially in clinical practice with difficult, acting-out patients) how the self-defeating, destructive aspects of such problems are rooted in disturbed object relations and structural deficiencies. Actually, setting aside his misleading and highly speculative conclusions about "death instinct," Freud's formulations about turning passive unpleasure into active mastery and the defensive function served by children's play had within them the anlage of a more contemporary theory of affects (Modell, 1984; Wilson & Malatesta, 1989) and the adaptive aspects of repetition. This emphasis of converting a passive experience of distress to an active one comes closer to capturing what we are trying to describe about addicts' experience with and perpetuation of suffering.

We are still in need of a compelling and comprehensive theory of repetition that more clearly elaborates on and accounts for object relational and structural factors, so as to explain the human penchant to court and hold onto painful affects. In what follows we will selectively examine some more recent observations, which provide a better explanation of the need to repeat painful experiences and patterns, including the patterns and reactions involved with addictions. Our emphasis is based on a view of repetition in which there is a need to repeatedly express, control, and resolve early disruptive maternal–child experiences, which are represented in patterns of affect expression and are attached to the dynamics and conflicts of more advanced phases of development. We hope to show how these observations provide a better basis to explain and understand addictive suffering.

The ubiquity of human suffering evident in all psychopathology is sadly often overlooked in substance dependent individuals because of the pejorative view of them as "pleasure seekers" or as "self-destructive characters." There is little in our clinical experience that suggests that individuals who become and remain addicted are governed by pleasure or self-destructive motives (Khantzian, 1975). Gedo (1979) has also argued against suggesting that the compulsion to repeat painful experiences or suffering derives from a death instinct or inverted aggression to expiate guilt. In fact, he believes that many aspects of repeating are best understood as automatic attempts to avoid "traumatic unpleasure" and to preserve self-organization. Least of all does the suffering have to do with attacks upon the self.

When it comes to understanding addiction, Freud's conjectures about the "death instinct," employing the motivational explanation of the pursuit of pleasure, do not serve us well today. Fairbairn's (1944) work is a helpful supplement and is quite useful in clarifying why people court distress in their troubled object relations. He believed the libido was object seeking, not pleasure seeking, in human life and that the essential striving of the child is not pleasure, but contact. The child's only choice, even if painful and ungratifying, is his or her parent, and if they are ungratifying, then the child establishes compensatory internal object relations and, despite frustration, seeks a more gratifying contact with the parent. Fairbairn called this an "obstinate attachment." Later, in adult life, allegiance and devotion are maintained to these early painful ties in the painful, self-defeating attachments and relationships that are repeatedly formed and reexperienced. Valenstein (1973) has provided additional useful insights about attachment to painful feelings, which are relevant to our understanding of addictive suffering. His observations derived from work with patients who remained tenaciously attached to their psychic pain in the transference. He believed that the attachment is an amplification of such patients' predilection "to exact a singular quality of pain from human relationships" (p. 366). Similar to Fairbairn, he linked qualities of affect response to the infant's earliest ties, which in turn influence later object representation and coalesce more around the *affective* correlates of experience than around cognitive elements. Given the preverbal nature of early life experiences, motor and affect referents may substitute for discrete memories and cognition. Along these lines, Modell (1984) has commented on patients who attempt in the treatment relationship to produce actively, negative affects that have been experienced passively. He linked his observations to Freud's paradigm of the repetition compulsion, which Modell believed had the rudiments of an object-related theory. He stated,

> It is the attempt to bring trauma, that is, pain experienced in the conflict with the external world, into the internal world and thus create the illusion of mastery and control. It is as if one protects oneself from trauma of overwhelming massive pain by inoculating oneself with repeated small doses. (Modell, 1984, p. 34)

Perhaps these observations about the early, preverbal origins of certain affect–action patterns might also help explain aspects of the antisocial personality disorder so often associated with addicts. That is, addicts' tendency to (alloplastically) work on and extract from their environment their needs and wants through action and activity might derive more from a generic absence of feelings than from—our usual understanding—an absence of guilt and shame. That is, the "self-organization" of such individuals probably embodies archaic affect experiences and behavioral patterns that derive from early experiences and, as Gedo has stated, are "a manifestation of a 'compulsion to repeat' certain patterns lacking in symbolic representation" (1986, p. 166).

Although there have been few elaborations or systematic attempts to explore the repetitious aspects of addictive behavior, especially concerning its maladaptive aspects, a number of psychoanalytic observers have implicitly or explicitly appreciated some of the repetitious elements in this phenomenon. Rado (1933) offered some insightful observations on the painfully repetitious and regressive cycles of addiction, but his formulations were heavily tinged with drive theory and reduced the repetitive aspects of addiction to this consideration alone. Weider and Kaplan (1969) considered the regressive and repetitious aspects of drug use once physical dependence occurs. He describes how artificial drive structures are established with their own rhythm and periodicity. Zinberg (1975) noted that virtually all addicts appear similar in their constant, magical expectations for gratification. He attributed this to the loss of ego autonomy secondary to artificial addictive drive cycles and social isolation. More recently, Wurmser (1986) described the cyclical aspects of addictive involvement as part of a neurotic equation. He described how mounting depressive and anxious affect as a consequence of an overbearing superego is overridden with defiant acts, bolstered by drug effect, only for an "inner judge" to return with greater condemnation when the drug effects wear off. With progression, this "return of the repressed" takes increasingly archaic forms. Much of the conflict and helplessness becomes externalized and plays itself out in shameful and humiliating encounters with loved ones and authority figures and in imposed external restrictions and confinement. Wurmser acknowledged recent developmental observations and their implications for affect theory. His formulations about how addicts externalize core phobic problems and the need for superego analysis of their conflicts is an excellent example of how primitive affect–action patterns may be played out, expressed, and resolved through later neurotic dynamics. Khantzian (1975, 1980) has emphasized how the chronic adoption of drug solutions produces a "dis-use atrophy" in ego/self capacities and malignantly combines with disturbances in need satisfaction and self-care capacities to make repeated reversions to drugs likely and compelling.

REPETITION AND ADDICTIVE SUFFERING

Many psychoanalytic formulations have stressed how addicts seek relief from painful affect with their drugs. We prefer to state that more than anything such individuals succeed in *changing* what or how they feel. Indeed, the most usual and apparent result is short-term relief; feeling better seems to be the main motivation for initially seeking out and using drugs. However, as we have indicated, addicts' own reports, clinical observation, and the natural course of their illness reveals that, more frequently, distress *results* from their acute and chronic drug use. Thus, the use of a drug comes to result in their feeling worse rather than better. They also discover that on different occasions drugs intensify or lessen their confusion around feelings. Whether the effects are positive or negative, they also invariably experience the acute and lingering distress of withdrawal if and when they have develop physical dependence on their drug. In brief, this partial list of short- and long-term consequences of drug dependency suggests that it cannot be reduced to simple motives of seeking pleasure or relief and that a more comprehensive formulation is needed to explain the complexities of how affect experience and dysfunction interact with drug effects and aftereffects to make reversion to drug use repetitiously compelling.

As with other aspects of mental life, symptoms, defenses, and particular adaptations may have more than one meaning or be multiply determined (Waelder, 1936). In the case of drug use, a person's aim may be different depending upon where they are in the course of their drug use and/or addictive illness. We have emphasized and given importance to the role of affect deficits and dysfunction because clinical evidence and observations reveal them to be central for explaining addicts' special relationship with suffering and their tendency to revert to or persist in using addictive drugs despite the obvious deleterious consequences.

In this chapter, we have discussed novel and recent formulations on affect deficits and dysfunction and on the nature of repetition in psychic suffering. These formulations provide a basis on which to better understand why substance-dependent individuals respond so persistently to inner distress and life events with action and drug solutions. Although addicts succeed in altering their distress, they also perpetuate it and often make it worse (from the vantage point of adaptation). As our previous discussion suggests, addicts are not alone in experiencing the internal world of feelings in vague, confusing, and bewildering ways, including ways in which they seem to be out of touch with and/or have no words for their feelings. Affect deficits and repetition provide a basis on which to explain why substance dependent individuals would readily accept, and perhaps even take advantage of, the suffering entailed with addiction as much as they rely on the relief-producing properties of these drugs. Advances in our biological understanding of neurotransmitters and the popularity of the disease concept of substance dependence have produced a strong tendency to discount psychological and developmental influences as etiological factors in addiction. It is another example of how our conceptualizations misguide us in selectively identifying certain factors to the exclusion of others. However, adopting a hierarchical and psychodynamic approach to these problems provides a perspective with which to appreciate within the psychological realm how developmental disturbances and traumatic events cause the deficits and dysfunction in affect experiences in addicts. Utilizing this perspective, the repetitious nature of addicts' reversion and attachment to the painful qualities of their drug use and related involvements becomes more understandable. Now, psychoanalysis needs to consider how alterations and dysfunction in affects govern repetitious attempts to resolve the human experience of suffering, including addictive suffering. Considered then from this vantage point, repetition and suffering for addicts is not best explained by destructive instincts, masochism, or inverted aggression but as an attempt to control or tolerate suffering that is otherwise experienced as being beyond the person's control.

Once addicts use and become involved with drugs, they discover that the drugs not only can produce relief but also produce and control the vagueness, confusion, and bewilderment associated with their feelings. That is, at the same time that addicts relieve distressing states with drug effects, they also convert the more vague and confusing aspects of their feeling life from a passive experience into an active one. Substance abusers actively replace preexisting passively experienced admixtures of pain, dysphoria, and emptiness with admixtures of analgesia, relief, dysphoria, and distress produced by the drug effects and aftereffects. The terms "altered states of consciousness" or "mood altering drugs" are commonly used to explain drug urges. In our opinion, the operative word is "alter" and that the motive to change "consciousness" or "mood" is misleading. More precisely, when individuals use drugs, they alter qualities and quantities of feelings, and more importantly, they succeed in substituting uncontrolled suffering with controlled suffering and replace a dysphoria that they do not understand with a drug-induced dysphoria that they do understand.

Finally, as we previously suggested, an appreciation of addicts' reasons for perpetuating their suffering at the same time that they relieve it could shed light on why repetition and suffering are so pervasive in all types of psychopathology and life in general. We believe our exploration of the borderlands of affect, repetition, and addiction have implications for better understanding the human tendency to suffer. These insights have potential for illuminating and better explaining some of the unique and idiosyncratic ways our patients in general repeat their suffering and distress. What this discussion suggests is that to some degree emotional suffering associated with psychopathology involves attempting to resolve deficits and dysfunction in affects, and one's symptom or disorder makes more manageable and understandable (for self and other) what would otherwise be confusing and nameless. This appreciation could lead us to reconsider how deficits and dysfunction in affect experience attach and play themselves out in addicts' difficulties with self-esteem, relationships, and self-care (Khantzian, 1978).

CONCLUSION

The repetitious cycles of involvement and reinvolvement with drug use and dependency are not so much related to pleasure seeking or self-defeating and self-destructive motives or, for that matter, to simply seeking relief from unpleasure. Rather, they represent a way of expressing and working out unresolved "affect–action" patterns and unusual qualities and dysfunction around affect experience that derive from earliest phases of development. Viewed then from this perspective, the painful, perpetuating aspects of addiction can be considered a form of substituted suffering—in which patients exchange their preexistent world of feelings, which are out of control, vague, and confusing, and thus overwhelming, for a life revolving around drugs, in which they repetitiously produce relief and suffering, which enables them to feel more in control and less confused and overwhelmed. It is little wonder then that the recovery movement (e.g., AA and NA) has been so successful, given its focus on how alcoholics and addicts have "lost control of their lives" and that recovery rests on persistently maintaining the aim of self-regulation as the most important requirement.

A hierarchical approach thus makes a great deal of sense in the understanding of addiction for several reasons. It helps to explain the "trade-off" of one form of suffering for another. Further, Modes I, II, and III tend to account for the data of interest to many object relations theorists, whereas Modes IV and V tend to account for the neuroses best known and studied by ego psychology. Thus, the hierarchical way of thinking about the mind and organizing clinical phenomena can encompass a broad array of clinical data, including that which is asymbolic and psychobiological. Even further, by viewing any addict as capable of functioning in any mode at any time, the model demonstrates sensitivity to the shifting, dynamic flux of personality dynamics that allows us to best conceptualize the complex nature of the addictive process. Thus, we can see how many of the specific hypotheses of many investigators concerning the psychic life of an addict can be found to be part of a larger and more encompassing explanation, each hypothesis addressed largely to the particular concerns of one mode or another. A detailed effort at linking modal concerns with the prevailing hypotheses of addiction can be found in Wilson et al. (1989). For example, Mode I longings for contact and an undifferentiated core craving for ecstacy can be seen in the hypothesis of hyposymbolization (Wurmser, 1974) and the dedifferentiation hypothesis of affects (Krystal, 1974). Mode II problems of pervasive oral neediness can encompass such hypotheses as Wieder and Kaplan's (1969) explanation of the pharmacogenic effect of drugs. Mode III phenomena can account for such hypotheses as Milkman and Frosch's (1973) hypothesis of heroin as a regulator of self-esteem.

Ironically, first succumbing to an addictive disorder and then recovering from it rests on how powerfully orienting and adaptive the drug experience is around one of the most disorienting aspects of addicts' lives—that is, their feelings. So we see that Dostoyevsky is only partially right: Addicts (and others) are indeed "in love with suffering," but this is because they cannot find comforting memories or words for feelings to guide them in courting a more suitable and satisfying companion than drugs.

REFERENCES

Fairbairn, W. R. (1944). Endopsychic structures considered in terms of object relations. In *Psychoanalytic studies of the personality*. London: Tavistock, 1952.

Freud, S. (1920). Beyond the pleasure principle. *Standard Edition* (Vol. 18, pp. 7–61). London: Hogarth Press, 1955.

Gedo, J. E. (1979). *Beyond interpretation: Toward a revised theory of psychoanalysis*. New York: International University Press.

Gedo, J. E. (1986). *Conceptual issues in psychoanalysis: Essays in history and method*. Hillsdale, NJ: Analytic Press.

Gedo, J. E., & Goldberg, A. (1973). *Models of the mind*. Chicago: University of Chicago Press.

Hendin, H. (1974). Students on heroin. *Journal of Nervous and Mental Diseases, 158*, 240–255.

Keller, D. (1989). *Affectivity and self–other differentiation in opiate versus cocaine abusers*. Unpublished doctoral dissertation, New School for Social Research, New York, NY.

Khantzian, E. J. (1972). A preliminary dynamic formulation of the psychopharmacologic action of methadone. In *Proceedings of the Fourth National Methadone Conference, San Francisco* (pp. 371–374). New York: National Association for the Prevention of Addiction to Narcotics.

Khantzian, E. J. (1974). Opiate addiction: A critique of theory and some implications for treatment. *American Journal of Psychotherapy, 28*, 59–70.

Khantzian, E. J. (1975). Self selection and progression in drug dependence. *Psychiatry Digest, 10*, 19–22.

Khantzian, E. J. (1978). The ego, the self and opiate addiction: Theoretical and treatment considerations. *International Review of Psycho-Analysis, 5,* 189–198.

Khantzian, E. J. (1979). Impulse problems in addiction: cause and effect relationships. In H. Wishnie (Ed.), *In working with the impulsive person* (pp. 97–112). New York: Plenum Press.

Khantzian, E. J. (1980). An ego-self theory of substance dependence. In D. J. Lettieri, M. Sayers, & H. W. Wallenstein (Eds.), *Theories of addiction* (pp. 29–33). NIDA Monograph No. 30. Rockville, MD: National Institute on Drug Abuse.

Khantzian, E. J. (1982). Psychological (structural) vulnerabilities and the specific appeal of narcotics. *Annals of the New York Academy of Sciences, 398,* 24–32.

Khantzian, E. J. (1985). The self-medication hypothesis of addictive disorders. *American Journal of Psychiatry, 142*(11), 1259–1264.

Khantzian, E. J. & Kates, W. W. (1978). Group treatment of unwilling addicted patients: programmatic and clinical aspects. *International Journal Group of Psychotherapy, 1*(1), 81–94.

Khantzian, E. J. & Treece, C. (1977). Psychodynamics of drug dependence: an overview. In J. D. Blaine & D. A. Julius (Eds.), *Psychodynamics of drug dependence* (pp. 101–107). NIDA Monograph No. 12. Rockville, MD: National Institute on Drug Abuse.

Krystal, H. (1974). The genetic development of affects and affect regression. *The Annual of Psychoanalysis, 2,* 98–106.

Krystal, H. (1982). Alexithymia and the effectiveness of psychoanalytic treatment. *International Journal of Psychotherapy, 9,* 353–378.

Krystal, H., & Raskin, H. A. (1970). *Drug dependence: Aspects of ego functions.* Detroit: Wayne State University Press.

Lichtenberg, J. D. (1983). *Psychoanalysis and infant research.* Hillsdale, NJ: Analytic Press.

Mahler, M. S. (1968). *On human symbosis and the vicissitudes of individuation.* New York: International University Press.

Martin, W. R., Haertzen, C. A., & Hewett, B. B. (1978). Psychopathology and pathophysiology of narcotic addicts, alcoholics, and drug abusers. In M. A. Lipton, A. DiMascio, & K. F. Killam (Eds.). *Psychopharmacology: A generation of progress* (pp. 1591–1602). New York: Raven Press.

Martin, W. R., Hewett, B. B., Baker, A. J., & Haertzen, C. A. (1977). Aspects of the psychopathology and pathophysiology of addiction. *Drug and Alcohol Dependence, 2,* 185–202.

Marty, P., & de M'Uzan, M. (1963). La pensée opératoire. *Revue Francaise de Psycho-Analyse, 27* (Suppl.), 345–356.

McAuliffe, W. E., Wechsler, H., Rohman, M., Soboroff, S. H., Fishman, P., Toth, D., & Friedman, R. (1984). Psychoactive drug use by young and future physicians. *Journal of Health and Social Behavior, 25,* 34–54.

McDougall, J. (1984). The "dis-affected" patient: Reflections on affect pathology. *Psychoanalytic Quarterly, 53,* 386–409.

Milkman, H., & Frosch, W. A. (1973). On the preferential abuse of heroin and amphetamine. *Journal of Nervous and Mental Diseases, 156,* 242– 248.

Modell, A. H. (1984). *Psychoanalysis in a new context.* New York: International Universities Press.

Nemiah, J. C. (1970). The psychological management and treatment of patients with peptic ulcer. *Advances in Psychosomatic Medicine, 6,* 169–173.

Nemiah, J.C. (1975). Denial revisited: Reflections on psychosomatic theory. *Psychotherapy and Psychosomatics, 26,* 140–147.

Rado, S. (1933). The psychoanalysis of pharmacothymia. *Psychoanalytic Quarterly, 2,* 1–23.

Sashin, J. I. (1985). Affect tolerance: A model of affect–response using catastrophe theory. *Journal of Social and Biological Structures, 8,* 175–202.

Sashin, J. I. (1986, November). *The relation between fantasy and the ability to feel affect.* Paper presented at Grand Rounds, The Cambridge Hospital, Cambridge, MA.

Sifneos, P. E. (1967). Clinical observations on some patients suffering from a variety of psychosomatic diseases. In *Proceedings of the Seventh European Conference on Psychosomatic Research* (pp. 452–458). Basel: S. Karger.

Valenstein, A. (1973). On attachment to painful feelings and the negative therapeutic reaction. *The Psychoanalytic Study of the Child, 26,* 365–392.

Waelder, R. (1936). The principle of multiple function: Observations on overdetermination. In S. Guttman (Ed.), *Psychoanalysis: Observation, theory, application* (pp. 68–83). New York: International Universities Press, 1976.

Weider, H., & Kaplan, E. (1969). Drug use in adolescents. *Psychoanalytic Study of the Child, 24,* 399–431.

Wilson, A., & Malatesta, M. (1989). Affect and the compulsion to repeat: Freud's repetition compulsion revisited. *Psychoanalysis and Contemporary Thought, 12,* 243–290.

Wilson, A., Passik, S., & Faude, J. (1990). Self-regulation and its failures. In J. Masling (Ed.), *Empirical studies of psychoanalytic theories* (Vol. 3, pp. 149–211). Hillsdale, NJ: Erlbaum.

Wilson, A., Passik, S., Faude, J., Gordon, E., & Abrams, J. (1989). A hierarchical model of opiate addiction: Failures of self-regulation as a central aspect of substance abuse. *Journal of Nervous and Mental Diseases, 177,* 390–399.

Wurmser, L. (1974). Psychoanalytic considerations of the etiology of compulsive drug use. *Journal of the American Psychoanalytic Association, 22,* 820–843.

Wurmser, L. (1986). Flight from conscience: Experiences with the psychoanalytic treatment of compulsive drug users. *Journal of Substance Abuse Treatment, 4,* 157–168.

Zinberg, N. E. (1975). Addiction and ego function. *Psychoanalytic Study of the Child, 30,* 567–588.

10

The Psychopathological Spectrum and the Hierarchical Model

MICHAEL ROBBINS

A quiet but significant theoretical revolution has been occurring within general psychiatry and psychoanalysis in the post–World War II decades. It has the potential for unlocking access to a number of hitherto impenetrable questions about the boundaries and limits of psychoanalytic theory. For example, do the serious personality disorders and psychoses, which superficially bear so little resemblance to psychoneurosis and which seem hardly comprehensible to many of us in terms of the classical model of drive, intrapsychic conflict, and defense, have a place within the scope of psychoanalysis? And what about those conditions that border on the organic or somatic, whether they be the so-called psychosomatic disorders or mental disorders with specific genetic or constitutional substrates and associated organic abnormalities such as schizophrenia? How does psychoanalysis deal with the boundaries between intrapsychic and interpersonal phenomena? Do theories of the dyad, the family, the group, the culture, and the society relate to those of psychoanalysis? The theoretical revolution to which I refer has to do with gradual introduction of the concept of hierarchical modeling, whose major architects are Werner (1948), Engel (1977, 1980), Weiss (1969, 1977), and one of the editors of this volume, Gedo, both with his early collaborator Goldberg (1973), and subsequently on his own (1979; 1984; 1986; Chapter 4, this volume).

Weiss and Engel postulate that nature is organized in a hierarchy of functionally interdependent dynamic systems, each of which requires a separate theoretical model for its comprehension. The person is the highest level of the organismic hierarchy and the lowest level of the social hierarchy. Engel's biopsychosocial model allows us to view *intersystemic* relations among psychoanalytic theories and theories of abutting disciplines (neurosciences, interpersonal or group process theories) in a more coherent and correlated manner, unfettered by pressures toward fantatical adherence to any single theory and to the simplistic reductionistic thinking that accompanies such misguided zeal. Gedo's epigenetic mind model hierarchy allows for a similar *intrasystemic* expansion within psychoanalytic theory, so that we may begin to account for what appear to be qualitative differences in mentation between neurotic, borderline, and narcissistic personalities and for some of the problems encountered in applying the classical neurosis model of mental function to more disturbed patients. In a bold stroke it frees psychoanalysis from the Procrustean bed of having to account for all forms of psychopathology with the conflict–defense neurosis model and potentially broadens the scope of psychoanalysis to encompass more primitive mental states as well as newer findings of infant research (see Lichtenberg Chapter 7, this volume). But it does not require that we throw out the metaphorical baby—Freud's neurosis theory, which in so many respects serves us well—with its bathwaters, and adopt in its stead a "new" psychoanalysis, as alternative formulations such as self psychology have done (see Robbins [1980, 1992a] and Bacal [1987] for a disussion of Kohut's nonacknowledgment of his own psychoanalytic theoretical roots), therein introducing problems perhaps more thorny than the ones they purport to solve.

In the broadest sense, the biopsychosocial hierarchy proposed by Engel and Weiss may be viewed as a complementary series of sciences or theories, which have in common their power to explicate the mysteries of the human person, both his or her inner workings and his or her social propensities. These theories nest within one another in a layered or stratified manner, from microscopic to macroscopic. Gedo's psychoanalytic mind model hierarchy may be conceptualized as nesting within that system level of Engel's biopsychosocial model that he reserves for theories of the self or person, bracketed at the lower or more microscopic level by the neurosciences and at the higher level by progressively macroscopic theories of persons in relation to one another: dyadic, familial, group, societal, and ultimately cultural. There appear to be both similarities and differences between, on one hand, the overall hierarchy of human sciences and theories that comprise the biopsychosocial model and, on the other, the subhierarchy of self-organization within psychoanalysis that Gedo has proposed. Wilson and Passik (Chapter 3, this volume) describe some of the general characteristics of hierarchical organizations: They are based on the observation of discontinuities in the course of development and on the postulate of emergent or nonreducible organizations, structures, or configurations that are contingent upon but qualitatively different from prior ones. The biopsychosocial hierarchy possesses properties both of stratification, layering, or magnitude and of time or evolution. The person may simultaneously be described in the terms of physics, neuroscience, psychoanalysis, group process, society, and culture; in fact, a description is incomplete without including all of these complementary levels. At each conceptual level, however, a developmental or evolutionary transformational process may also be observed. And in the case of individual development a certain sophistication of organization is necessary at the biological level before it is possible to perceive emergent self-organizations at the psychoanalytic level; and considerable development of the self-system is required before it is meaningful or useful to utilize theories of groups or of culture.

It is in regard to the developmental fate of earlier, underlying, or simpler organizations, and the scientific theories that represent them, that there may be some difference between the biopsychosocial model and Gedo's epigenetic hierarchy, but this may be nothing more than the difference between hierarchical systems dimensions of time and stratification. That is to say, in Gedo's system, as the structural organization of the person evolves, more primitive structures vanish and the models needed to account for them are no longer relevant except under pathological conditions such as arrest or regression. New structural organizations attain a relative autonomy from older ones. In the biopsychosocial model the "higher level" sciences become applicable as development progresses, but the "lower level" and "more" organic phenomena for which they account continue to exist, and the sciences that account for them remain every bit as important. Not only do the higher levels never entirely attain autonomy from the lower ones, but it is necessary to understand something of the nature and shape of the lower ones in order to construct higher-level sciences that are useful.

Gedo defines his epigenetic hierarchy in terms of five stages or modes and their related developmental achievements, which he believes emerge more or less sequentially in the normal course of infancy and childhood and undergird qualitatively new and different ways of thinking and feeling. These are: state regulation or homeostasis; integration (or cohesion of the self); self-esteem regulation, including acceptance of reality and relinquishment of illusion and grandiosity; intrapsychic conflict and defense; and self-actualization beyond conflict. It is apparent that some of his choices reflect efforts to incorporate the contributions of Kleinians and Kernberg, as well as

Kohut, and to frame the result in a context of his own, including such ideas as that motivational theory ought to be based on the concept of a broad spectrum of organismic aims and goals rather than on an outmoded scientistic theory of drives or a schema limited to ambitions and ideals.

Others have proposed—or appear to have proposed—different models of mentation to account for more primitive forms of psychopathology. Kernberg, for example, holds that "splitting" and projective identification are characteristic of borderline personalities, although it is worthy of note that his neo-Kleinian theory is commonly misunderstood as being different from the neurosis model of the mind, when in fact it is a classical theory of drive, conflict, and defense, in which "splitting" refers to a primitive defensive operation and not to a stage of incoherence or fragmentation of self. Kohut, in contrast, has proposed a genuinely nonneurotic model in which intrapsychic organization is predicated not on drive organization, conflict, and defense, but on the achievement of self-cohesion around ambitions and ideals, in relation to empathic selfobjects. In his schema there is scant place for object relations, and phenomena reflective of absence of integration are considered meaningless by-products of the failure of self-cohesion. Although Kohut is innovative insofar as he has recognized the need for a model of mind other than the neurotic, he remains traditional insofar as he believes that one must choose a single model of mind to account for all conditions, regardless of its limits.

I have attempted to apply the hierarchical model to the problem of primitive personality organization (Robbins, 1982, 1983, 1988, 1989; Chapter 8, this volume). Although Kernberg (1970) and Meissner (1984) have attempted to expand and refine the distinctions between the various serious character and personality disturbances, most particularly the borderline and narcissistic conditions, few efforts have been made to compare and contrast conditions spanning the spectrum of psychopathology and to test the general applicability of Gedo's propositions in accounting for similarities and differences among a wide range of conditions.

Despite the extraordinary breadth of his view, Gedo has concluded that his own clinical experience, which comprises office psychoanalysis exclusively, is insufficient for him to attempt to include schizophrenia within the confines of his model hierarchy (1988, p. 187). This is consistent with the position of most analysts, who, with the exception of the two decades or so following World War II, have adhered to Freud's model of office practice, as well as his beliefs about the nature of schizophrenia, and have not involved themselves in the conceptualization or treatment of that condition. Freud was never satisfied that schizophrenia is comprehensible with the same theoretical frame of reference as the neuroses, for he believed, incorrectly, that schizophrenics were incapable of forming transferences, and he speculated about such fundamental differences as weakness of libidinal cathexis of object representations (1915) or an ego that repudiated reality rather than attempt to reconcile itself with it (1924a, 1924b). A number of analysts (Hendrick, 1951; Federn, 1952; Hartmann, 1953; Jacobson, 1953; Meehl, 1962; Mahler, 1968; Kernberg, 1972; Grinker, 1973; London, 1973; Stierlin, 1975; Wexler, 1971, 1975; Holzman [see Gunderson, 1974]; Grotstein, 1977) have agreed with Freud that there is a fundamental difference between the mechanisms of neurosis and schizophrenia, but comprehensive models of schizophrenia have not developed out of their speculations, and for the most part the idea that schizophrenia is characterized by a particular vulnerability or deficit has been a road not taken, and schizophrenia has increasingly been relegated to the fringes of the psychoanalytic repertory, if not orphaned entirely and left to become a ward of biological psychiatry.

In this chapter I should like to reexamine some of the issues relevant to an epigenetic model hierarchy from the perspective of my own observations and hypotheses about primitive personality, as well as my clinical experience with schizophrenics. I should like to detail some of the differences in mental structure and function I have observed (1) between neurotics and primitive personalities, (2) between the borderline and narcissistic groups within the primitive personality spectrum, and (3) between the primitive personalities and schizophrenics. I shall attempt to abstract some of the variables that I find useful in discriminating among these conditions. Finally I shall discuss some of the implications of my observations and abstractions for the general notion of a model hierarchy, and for Gedo's epigenetic hierarchy in particular. Some of this is a summary of conclusions from other papers (see Robbins [1982, 1983, 1988, 1989] for detailed descriptions of primitive personality organization and Robbins [1992b, 1993] for a focus on schizophrenia).

When I refer to psychopathological entities I am adhering to the descriptive definitions of DSM-III except in the case of manic–depressive psychosis. I use the term primitive personality organization, which Werner first employed (1948), to group borderline, narcissistic, paranoid, and schizoid personalities, which share certain common features (see Khan, 1960; Kernberg, 1966, 1967; Kohut, 1971; Gunderson & Kolb, 1978; Robbins, 1982, 1983). I should like to emphasize two points regarding the observations I am about to present: First, they represent an effort to condense a vast amount of material and present an overview of phenomenological similarities and differences that have impressed me in my encounters with patients from these various categories. I do not have the space to attempt a detailed exposition of any of the observations or to present case illustrations. I can only apologize in advance if one result of this condensation is a certain unsubstantiated or dogmatic quality. For detail I refer the reader to Robbins (1982, 1983, 1989, 1993). Second, an overview of this sort entails considerable abstraction and hypothesis, therefore it is presented more in the spirit of raising issues and promoting discussion than making factual assertions.

PSYCHONEUROSIS AND PRIMITIVE PERSONALITY ORGANIZATION

The ideas in this section are derived from a series of papers, but primarily from Robbins (1989). I will begin by noting three ways in which primitive personalities differ from neurotics.

First, primitive personalities show less psychic integration under the aegis of a constant sense of self, as many observers from disparate theoretical camps, including Kernberg, Kohut, and Gedo, have noted. The consciousness of the primitive personality is dominated by one or another extreme idea, without concurrent awareness of the other pole, which exclusively dominates consciousness at other times. Or, to say it differently, the individual's self-sense is inconstant and contradictory. In this mode of thinking, contradictory elements are not integrated, with the result that the individual is incapable of experiencing intrapsychic conflict or emotional ambivalence. While the observer of contradiction in behavior and thinking tends to empathically or projectively assume the existence of intrapsychic conflict, and in neurotics and ordinary character disorder patients exploration of associations and defenses confirms such an assumption, similar work with primitive personalities fails to reveal intrapsychic linkage between what appears to the observer as conflicting states of mind. Some minimal integration is suggested, however, by the symbiotic bonds these patients form and the sensorimotor–affective interactions with noninternalized aspects of self perceived in the object (Robbins [1981], after Piaget). This sensorimotor–affective mode of thought is related to developmental precursors of defensive projection and defensive introjection (displacement and condensation, respectively, according to Sandler and A. Freud, 1983).

Second, primitive personalities show incomplete differentiation of self from object, of thought from action, and of stable intrapsychic representations and structures from the total mental matrix. Mental representations are undeveloped, particularly in the areas of object relations and of affects (see Chapter 8, this volume). The results are problems of inconstancy of self-sense and of objects, lack of impulse control, and resultant destructive expression of affect because rage is poorly represented and its control relatively unstructured and because there is difficulty with self- or tension-regulation. The "unconsciousness" or unawareness that characterizes such individuals is not dynamic, based on repression, but is due to lack of ability to differentiate or make distinctions and a relative absence of articulated control structures.

Third, there is a qualitative difference in object relations between neurotics and primitive personalities. Pathological symbiosis results from the primitiveness of cognition and affect, particularly from the relative undevelopment of integration and differentiation, which I have described elsewhere (Robbins, 1981). As I mentioned earlier, however, not all manifestations of primitive personality can be conceptualized in terms of arrested development. The symbiotic relationships of the primitive personality do not have a normal infantile counterpart. While the pathological symbiotic relationships deal with elements of thought and feeling that have not been maturely differentiated and integrated, as do the symbiotic relations of normal infants, and in each instance an incompletely differentiated object is required to compensate for the subject's lack of integration, they include unique elements of adaptation to the pathogenic parenting to which these individuals were subjected as infants and children. The incompletely integrated psyche of the primitive personality requires aliment for a self-destructive introject in order to maintain a sense of identity, and, reciprocally, requires an absorbing, nonreflecting mirror or shell to assimilate and struggle with uninternalized dysphoric affects in order to maintain a sense of completeness. The result is reciprocal possession configurations based on predefensive projection and introjection, respectively, instead of differentiated whole object relationships and integrated poles of conflict and ambivalence.

NARCISSISTIC AND BORDERLINE PERSONALITIES

The observations in this section derive primarily from my 1982 paper. Despite the overall similarity between narcissistic and borderline personality organization, insofar as they share, to a greater or lesser degree, the characteristics listed in the preceding section, there are significant differences between the two conditions. The differences, however, are not those that have been touted by the self psychologists, that is, integration versus fragmentation of a cohesive self and presence versus absence of a symbiotic or selfobject relationship. Both borderline and narcissistic personalities have at least two distinctive conscious variants of sense of self, and persons of both diagnostic groups are unaware of an internal disjunction or contradiction. That is, neither narcissistic nor borderline personalities have achieved mature intrapsychic integration. Both require symbiotic objects on which to project, perceive, and enact loosely integrated aspects of self in an effort to repair and compensate for deficiencies in emotional representation and regulation, and deficiencies in the narcissistic area of self-esteem. The symbiotic transferences of borderlines may be more difficult to identify because of their chaotic and destructive appearance. As for the symbiotic transferences formed by narcissistic personalities, they are not abortive efforts to resume normal development. Unless their destructive aspects are interpreted and modified, they lack the developmental potential Kohut attributes to them (see my 1982 discussion of Kohut's two analyses of Mr. Z).

Let us contrast the functioning of the two symbiotic structures, possessor and possessed, in borderlines and narcissistic personalities. Borderline personalities, functioning in the possessor mode, aggressively recruit specific attentive and concerned objects in their quest to assimilate good feelings. Because they are unable to represent and sustain good feelings or self-esteem of their own, their quest is inevitably frustrated, and in reality, unbeknownst to them, they require the object as a screen on which to enact their unrepresented rage and associated dysphoric feelings. Although they attack and devalue such a person, and coerce that person to own and process the projected rage and rejection, the person remains an important aspect of the undifferentiated self and the unintegrated affective configuration, and the symbiotic linkage provides borderline personalities with a minimal, albeit unconflicted, integration with their own thoughts and feelings. The object of the borderlines' possessive inclinations is inconstantly perceived, shifting between a valence of desirability, which causes borderlines to act seductively because of perceived need-gratifying potential, and a valence of undesirability because borderlines are unable to represent and sustain either positive loving feelings or self-esteem, and instead experience rage and frustration that is projected and enacted, leading to attack and rejection of the object. As a result, the symbiotic object of borderline possessors is not readily able to exercise a effective caregiving function and serves only as emotional waste container for feelings of rage, devaluation, and rejection.

Reciprocally, borderlines require one or more specific familiar (parent-like) objects who are actively recruited for adaptive enactment of the introjective configuration (possessed). The attributions of badness and devaluation made by the selected object are used introjectively as aliment for maintenance of a badness identity, based on dysphoric feelings and self-devaluation, often construed delusionally and associated with destructive psychological and physical attacks on the self. The introjective attacks on themselves comprise enactments of unrepresented precusers of rage and also have a primitive self-control or self-regulatory aspect insofar as they curtail autonomous expression of thoughts and feelings as more mature ego and superego functions might be expected to do, albeit in a more selective and constructive manner.

The borderline configurations of gratification-demanding, hostility-enacting and projecting (badness attributing) possessor, on the one hand, and blame-taking, "badness" introjecting possessed, on the other, may occur in separate relationships, or may alternate or occur simultaneously within a given relationship as roles shift projectively and introjectively, lending a further sense of chaos, inconstancy, and instability to borderline relationships. In other words, borderlines are generally unable to achieve stability in their efforts to use an object to substitute for unrepresented positive feelings, to induce even transient archaic forms of self-esteem, and to serve in the stead of absent intrapsychic structures related to the representation and control of rage. Nonetheless, if therapeutically contained and mirrored back to borderlines, the projected–introjected–enacted cognitive and affective elements are potentially available for internalization, representation, and growth, in ways not qualitatively dissimilar to those of the mirroring mother who assists her infant to identify and control its emotions.

By contrast, the object necessary to sustain narcissists' grandiosity by flattery satisfies the narcissist's unacknowledged dependency needs by caregiving ministration. And this object is the repository for the narcissists' projected feelings of devaluation (what Morrison, 1989, refers to as narcissistic shame). The object of the narcissist's possessor configuration performs an essential stabilizing and containing function and does not, under ordinary circumstances, arouse frustration and rage as does the object of the borderlines' possessor configuration. As a result, the object is sustained and even cared for with a certain constancy by narcissistic personalities, albeit with a degree of devaluation consisting of projection of the negative pole of self-esteem (devaluation or shame) as well as the narcissists' denied dependency. It is possible for an object to satisfy the basic dependency needs of narcissistic personalities as well as their archaic grandiosity, while introjectively containing the narcissists' projected devaluation and dependency feelings, so that rage that would otherwise need to be projected and enacted were these to be faced does not play a significant role except under circumstances of symbiotic object failure and frustration. This suggests that with suitable assistance, narcissistic personalities are capable of a degree of state regulation, of representational and structural constancy, and a modicum of archaic self-esteem beyond that of borderlines. The self-sense of narcissistic personalities is more stable than that of borderlines because dependency needs, although denied and projected, can be met and grandiosity sustained so long as feelings of devaluation or shame can be kept out of awareness. In their possessed configuration, in another concurrent relationship, narcissistic personalities act as the devalued possession of another narcissist, mirroring that person's grandiosity and servicing his or her needs. In this role, as well, there is a certain stability. Though the introjected devaluation is consistent with the other pole of narcissists' archaic self-esteem, they are simultaneously valued by the object for the important function they serve.

The differences between the two conditions, borderline and narcissistic, include that the symbiotic relations of narcissistic personalities have a greater degree of self and object constancy, better self–object differentiation, and consequently greater stability and durability. The objects of both narcissistic and borderline personalities are chosen because of unconsciously perceived resemblances to and differences from parental figures, but while the relationships of the borderline prove almost entirely maladaptive from an adult social standpoint, no matter how effective they may be in creating the "split" senses of self, the analogous possession relationships of narcissistic personalities perform constructive, adaptive functions mirroring their grandiosity and servicing their dependent needs. Perhaps this is why Kohut believed such relationships are reflective of arrested stages of normal development. With the assistance of a symbiotic object, narcissistic personalities are able to maintain inner states of tension regulation, dependent satisfaction, and archaic self-esteem; they can approximate stable structures, defined as functions with a slow rate of change, and achieve rudimentary representational constancy. Sensorimotor–affective thinking is less pronounced than in borderlines, and as a result, impulse control tends to be better. Like borderlines, however, they cannot represent, sustain, and control basic affects such as love and rage. Neither knows much about feelings as stable internal dispositions, although borderlines characteristically emote negatively while attributing the negativism to others. Whereas the self-esteem system of borderlines is constantly one of badness and self-devaluation or shame, narcissistic personalities, with assistance, vacillate between extremes of grandiosity and self-devaluation, and they can sustain the former sense of self for periods of time. The configurations of grandiose possessor, superior to human neediness, and devalued, dependent, and grandiosity-mirroring possession are assigned to self and object in separate relationships; that is, narcissistic personalities take one role in one relationship and the other in another, and the roles do not oscillate or occur simultaneously within a single relationship, as is the case with borderlines. For this reason the object relations of narcissistic personalities have greater constancy and stability, are more constructive, and are less confusing and chaotic than those of borderlines.

SCHIZOPHRENIA AND PRIMITIVE PERSONALITY ORGANIZATION

The manifest and frightening impression of unfamiliarity and bizarreness conveyed by schizophrenics has effectively discouraged most efforts to study them in depth as human beings. However, if one is able to develop a relationship with a schizophrenic, it is possible to observe the workings of more fundamental processes. It is some of these that I now attempt to summarize. The reader will note a considerable resemblance to some of the experimental findings noted by Grand, Feiner, and Reisner (Chapter 2, this volume), particularly with regard to phenomena of integration and differentiation, goal-directedness, and attitude toward or use of objects.

In schizophrenia, lack of integration and differentiation, and resultant chaos, disorganization, and instability, are even more severe than in borderline personalities, although this may be superficially masked by the pseudostability of delusional ideation. Schizophrenics have not even developed the capacity to be instrumentally effective sensorimotor–affective thinkers. They do not use the environment adaptively as a screen for enactment of the workings of their minds, as do primitive personalities. In ordinary development, the most primitive form of sensorimotor–affective thinking does not involve differentiation among objects, that is, anything can be aliment for the mouth-sucking schema, but soon, through a process of assimilation and accommodation, infants come to have stable recognition representations, however primitive, which guide their enactments toward objects that will better serve as aliment for their ongoing cognitive schemata and away from ones who will not. Schizophrenics, unlike primitive personalities, cannot differentiate or discriminate such crucial characteristics of persons they might potentially relate to as their capacity to pay attention and to be empathic or their degree of objectivity and firmness of personal boundaries. While primitive personalities cultivate the obligatory symbiotic linkages I have described and act as though they cannot survive without others no matter how troubled their relationships with them may seem, schizophrenics are passive and make no effort to selectively recruit others into their cognitive–affective schemata except, on occasion, in a personally indiscriminate manner as props for delusional enactments. Gedo's conclusion that the most primitive mental state is characterized by difficulties with tension and state regulation, as well as absence of integration, might imply that schizophrenics would welcome a holding object, but they tend to be rejecting or indifferent, as countless observers, beginning with Freud, have noted. The schizophrenic is not even sufficiently stable, differentiated and integrated to enter into a symbiotic relationship without extraordinary therapeutic assistance.

Nevertheless, although Freud considered schizophrenia to be a "narcissistic neurosis," and schizophrenics to be unrelated to others and incapable of forming transferences, many subsequent analysts have demonstrated that this is not the case. Schizophrenics' passivity, arcane thinking, and absence of specific relationships present an appearance of unrelatedness that is deceiving, as is known by anyone who has participated in family therapy and observed how exquisitely albeit indirectly responsive schizophrenics are to the vicissitudes of family dynamics.

If schizophrenics can be engaged, the therapist may discover an involvement with their primary object that contains within it prototypic ingredients of the possessed symbiotic configuration of primitive personalities. Both primitive personalities and schizophrenics have a basic adaptive stance toward the world involving introjection of attributions placed upon them in reality or in fantasy and related self-destructive enactments. Schizophrenic ineptitude or disability with regard to self-care is accompanied by primitive narcissistic thinking—self-devaluation and grandiosity—in relation to family members who infantilize them and thus covertly devalue them and simultaneously treat them as special and even extraordinary.

The possessed configuration of schizophrenics differs from that of primitive personalities insofar as it is not "transference ready." Several cognitive, affective, and behavioral deficits appear to account for this fact. These include: inability to differentiate a specific object, in this case a familiar (parent-like) one; inability to displace the primitive possessed symbiotic template to a specific object so that a transference may form; and, perhaps, inability to mentally represent such a template as well.

Passivity *pervades all aspects of the schizophrenic personality*, in contrast to the situation of the primitive personality, who manifests, alongside a more superficially passive possessed configuration, an unintegrated aggressive, adaptive possessor configuration. Schizophrenics are unable to utilize aggression externally and adaptively. The cognitive, affective, and behavioral deficits that differentiate schizophrenics from primitive personalities with regard to a possessor symbiotic configuration include: inability to differentiate a strange, nonparental object (one who cares, pays attention, gives accurate mirroring feedback rather than attributions); inability to actively recruit an object; inability to actively, externally, and adaptively mobilize aggression in the service of identity maintenance, however pathological; inability to integrate mental processes sufficiently to make adaptive projective use of an object for sensorimotor-affective enactments; and, in fact, an almost total repudiation of mind, so that there is no interest in having an object as possession to act as precursor or container for not-yet-internalized mental contents and processes, such as rage and its control.

Instead, unrepresented aggression is diffusely directed internally, toward their mental and emotional processes and toward persons who attend to these. One of the most striking characteristics that emerges only if one is so fortunate as to engage in therapeutic relationships with schizophrenics is the powerful attacks they make on the use of their mind: their cognitive–affective nihilism and urge toward mindlessness, mental anesthesia, or death; their deep-seated repugnance to think and bear feelings about the self and the object world; and their aversion to caring others who would help them attend to their thoughts and feelings. This is in contrast to the weakly integrated sensorimotor–affective symbiotic linkage primitive personalities maintain toward their own disquieting thoughts and feelings, with the help of an adaptable symbiotic object, or the self-attack and devaluation primitive personalities may adaptively experience with the "help" of a possessing symbiotic object. The schizophrenics' diffuse attack on thinking, feeling, and relating to another person who cares enough to pay attention and enhance their self-awareness, a form of self-destruction beyond symbiosis, is the very psychotic core.

Another way to look at the difference between primitive person alities and schizophrenics is to say that schizophrenics lack any active adaptive thrust to separate from their family and to grow psychologically. The family is equivalent to the world, and vice versa, and schizophrenics engage in a passive self-destructive adaptation to it. Unlike primitive personalities, they cannot differentiate specific individuals who psychologically resemble parents so as to engage in extrafamilial relationships and at least give the appearance of separation and autonomy. Nor can they discriminate and identify persons whose psychology differs from that of their parents and whose attention might enable them to resume the aborted infantile task of identifying and processing their dysphoric affects and unmet needs and working out their unstable and polarized self-esteem.

It may be instructive to contrast this view of primitive personality organization and schizophrenia with that of the Kleinian school, which has influenced Searles (1965), who, to my mind, has been the most successful analyst to date in describing the thinking and relationships of schizophrenics. Kleinians describe a primitive paranoid–schizoid position characterized by splitting and unmitigated rage and hatred, in which whole objects are psychically annihilated, and by means of projective identification, "bad" part-object relations are split off or sequestered from "good" ones. This is succeeded in development by the so-called "depressive" position characterized by psychological containment of rage, resulting in object constancy, ambivalence, guilt and reparative efforts, and whole object relations. How borderline personality is to be distinguished from schizophrenia in such a schema is not clear; probably the distinction is quantitative, related to the extent of splitting or fragmentation and projective identification. What I am suggesting instead is that there is a qualitative distinction between the structural organization and object relations of primitive personalities and schizophrenics. To view the matter in Kleinian terms, schizophrenics are unable to sequester good feeling by splitting of psychic structures and effective projection of rage. While for schizophrenics there is projection of aggression in the form of delusions and hallucinations, it is adaptively ineffective because it is integrated neither with subject nor object. The sine qua non of projective identification, a containing object, is missing. In lieu of a symbiotic structure, which recruits objects and projectively seeks to contain and process dysphoric affects such as rage in order to maintain an object related sense of self or identity, there is only a psychotic core, consisting of diffuse internalization of rage, directed at thinking, feeling, and any object relating that enhances self-awareness. Although the psychotic core might be considered a process with a slow rate of change, I do not think it can be considered a psychic structure, insofar as structure connotes building or construction. Nor do I think of it as a death instinct, for it has a primitive adaptive aspect (see Robbins [1988] for more elaboration of this point). In the course of treatment of schizophrenia various unintegrated parts or "splits" may develop: an object-specific possessed configuration, an activation of the diffuse rage of the psychotic core, object-specific rage, and new caring and loving feelings involving self and object.

Before summarizing my observations, I should like to say an even more speculative word about manic–depressive psychosis. The diagnostic criteria for this illness have changed, and the DSM-III criteria that reflect current trends in diagnosis include under this major affective rubric many illnesses that I would define in the "old-fashioned" manner as acute schizophrenic episodes or schizoaffective illnesses. According to the current classificatory vogue, however, schizophrenia is diagnosed when there are predominantly cognitive problems and substantial "negative symptoms" (flatness, apathy, withdrawal, etc.), and manic–depressive illness tends to be equated with psychosis with manifest affect. I think this is a false dichotomy, for problems representing, structuring, and controlling affect pervade all these conditions, manifesting themselves sometimes in excessive emoting and at other times in seeming absence of affect.

I diagnose manic–depressive psychosis when I observe major mood swings that have prolonged amplitude, in the course of which many months of deep depression are followed in cyclic alternation by many months of increasingly expansive grandiose thinking, paranoid attitudes, and controlling behavior, associated with flight of ideas, diminished need for sleep, sprees of constant activity, and voracious consumption. Hypomanic patients are often extremely creative and productive, and even in the manic phase—in contrast with disorganized inept schizophrenics—they tend to dominate and control social settings and to be perceived by many as plausible, normal, even exceptional. Many socially productive and even creative individuals have been afflicted with this condition, which has been inextricably intertwined with both their productivity and social charisma. This form of illness is infrequently encountered. It is similar to the borderline personality insofar as there are cyclic alternations between possessed and possessor behavior (depressed and manic phases, respectively), but different insofar as these cycles are prolonged in amplitude rather than rapidly alternating or even simultaneously enacted as one encounters in the primitive personality disorders.

SUMMARY OF RELATIONSHIPS AMONG MAJOR PATHOLOGICAL ENTITIES

One thing that should be apparent from this brief and by no means comprehensive discussion is that many cognitive, affective, and behavioral variables are involved in distinguishing between the major pathological entities. I do not find it possible to relate a given illness to a single developmental task or pathological process, such as, to borrow some oversimplifying cliches to say that borderline pathology is the result of splitting or failure of integration, narcissistic pathology is the failure of self-cohesion or a defense against the depressive position, schizophrenia is the result of decathexis of the object world, and mania is a primitive defensive denial of depression. As one traces the primitivization of thinking, feeling, and behavior from neurosis to schizophrenia, one encounters cognitive and affective peculiarities at once more numerous, severe, global, and difficult to distinguish from one another. My observations seem to support the general consensus that narcissistic personality organization is more mature with regard to self-regulation, differentiation, structuralization, and mental representation than borderline organization. Moreover, there is some suggestion that there may be qualitative similarities between narcissistic personality and schizophrenia, on one hand, and borderline personality and manic–depressive illness, on another.

It is possible to identify a number of variables that may be viewed as continua on which a personality profile may be constructed and the major disorders may be located. The real difficulty is to ascertain which of these variables are truly separate and independent and which are merely other names for or aspects of the same thing. This problem is compounded if one conceives of the earliest phases of development as emerging from an undifferentiated matrix as the infant utilizes his or her considerable innate sensory, perceptual, and cognitive capacities in the context of a sustaining and regulating object relationship. The differentiation–integration process is probably a central variable both in normal development and in the various psychopathological states. Werner (1948) has suggested that "the development of biological forms is expressed in an *increasing differentiation* of parts and an *increasing subordination*, or *hierarchization* . . . an ordering and grouping of parts in terms of the whole organism" (p. 41), and that "the fundamental law of development [is] increase of differentiation and hierarchic integration" (p. 44). I think of differentiation and integration as aspects of a unitary process. Only insofar as aspects of mind become representationally differentiated can they also become integrated or structured into patterned complex configurations. In turn, the configuration or organization of differentiated entities is part of their further differentiation from one another; the building of structures and complex representations establishes their separateness and distinctiveness. On the continuum of the variable differentiation–integration can be located all of the illnesses ranging from the extreme disorganization, undifferentiation, absence of structure and representation, and inconstancy and state instability of schizophrenia—in which intrapsychic linkage to affect-laden mental contents and related linkage to objects is virtually absent—to the structured psychic organization of neurosis—characterized by integration in the form of intrapsychic conflict and defense, and mature ambivalence (where the multiple feelings are enriching rather than destructively fragmenting).

Symbiosis is the most primitive form of object relationship, and in conditions such as primitive personality organization, characterized by incomplete differentiation and integration, where autonomous self-regulation is deficient or compromised, symbiotic objects are required to maintain tenuous integration and to preserve both a sense of self and the illusion of autonomy. The linkage of mind to external object compensates for absent psychic structuralization. This is why I consider primitive personality organization to be an interpersonal or adaptive as well as an intrapsychic disturbance. Through sensorimotor–affective thinking (Robbins, 1981), the symbiotic relationship enables the first stage of integration and internalization, or connection between as yet self–object undifferentiated aspects of mind. Looked at in this manner, relating to others involves differentiating them from oneself, which in turn involves resolution of symbiosis by integration of mind. A more extreme undifferentiation of self from object and absence of integration of mental content is characteristic of schizophrenic delusions and hallucinations. They reflect a basic failure of differentiation of self from nonself and a loss of integration between mentation and self even more profound than the projection or introjection with maintenance of relatedness that chararacterizes the primitive personality. Some of the characteristic deficits in schizophrenia, such as incapacity to perceive strangeness or unfamiliarity, difficulties with state and tension regulation, reflective incapacity, and extreme representational inconstancy, are probably also aspects of failure of differentiation–integration. Sensorimotor–affective thinking is characteristic of early stages of differentiation–integration. The schizophrenic is barely able to utilize this modality and does not use the animate or inanimate environment instrumentally. The capacity is more highly developed in the symbiotic possession relationships of the borderline. The neurotic has more or less completed the task of internalizing symbolic process, has relinquished sensorimotor–affective thought and symbiotic objects, is able to self-regulate, albeit not without conflict, and can pursue relationships for purposes of gratification and not as obligatory life support.

The major illnesses differ insofar as the representation, control, and expression of affect is concerned, and this is also closely related to differentiation and integration. They range from schizophrenia, which involves a basic repudiation of mental life, an inability to take initiative and express aggression in a socially adaptive manner, an inability to love; through the primitive personality disturbances, where affect representation is absent or rudimentary, and symbiotic objects are used as loosely integrated containers or precursors of noninternalized affects and emotions, particularly dependency and aggression; to the neuroses, where affects are represented, conflicts among cognitive–affective configurations are ubiquitous, and complex integrative defensive and adaptive processes are available to resolve these conflicts.

As I have implied elsewhere, valuable as it may be for heuristic purposes, the complete disjunction Kohut postulates between so-called narcissistic disturbances and pathologies of object relations is not supported by clinical data. Self-esteem regulation and stability, once again related to differentiation–integration, is a major problem in all illness, with the possible exception of neurosis: it is not simply a problem that appears in the form of tendencies toward unrealistic grandiose or idealizing thinking once integration and self-cohesion occurs. Nor is pathological narcissism simply to be equated with grandiosity and idealization. Coexistent but unintegrated extremes of grandiosity and devaluation or shame are found in the unstable and at times chaotic self and object representations of all primitive personalities and, in more extreme form, in schizophrenia. On the other hand, disturbances of object relationship and affect are also characteristic of the narcissistic personality.

The pathological entities are distinctive with regard to object relations, as well, ranging from the passive, global, undifferentiated, nontransference-ready adaptation of the schizophrenic, who is incapable of making active use of an object; to the active but pathological symbiotic relationships of the borderline, which are adaptive but primitive on the differentiation–integration continuum, lacking constancy and stability even with the assistance of an object; to the symbiotic relationships of the narcissistic personality, which are somewhat more constant and stable, enable maintenance of a sense of self, however polarized and unrealistic, as well as some basic need satisfaction, and are more intrapsychically and interpersonally constructive, although they do not allow for mutual autonomy; to the whole, constant, at times loving but conflicted relationships of the neurotic.

IMPLICATIONS FOR AN EPIGENETIC HIERARCHICAL MODEL OF MIND

What conclusions can be drawn from what appear to be qualitative differences in mental organization and function that characterize the major psychopathological entities?

One danger of overly rigid or concrete adherence to a hierarchical model is that it may lead to a misconception of the complex, multivariate, interactive, and transformational process of development as a series of concrete, all-or-nothing sequential milestones, each based on a single variable. Probably the notion that a single variable may be responsible for a qualitative reorganization of thinking is a heuristic oversimplification. A hierarchical model simply helps to focus our attention on a few selected tasks in a complex developmental process and to suggest something of the way they evolve and interact with other tasks and achievements. It is not easy to decide which variables are central in an organizational schema and which subordinate. For instance, Gedo's schema omits the important variable of psychological differentiation, which I have suggested is a facet of integration. My experience with adults with various forms of psychopathology is that problems with several variables are commonly encountered simultaneously, and I would guess they are not resolved in a one-at-a-time, all-or-nothing sequence in normal development, either. Gedo makes a similar observation about the simultaneous functioning of different aspects of personality at different levels of organization, although he invokes the explanatory concept of vertical dissociation to account for unevenness of maturation, whereas I think it may suffice to view concurrent and continuing evolution of several variables as an expectable consequence of the complexity of mind and of the unfolding of differentiation–integration. Developmental inconsistencies will be more pronounced in instances where there has been insufficient caregiving or interference from pathological relationships. The observation of uneven maturation leads Gedo to another conclusion with which I agree, that it is not sufficient to equate psychopathological entities with disturbances of single developmental variables, for example, borderline personality with problems at Level II in his schema, narcissistic personality with problems at Level III, neurotic with Level IV, and the like, although for purposes of diagnosis and treatment planning there are times when it may be useful to make such oversimplifications.

The notion of a common developmental sequence in human beings rests implicitly on a postulate of common beginnings, about which Freud himself articulated doubts when he formulated the concept of a complemental series (1916–1917), and genetic research challenges increasingly, not only in the case of schizophrenia (Robbins, in press) but in the neuroses and character disorders as well (Pardes, Kaufman, Pincus, & West, 1989). There is increasing evidence for a genetic substrate to much of human personality, normal and pathological, and a hierarchical model ought to take into account genotypic differences and activation of phenotypes in the context of deficient or disturbing early object relations (see Robbins, 1992b). So there may be multiple developmental pathways rather than a single one.

The contention of the biologist Weiss, the psychiatrist Engel, and most recently the psychoanalyst Gedo that living systems are organized in transformational hierarchies, and Gedo's application of an epigenetic hierarchical model to normal development and psychopathology, now seem substantiated beyond reasonable doubt, as the various contributions in this volume attest. It remains to be seen, however, whether the same model that encompasses normal development will suffice to account for the spectrum of psychopathology. Proponents of this idea maintain that adult pathology has a normal infantile counterpart, and they rely on concepts of arrest, fixation, and regression in mapping infantile pathogenesis and adult onset of illness. I have described reasons for doubting the assumption of isomorphism between psychopathology and persistence of or return to more infantile modes of thinking and acting. In attempting to resolve this problem and construct accurate models of normal and pathological development and regression, we encounter significant difficulties regardless of whether we proceed from the data of infant observation or from that of analysis of pathological adults. Prospective theorizing about adult pathology from infant observation encounters difficulties in discriminating normal development and its vicissitudes from the antecedents of the various forms of adult pathology, as well as the very impossibility of extrapolating more mature modes of organization from more primitive ones, which led to the necessity of a hierarchical model to begin with. Retrospective theorizing about infancy from analysis of adult pathology encounters the problem of pathomorphism, that is, reconstruction of normal development from pathological adults (Peterfreund, 1978) and the related possibility that there is no such thing as normal neurosis or psychosis of infancy and that regression is not simply a retracing of previous developmental pathways (Fairbairn, 1952; Kohut, 1971, 1977). What is missing is the possibility of abnormal or deviant development (Robbins, 1981, 1983, 1989) and, conversely, of forms of regressive primitivization or pathological change that do not retrace previous developmental pathways.

To be more specific, not all the variables distinguishing patients with major pathological diagnoses seem relevant to normal infant development. While such variables as presence or absence of affect representations and sensorimotor–affective thinking appear to have normal infant counterparts, other elements may not. Of these I shall mention three: the symbioses that characterize some of the major primitive pathologies, aberrations of self-esteem (including grandiosity and devaluation), and failures of integration.

Pathological symbiotic relationships that compensate for developmental failures at preneurotic levels of function, for example, are not simply perseverations of developmentally normal symbiosis, but are unique configurations, as I have already indicated. My clinical observations, contrary to those of Kohut, lead me to doubt that concurrent extremes of self-esteem from grandiosity to extreme and destructive devaluation are normal in infancy. And disintegration of aims and goals may not be a normal part of childhood, either. Certainly small children do not demonstrate the singularity and socialization of goal directedness and purpose that may characterize *some* mature adults, but can we truly say they are psychologically disorganized and unintegrated as opposed to proceeding from less mature forms of differentiation and integration to more mature ones? It does not necessarily follow from the fact that integration is one of the emergent principles of human development that the infantile psyche is normally disintegrated or unintegrated. The normal infant is also psychically undifferentiated, though possessing innnate capacities to make distinctions. It is only as differentiation occurs that organization and integration can follow; *in the undifferentiated state disintegration is a meaningless concept.* Perhaps, as Fairbairn (1952) suggests, the phenomenon of unintegration is encountered only in pathological situations.

Efforts to define normal and psychopathological development and to relate the two, whether through infant observation or through reconstruction from analyses of pathological adults, both face the barrier that is the very rationale for an epigenetic hierarchical model, namely the discontinuous nature of development with its succession of new organizations. Complex organizations are not retrospectively reducible to their original constituents. Although one may speculate, it is not possible to reconstruct with accuracy the sequences and elements involved in the composition of a complex work of art. Nor, conversely, is it possible to predict and construct future organizations from current components as LaPlace's naive deterministic theory of emergent evolution holds. The only solution to this problem would appear to be vast, long-range, and detailed studies of the life cycle, which sound more wishful than practical when one considers how difficult it is to study in depth for a few years any group of pathological adults or seemingly normal or "at risk" infants.

Meanwhile I think it is important that an epigenetic hierarchical model of the mind attempt to map pathological developmental and regressive pathways as well as normal ones and to recognize that there may be constitutional differences in our beginnings—all men are not created equal. There needs to be a place in the model for developmental deviance under the stress of unusual biological and/or environmental conditions. This simply means that making a model hierarchy is a complex, multivariable, multipath endeavor and that the concept of epigenesis should be considered in its most general sense, and not simply equated with a single pathway or a linear sequence.

Notwithstanding my questions about the details of his schema, Gedo's epigenetic hierarchy of mental development and self-formation, following Weiss's human systems hierarchy and Engel's biopsychosocial model, accounts better than any other psychoanalytic theory for what I suggest is an indisputable fact, namely that all human beings do not think in qualitatively similar ways. Primitive mentation is a reality, not simply a theoretical fantasy that reflects a failure on the part of some analysts to appreciate the ubiquity of intrapsychic conflict, defense, and the dynamic unconscious. The detailed specification of these differences in the way people think is essential to the understanding and treatment of more serious forms of mental illness. The task that Gedo has begun, to develop such a comprehensive model that encompasses disturbances in self-care and interpersonal skills as well as conditions characterized by inhibitions, symptoms, and intrapsychic conflict, should be one of the most exciting challenges for psychoanalysis in the decades to come.

REFERENCES

Bacal, H. (1987). British object relations theorists and self-psychology: Some critical reflections. *International Journal of Psycho-Analysis, 68,* 81–98.
Engel, G. L. (1977). The need for a new medical model: A challenge for biomedicine. *Science, 196,* 129–136.

Engel, G. L. (1980). The clinical application of the biopsychosocial model. *American Journal of Psychiatry, 137,* 535–544.

Fairbairn, W. R. D. (1952). *Psychoanalytic studies of the personality.* London: Tavistock.

Federn, P. (1952). *Ego psychology and the psychoses.* New York: Basic Books.

Freud, S. (1915). The unconscious. *Standard Edition* (Vol. 14, pp. 159–216). London: Hogarth Press, 1966.

Freud, S. (1916–1917). Introductory lectures on psycho-analysis. *Standard Edition* (Vols. 15 & 16). London: Hogarth Press, 1966.

Freud, S. (1924a). Neurosis and psychosis. *Standard Edition* (Vol. 19, pp. 149–156). London: Hogarth Press, 1966.

Freud, S. (1924b). The loss of reality in neurosis and psychosis. *Standard Edition* (Vol. 19, pp. 183–190). London: Hogarth Press, 1966.

Gedo, J. (1979). *Beyond interpretation.* New York: International Universities Press.

Gedo, J. (1984). *Psychoanalysis and its discontents.* New York: Guilford Press.

Gedo, J. (1986). *Conceptual issues in psychoanalysis.* Hillsdale, NJ: Analytic Press.

Gedo, J. (1988). *The mind in disorder.* Hillsdale, NJ: Analytic Press.

Gedo, J., & Goldberg, A. (1973). *Models of the mind.* Chicago: University of Chicago Press.

Grinker, R. (1973). Changing styles in psychoses and borderline states. *Psychiatry, 130,* 151–152.

Grotstein, J. (1977). The psychoanalytic concept of schizophrenia. II: Reconciliation. *International Journal of Psycho-Analysis, 58,* 427–452.

Gunderson, J. (Reporter). (1974). The influence of theoretical models of schizophrenia on treatment practice. *Journal of the American Psychoanalytic Association, 22,* 182–199.

Gunderson, J., & Kolb, J. (1978). Discriminating features of borderline patients. *American Journal of Psychiatry, 135,* 792–796.

Hartmann, H. (1953). Contribution to the metapsychology of schizophrenia. *Psychoanalytic Study of the Child, 8,* 177–198.

Hendrick, I. (1951). Early development of the ego: Identification in infancy. *Psychoanalytic Quarterly, 20,* 44–61.

Jacobson, E. (1953). Metapsychology of psychotic depression. In P. Greenacre (Ed.), *Affective disorders* (pp. 49–83). New York: International Universities Press.

Kernberg, O. (1966). Structural derivatives of object relations. *International Journal of Psycho-Analysis, 47,* 236–253.

Kernberg, O. (1967). Borderline personality organization. *Journal of American Psychoanalytic Association, 15,* 641–685.

Kernberg, O. (1970). A psychoanalytic classification of character pathology. *Journal of American Psychoanalytic Association, 18,* 800–822.

Kernberg, O. (1972). Early ego integration and object relations. *Annual of the New York Academy of Science, 193,* 233–247.

Khan, M. (1960). Clinical aspects of the schizoid personality: Affects and technique. In *The privacy of the self* (pp. 13–26). New York: International Universities Press.

Kohut, H. (1971). *The analysis of the self.* New York: International Universities Press.

Kohut, H. (1977). *The restoration of the self.* New York: International Universities Press.

London, N. (1973). An essay on psychoanalytic theory: Two theories of schizophrenia. Part II: Discussion and restatement of the specific theory of schizophrenia. *International Journal of Psycho-Analysis, 54,* 179–193.

Mahler, M. (1968). *On human symbiosis and the viscissitudes of individuation. Vol. 1: Infantile psychosis.* New York: International Universities Press.

Meehl, P. (1962). Schizotaxia, schizotypy, and schizophrenia. *American Psychologist, 17,* 827–837.

Meissner, W. (1984). *The borderline spectrum.* New York: Aronson.

Morrison, A. (1989). *Shame: The underside of narcissism.* Hillsdale, NJ: Analytic Press.

Pardes, H., Kaufman, C., Pincus, H., & West, A. (1989). Genetics and psychiatry: Past discoveries, current dilemmas, and future directions. *American Journal of Psychiatry, 146,* 435–443.

Peterfreund, E. (1978). Some critical comments on psychoanalytic conceptualizations on infancy. *International Journal of Psycho-Analysis, 59,* 427–441.

Robbins, M. (1980). Current controversy in object relations theory as outgrowth of a schism between Klein and Fairbairn. *International Journal of Psycho-Analysis, 61,* 477–491.

Robbins, M. (1981). The symbiosis concept and the commencement of normal and pathological ego functioning and object relations. II: Developments subsequent to infancy and pathological processes. *International Review of Psycho-Analysis, 8,* 379–391.

Robbins, M. (1982). Narcissistic personality as a symbiotic character disorder. *International Journal of Psycho-Analysis, 63,* 457–473.

Robbins, M. (1983). Toward a new mind model for the primitive personalities. *International Journal of Psycho-Analysis, 64,* 127–148.

Robbins, M. (1988). The adaptive significance of destructiveness in primitive personalities. *Journal of the American Psychoanalytic Association, 36,* 627–652.

Robbins, M. (1989). Primitive personality organization as an interpersonally adaptive modification of cognition and affect. *International Journal of Psycho-Analysis, 70,* 443–459.

Robbins, M. (1992a). A Fairbairnian object–relations perspective on self-psychology. *American Journal of Psychoanalysis, 52,* 247–261.

Robbins, M. (1992b). Psychoanalytic and biological approaches to mental illness: Schizophrenia. *Journal of the American Psychoanalytic Association, 40,* 425–454.

Robbins, M. (1993). *Schizophrenia and the human sciences.* New York: Guilford Press.

Sandler, J., & Freud, A. (1983). Discussions in the Hampstead Index of *The ego and the mechanisms of defense. Journal of the American Psychoanalytic Association, 31*(Suppl.), 19–146.

Stierlin, H. (1975). Schizophrenic core disturbances. In J. Gunderson & L. Mosher (Eds.), *Psychotherapy of schizophrenia* (pp. 317–322). New York: Aronson.

Weiss, P. (1969). The living system: Determinism stratified. In A. Koestler & J. Smythies (Eds.), *Beyond reductionism* (pp. 3–55). New York: Macmillan.

Weiss, P. (1977). The system of nature and the nature of systems: Empirical wholism and practical reductionism harmonized. In K. Schaefer, H. Hensel, & R. Brady (Eds.), *Toward a man-centered medical science* (pp. 17–64). Mt. Kisco, NY: Futura.

Werner, H. (1948). *Comparative psychology of mental development.* New York: International Universities Press.

Wexler, M. (1971). Schizophrenia: Conflict and deficiency. *Psychoanalytic Quarterly, 40,* 83–99.

Wexler, M. (1975). The evolution of a deficiency view of schizophrenia. In J. Gunderson & L. Mosher (Eds.), *Psychotherapy of schizophrenia* (pp. 161–174). New York: Aronson.

IV

Overview

11

Hierarchical Concepts in Psychoanalysis

ARNOLD WILSON AND JOHN E. GEDO

We live at a time when the boundaries between many scientific disciplines seem to be more permeable than ever before. This is equally true about psychoanalysis and all the various social sciences. Many of these boundaries, it is now clear, were man-made and not inherent within the phenomena studied. These days it is hard to recognize what had not long ago been implicitly agreed-upon areas of inquiry. We read journals and accept at face value such areas of investigation as "cultural psychology" or "psychoimmunology," and even recognize that what would have once seemed an oxymoron is now a specific domain at the cutting edge of scientific investigation. There is a renewal of interest in the relationship between method and data within and between disciplines, contributing to the generalized breakdown of many disciplinary boundaries that only a decade ago looked secure.

Perhaps one of the most dramatic changes sweeping across the fields previously demarcated by these boundaries in the last decade has been the increased concern with *how* we know what we know, rather than simply *what* we know. More and more, the telling discussions within and between most social and human sciences have been concerned with issues of method and epistemology. It is not at all unusual to hear in the essence of these debates a raft of new phrases, such as "pluralism," "relativism," or "constructivism," that reflect this concern. The tension between the wish for certainty and the inevitability of uncertainty in how and what is known is at the heart of much of this controversy, permeating postmodern art, science, and literature.

At present and for the foreseeable future, there is within what is called science (see Lakatos, 1978) no single diacritical marker that pinpoints any particular method as distinctively scientific and without qualification preferable under all circumstances to any other. Tension about these uncertainties permeates our volume, marking psychoanalysis as a body of method and knowledge swept along by contemporary currents, and unable to protect its flank through any dogmatic assertion of privilege.

However, for psychoanalysis to travel these newly paved roads, a significant journey must be carefully planned lest the itinerary go awry. Welcoming multiple methods does not necessarily imply that these are equally valid under all conditions. In other words, it is one thing to be relativistic, another to be pluralistic. From our viewpoint, the ominous specter of relativism permeates many recent attempts to recast psychoanalysis—a development we find of dubious value. Most relativistic approaches question the possibility that any position can embody a clear truth value, and thus attempt to subvert all scientific effort. Appeals to relativism in psychoanalysis have promoted rationalizations for sloppy thinking and the use of superficial and boring slogans through appeals to crutches like "unfettered complexity," the alleged limitations imposed on method by "the stance of the observer" or by a "multiplicity of knowers" or "inter-subjectivities"—each of whom purportedly embodies a separate and equally valid version of truth.

One of the most important differences between ideology and science is that science (in contrast to ideology) must be relentless in its efforts to avert self-deception. Psychoanalysis must avoid lapsing into using any of the current ideologies surrounding relativism. We do not advocate relinquishing the tenacity that empowers critical, clear, and original thinking.

In an examination of the transfiguration of metapsychology, Holt (1981) outlined, as follows, four major positions on the question, What kind of science is psychoanalysis?: (1) Is it a natural science (e.g., Freud, Hartmann); (2) Is it a social/behavioral science (e.g., Gill); (3) Is it a humanistic or hermeneutic science (e.g., Schafer, Spence); (4) Is it some amalgam of natural, social, and hermeneutic science (e.g., Modell, Brenner, Wallerstein)? The assumptions brought to bear from each position will have radical implications for how psychoanalytic theory and practice will proceed.

Yet it strains belief to imagine that any one of these positions, represented by the distinguished practitioners listed, is *not* psycho-analysis, despite the multiplicity of methods advocated. Nor are any of them "wrong" when they stake out their positions. Taken together they constitute an ecumenical position on the methodology of psychoanalysis as science; were any to emerge as the sole approach to psychoanalysis, our field would be the poorer. It is through dialogue between and within their respective points of view that the field will flourish. Elements of each of these positions can be discerned in the chapters in this volume. We anticipate that they will coexist dialogically and not always comfortably.

Because of the advantages of ecumenicism, we think that psychoanalysis would thrive in a pluralistic (but not relativistic) world. As we define it, a pluralistic view holds that two or more seemingly conflicting positions can both stake claims to truthfulness. At the same time, pluralism encourages critical evaluation of the various positions, most usefully through a recognition of each other's assumptions as well as assertions. Useful critiques engage assumptions side-by-side with assertions, strong points side-by-side with vulnerabilities. The notion is attributed to Hegel that if a theory one is not sympathetic to is worth taking up in the form of a critique, one should immerse oneself in it, enter into the theory's strength, try to understand it from within rather than without, give it the most generous possible reading, and *then* find where it can be criticized. By entertaining the strength of the adversarial position, one's critique is likewise strengthened. This notion has been termed "the method of immanent critique" by the Frankfurt critical theory group. We seek to represent and advance this method of critique among the multiple methods in a necessarily pluralistic psychoanalysis.

Booth (1979) has described what he terms a "methodological pluralism." In this book we have sought to promote a defensible methodological pluralism that bears on a hierarchical conception of psychoanalysis. In agreement with Schafer (1990), we believe that it is through principled critique between theoretical and methodological positions, rather than through assertion of common ground (see Wallerstein, 1990), that psychoanalysis is now in a position to evolve.

Further, we identify another task that hierarchical approaches stand to accomplish—reconciling multiple "models" within psychoanalysis. In the philosophy of science, the investigation of models within any area of inquiry is seen as the center of the effort to understand the essence of that area. The empirical discoveries made by psychoanalysis, as in any science, are often coherent or verifiable only within the framework of a superordinate model (Black, 1962; Pepper, 1972). Out-of-model discoveries often appear untenable or implausible until they are evaluated within a particular operative model or are translated into the terms of a particular operative model. Psychoanalysis is permeated by multiple models, existing at multiple levels of abstraction. Further, the anatomy of any systematically articulated model is seen as explicitly hierarchical in nature (Black, 1962). Models can exist on several levels, from inclusive metaphysical models to narrowly circumscribed models of specific features of a theory (Reese and Overton, 1972). Different levels of models can be characterized by different degrees of generality, openness, and vagueness.

Thus, we suggest that a hierarchical approach within psychoanalysis could usefully focus on the reconciliation of models that incorporate specific schools of thought or theories. Models are distinguished from schools of thought and theories. A school of thought generally coalesces out of political allegiances. In psychoanalysis, self psychology has evolved into a school of thought, not a model. A model should also be distinguished from a theory. Any theory presupposes a more general model according to which its theoretical concepts are formulated. Models provide a context within which to develop theories. Within theories, more specific forms of the model are then specified and hypotheses elaborated. Models form, reform, and constitute data. They are often invisible, and yet they determine the way one looks at the world and what is adduced as important. Models lend themselves to new ways of looking at things, and to comprehensibility, but not necessarily to new or original data. Yet, at the same time, the use of a model may interfere with the comprehension of knowledge from the perspective of other models (Toulmin, 1961). The view from one model may make the view from another model look silly, oversimplistic, or trivial. Any deductions based on a model must be tested against the data which emerge from the model itself. A model is judged by the criteria of usefulness—a theory by criteria of truthfulness. A model is not intended to be a description of reality but rather a representation of the features of what is essential for understanding a particular problem. A model works by metaphor but should be distinguished from metaphor. In contrast to metaphor as a trope, a model is a systematically developed and elaborated metaphor that suggests new ways of looking at a problem. A model involves an original domain of study, a purpose, and conventions of interpretation.

Despite the aspects of divergence amongst the chapters in this volume, there are also certain threads that tie them together. All in one way or another are wrestling with the following issues: (1) The integration of contemporary scientistic formulations and the expunging of classical metapsychological formulations; (2) The role of hierarchies within their respective approaches to psychoanalysis; (3) The question of whether and how to privilege one hierarchic level (e.g., classical theorists have historically privileged the Oedipal, while those who take stock of infant research have drifted into privileging the earliest level) over all others; and (4) The overall role and value of the metaphor of human development for psychoanalysis, both for theory and for the explication of clinical process.

In virtually all scientific inquiry the method used to assess data will in part determine the nature and form of the data found. There are no theory-free (Bernstein, 1983) or method-free (Feyerabend, 1975) data. Thus, a crucial question to be asked of any method is whether it is appropriate to the domain in which the questions lie that it seeks to answer. In this book, Wilson and Passik, Bucci, and Grand, Feiner, and Reisner, have opted for the systematic, publicly verifiable, replicable, experimental approach to the exploration of hierarchies in psychoanalysis, which is characteristic of the lower procedural levels of model building.

Methods imported from harder science have proved increasingly useful within psychoanalysis in recent years, although they certainly are not at present decisive. These include the classic experimental method as well as others. Edelson (1984) has shown that psychoanalytic hypotheses can and have been tested for degrees of comparative support in the clinical situation throughout the history of the field. He concludes that systematic tests of comparative support of competing psychoanalytic hypotheses has had and, by extrapolation will have, an important role in the evolution of cumulative knowledge. Further, these tests can (but do not necessarily have to) enlist statistical techniques, for hypothesis testing can be embodied by the manner in which any argument, including the case study, is written and contested.

Bucci states a case for "referential activity" (RA) bridging verbal and nonverbal coding systems as a key phenomenon in psychoanalysis. Her approach is predicated on the possibility of articulating an interface between cognitive science and psychoanalysis. She postulates two distinct universal systems for processing information—the verbal and nonverbal. Referential activity is a third key system, one which has the task of linking the verbal and nonverbal systems, thereby allowing for a meaningful translation between these different ways of coding information.

The most important task of clinical psychoanalysis, in Bucci's opinion, is for the analysand to articulate and the analyst to enlarge through interpretation the patient's referential activity, thereby expanding the linkage between the verbal and nonverbal systems. Expanding RA amounts to structural change. The expansion of RA takes place in phases that can be identified and promoted by the analyst. In this view, free association, defenses, and interpretation have quite different modes of action than other approaches to analysis attribute to them. Free association, for example, allows for the progressive relaxation of the verbal code and the temporary emergence of the nonverbal code, which can then "speak" through language as much as that is possible. In this conceptualization, repression can be viewed as the inhibition of referential connections.

Bucci expresses two particular qualifications about her views that depart from an epigenetic perspective. First, while she speaks of a purely psychological domain, she suggests that it is meaningless to postulate *shifts* between biological and psychological domains, since all that occurs is a kind of translation from the terms of one domain into another. (This issue was previously discussed in a scholarly way by Rubenstein [1976], whose call for a protoneurophysiological approach to theory construction properly attracted a good deal of attention.) Second, she calls her approach "quasi-epigenetic," because she asserts that the nonverbal domain utilizes parallel rather than hierarchical organizational arrangements.

We take a different view about these qualifications. It is by now a virtual truism that psychoanalysis requires a theory of thought organization that can oscillate between the supremely insightful and the blatantly somatic, as expressed in such phenomena as hypochondriasis, body symptoms, or conversion reactions. What we are looking for is a way of explicating how meaning can be encoded in ways that implicate the body and the brain. In other words, a "monistic" mind/body (after Langer, 1951) position is required.[1] In one attempt to grapple with this problem, Basch (1976) argues that the difference between mind and brain is a semantic confusion, and the former is merely an emergent quality of the latter. This argument begs the question, for the firing of cells that are activated as part of a mental operation does not in and of itself equal a thought. To speak of mind and brain as separate domains, through which the same phenomena are merely recast, forecloses on some of the most interesting and progressive questions being asked of modern brain science and psychoanalysis, an example of which is provided by Levin in this volume.

Bucci also asserts that her approach is quasi-epigenetic because the nonverbal system depends on parallel processing, and thus is not organized hierarchically, in contrast to the logical (verbal) system, which is hierarchical in nature. She thereby implies that the nonverbal system cannot be characterized by developmental/maturational criteria. We suggest that the independent line postulated for the nonverbal system does not preclude a hierarchical organization; it only requires a reconceptualization in terms of its independent status from the maturational line of the verbal system. Just as one can attribute more as well as less advanced aspects to the verbal system, so too one might attribute similar markers to the nonverbal system, and link them with the parallel processes that define their interrelatedness. The parallel processing code of Paivio must have a hierarchical structure that can be usefully specified.

Finally, the concept of referential activity fits into an epigenetic framework precisely by virtue of the fact that when this new capacity enables the individual to link previously unconnected information processing systems (verbal with nonverbal), internal communication is so greatly enhanced that the resultant functional mode is decisively different from what preceded it. In other words, conditions wherein nonverbal and verbal systems are merely available in parallel are superseded by RA if development proceeds optimally. The failure to take this maturational step (even about portions of the nonverbal system) constitutes the persistence of a relatively archaic mode of organization. In view of the fact that nonverbal systems operate from birth and verbal ones become available many months later, the epigenesis can be characterized as a stage of nonverbal processing, followed by a dual system, and ending with the acquisition of RA.

Jerome Frank, an early pioneer in psychotherapy research, conceived of "nonspecific factors" in an effort to articulate the subtle ways in which therapy works. As we learn more and more about the activities of the mind and the brain, and how they find expression in the analytic process, we can scientifically depict the anatomy of the processes that had heretofore been considered nonspecific, and thereafter name them. Bucci's formulations represent one of the most elegant descriptions we have yet encountered of one such nonspecific factor contributing to therapeutic change. "Only connect," she counsels, and this is enough for psychoanalysis to proceed. At long last, psychoanalysis has a persuasive theoretical argument for how and why this simple task of connecting, using only words, leads to the complicated set of phenomena grouped under the rubric "analytic change."

Grand et al. describe a structured interview organized around the identification of symptoms which, they assert, allows for a classification according to an epigenetically defined level of functioning. Accordingly, they have developed the LIF (Level of Integrative Failure) questionnaire that allows for this classification. Although their approach emphasizes symptoms and not personality organization, they do note that the two should in great measure prove to be parallel. Human development is important for this scheme to the extent that its unfolding is parallel to levels of integrative functioning, which becomes recapitulated in the regressions of adults. Six levels of integrative failure are identified. After an extensive review of the underlying theoretical propositions, a small pilot project is described which demonstrates a potential application of the LIF.

In their work, Grand et al. shift the focus to symptoms and thereby seek to move the inferential process away from the level of the hypothetical construct. They jettison the notion of organization used by Gedo and Goldberg (1973), for example, in an earlier hierarchical scheme, in favor of the symptom. Thus, one might locate their effort as midway between a psychoanalytic and descriptive psychiatric orientation, between what is inferred and what is observed. This interesting choice seems to us to be ambitious and worthy of special note. Their effort to link epigenesis, levels of organization, and manifest symptoms represents a valuable effort to link what some consider to be divaricating phenomena. It is fascinating to follow how they tie together symptoms with such psychoanalytic postulates as tension regulation and the acquisition of psychic boundaries. However, further empirical work is clearly required before one can evaluate the validity of their proposals. Their view of symptoms as departures from the processes of normal development is also worthy of consideration and requires fuller explication. Of course, the history of psychoanalytic explanation is largely based on the obverse of their proposition; that is, normal development has usually been inferred from constellations of pathologies. Nevertheless, their program is a stellar example of the type of empirical research that can lend support to a hierarchical conception of psychoanalysis, and one that might serve as a bridge to a psychiatric view of symptoms.

In their chapter, Wilson and Passik describe the development of a different theoretical system, which they term the EARS, an acronym for Epigenetic Assessment Rating System. The EARS has been applied to the speech samples of a TAT, a RAPS, a 5-minute monologue, and a transcript from a psychoanalytic hour. Each EARS score is broken down into ten dimensions. The authors then report the results from several studies, from first generation validation efforts to second generation attempts to deepen external validity.

The findings of Bucci, Wilson and Passik, and Grand et al. are interesting, but one is still left with questions, particularly about the significance of their research for clinical work. There is no inherent superiority in statistics, control groups, and well controlled research designs over anecdotal vignettes or fairy tales; method is not meant to be applied as a sacred ritual. Rather, method must be fitted to a domain of theory and evidence. Do these studies tell us something psychoanalytic that cannot be known in any other way? We think so. In its own way, each contributes to the ongoing articulation of a pluralistic and hierarchical conception of psychoanalytic data. In particular, a case can be made that these approaches better lend themselves to what Reichenbach (1938) termed the "context of justification" rather than to the "context of discovery," that is, to the testing and evaluation of hypotheses rather than to the generation of new ideas. Both contexts play a necessary role in the orderly evolution of scientific hypotheses.

After reviewing the research contributions, let us examine the theoretical/historical considerations. Gedo provides a history of the evolution of his ideas about hierarchical conceptualization in psychoanalysis. In an intellectual/autobiographical essay, Gedo traces his hierarchical conception from its earliest form when the monograph, *Models of the Mind*, written in conjunction with Arnold Goldberg, represented a first effort to knit together Freud's models of metapsychology with developmental modes. Gradually, Gedo's hierarchical model evolved and became independent of the Freudian enterprise until it reached its most recent statement, one that illuminates many phenomena, but is most innovative in his description of how psychobiological repetition erupts into the provinces of human subjectivity. Many of the chapters in this volume systematically take up Gedo's position.

In one of these chapters, Levin examines some aspects of the interface between linguistics and psychoanalysis. He attempts to show that "natural languages" framed by brain neurobiology are hierarchical, organized at various levels that are strikingly similar to the levels of Gedo's model. In particular, Levin notes the activity of the prefrontal cortex in unifying goal-directed activities.

In his investigation of hierarchies, Grossman returns to Freud's monograph *On Aphasia* (1888) and shows that Freud's earliest metapsychological considerations involved developing a hierarchical theory of mental representation. Grossman then traces the influence of this early model on Freud's later theorizing; he concludes that the hierarchical model developed in *On Aphasia* is the heretofore unrecognized unifying element knitting together Freud's metapsychology. He also suggests that a hierarchical approach unifies the more abstract aspects of Freud's theories and their clinical applications.

Lichtenberg has contributed a chapter in which he further develops the ideas about motivational systems proposed in his recent book about the same subject. In this paper, he shows how each motivational system can be seen as hierarchically ordered. He depicts how the organizing principles of self-organization, self-stabilization, dialectical tension, and hierarchical arrangement are central for the understanding of each of five motivational systems. He concludes that hierarchical self-organization is the initiator and integrator of all motivation.

Thus far, Lichtenberg has failed to clarify the relationship between his concept of "self" and "motivation" and the definitions of these same terms utilized by other psychoanalytic authors. When many (although not all) psychoanalysts talk about motivation, they are generally referring to some concept of drive, instinct, or wish. Lichtenberg, by contrast, refers to motivational systems which, either in isolation or in unison with another system, "govern experience." Where are the motives in the systems? Moreover, Lichtenberg's "self" must be understood as being hierarchically different from many other concepts of self. For example, it is necessary to specify how his "self" contains an unconscious that has some sort of transformational relationship to a conscious component in any of the motivational systems. Lichtenberg's "self" appears to have more correspondence to the lower presubjective modes than to the subjective modes of other hierarchies in this volume. One looks for and wonders where are the motivations generally attributed to superego and ego-ideal in traditional psychoanalytic theory. Nevertherless, it is greatly to Lichtenberg's credit that he has taken observational infant research as far as he has, perhaps farther than anyone else on the contemporary scene struggling with the integration of this body of knowledge with clinical concerns. We look forward to the continuing evolution of his ideas in this area.

The chapters of this volume investigating hierarchical aspects of psychoanalysis through a theoretical approach contribute to the methodological pluralism we espouse. In our opinion, the four chapters taken together constitute a strong argument for hierarchies as an indispensable aspect of all psychoanalytic theorizing, from Grossman's reading of Freud to Gedo's pluralistic effort to integrate competing conceptualizations, Levin's appropriation of neurolinguistics for psychoanalysis, and Lichtenberg's reconstrual of motivation along the lines of the findings of infancy research. In contrast to the research contributions, each can be seen as contributing more to the "context of discovery" than to the "context of justification," as Reichenbach distinguished them. Such approaches are characteristic of the higher levels of model building, in which a known system of concepts depicts new realms of application by analogic extension. What remains to be explored about the value of hierarchical considerations in psychoanalysis is applicability to the essential native data base of psychoanalysis, that is, to findings from the clinical situation.

Clinical vignettes are offered from within the clinical situation, formulated in accord with preferences for particular clinical theories. Issues of technique and clinical considerations flow from the vignettes and theory adduced. We agree with those analysts who speak of the uniqueness of the "psychoanalytic method" (e.g., Brenner, 1982) and claim that this observational method yields a unique form of data unobtainable under any other circumstances. We part company with the view that psychoanalytic observations are therefore not comparable with other forms of data obtained under other methodological circumstances. We find this an isolationist solution, but are sympathetic to the problem that it attempts to solve; psychoanalysis has too often been undermined by basing far too many of its efforts at adjudication of pressing problems upon second-order evidential reports, one-step removed from the unique occurrences themselves, via a careless (or parsimonious) integration with oversimplistic formulations or a description or interpretation of evidence rather than a public or verbatim account of evidence. We applaud the effort to convert second order evidence (the case study) into empirical evidence that possesses true testability, verifiability, and sound scientific status, and to provide the basis for a fair and sound critical examination of our theories. The way to get there is through the public unpacking of our private data base, which is whatever occurs in the analytic setting itself, of what we do, how we do it, and what happens when we do it. To study the psychoanalytic process, we must directly raise a periscope into the analytic encounter, see psychoanalysis in action rather than indirectly hear people talk about it, and to articulate principled ways of speaking about it and studying it that do not do violence to the healing art that is clinical psychoanalysis. On this issue there is remarkable consensus even between such natural adversaries as hermeneuticists and "harder" scientists.

Although the clinical reports in this volume do not meet these ideal criteria, the two chapters by Robbins and the one by Khantzian and Wilson approach hierarchies in psychoanalysis by discussing their clinical work in terms of the differing theories that they believe yield better results with different kinds of patients. Their chapters are filled with clinically germane issues, debates, and conclusions. All three of these clinical contributions consider patients who are often regarded as unanalyzable. In drawing from hierarchical conceptions, they suggest ways of thinking about psychoanalysis not widely taught in clinical training, but congruent with Gedo's position. From our perspective, perhaps equally important is that to some extent, each author struggles to integrate modern research findings and hard data in order to guide the inductive leaps within the realities of the clinical situation.

In the first of two chapters in this volume, Robbins focuses on affect disturbances in primitive personalities as his avenue into hierarchical considerations in psychoanalysis. Robbins postulates that the capacity to mentally represent affects (i.e., to develop a symbolic system to designate them) constitutes a crucial nodal point in development. From a hierarchical viewpoint, the acquisition of this capacity marks progression from a "primitive" organization of the personality to a more differentiated mode of functioning, character-ized by pathologies more clearly in focus in previous psychoanalytic discourse.

Khantzian and Wilson focus on affect disturbances in the pre-subjective modes prevalent in addicts. They recast the major theories of addiction into hierarchical terms, and emphasize the ways in which addicts can misleadingly appear to be more advanced in development than they in fact are. In particular, they focus on a "trade-off" addicts engage in, through which higher forms of organization mask earlier, presubjective, affective impairments. These earlier impairments are components of wider immersion in failures of self-regulation, which are compensated for not by recruiting another person (as in certain personality disorders), but rather through the medicative effects of the narcotic. The authors contrast this hierarchical view with the theories heretofore found putatively applicable with addicts (e.g., as pleasure seekers, or as masochistic), and suggest that these views bent clinical data to fit theory, rather than vice versa.

In his second contribution to the volume, Robbins evaluates hierarchical considerations as they apply to the more severe spectrum of psychopathologies, ranging from narcissistic to borderline and schizophrenic states. He identifies such an approach as a paradig-matic one that represents a point of departure from a psychoanalysis that limits itself to the conflict neuroses of the structural model, or the drive-defense considerations that have their origins in topographical views. In particular, he notes how developmental phenomena refer-able to incomplete self–other differentiation and primitive object relations are well handled by a hierarchical model.

However, to handle the detailed clinical data Robbins adduces from his range of severe pathologies, a model finer-grained than the five-modal hierarchies used by Gedo or Wilson and Passik may be required. It will be recalled that Grand et al., who also dealt with a patient population with severe impairments, found it necessary to devise a 6-modal schema for the LIF. It remains to be seen whether that solution would be suitable in terms of Robbins's requirements. The question remains open as to the relative utility of schemata offering greater complexity or easier applicability. Certainly, the complexities introduced by hierarchical schemata as described throughout this volume present novel challenges to clinicians, who even before thinking hierarchically already had to juggle a fantastic amount of information while trying to make sense of their patients' free associations.

NOTE

1. It is not widely recognized that this same debate raged in the philosophical exchanges between Leibnitz and Spinoza centuries ago, where the protagonists staked out such positions as "mind–body dualism" and "mind-body parallelism"!

REFERENCES

Basch, M. (1976). Psychoanalysis and communication science. *Annual of Psychoanalysis, 4,* 385–422.

Bernstein, R. (1983). *Beyond objectivism and relativism.* Philadelphia: University of Pennsylvania Press.

Black, M. (1962). *Models and metaphor.* Ithaca, NY: Cornell University Press.

Booth, W. (1979). *Critical understanding: The power and limits of pluralism.* Chicago: University of Chicago Press.

Brenner, C. (1983). *The mind in conflict.* New York: International Universities Press.

Edelson, M. (1984). *Hypothesis and evidence in psychoanalysis.* Chicago: University of Chicago Press.

Feyarabend, P. (1975). *Against method.* New York: Verso.

Gedo, J., & Goldberg, A. (1973). *Models of the mind.* Chicago: University of Chicago Press.

Holt, R. (1981). The death and transfiguration of metapsychology. *International Review of Psycho-Analysis, 8,* 129–144.

Lakatos, I. (1978). *The methodology of scientific research programs.* Cambridge: Cambridge University Press.

Langer, S. (1951). *Philosophy in a new key.* Cambridge, MA: Harvard University Press.

Pepper, S. (1972). *World hypotheses: A study in evidence.* Berkeley: University of California Press.

Reese, H. W., & Overton, W. (1972). On paradigm shifts. *American Psychologist, 27,* 1197–1199.

Reichenbach, H. (1938). *Experience and prediction*. Chicago: University of Chicago Press.

Rubenstein, B. (1976). On the possibility of a strictly clinical psychoanalytic theory: An essay in the philosophy of psychoanalysis. In M. M. Gill & P. S. Holzman (Eds.), *Psychology versus metapsychology: Psychoanalytic essays in honor of George S. Klein* (pp. 229–264). New York: International Universities Press.

Schafer, R. (1990). The search for common ground. *International Journal of Psycho-Analysis, 71*, 49–52.

Toulmin, S. (1961). *Foresight and understanding*. New York: Harper and Row.

Wallerstein, R. (1990). Psychoanalysis: The common ground. *International Journal of Psycho-Analysis, 71*, 3–20.

Index

n. indicates entries found in endnotes

Abandonment, panic of, 11, 54
  in borderline personality disorder, 70, 72
Acting out, 42, 43, 72
Adaptation, 157, 186, 301
  crises, 49, 53
  in developmental process, 51–52
  and substance abuse, 266, 270
  symbiotic, 145, 254
Addictive behaviors, 143, 227, 267–268, 275, 278–279, 281, 322; *see also* Substance abuse
  dual aspect of, 263–264, 270
  hypotheses of, 265–266, 281
Adler, A., 154
Adolescence
  affect representation in, 252
  transitions in, 217
Advances in Clinical Psychoanalysis (Gedo), 144
Affect
  abnormal, 114
  deficits, 271, 278, 279
  expression/tolerance; *see* Thematic Apperception Test, and Epigenetic Assessment Rating Scale
  in infants, 251
  and integrative failure, 53–57, 251; *see also* Affect representation
  labile, 53, 70
  negative, 266–267, 268, 294
  pharmacologically induced, 107
  and stimulus barrier, 272, 273

Affect representation, 236, 238–259, 301, 322
  case studies of, 241–246, 247–248, 250–251, 255–259
  development of, 251–254
Aggression, 296, 301; *see also* Hostility
Aibel, I., 72*n.*
Alexander, F., 130
Alexthymia, 107, 111, 239, 270, 272
Alogia, 114
Analogy, 189–192
Anger; *see also* Rage
  deflected toward oneself, 11, 240; *see also* Hostility, introjected
  paranoid, 272
  unawareness of, 240, 243, 247–248, 256
Anhedonia, 237
Annihilation anxiety, 11, 54
Antisocial personality disorder, 276
Anxiety
  in infants, 212–214
  in integrative failure, 54, 56, 69
  moral, 88, 98
Aphasia, 195*n.*; see also On Aphasia
Apraxia, 146
Associated meanings, 220, 226
Attachment, 87, 115, 213, 222, 249
  "obstinate," 275
  to suffering, 263–264, 268, 270, 275–276
Attention, 160, 219–220
Autism, 53, 58, 72
"Autobiographical Study" (S. Freud), 185
Autonomic activation, 5, 6, 11
Autonomy, 88, 99
  illusion of, 300